# COLLOQUIAL ENGLISH

Drawing on vast amounts of new data from live, unscripted radio and TV broadcasts, and the internet, this is a brilliant and original analysis of colloquial English, revealing unusual and largely unreported types of clause structure. Andrew Radford debunks the myth that colloquial English has a substandard, simplified grammar, and shows that it has a coherent and complex structure of its own. The book develops a theoretically sophisticated account of structure and variation in colloquial English, advancing an area that has been investigated from other perspectives, such as corpus linguistics or conversational analysis, but never before in such detail from a formal syntactic viewpoint.

ANDREW RADFORD is Emeritus Professor at the University of Essex. He has written nine books on syntactic theory and English syntax, including *Syntactic Theory and the Structure of English* (1997), *Minimalist Syntax* (2004) and *Analysing English Sentences* (2016), all published by Cambridge University Press.

# *Colloquial English*

## In this series

*Earlier issues not listed are also available*

# COLLOQUIAL ENGLISH

## STRUCTURE AND VARIATION

ANDREW RADFORD

*University of Essex*

CAMBRIDGE
UNIVERSITY PRESS

# CAMBRIDGE
UNIVERSITY PRESS

University Printing House, Cambridge CB2 8BS, United Kingdom

One Liberty Plaza, 20th Floor, New York, NY 10006, USA

477 Williamstown Road, Port Melbourne, VIC 3207, Australia

314–321, 3rd Floor, Plot 3, Splendor Forum, Jasola District Centre,
New Delhi – 110025, India

79 Anson Road, #06–04/06, Singapore 079906

Cambridge University Press is part of the University of Cambridge.

It furthers the University's mission by disseminating knowledge in the pursuit of
education, learning, and research at the highest international levels of excellence.

www.cambridge.org
Information on this title: www.cambridge.org/9781108428057
DOI: 10.1017/9781108552202

First published 2018

Printed in the United Kingdom by Clays, St Ives plc

*A catalogue record for this publication is available from the British Library.*

*Library of Congress Cataloging-in-Publication Data*
Names: Radford, Andrew, author.
Title: Colloquial English : structure and variation / Andrew Radford.
Description: Cambridge, United Kingdom : Cambridge University Press, [2018] |
Series: Cambridge studies in linguistics
Identifiers: LCCN 2017058251 | ISBN 9781108428057 (hardback)
Subjects: LCSH: English language – Variation. | English language – Spoken
English. | English language – Grammar. | Conversation analysis – Data processing.
| Linguistic change. | Communication models.
Classification: LCC PE1074.7 .R36 2018 | DDC 425–dc23
LC record available at https://lccn.loc.gov/2017058251

ISBN 978-1-108-42805-7 Hardback
ISBN 978-1-108-44869-7 Paperback

This book is dedicated to my dear wife Khadija, whose unswerving and enduring love, friendship and selflessness have supported my research, and whose winning smile and irresistible laughter have lit up life in Grey Britain for the past four decades. Words can never express my feelings for you and the profound debt I owe you.

# Contents

# *Acknowledgements*

This book has greatly benefited from invaluable help provided by numerous people. I will not attempt to list them all here, but special thanks are due to the following (listed alphabetically, by surname) for helpful observations, suggestions, references or data.

Paolo Acquaviva, Enam Al-Wer, Merete Anderssen, Doug Arnold, Martin Atkinson, Sjef Barbiers, Gavin Barry, Josef Bayer, Paola Benincà, Bob Borsley, Oliver Boxell, Memo Cinque, Chris Collins, Stephen Crain, Silvio Cruschina, Peter Culicover, Simone De Cia, Yoshio Endo, Claudia Felser, Ángel Gallego, Teresa Guasti, Liliane Haegeman, Roger Hawkins, Alison Henry, Maria Lluïsa Hernanz Carbó, Wolfram Hinzen, Philip Hofmeister, Anders Holmberg, Georgios Ioannou, Eiichi Iwasaki, Ángel Jiménez-Fernández, Wyn Johnson, Mike Jones, Marie Labelle, Richard Larson, Adam Ledgeway, Mireia Llinàs-Grau, Jim McCloskey, Jaume Mateu, Jamal Ouhalla, Susan Pintzuk, Gemma Rigau, Ian Roberts, Tom Roeper, Luigi Rizzi, Louisa Sadler, Andrew Spencer and Julio Villa-García.

More specific contributions are acknowledged at appropriate points in the text. I should also like to thank anonymous referees for helpful comments (particularly on the organisation of the text), Neil Smith and Andrew Winnard for encouraging me to publish my work as a research monograph with Cambridge University Press, and Anna Oxbury for invaluable help with copy-editing.

In addition, I would like to thank the University of Essex for granting me a period of research leave which enabled me to undertake much of the groundwork for the research findings reported here, and for allowing me to continue to use their research facilities after my retirement, in my capacity as Emeritus Professor.

I would also like to express my retrospective thanks to those teachers who (half a century ago) played a formative role in my undergraduate and graduate education at (Trinity College) Cambridge, and inspired me to go on and pursue research. These include Prof. Pat Boyde (eminent Dante scholar) and the late

Prof. Ralph Leigh (eminent Rousseau scholar) who were perceptive enough to see that I had no literary soul and encouraged me to pursue philology and linguistics rather than Dante and Racine; the late Prof. Peter Rickard (eminent French philologist) and the late Dr Joe Cremona (eminent Romance philologist) who inspired my interest in Romance philology and awakened in me a fascination with linguistic data; and Prof. Pieter Seuren (eminent syntactician) who guided and inspired my graduate work on syntax. The debt I owe to all of you is incalculable.

And finally, a special word of thanks to all the broadcasters who have not only entertained me so richly over the past decade, but have also provided a fertile source of data for my research. I can't thank them all here, but I'd like to single out a few favourites: Alan Green, Tim Vickery, Geoff Boycott, Jonathan Agnew and the late Jimmy Armfield and Graham Taylor. What a massive job (%that) you guys do in sharing your wisdom and wit with us, and in always giving 110%!

# *Prologue*

Over the past four decades, I have produced a series of books characterising aspects of the syntax of standard English (Radford 1981, 1988, 1997a, 1997b, 2004a, 2004b, 2009a, 2009b, 2016). During that time, I have become increasingly aware (mainly from paying close attention to the language used on popular British radio and TV stations) that in colloquial English we find non-canonical structures (i.e. structures not reported in grammars of standard varieties of English) which are very different in nature from the structures found in the kind of standard English used e.g. in national newspapers or news bulletins on radio and TV. I have used occasional examples of such colloquial English structures as the basis of some of the exercise material in my syntax books, asking readers to describe how the non-canonical structures in the exercise material differ from the canonical structures described in the main text. Examples of non-canonical structures mentioned in earlier books of mine are given below (where the constituents of interest are highlighted in bold or italics):

(1)  a. *What a mine of useless information* **that** I am (Sir Terry Wogan, BBC Radio 2; Radford 1988: 501)
  b. Let's find out **how good** you are *a driver* (Jeremy Clarkson, BBC2 TV; Radford 2009a: 426)
  c. That's the guy **who** I think*'s sister* is the lead singer in a new band (Radio presenter, Top Shop, Oxford Street, London; Radford 1988: 526)
  d. *What* is thought **has** happened to him? (Reporter, BBC Radio 5; Radford 2004a: 429)
  e. *To which* of these groups do you consider that you belong **to**? (Form issued by the Council in the town where I live; Radford 2009a: 233)
  f. I hit **shots** that I know I can hit *shots* (Tiger Woods, BBC Radio 5; Radford 2016: 313)
  g. This information is asked for on the census-form, [**which** they threaten to fine you up to a thousand pounds if you don't fill *the thing* in] (Civil Liberty spokesman, BBC Radio 5; Radford 2016: 477)

1

Such structures are interesting for (at least) five different reasons.

One is that they raise the question of whether (as prescriptivists would have us believe), non-canonical structures like those above are simply instances of 'sloppy grammar' produced by people who have an inadequate mastery of the syntax of 'proper English', so that sentences like those in (1) have no real structure (or have a 'wild' structure not conforming to principles of Universal Grammar (UG)). In this monograph, I shall argue strongly against this view, and instead maintain that they have a UG-compliant structure of their own, and that studying this structure closely tells us a great deal about parametric variation in syntax.

A second reason why non-canonical structures like those in (1) are interesting is that they have the potential to raise challenging descriptive questions about the structure of particular types of phrase or sentence. By way of illustration, consider the WH+COMP structure in (1a), where an (italicised) wh-phrase is followed by a (bold-printed) overt complementiser. One descriptive question which this raises is how an overt complementiser like *that* comes to be used in a main-clause wh-exclamative structure, when overt complementisers in English are generally not used in wh-clauses, nor in main clauses either. Could the answer be (as suggested by Zwicky 2002: 227) that (1a) is a reduced variant of a cleft sentence structure such as 'What a mine of useless information *it is* that I am', with the (italicised) *it is* string undergoing deletion in the phonology?

A third reason why non-canonical structures are interesting is that they can potentially cast light on theoretical issues. For example, the possibility of extracting *how good* out of the phrase *how good a driver* in (1b) calls into question the robustness of the claim made by Bošković (2005, 2008a, 2009a) that languages with (definite/indefinite) articles disallow left branch extractions – and indeed the same could be said about extraction of *who* out of the DP *who's sister* in (1c). As a further example, consider a sentence like (1d). What appears to happen here is that *what* originates as an argument of the verb *happen* and then (via successive movement operations) becomes first the subject of *has* and then the subject of *is*. However, this latter movement provides an apparent empirical challenge to two principles widely considered to be universal. One is the Phase Impenetrability Condition/PIC of Chomsky (1998) under which a constituent c-commanded by a phase head P is impenetrable to any constituent c-commanding the maximal projection of P. If all finite clauses are CPs and all CPs are phases (as Chomsky claims), PIC would bar T-*has* from attracting *what* to move from being the specifier of T-*is* to becoming the specifier of T-*has*, because there is a CP phase boundary intervening between the two. Furthermore, the same movement would also violate the Inactivity Condition of Chomsky (2008: 150) which makes an A-chain inactive for further syntactic operations once its uninterpretable features have been valued: this is because the uninterpretable case feature on *what* will be valued by agreement with T-*is* and thereafter be inactive and so unable to be attracted by T-*has*. Thus, sentences like (1d) can potentially force us to re-evaluate the putative universality of fundamental principles.[1]

A fourth reason why non-canonical structures are interesting is that they offer the potential to shed light on the nature of microvariation in English, and thereby contribute to our understanding of microcomparative syntax. They also raise the sociolinguistic issue of whether (some) such structures are restricted to use in certain 'fringe' registers or varieties of English, as is often claimed. A case in point is provided by WH+COMP structures like (1a), where a wh-constituent is followed by an overt complementiser. Such WH+COMP structures are generally considered to be restricted to use in a handful of varieties of English. For example, they are reported as characteristic of Irish English in Henry (1995); and Zwicky (2002: 227) remarks that the speaker who produced sentence (1a) is 'not only a speaker of Irish English, but a proud speaker of this variety, given to exaggerating his Irishness'. However, data I have collected from live, unscripted radio and TV broadcasts suggest that such structures are used by a far broader spectrum of speakers from diverse social and geographical backgrounds.

A fifth reason why non-canonical structures are of interest is that they raise the psycholinguistic question of whether (some) such sentences could be the result of processing errors – e.g. blends or memory lapses. For example, a sentence like (1d) could in principle be the result of a blend between an impersonal passive like *What is it thought has happened to him?* and an infinitival structure like *What is thought to have happened to him?* In much the same way, a preposition doubling structure like (1e) could in principle result from a memory lapse, if (when reaching the end of the sentence), the speaker forgets having pronounced a copy of the preposition at the beginning of the sentence and spells it out again at the end of the sentence.

So, as we see from the foregoing discussion, non-canonical structures are of interest from five different perspectives (prescriptive, descriptive, theoretical, sociolinguistic and psycholinguistic). This book aims to characterise a set of

---

[1] See Danckaert et al. (2016) for an an interesting account of this type of structure.

non-canonical syntactic structures found in colloquial English. The data used here come mainly from recordings which I have made of popular programmes on British radio and TV stations over the past decade, using live, unscripted broadcasts in order to avoid possible prescriptive influences from copy-editors. Typical sources were popular sports broadcasts from BBC Radio 5, BBC Radio 5 Sports Extra, BBC World Service, Talksport Radio, BBC TV, ITV, Sky Sports TV and BT TV. Programmes recorded included discussion forums, phone-ins and sports commentaries. The data were collected in an informal (unscientific) manner and transcribed orthographically by me. For obvious reasons, I excluded utterances containing dysfluencies (e.g. incomplete sentences), as well as structures produced by non-native speakers. These broadcast data are (where appropriate) supplemented and complemented by data from other sources (e.g. internet data).[2]

Although I have collected data on numerous non-canonical structures over the past decade, in this book I focus on aspects of the cartography of the clause periphery in colloquial English (i.e. that part of the structure on the lefthand edge of the clause, preceding the subject). This gives the book a novel focus in two respects: firstly because there is relatively little cartographic work on English, and secondly because there is even less work based on spoken language data. The book is organised into four core chapters as follows. Chapter 1 presents an overview of research into the clause periphery in English since the 1950s. Chapters 2–4 take a detailed look at the syntax of topics, complementisers, and *how come*, examining where they are positioned with respect to a variety of other peripheral constituents in colloquial English, and how they are derived. More specifically, chapter 2 examines the syntax of three types of topic found in colloquial English, which differ in whether they are linked to their associated proposition syntactically (via a gap), lexically (via a resumptive expression), or pragmatically (via a chain of pragmatic inferencing). Chapter 3 deals with complementiser spellout in colloquial English: it focuses mainly on non-canonical uses of the

---

[2] As should be obvious, there are methodological shortcomings in using a randomly collected set of anecdotal data. For a discussion of the relative merits and reliability of different methods of collecting linguistic data, see Schütze (1996), Cowart (1997), Hoffmann (2011: ch. 2), Weskott & Fanselow (2011), Schütze & Sprouse (2014), Radford (2016: 1–9). On the drawbacks of collecting linguistic data from a corpus (or from the web), see Schütze (2009). For a defence of the use of introspective judgement data rather than other sources of data, see Newmeyer (2003, 2005, 2006a, 2006b) on usage-based data, and Sprouse (2011), Sprouse et al. (2013), and Sprouse & Almeida (2011a, 2011b, 2012a, 2012b) on experimental data. For evidence that linguists may give different grammaticality judgements about sentences than non-linguists, see Dąbrowska (2010).

complementiser *that*, offering an account of how *that* comes to occupy a wide range of positions within the clause periphery in colloquial English. Chapter 4 deals with the syntax of *how come* clauses, and discusses variation in their use in respect of whether *how come* can or cannot be followed by *that*, and whether or not *how come* triggers Auxiliary Inversion. The book concludes with a brief Epilogue highlighting key aspects of the research findings reported here.

This book follows in the footsteps of a burgeoning tradition of work which adopts a theoretical approach to the syntax of register variation. In this sense, it is cast in the mould of research on registers such as diary styles (Haegeman 1990a, 1990b, 1997, 2000b, 2013; Matushansky 1995; Horsey 1998; Haegeman & Ihsane 1999, 2001), newspaper headlines (Simon-Vandenbergen 1981; Stowell 1991, 1996), recipe books and instruction manuals (Haegeman 1987; Massam 1989; Massam & Roberge 1989; Culy 1996; Sigurdsson & Maling 2007), note-taking (Janda 1985), telegrams and text messages (Barton 1998), telephone conversations (Hopper 1992), online blogs (Teddiman & Newman 2010), and emails/ postcards (Nariyama 2006). It is also in the same mould as research on specific syntactic phenomena such as subject, object and article drop (Weir 2008, 2009, 2012, 2014b, 2018), non-standard patterns of agreement (Adger & Smith 2010), and extra *be* constructions (Massam 2017). However, it differs from (most of) the above in that it is not an article focusing on one specific register or phenomenon, but rather a monograph-level study which explores the syntax of (a range of different constituents within) the clause periphery in everyday spoken English.

In this sense, the present book can more readily be compared with Alison Henry's (1995) seminal monograph on Belfast English, which offered a minimalist perspective on the syntax of subject–verb agreement, imperative subjects, *for-to* infinitives, interrogative inversion and contact relatives in Belfast English; however, it differs from her book in having a more unitary focus (on the clause periphery), and in looking at non-standard, non-dialectal variation rather than focusing on one specific dialect. A more recent comparison could be drawn with Liliane Haegeman's (2012) cartographic study of the left periphery in English; however, it differs in that her study focuses mainly on adverbial clauses and uses data from print media, whereas the present book covers a wider range of peripheral structures, and utilises data from spoken English.

Overall, this book has four main goals. One is the goal of dispelling the prescriptive myth that colloquial English is an inferior form of speech characterised by sloppiness and an absence of 'proper grammar'. The second is the descriptive goal of increasing awareness of the wide range of structural variation found in non-dialectal forms of colloquial English, and showing that this variation can be characterised in formal syntactic terms. The third is the theoretical goal of showing how the syntax of non-canonical structures can contribute to debates in contemporary theoretical linguistics. And the fourth is the methodological goal of showing how a usage-based approach can contribute an invaluable source of data which complements other (e.g. introspective and experimental) approaches and lead to a deeper understanding of the nature of syntactic structure and variation in contemporary colloquial English.

I hope this book will inspire, inform and guide researchers working on one or more of the topics covered in it, and will serve as a useful source for (graduate or advanced undergraduate) research seminars on syntactic theory and English syntax. I also hope that you will have as much fun reading it as I had collecting and collating the data!

# 1 *Background*

## 1.1 Introduction

The locus of the syntactic variation discussed in this book is the clause periphery – i.e. that part of the structure on the left edge of the clause, preceding the subject. More specifically, the book discusses the position occupied by a range of peripheral constituents and how they get there, dealing with topics in Chapter 2, complementisers in Chapter 3 and *how come* in Chapter 4. Since the research reported in Chapters 2–4 requires a good understanding of the syntax of the clause periphery, I use this chapter to present an overview of a range of approaches to the syntax of the clause periphery in research over the past 60 years or so. In §1.2, I look at how peripheral material was treated in the S-analysis of clause structure in work in the 1950s and 1960s, before turning to examine S'- and S"-analyses in work in the 1970s. In §1.3, I go on to outline the CP-analysis of the periphery in work in the 1980s, and the use of CP recursion to handle structures containing multiple peripheral constituents. In §1.4, I discuss the rationale for positing a more articulated structure for the periphery in cartographic work from the 1990s on. In §1.5 I look at the structure of defective clauses which have a truncated periphery.

## 1.2 S-, S'- and S"-analyses

In early work in generative grammar in the 1950s and 1960s (e.g. Chomsky 1955, 1957, 1964, 1965, 1966; Lees 1960; Rosenbaum 1965, 1967; Ross 1967) clauses were taken to be S-constituents generated by a phrase structure rule such as S → NP AUX VP (Chomsky 1965: 68) which can be seen in contemporary terms as specifying that S is formed by merging (i.e. combining) NP, AUX and VP.[1] Peripheral constituents preceding the subject were generally

---

[1] To simplify discussion, I set aside numerous theoretical issues and details of descriptive implementation throughout – e.g. the fact that some researchers took AUX to be a constituent of V or VP (see e.g. Chomsky 1964: 36), some grouped AUX and VP into a separate constituent

treated as being introduced by transformations positioning them on the left edge of S. For example, complementisers (in the analysis of Rosenbaum 1967) were absent from the underlying structure, and inserted on the left edge of S via a Complementiser Placement transformation. On this view, the bracketed complement clause in a sentence like (1a) below would have the flat structure shown in simplified form in (1b), with the italicised complementiser being positioned on the edge of S:

(1)    a.  It is likely [*that* Harry will sue Larry]
       b.

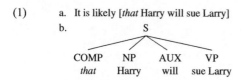

Emonds (1970) assumed a similar structure, while taking COMP to be introduced by a phrase structure rule like S → COMP NP AUX VP.

Other peripheral constituents were analysed as coming to be positioned on the edge of S via movement operations. For example, Chomsky (1955; 1975: 440) takes relative pronouns to be moved to the front of the S-constituent containing them by a Wh-Movement transformation ($T_W$), so that the bracketed relative clause in a sentence like (2a) below would have a superficial structure along the lines of (2b), with the italicised relative pronoun positioned on the edge of S:

(2)    a.  Documents were stolen from my house [*which* I had taken home]
       b.

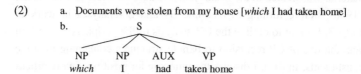

Similarly, a wh-question such as (3a) below was taken by Chomsky (1957: 69; 1975: 433) to involve an Auxiliary Inversion transformation ($T_Q$) positioning the (bold-printed) inverted auxiliary to the left of the subject, and subsequent Wh-Movement ($T_W$) positioning an (italicised) interrogative wh-constituent to the left of the inverted auxiliary, so deriving the structure shown in simplified form in (3b):

(3)    a.  *What* **has** John told Mary?
       b.

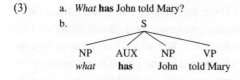

---

(e.g. the predicate phrase constituent of Chomsky 1965: 102) and some decomposed AUX into other constituents (like T, M, C).

Hooper & Thompson (1973: 466) propose an analogous structure for sentences involving Negative Constituent Preposing and Auxiliary Inversion, and suggest that a sentence like (4a) below has the structure (4b):

(4)  a.  *Never* **have** I had to borrow money
     b.

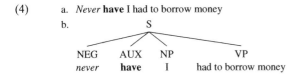

In a similar vein, Ross (1967: 209, 310) and Emonds (1970: 24) take Topicalisation to be an operation which moves an (italicised) topic to the edge of S, so that a clause like that in (5a) below has the structure in (5b):

(5)  a.  *These points*, we can discuss later
     b.

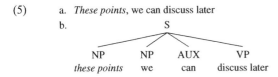

In much the same way, Emonds (1970: 25) treats left-dislocated constituents as positioned on the edge of S. Likewise, Ross (1967: 309) treats Adverb Preposing in a clause like that bracketed in (6a) below as involving movement of the (italicised) adverb to a position between the (bold-printed) complementiser and the (underlined) subject, so resulting in a structure like that in (6b):

(6)  a.  I promised [**that** *tomorrow* <u>he</u> would be there]
     b.

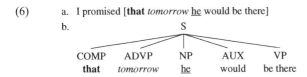

And Emonds (1970: 24) takes VP Preposing in a sentence like (7a) below to involve 'preposing a VP to the front of an S' (ibid.), so resulting in a structure like (7b):

(7)  a.  John intends to make a table, and [*make one* he will]
     b.

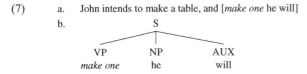

There is little point in accumulating further specific examples: the more general point illustrated in (1–7) above is that peripheral constituents in work of this era were generally treated as positioned on the edge of S, serving as daughters of S and sisters of the subject.

A step change in research on the periphery came with work on the syntax of questions by Katz & Postal (1964), refined in later work by Chomsky (1968), Jacobs & Rosenbaum (1968) and Baker (1970). They posited that wh-questions contain an S-initial question morpheme (designated as Q), generated by a phrase structure rule of the form S → (Q) NP AUX VP (Chomsky 1972: 144). Thus, the underlying structure of a sentence like (8a) below would be as shown in simplified form in (8b):

(8)     a.  What will they do?
        b.              S

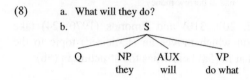

        Q      NP      AUX      VP
              they     will    do what

The Q-morpheme serves the semantic function of being a question operator and the syntactic function of serving as a trigger both for AUX Inversion and Wh-Movement. Q first attracts the auxiliary *will* to move to a position immediately following Q, so deriving:

(9)                      S

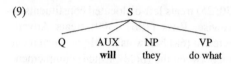

        Q      AUX      NP      VP
              **will**    they    do what

Subsequently, Q attracts the interrogative constituent *what* to move into the Q position and replace Q, so deriving the structure in (10) below (simplified, inter alia, by not showing the gap created by movement of *what*):

(10)                     S

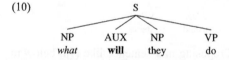

        NP      AUX      NP      VP
       *what*   **will**   they     do

Baker (1970: 209) argues that the Q-replacement analysis provides 'an explanation for the fact that only one questioned constituent may be moved'. He further posits (1970: 207) that the complementisers *if/whether* are 'lexical realizations of the Q morpheme', and claims that this accounts for why *if/ whether* and wh-constituents are mutually exclusive (e.g. in a sentence like '*I wonder *who* **whether/if** he saw').[2]

---

[2] Taking a rather different approach, Chomsky (1972) treats Q as a morpheme attracting (and being substituted by) a fronted auxiliary in questions, suggesting that Auxiliary Inversion 'replaces Q by Aux' (1972: 148). As pointed out by Ioannou (2011), the Q-analysis raised the dilemma of whether Q was replaced by a fronted auxiliary or by a fronted wh-constituent.

A related approach is adopted by Emonds (1970), who takes COMP to be the constituent that attracts wh-constituents (in interrogatives, relatives and exclamatives) to move to the periphery. More specifically, Emonds supposes that COMP is base-generated on the edge of S and can either be filled by an overt complementiser, or be expanded into an empty NP, PP or AP constituent which can subsequently be filled by a wh-constituent of the same category moving into the vacant NP/PP/AP position in COMP. This means that a relative clause like that bracketed in (11a) below will have a structure along the lines of (11b), with the italicised relative PP positioned on the edge of S:

(11)   a.   This is the hotel [*in which* he is staying]

   b.

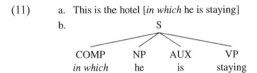

This analysis accounts for the restriction that only one wh-constituent is preposed in wh-clauses, and the further restriction that COMP cannot contain both an overt wh-constituent and an overt complementiser.

   A key characteristic of the S-analysis of clause structure was the assumption that all peripheral constituents are positioned on the edge of S and thus are immediately contained in the same S-projection as (and hence are sisters of) the subject and auxiliary. However, some work towards the end of the S-era treated phrasal peripheral constituents as adjoined to S. For example, Ross (1967: 288) took AUX Inversion to involve inverting auxiliary and subject, but took Wh-Movement to involve adjunction of a wh-phrase to S. Under Ross' analysis, a sentence like (12a) below would have the structure in (12b), with the bold-printed inverted auxiliary immediately contained within a lower S-constituent and the italicised wh-phrase within a higher one:

(12)   a.   *Which car* **will** Sam pick up?

   b.

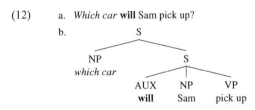

This results in a structure in which the wh-phrase comes to occupy a position higher than the subject and auxiliary. It also marks a move away from the earlier assumption that clauses have a flat structure, towards a more hierarchical structure.

The assumption that the clause periphery has a hierarchical structure was taken a step further in seminal work by Bresnan (1970, 1972, 1976, 1979). She argued that COMP is contained within a higher clausal projection termed S'/ S-bar, introduced into the derivation by the phrase structure rule S' → COMP S (Bresnan 1972: 29). On this view, the clause bracketed in (13a) below would have the structure in (13b):

(13)    a.  I feel sure [that Mary will agree]
        b.

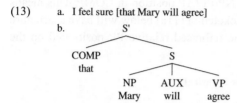

Evidence in support of postulating two different types of clausal projection (S and S-bar) comes from data such as the following:

(14)    a.  I've been wondering **whether** (but am not entirely sure **that**) *the President will approve the project* (Radford 1988: 293)
        b.  I wonder **whether** John likes fish and (**\*whether**) *Mary meat* (Radford 1988: 294)
        c.  Mary says **that** John, she doesn't know, but (**\*that**) *she'd like to see drunk* (Rochemont 1989: 149)

The S-bar analysis can account for such data by positing that the italicised shared string in (14a) is an S-constituent, and that Gapping in structures like (14b) and Topicalisation in structures like (14c) can only apply where S-constituents are coordinated. By contrast, it is not immediately obvious how data like (14) could be accounted for under the S-analysis.

Adopting the S-bar analysis, Bresnan takes Wh-Movement to be a 'COMP-attraction transformation' (1972: 42) which serves the function of 'moving a constituent ... into COMP position' (ibid.). The analysis of COMP as the landing site for preposed wh-constituents was widely adopted in subsequent work (e.g. Chomsky 1973, 1977a, 1977b). Noting that there are languages (and varieties of English) which permit structures in which a wh-constituent is positioned to the left of an overt complementiser, Chomsky & Lasnik (1977: 434) hypothesised that '*Wh* Movement places a *wh*-phrase to the left of the complementiser in COMP' (1977: 446). This means that in embedded questions like (15a) below, the wh-constituent *which dress* will be positioned to the left of a null complementiser. Chomsky (1980: 5 and 1981: 47) takes the wh-constituent to adjoin to COMP. On this view, the clause bracketed in (15a) below will have the structure (15b):

(15)   a.   I can't remember [which dress Mary was wearing]

   b.

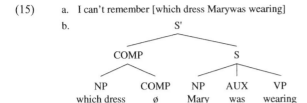

In a similar vein, Higgins (1973) took Topicalisation to involve movement of a topic into COMP.

However, not all work of the S-bar era assumed that movement to the periphery involved attraction to COMP. For example, Baltin (1982) treated Topicalisation as involving adjunction to S, and Wh-Movement as involving adjunction to S-bar. This would mean that a clause like that bracketed in (15a) has the structure in (16) below:

(16)

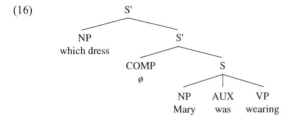

Overall, despite some differences of detail and implementation, work of this era generally assumed that all peripheral constituents could be accommodated within an analysis which posited two different clausal projections (an S-nucleus and an S-bar periphery).

However, this assumption was called into question in work by Chomsky (1977b), who argued for the postulation of a third clausal projection: more specifically, he argued that fronted and dislocated topics are contained within a superordinate S''/S-double-bar constituent immediately containing S'. He proposed that the topic is directly generated in situ, and is associated either with an in situ resumptive pronoun (in the case of Left Dislocation), or with a null operator that moves from its initial position within S to its derived position in COMP (in the case of Topicalisation).[3] On this analysis, Topicalisation in (17a) below will involve the structure in (17b), where *Op* is a fronted null operator adjoined to a null complementiser:

---

[3] But see Rivero (1980: 380) for an argument from Spanish against the claim that Topicalisation involves movement of a null operator.

(17)   a.  This book, you should read

b.

```
                      S"
              _____
            NP              S'
         this book     _____
                    COMP          S
                    Op+ø     _____
                          NP    AUX    VP
                         you   should  read
```

And Left Dislocation in (18a) below will have the (simplified) structure in (18b) if we take COMP to contain an inverted auxiliary which moves into COMP (Williams 1974; den Besten 1983), with a fronted wh-constituent adjoined to it:[4]

(18)   a.  This kind of book, who would you buy it for?

b.

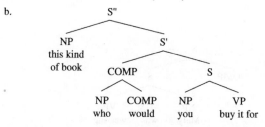

Thus, the S"-analysis provides for two different peripheral projections within clauses – namely S' and S". However, as we will see in the next section, the S-, S'- and S"-analyses were subsequently abandoned in the light of new ideas which led to the development of a CP analysis of the clause periphery in the 1980s.

## 1.3   CP Analyses

Theoretical developments in the early 1980s sounded the death knell of the S-, S'- and S"-analyses of clause structure outlined in the two previous sections, because they fell foul of a range of different constraints. One such was an Endocentricity Constraint to the effect that all phrases and clauses are projections of a zero-level head (i.e. a lexical item/word or inflectional affix), and conversely all zero-level heads (including functors) project into phrases. This ruled out S'- and S"-projections, since they were headed by an

---

[4] Baltin (1982) proposes an alternative analysis of Auxiliary Inversion under which the auxiliary moves to the lefthand edge of S, and does not move into COMP.

S-constituent which is clearly not a word or affix; it also ruled out S, because this is neither a zero-level category, nor (if analysed as S) a projection of one. Conversely, it also meant that functors (including auxiliaries, complementisers and determiners) project into phrases, and this resulted in inflected auxiliaries and inflectional affixes (categorised as INFL/I constituents in Chomsky 1981) projecting into IP (Chomsky 1981: 52), complementisers projecting into CP (Chomsky 1981: 274) and determiners projecting into DP (Abney 1987).

A second constraint which had important repercussions for the analysis of the clause periphery was the Binarity Constraint of Kayne (1984), requiring all syntactic structure to be binary-branching. This ruled out the traditional ternary-branching (NP+AUX+VP) analyses of S, and likewise ruled out the possibility of transformations moving other constituents to the edge of S (because this would result in structures which were not binary-branching).

A third constraint which had radical consequences for the structure of the periphery was the Like-Attracts-Like Constraint/LALC of Baltin (1982: 2), requiring that 'When they move, phrasal categories adjoin to phrasal categories, and non-phrasal categories adjoin to non-phrasal categories.' Since only heads and maximal projections can undergo movement (not intermediate projections), LALC allows only adjunction of one head to another, or of one maximal projection to another – and indeed this assumption is adopted in Chomsky (1986: 71, 73). For obvious reasons, LALC rules out the possibility of Wh-Movement involving adjunction to COMP, since this would involve a maximal projection (e.g. the wh-phrase *which dress* in 15b) adjoining to a COMP head.

A fourth constraint which had important implications for the analysis of the periphery was the No-Adjunction-to-Arguments Constraint posited by Chomsky (1986: 6), barring adjunction to arguments (and reformulated by McCloskey 1992: 9 as barring adjunction to a phrase s-selected by a lexical head). This constraint was widely invoked to account for contrasts such as the following:

(19)   a. We all agree [**that** *behaviour like this*, we simply cannot tolerate]
       b. *We all agree [*behaviour like this*, **that** we simply cannot tolerate]

In (19), the *that*-clause is an s-selected argument of the lexical head *agree*, and the Adjunction Constraint thus prevents the italicised fronted topic from being adjoined to the overall *that*-clause (i.e. to S-bar) in (19b), while permitting it to be adjoined to the S-constituent beginning with *we* in (19a). However, the very same constraint also means that Wh-Movement in embedded argument clauses can no longer be treated as adjunction to S under the S-analysis of clauses (as in 20a below) or as adjunction to S-bar under the S-bar analysis of clauses (as in 20b):

(20)    a.  I can't remember [$_S$ *which dress* [$_S$ Mary was wearing]]
        b.  I can't remember [$_{S'}$ *which dress* [$_{S'}$ Mary was wearing]]

Analyses like those in (20) are ruled out because they involve adjunction to a clause which is an argument of the lexical head *remember*.

A fifth constraint which undermined earlier analyses of clause structure was the requirement imposed in Trace Theory (Fiengo 1977) that a moved constituent should c-command its trace (i.e. the gap that it leaves behind when it moves). This rules out S-bar structures like (18b) because *who* would not c-command its trace. Furthermore, if the stronger requirement were imposed that a moved constituent should asymmetrically c-command its trace, it would also rule out taking peripheral constituents to be moved to the front of S, as in (10).

A sixth constraint with radical implications for the analysis of clause structure was the Linear Correspondence Axiom/LCA of Kayne (1994), specifying that linear ordering at PF is determined by asymmetric c-command relations between constituents. It follows from LCA that 'specifiers are an instance of adjunction, and that no phrase can have more than one other phrase adjoined to it' (Kayne 1994: xvi). This means that clauses with multiple constituents in their periphery cannot be treated as S- or S-bar constituents with multiple constituents adjoined to them.

A seventh constraint (or more properly, PF filter) which impacted on the structure of the periphery was the Doubly Filled COMP Filter of Chomsky & Lasnik (1977), which Chomsky (1981: 243) formulated as in (21) below (where $\alpha$ and $\beta$ are overt constituents):

(21)    **Doubly Filled COMP Filter/DFCF**
        *[$_{COMP}$ $\alpha$ $\beta$]

DFCF rules out the possibility of structures like (18b) in which COMP contains both an overt auxiliary and an overt wh-constituent.

Constraints such as those mentioned above undermined earlier analyses of clause structure and led to the development of a new binary-branching CP/IP analysis of clause structure in which the clause periphery is treated as a CP headed by a complementiser constituent which came to be abbreviated as C rather than COMP, and the clause nucleus is treated as an IP constituent headed by an INFL(ection) constituent which came to be abbreviated as I. Under this analysis, peripheral constituents were generally taken to be positioned on the edge of CP: for instance, complementisers were analysed as base-generated in the head C position of CP, inverted auxiliaries as moving from the head I position of IP to adjoin to a null complementiser in C, and fronted wh-phrases as moving into spec-CP (the specifier position within CP). This meant that the periphery of a sentence like (22a) below had the CP structure shown in simplified form in (22b), with nominals like *which dress* and *Mary* now treated as DPs rather than as NPs (the DP containing *Mary* being headed by a null determiner, the symbol ø being used to denote a null head, and — denoting a gap left behind by movement):

(22)    a.    Which dress was Mary wearing?

        b.

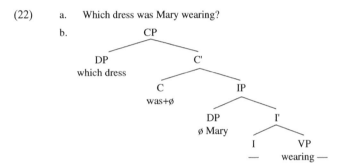

An analysis like that in (22b) satisfies the Endocentricity Constraint in that clauses are treated as projections of I/INFL and C/COMP, and conversely functors like C, I and D project into phrases. It also satisfies the Binarity Constraint, since all non-terminal nodes in (22b) are binary-branching. In addition, it satisfies the Like-Attracts-Like Constraint because e.g. AUX-Inversion is treated as adjunction of the I-head *was* to a null C-head. Furthermore, it satisfies the No-Adjunction-To-Arguments Constraint, because in an embedded clause like that bracketed in (15a) 'I can't remember [which dress Mary was wearing]', the fronted wh-phrase moves into spec-CP and does not adjoin to the CP argument itself. Moreover, (22) satisfies the c-command requirement on traces, since the moved DP *which dress* asymmetrically c-commands its trace.[5] In addition, it satisfies the Linear Correspondence Axiom,

---

[5] A potential complication is that the inverted auxiliary does not c-command its trace, if adjoined to a null complementiser. There are a variety of ways of dealing with this (e.g. by making a technical modification to the definition of the c-command relation, or by supposing that the null complementiser is deleted, or by taking Auxiliary Inversion to be the kind of operation which does not leave a trace behind), but I will not pursue this matter further here.

because both CP and IP have only one specifier/adjunct each. And finally, (22b) also satisfies the Doubly Filled COMP Filter because the C(OMP) node contains only one overt constituent – namely the inverted auxiliary: by contrast, the filter correctly prevents an inverted auxiliary from adjoining to an overt complementiser, so ruling out sentences like *'I wondered **if** *was* he leaving'.

The CP analysis in (22b) makes two different types of position available in the clause periphery: (i) the C position in CP housing heads positioned in the periphery (e.g. complementisers and inverted auxiliaries); and (ii) the specifier position in CP housing phrases (or, more technically, maximal projections) positioned in the periphery, such as fronted wh-constituents. However (as we'll see in the remainder of this section), a number of linguists subsequently identified a range of types of clause whose periphery could not be given a straightforward characterisation in terms of a single CP constituent, and (for the most part) proposed to handle them in terms of CP recursion.

As a case in point, consider a multiple-complementiser structure like the bracketed complement clause in (23a) below, which McCloskey (1992) argues to have a CP recursion structure along the lines of (23b), in which each of the complementisers heads a separate CP projection and the underlined subordinate clause (which, for concreteness, I take to be a SUBP headed by the SUB/subordinating conjunction *when*) is adjoined to the lower CP (below denoted as $CP_2$):

(23)

a.    She maintained [**that** <u>when they arrived</u> *that* they should be welcomed] (McCloskey 1992: 21, fn.13, attributing the example to Richie Kayne)

b.

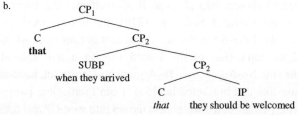

A structure like (23b) will not violate the Adjunction Constraint, since (under McCloskey's analysis) the *when*-clause is adjoined to an inner CP which is not an argument (by virtue of being the complement of a functional head, not of a lexical head).

However, (23b) will violate the Doubly Filled COMP filter, if this is translated into the CP framework in the manner specified below:

(24)    **Doubly Filled COMP Filter/DFCF** (CP version)
        The edge of a CP headed by an overt complementiser (like *that/for/if/whether*)
        cannot contain any other overt constituent

Formulating DFCF as in (24) will allow structures like (22b) where C contains
an inverted auxiliary while excluding structures like (23b) where C contains an
overt complementiser. One way of avoiding violation of DFCF in clauses like
that bracketed in (23a) is to posit an even more complex CP recursion structure
like (25) below in which the *when*-clause is contained within a separate CP
projection of its own:

(25)

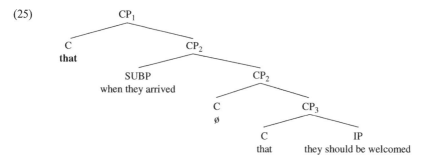

There would then be no DFCF violation because the edge of each CP would
contain only one overt constituent.

   In a similar vein, a number of linguists argued that a CP recursion analysis is
appropriate for embedded clauses containing a complementiser followed by
additional peripheral material. For example, Authier (1992: 331) argued that
clauses like that bracketed in (26a) below containing a fronted focused negative
phrase and an inverted auxiliary can be handled in terms of a CP recursion
analysis like (26b):

(26) a.    John swore [that under no circumstances would he accept their offer]

   b.

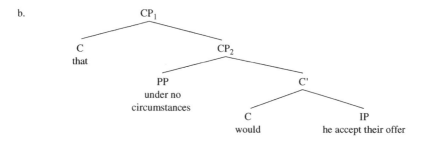

Authier (1992: 333) proposes a similar analysis for complementiser+topic structures, under which a clause like that bracketed in (27a) below will have the CP recursion structure in (27b):

(27)  a.    It's true [that this book, he read thoroughly]

b.

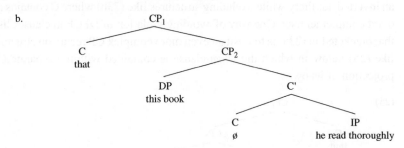

The key assumption made in analyses like (26) and (27) is that clauses with a periphery containing a complementiser followed by some other peripheral constituent involve CP recursion.

In much the same way, Browning (1996) argued that CP recursion can account for why intervening constituents ameliorate *that*-trace effects in *that*-clauses like those bracketed below (simplified in numerous ways, including by showing only the initial trace *t* of the moved wh-pronoun *who*):

(28)    a.  *Robin met the man who Leslie said [CP [C **that**] *t* was mayor of the city]
        b.  Robin met the man who Leslie said [CP [C **that**] [CP for all intents and purposes [C ø] *t* was mayor of the city]]

Under Browning's analysis, the *that*-clause in (28a) contains a single CP projection headed by *that*, and the complementiser *that* is immediately adjacent to the trace *t*, so inducing a violation of the COMP-Trace Filter/ CTF of Chomsky & Lasnik (1977: 451), which rules out superficial structures in which an overt complementiser is immediately followed by a trace. By contrast, the *that*-clause in (28b) contains two CP projections – an outer one with *that* as its head, and an inner one with a null complementiser as its head and the PP *for all intents and purposes* as its specifier; there is no CTF violation in the double-CP structure in (28b), since the trace is immediately preceded by a null complementiser, not by the overt complementiser *that*.

A further type of clause structure which has been argued to require a CP recursion analysis is an elliptical structure termed Swiping by Ross (1969). This is illustrated in (29) below (from Hartman & Ai, 2009), where the bracketed clause is said to have undergone Swiping (an operation which involves fronting of a head-last wh-PP containing a preposition positioned after its wh-complement, and deletion of the material marked by ~~strikethrough~~):

(29)     He fought in the civil war, but I don't know [*which side for* ~~he fought~~]

Under the analysis of Swiping proposed by van Craenenbroek (2004, 2010), the italicised elliptical clause is a CP-recursion structure. The DP *which side* originates as the complement of the preposition *for*, and the whole PP moves to become the specifier of an inner CP, so resulting in the structure shown in simplified form below:

(30)

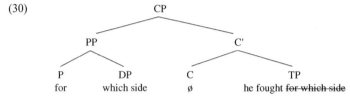

The CP in (30) is embedded as the complement of a null complementiser which then attracts the wh-DP *which side* to become its specifier, in the manner shown by the arrow in (31) below. In the PF component, the TP complement of the lower CP subsequently undergoes a form of ellipsis known as Sluicing, ensuring that the constituents of TP receive a silent spellout (marked by strikethrough below). The italicised string in (29) thus has the superficial structure shown below:

(31)

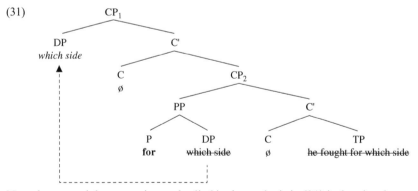

Note that a crucial assumption embodied in the analysis in (31) is that the clause periphery in cases of Swiping has a CP recursion structure.

The general point illustrated above is that a range of different structures involving multiple peripheral constituents have been argued to involve CP recursion. Indeed, if we were to generalise the Doubly Filled COMP Filter (24) and follow Koopman (2000) in postulating a Generalized Doubly Filled Comp Filter which bars the edge of a given CP from containing more than one overt constituent, it follows that every overt peripheral constituent will be contained in a separate CP. As noted by Koopman (2000: 343), this will mean that the periphery of a root question such as (32a) below will require a CP recursion structure like (32b), with the auxiliary and wh-constituent contained in separate CP projections:

(32)    a.  Who did you see?
        b.  [CP2 Who [C ø] [CP1 [C did] you see]]

Koopman (2000: 342) argues that a CP recursion analysis will also be required in structures where peripheral constituents precede overt complementisers. As noted by Hallman (1997: 91), this would mean that a Belfast English interrogative clause like that bracketed in (33a) below would have a CP recursion structure along the lines of (33b):

(33)    a.  I wonder [*what street* **that** he lives in] (Henry, 1995: 89)
        b.  [CP2 *what street* [C ø] [CP1 [C **that**] he lives in]]

On this analysis, *what street* is the specifier of an outer CP and *that* the head of an inner CP.

There seems little point in providing further examples of CP recursion structures here. The general point illustrated above is that much work from the 1980s on analysed the periphery of clauses containing multiple peripheral constituents as comprising recursive CP projections. However, the CP recursion analysis was subsequently criticised by a number of linguists as being unable to provide a principled account of restrictions on the range and ordering of constituents in the periphery. We'll look at these criticisms and the conclusions they led to in the next section.

## 1.4    The Cartographic Approach

From the end of the 1980s on, awareness developed of potential problems with the CP recursion analysis of the periphery. For example, Authier (1992) and Watanabe (1993b) observed that topics (and certain other peripheral projections) are barred from occurring in structures like those asterisked below (examples from Maki & Kaiser 1998: 291):

(34)    a.  John believes **that**/*ø *this book*, Mary wrote
        b.  *John regrets **that** *this book*, Mary wrote
        c.  *John believes the rumor **that** *this book*, Mary wrote
        d.  ***Before** *this book*, Mary wrote, John had been a student
        e.  ***That** *this book*, Mary wrote is true

If we adopt a CP recursion analysis in which each of the highlighted peripheral constituents is contained in a separate CP projection headed by a bold-printed complementiser, it is not obvious why a CP containing a topic should not be able to appear after a null C in (34a), or after a factive complementiser in (34b), or after a complementiser introducing a noun complement clause in (34c), or after a complementiser introducing a subordinate clause in (34d), or after a complementiser introducing a subject clause[6] in (34e).

There have been a number of attempts to develop a constraint which will account for some or all of the restrictions illustrated in (34). Iatridou (1991) argues that CP-recursion is limited to environments where the recursive CP is governed by a selecting verb; likewise, Iatridou & Kroch (1992: 5) suggest that 'CP recursion occurs only when the embedded clause is governed by a local L-marking verb'[7] although they subsequently offer the qualification that 'perhaps any +V lexical category' can license a second CP complement (1992: 18). In a similar vein, Maki & Kaiser (1998: 291) suggest that only an embedded CP which is L-marked and has an overt edge (i.e. has an overt head or specifier) allows a CP complement. The overt edge condition will rule out use of a null complementiser in (34a), while the L-marking condition will rule out (34c, d) if nouns and prepositions/subordinating conjunctions do not L-mark their complements.

However, this still leaves (34b) unaccounted for, since *regret* L-marks its *that*-clause complement. Watanabe (1993a: 131) deals with this problem by positing that factive clauses contain an additional CP projection with a null factive operator as its specifier, positioned below the CP containing *that*: he further conjectures (ibid.) that 'CP recursion is allowed only once' (a restriction which would follow from the assumption that only an L-marked CP can have a CP complement). This means that the periphery of the embedded clause in (34b) would require an illicit triple-CP structure, with one CP housing the complementiser *that*, another housing the null factive operator and a third housing the topic.

Further problems posed by the CP-recursion analysis of the periphery were highlighted by Lasnik & Saito (1992). They argued that the

---

[6] It should be noted, however, that what appear to be clausal subjects like the underlined in *That the defendant is guilty has been proved beyond all reasonable doubt* have been argued to be peripheral topics by Emonds (1976), Koster (1978), Williams (1980), Stowell (1981), Safir (1986), Bresnan (1994), Postal (1998) Alrenga (2005) and Haegeman (2012: 6.4.2).

[7] According to Chomsky (1986: 14) a constituent is L-marked if it is theta-marked by (and is the sister of) a lexical category.

ungrammaticality of sentences like (35a) below shows that recursion of dislocated topics is not permitted in English, while the ungrammaticality of (35b) shows that dislocated topics do not occur in embedded clauses:

(35)    a. *\*John*, **Mary**, he likes her (Lasnik & Saito, 1992: 79, ex. 47)
        b. \*I believe **that** *this book*, you should read it (Lasnik & Saito, 1992: 77, ex. 42)

If dislocated topics are housed in spec-CP and CP recursion is permitted, there is no obvious way of ruling out topic recursion in sentences like (35a), or topic embedding in sentences like (35b). By contrast (Lasnik & Saito note), this problem can be overcome if dislocated topics are housed in a dedicated topic projection (which they term TP, but which I shall here denote as TOPP, in order to avoid confusion with the widespread use of TP to denote a Tense Projection). If phrase structure rules (or selectional constraints) specify that a TOPP can only take an IP as its complement, if (non-defective) embedded clauses are CPs, and if CP never permits a TOPP complement, this will rule out the possibility of both types of structure in (35).[8]

In a similar vein, Pesetsky (1989) noted that the CP recursion analysis faces problems in accounting for why topics occur after (but not before) wh-phrases in structures like (36) below, but the converse order is found in (37):

(36)    a. ?I wonder **to whom** *this book* we should give (Pesetsky 1989: 13, ex. 41b)
        b. \*I wonder *this book* **to whom** we should give (Pesetsky 1989: 13, ex. 42a)

(37)    a. ?*This book*, **to whom** should we give? (Pesetsky 1989: 13, ex. 39b)
        b. \***To whom** should *this book*, Bill give? (Pesetsky 1989: 13, ex. 40c)

Similarly, Watanabe (1993a) observed that the CP recursion analysis seemingly can't explain why fronted topics are positioned after (but not before) complementisers in structures such as (38) below:

(38)    a. John said **that** *this book*, Mary should have read (Watanabe 1993a: 127, ex. A16a)
        b. \*John said *this book*, **that** Mary should have read (Watanabe 1993a: 127, ex. A16b)

If each of the peripheral constituents highlighted in (36–8) above is positioned on the edge of a separate CP projection and if CPs can be recursively stacked, it

---

[8] On the claim that (cross-linguistically) topics serve as specifiers of a TOPP, see Grewendorf (2002), Grohmann (2006) and Platzack (2001, 2004). In §2.5, we will see that sentences like (35b) do in fact occur in colloquial English.

is not clear how the relevant restrictions are to be handled. As noted by Müller (1995: 344), under the CP recursion analysis, there is 'no obvious way to distinguish between the landing site of Wh-Movement and the landing site of topicalisation'.

By contrast, if a CP with a topic specifier is treated as a topic projection and a CP with an interrogative specifier is treated as an interrogative projection, the data can be given a relatively straightforward characterisation. Thus, we can handle (36) by supposing that the verb *wonder* selects an interrogative projection as its complement (not a topic projection).[9] In relation to (37), we can posit that an interrogative projection allows a topic projection as its complement, but that the converse ordering is not possible in a root clause because the intervening topic projection blocks the inverted auxiliary *should* from moving into the head position in the interrogative projection containing *to whom*. And in much the same way, we can handle (38) by positing that the verb *say* selects a declarative projection as its complement, not a topic projection.

A further set of data which prove problematic to handle in a CP recursion analysis concern the observation made by Rizzi (1997: 301) that complementisers like *that* and *for* occupy different positions with respect to peripheral adverbials, as illustrated by the clauses bracketed below:

(39)  a. She is anxious [**that** *John* should leave tomorrow]
  b. She is anxious [**that**, tomorrow, *John* should leave]

(40)  a. She is anxious [**for** *John* to leave tomorrow]
  b. *She is anxious [**for**, tomorrow, *John* to leave]

As (39b) illustrates, a peripheral adverb like *tomorrow* can intrude between the declarative complementiser *that* and the subject *John*, but not between the infinitival complementiser *for* and *John*. This is difficult to account for in a principled fashion under a CP recursion analysis in which each of the highlighted constituents is contained in a separate CP. By contrast, the data can be accommodated in a relatively straightforward fashion if the two types of complementiser represent two different types of peripheral head, with *that* marking declarative force (or clause type[10]), and *for* marking (non-)finiteness. We can then suppose that a force-marking head like *that* occupies the highest position in the periphery (as the head of FORCEP) and so can precede

---

[9] However, this only holds if we suppose that interrogative operators in embedded questions occupy spec-FORCEP – not if they occupy some lower position in the periphery.
[10] Although Rizzi treats force and type as equivalent terms, Huddleston (1994) highlights important differences between the two notions – though I will set this issue aside here.

a peripheral adverbial like *tomorrow*, whereas a head like *for* which marks non-finiteness occupies the lowest position in the periphery (as the head of a FINP/finiteness projection) and so must immediately precede the clause subject.

The key insight underlying the idea of splitting up CP into a number of distinct types of projection is that each different type of peripheral constituent occupies a specific position on the edge of a *dedicated* functional projection (i.e. a functional projection which is dedicated to housing a constituent of the relevant type on the edge of the projection). This implies that a peripheral topic will appear on the edge of a topic projection, a peripheral focused constituent on the edge of a focus projection ... and so on. For obvious reasons, this has been dubbed the 'split CP' analysis, because it involves splitting what had previously been treated as a single type of peripheral constituent (= CP) into a number of different types of projection (a topic phrase, focus phrase etc.), each housing a different type of peripheral constituent. The approach has been developed in work by Luigi Rizzi over the past three decades (see Rizzi 1996, 1997, 2000a, 2000b, 2001, 2004a, 2004b, 2005, 2006a, 2006b, 2006c, 2010, 2011, 2012, 2013a, 2013b, 2013c, 2014a, 2014b, 2015a, 2015b; Rizzi & Shlonsky 2006, 2007; Cinque & Rizzi 2008; Rizzi & Cinque 2016; Rizzi & Bocci 2017), and built on by many other researchers.[11] It has been termed *cartographic* since its aim is to devise a 'map of the left periphery' (Rizzi 1997: 282). A wide range of different types of peripheral projection have been posited by different authors in different papers: here, I will concentrate on some of the main types of peripheral projection which have played a prominent role in Rizzi's own work.

---

[11] These include Aboh (2004, 2005, 2006, 2010), Badan (2007), Badan & Del Gobbo (2010), Baltin (2010), Belletti (2004a, 2004b, 2009), Benincà (2001, 2006, 2010, 2012a, 2012b), Benincà & Cinque (2010), Benincà & Munaro (2010), Benincà & Poletto (2004), Bianchi & Frascarelli (2010), Biloa (2013), Bocci (2004, 2007, 2009, 2013), Cardinaletti (2004, 2009), Cinque (2002), Cinque & Rizzi (2008, 2010), Cruschina (2006, 2008, 2010a, 2010b, 2011a, 2011b, 2012), Cruschina & Remberger (2008), Danckaert (2011, 2012), Demonte & Fernández Soriano (2009, 2013, 2014), Durrleman (2008), Endo (2007, 2014), Franco (2009), Frascarelli & Hinterhölzl (2007), Frascarelli & Puglielli (2007), Garzonio (2005), Grewendorf (2002), Grewendorf & Poletto (2009), Haegeman (2000a, 2003, 2004, 2006a, 2006b, 2007, 2009, 2010, 2012), Jayaseelan (2008), Jiménez-Fernández (2011, 2015), Krapova (2002), Krapova & Cinque (2008), Laenzlinger (1999), Legate (2002), Munaro (2003), Nye (2013), Paoli (2003, 2007), Paul (2005, 2014), Pearce (1999), Poletto (2000), Puskás (2000), Roberts (2004), Roussou (2000), Salvi (2005), Shlonsky (1997, 2010, 2014), Speas & Tenny (2003), Torrence (2013), Tsai (2008), Villa-García (2010, 2011a, 2011b, 2012a, 2012b, 2012c, 2015), Villalba (2000). For overviews of the relevant literature, see Cinque & Rizzi (2010), Shlonsky (2010), Rizzi (2013a), Rizzi & Cinque (2016), Rizzi & Bocci (2017).

Rizzi argues that each dedicated peripheral head typically[12] carries an edge feature which requires it to project a particular kind of specifier on the edge of the relevant projection. If we use the traditional label C to denote a peripheral head, we can say that a C with a topic feature (TOP) houses a topic (i.e. requires a topic to be projected on the edge of the projection as its specifier),[13] a C with a focus feature (FOC) houses a focused constituent, a C with a question feature (Q) houses an interrogative constituent,[14] a C with a relative feature (REL) houses a relativised constituent, a C with an exclamative feature (EXCL) houses an exclamative constituent, a C with a modifier feature (MOD) houses an adverbial modifying the clause, and so on. The head of each such projection will assign its specifier and complement a specific interpretation at the semantics interface: for instance, the head of the topic projection tells the semantic component that 'my specifier is to be interpreted as the topic, and my complement as the comment' (Cinque & Rizzi 2010: 51). In a similar way, a focus head 'assigns the focus interpretation to its specifier, and the presupposition interpretation to its complement' (ibid.), where the presupposition constitutes 'new information, information assumed not to be shared by the interlocutor' (Rizzi 2014b: 8). A key assumption in this approach is that (in conformity with the Linear Correspondence Axiom of Kayne 1994), no peripheral projection can have more than one specifier/adjunct.

Two different (but equivalent) types of notation have been used in the relevant literature to differentiate various types of peripheral head. One

---

[12] However, FIN and FORCE heads are distinct, in that they never house a specific type of specifier, but rather serve as a projection through which other constituents can transit. Thus, Rizzi and Shlonky (2006: 348) note that 'FIN is not a criterial head', in the sense that 'it is not a head which assigns any special interpretive property to its Spec' – though this position seems to be at odds with the claim made in Rizzi (1997: 308) that fronted topic arguments are directly merged in spec-TOPP and associated with an operator which moves to spec-FINP (which would mean that spec-FINP is the criterial position for the relevant operator). Similarly, Watanabe (1993a: 128) observes that declarative *that* never projects a specifier. This could be seen as equivalent to positing that FORCE and FIN are phase heads, in terms of the theory of phases developed in Chomsky (1998, 2008).

[13] I set aside here the possibility that there may be more than one different type of topic, and consequently more than one type of topic projection: for discussion, see Belletti (2004a), Benincà & Poletto (2004), Bianchi & Frascarelli (2010), Frascarelli & Hinterhölzl (2007) and Samek-Lodovici (2006, 2009); see also §2.2.

[14] However, Rizzi & Bocci (2017) argue that wh-question operators are focused in root questions (and so move to the edge of FOCP), and that it is only in embedded questions that wh-question operators move to the edge of a QP/question projection. Nonetheless, they show *which book* moving to the edge of Q-projection in a root question in *Which book should you read?* (2017: 13). In earlier work (e.g. Rizzi 2001), the relevant wh-question projection was labelled WHP (a convention which I shall use in this book, since it avoids confusion with the use of QP to denote a quantifier phrase).

convention (used inter alia in Rizzi 2006a) takes (e.g.) the head of an inter-rogative projection to be a C constituent carrying a Q(uestion)-feature, denoted as $C_Q$. On this view, the interrogative projection in a complement clause like that bracketed in (41a) below has the structure shown in simplified form by the bracketing in (41b) (where $t$ is a trace of the fronted wh-phrase *which book*, representing a null copy of the fronted constituent):

(41)    a. Bill wonders [which book she read]
        b. Bill wonders [which book $C_Q$ [she read $t$]] (Rizzi 2006a: 112, ex. 31)

An alternative convention (used e.g. in Rizzi 2011) takes the relevant periph-eral head to carry the label Q, so that the bracketed clause in (41a) instead has the structure shown below:

(42)    Bill wonders [which book Q [she read $t$]] (adapted from Rizzi 2011:1)

The two labelling conventions used in (41b) and (42) can be regarded as extensionally equivalent (hence interchangeable) for present purposes.[15]

Rizzi (2014b) argues that the postulation of a range of different types of peripheral head hosting different types of specifier gains cross-linguistic support from structures in other languages like those bracketed below which contain a bold-printed peripheral head with an italicised specifier:

---

[15] It could be argued that the notation in (41b) is preferable, since it enables us to draw a distinction between (e.g.) an interrogative clause (like that italicised in 'I don't know *which he chose*') and an interrogative nominal (like *which book?*), by positing that the clause is a projection of a $C_Q$ head (i.e. of an interrogative complementiser) whereas the nominal is a projection of a $D_Q$ head (i.e. of an interrogative determiner). A similar labelling dilemma could be argued to arise in relation to differentiating between clausal and nominal topic structures, if the two italicised expressions in the structure bracketed below are topics associated with the underlined DP:

> (i) Arsenal fans have been scathing about [*Arsène Wenger, his side*, the way it's been set up] (Andy Goldstein, Talksport Radio)

If so, labelling the bracketed structure as a projection of a TOP head would fail to differentiate between topic-containing nominals like that in (i) above, and topic-containing clauses like that in (ii) below:

> (ii) *Arsène Wenger, his side*, Arsenal fans have been scathing about the way it's been set up

We could differentiate the two types of structure if clausal topic structures are CPs with a $C_{TOP}$ head, and nominal topic structures are DPs with a $D_{TOP}$ head. It should nevertheless be noted that it is by no means clear that the bracketed string in (i) is a topic structure; it could alternatively be a string of three separate DPs (serving as parallel complements, each being an elaboration of the content of the previous one).

(43) a. Ik weet niet [*wie* **of** [Jan gezien heeft]] (Dutch, Haegeman 1994: 382)
 I know not who Q Jan seen has
 'I don't know who Jan has seen'
 b. Un sè [do [*dan lo* **yà** [Kofi hu ì]]] (Gungbe, Aboh 2004)
 I heard that snake the TOP Kofi killed it
 'I heard that the snake, Kofi killed it'
 c. Un sè [do [*dan lo* **wè** [Kofi hu]]] (Gungbe, Aboh 2004)
 I heard that snake the FOC Kofi killed
 'I heard that the snake, Kofi killed'
 d. Der Mantl [*den* **wo** [dea Hons gfundn hot]] (Bavarian, Bayer 1984b)
 The coat which REL the Hans found has
 'The coat which Hans has found'
 e. [*Che bel libro* **che** [ho letto]]! (Italian)
 What nice book EXCL I.have read
 'What a nice book I read'

In such sentences, each of the italicised constituents serves as the specifier of a (bold-printed) dedicated peripheral head (*wie*$_{who}$ serving as the specifier of the interrogative head *of*$_{if}$, *dan*$_{snake}$ *lo*$_{the}$ as the specifier of the topic head *yà* or the focus head *wè*, *den*$_{which}$ as the specifier of the relative head *wo*$_{where}$, and *che*$_{what}$ *bel*$_{nice}$ *libro*$_{book}$ as the specifier of the exclamative head *che*$_{that}$, this being taken to be a 'a lexicalization of the EXCL head' in Rizzi 2011: 8).

Constituents occupying the specifier position of a peripheral projection do so in order to satisfy a requirement for them to occupy a criterial position in a spec–head relation with a matching head (Rizzi 1997: 282): e.g. a peripheral topic must occupy the specifier position in a topic projection in order to be in a spec–head relation with a topic head. Once a constituent is in its criterial position, it is thereby frozen in place in consequence of a constraint termed the Criterial Freezing Condition in Rizzi (2005, 2006a, 2010, 2014a, 2014b) and Rizzi & Shlonsky (2006, 2007). For present purposes, this constraint can be formulated as follows:

(44) **Criterial Freezing Condition/CFC**
 A constituent which occupies its criterial position is frozen in place

The effect of CFC can be illustrated by the contrast below:

(45) a. Did you ask [*where* he had been —]?
 b. *Where* did you ask [— he had been —]?

The interrogative operator *where* will move from the gap position in (45a) above to its criterial position on the edge of the bracketed interrogative clause. This means that in consequence of CFC, *where* is frozen in place and cannot subsequently move to the front of the main clause as in (45b).

An interesting question arising from the postulation of a wide variety of different types of peripheral projection is what determines the range of positions which they can occupy. Rizzi has used a template as an informal descriptive device designed to represent the relative positions occupied by different functional heads in the clause periphery. He has refined the template considerably over the years, as can be seen by the different versions given below (where TOP = Topic, FOC = Focus, INT = Interrogative, MOD = Modifier, FIN = Finiteness, and a star is used to mark the possibility of having one or more heads of the relevant type):[16]

(46)    a. FORCE > TOP* > FOC > TOP* > FIN (Rizzi 1997)
        b. FORCE > TOP* > INT > TOP* > FOC > TOP* > FIN (Rizzi 2001)
        c. FORCE > TOP* > INT > TOP* > FOC > TOP* > MOD* > TOP* > FIN
           (Rizzi 2015a)

However, it should be noted that Rizzi has repeatedly stressed that such templates have the status of descriptive artefacts rather than theoretical postulates. In other words, the relative ordering of different types of peripheral constituent (and possible combinations of them) are determined by a range of independent factors (e.g. interface requirements, or locality principles). For example, semantic factors determine that no clause can contain more than one FORCEP projection (since no clause can be of two different types), and no more than one FOC projection (because the complement of a focus head is a presupposition, and FOCP recursion would thus lead to an 'interpretive clash', according to Rizzi 1997: 297). In addition, selectional requirements (e.g. the requirement for *announce* to have a declarative complement) mean that FORCEP will be the highest projection in embedded clauses, because 'verbs select for declaratives or questions, not for clauses with or without topic (or focus)' (Rizzi 1997: 301). Likewise, if (accusative) case assignment requires adjacency between case assigner and case assignee,[17] this

---

[16] It seems clear that such templates will need further refinement, since they do not include the REL(ative), EXCL(amative) and Q(uestion) heads which Rizzi posits in other work (e.g. 2012, 2015a). Furthermore, Rizzi (2014a) allows for FINP recursion structures of the form FINP > MODP > FINP. MODP is a projection which houses circumstantial adjuncts: a variant of it is the SCP/scene-setting projection of Haegeman (2000a).

[17] See Chomsky (1980, 1981) and Stowell (1981), and in particular the remark by Chomsky (1981: 94) that 'Case-assignment for English involves a condition of adjacency: that is, Case is

means that FINP must be the lowest projection in the periphery of a clause like that in 'She's keen **for** (*immediately) *him* to leave', in order for the FIN head *for* to be immediately adjacent (and thus able to assign accusative case) to the subject *him* (as noted by Rizzi 1997: 301). A third factor limiting possible orderings and combinations of peripheral projections are locality constraints (see Abels 2012 for discussion). For example (as noted by Rizzi 1997: 303), an intervening peripheral adverb blocks AUX Inversion in a conditional structure like *Had (*yesterday) John done that* ..., because the Head Movement Constraint of Travis (1984) requires successive-cyclic movement of the auxiliary, but the auxiliary cannot transit through the inert head of the peripheral projection housing the adverb *yesterday*. And structures like (47) below in which one fronted argument crosses another:

(47)     *He is someone *who* **nothing** dare anyone say to

will be barred by a constraint preventing a constituent from moving across an intervening constituent of a similar kind, which Abels (2012: 247) characterises succinctly as follows:

(48)     **Intervention Constraint**[18]
         Likes cannot cross likes

The constraint (48) will prevent the relative argument *who* crossing the fronted negative argument *nothing*, since the two are alike in respect of both being argumental operators undergoing A-bar movement.

---

assigned by V or P to an adjacent NP.' I note, however, that my broadcast English data contain the following example in which an (underlined) adverb intervenes between a (bold-printed) transitive complementiser and the (italicised) subject that it assigns accusative case to:

(i)  It's time **for** <u>now</u> *Rooney* to go (Darren Gough, TalkSport Radio)

If we follow Rizzi (2014a) in allowing FINP recursion structures of the form FINP+MODP+FINP, it could be that the *for*-clause in (i) has the structure below:

(ii)  [$_{FINP}$ for [$_{MODP}$ now [$_{FINP}$ ø [$_{TP}$ Rooney to go]]]]

If so, the lower FIN head may be the case assigner for *Rooney* (and indeed *for* could in principle originate there, and move from the lower to the higher FIN position).

[18] For discussion of intervention effects, see Starke (2001), Boeckx & Jeong (2004), Rizzi (2004b), Endo (2007), Friedmann et al. (2009), Haegeman (2012), and Haegeman et al. (2014). An interesting structure from my broadcast English data which potentially violates the constraint (by moving an italicised interrogative operator across a bold-printed one) is the following:

(i)  The pollsters are still adjusting *how many states* **who**'s gonna get (Sandy Warr, Talksport Radio)

## 1.5    Truncated Clauses

Although complete clauses have the status of FORCEP projections able to house a full range of peripheral constituents (e.g. topics and/or focused constituents), there are also a class of truncated clauses whose periphery projects only as far as the FINP projection. These include bare declarative complement clauses (i.e. those not introduced by an overt complementiser like *that*). Rizzi & Shlonsky (2007) and Rizzi (2014a) posit that bare declarative complement clauses are truncated at the FINP level (in the sense that they project only as far as FINP): accordingly, Rizzi (2014a: 30) claims that 'finite clauses with null complementisers in English involve truncation of the higher structure of the C system, of Force (hence the absence of the declarative force marker *that*) and of the Topic-Focus system' and thus contain only 'a vestigial presence of the C-system' comprising a projection of 'the lowest head, Fin'.[19]

We can illustrate the difference between complete and truncated clauses in relation to the contrast between (49) and (50) below (cf. 34a above):

(49)    a. John believes [**that** Mary wrote this book]
        b. John believes [**that** *this book*, Mary wrote]

(50)    a. John believes [Mary wrote this book]
        b. *John believes [*this book*, Mary wrote][20]

Given Rizzi's assumptions, the *that*-clauses in (49a/b) will be FORCEP constituents with the respective peripheral structures bracketed in (51a/b) below:

(51)    a. John believes [$_{FORCEP}$ [$_{FORCE}$ **that**] [$_{FINP}$ [$_{FIN}$ ø] Mary wrote this book]]
        b. John believes [$_{FORCEP}$ [$_{FORCE}$ **that**] [$_{TOPP}$ *this book* [$_{TOP}$ ø] [$_{FINP}$ [$_{FIN}$ ø] Mary wrote]]]

Since (by hypothesis) a complete clause (= FORCEP) can contain a medial peripheral projection like TOPP, and since a declarative FORCE head in a complement clause is spelled out as *that*, the *that*-clause in (49b/51b) can contain an (italicised) peripheral topic.

---

[19] A related proposal is made by de Cuba & MacDonald (2013a, 2013b), who draw a distinction between referential clauses (which they claim to lack illocutionary force, and take to be truncated clauses with the status of FINP), and non-referential clauses (which denote a speech act and have the status of FORCEP).

[20] For expository purposes, let us assume for the time being that sentences like this are ungrammatical, although in Chapter 3 we will see that there are speakers who produce such sentences.

But now consider the sentences in (50). Since the complement clauses in (50a, b) do not contain *that*, they are not FORCEP constituents (if we take *that* to always spell out a FORCE head). Hence, they must be constituents smaller than FORCEP, as shown below:

(52)  a. John believes [$_{FINP}$ [$_{FIN}$ ø] Mary wrote this book]
   b. *John believes [$_{TOPP}$ *this book* [$_{TOP}$ ø] [$_{FINP}$ [$_{FIN}$ ø] Mary wrote]]

(52a) is grammatical because a bridge verb like *believe* (unlike a non-bridge verb like *quip*) can select a truncated clause/FINP as its complement.[21] By contrast, (52b) is ungrammatical because (by hypothesis) only a complete clause projecting a FORCEP constituent can contain a medial projection like TOPP, not a defective clause: since there is no FORCEP to license it in (52b), the TOPP projection is therefore unlicensed. We can reach the same conclusion by a different route. For a structure like (52b) to be grammatical would require us to suppose that verbs (like *believe*) can select for a TOPP complement. However, as noted by Rizzi (1997: 310) in relation to such structures 'The higher verb selects for the specification of Force, not the TopP: verbs select for declaratives or questions, not for clauses with or without topic (or focus).'

Complete and truncated clauses differ in that (in standard varieties of English), truncated clauses (like that bracketed in 53a) below allow subject extraction, but complete clauses (like that bracketed in 53b) do not (in standard varieties of English):

(53)  a. Who do you think [*t* will come]?
   b. *Who do you think [that will come]?

This phenomenon is widely known as the '*that*-trace effect', because the bracketed clause in (53b) contains an illicit structure in which the complementiser *that* is immediately followed by a trace of the extracted subject *who*. I will sketch Rizzi's account of this phenomenon, because this will turn out to be central to analyses discussed in later chapters (e.g. Endo's 2014, 2015a, 2015b, 2017 analysis of *how come* questions).

---

[21] A bridge verb is a verb (like *say*) which allows (italicised) material to be extracted out of its (bracketed) complement (thereby bridging the boundary between the two clauses), whereas a non-bridge verb (like *quip*) does not – as illustrated below

(i)  *What* did Mike **say/*quip** [that she had done —]?

It is widely assumed that bridge verbs can select a bare clausal complement, but non-bridge verbs cannot.

Rizzi posits that the the subject *who* in (53) originates within VP as an internal argument (and complement) of the unaccusative verb *come*. The TP *will come who* is merged as the complement of the subject projection posited by Rizzi (2005) and Rizzi & Shlonsky (2006, 2007), which is taken to involve 'a SUBJ head in the high part of the IP system' (Rizzi 2005: 212), with T/I moving to SUBJ (according to Rizzi & Shlonsky 2006), and the subject moving to spec-SUBJP and thereby coming to occupy its criterial position in the periphery, which is 'a position dedicated to a special interpretive property of the scope-discourse kind ("aboutness")', according to Rizzi (2005: 213).[22] This SUBJP constituent is in turn merged with a FIN head which is taken by Rizzi & Shlonsky (2007) to carry the feature [+N] marking it as nominal, together with an unvalued number agreement feature [αPl(ural)]. The subject *who* does not move into spec-SUBJP since if it did so, it would be in a criterial position for a subject and thus be frozen in place by the CFC (44), and hence be unable to be extracted (so wrongly predicting that 53a is ungrammatical). Instead, *who* 'skips over' SUBJP and moves directly into spec-FINP in order to value the unvalued number feature on FIN (which 'has an unvalued number feature which is valued when the subject moves to its Spec' according to Rizzi & Shlonsky 2007: 19), so giving rise to the structure below:

(54)    Who do you think [$_{FINP}$ *who* [$_{FIN}$ ø] [$_{SUBJ}$ [$_{SUBJ}$ ø] [$_{TP}$ [$_T$ will] come ~~who~~]]]

Subsequently, *who* can move out of FINP into the matrix clause, ultimately coming to occupy its criterial position in spec-FOCP in the matrix clause.[23] The SUBJ head must fulfil the requirement (imposed by the Subject Criterion) that it be locally c-commanded by a nominal constituent, and this requirement is satisfied by the (expletive) nominal FIN head in (54).[24] On the assumption

---

[22] Shlonsky (2014) takes the Subject Projection to be a projection of a person feature, while Rizzi (2015a) takes it to be a projection of a D head. However, I shall continue to use the more transparent label SUBJP here.

[23] Various details are glossed over here, including whether the subject moves to spec-FINP in the embedded clause directly from its thematic position in VP complement position or transits through one or more functional projections below SUBJP, and whether *who* transits through the edge of the matrix vP.

[24] An alternative analysis would be to suppose that SUBJP has a null expletive pronoun as its specifier, and this expletive satisfies the criterial requirement for SUBJ to have a subject – as suggested for Italian structures like that below in Rizzi & Shlonsky (2007:11):

(i)  Chi **credi** [che [*pro* SUBJ [vincerà]]]
     'Who do you think that will win?'

However, neither way of satisfying the Subject Criterion (whether by a nominal FIN or by a null expletive pronoun subject *pro*) would seem straightforwardly consistent with the general

that the complementiser *that* cannot lexicalise a nominal FIN carrying agreement features, it follows that the complementiser *that* can't be used in a truncated clause structure like (54).[25]

But now consider what bars subject extraction out of a complete clause like that bracketed in (53b) *'Who do you think [that will come]?' The embedded clause cannot be treated as a truncated FINP structure like that below:

(55)     Who do you think [FINP *who* [FIN that] [SUBJP [SUBJ ø] [TP [T will] come ~~who~~]]]

This is because (for reasons outlined in the preceding paragraph) only a nominal FIN can attract a subject to move to spec-FINP, and (by hypothesis) *that* cannot be used to lexicalise a nominal FIN. However, an alternative derivation which has to be ruled out is one whereby the complement clause is a complete clause in which *that* is a FORCE head which selects a FINP complement with a nominal head, with *who* escaping out of the embedded clause by transiting through spec-FINP and spec-FORCEP, as below:

(56)     Who do you think [FORCEP ~~who~~ [FORCE that] [FINP ~~who~~ [FIN ø] [SUBJP [SUBJ ø]
         [TP [T will] come ~~who~~]]]]

What blocks such a derivation? Rizzi & Shlonsky (2007: 32) suggest that (because it marks both finiteness and declarative force) '*that* is first merged in Fin, to express finiteness, and then moves to Force to check the Force

assumption that a criterial head is one which assigns a special interpretive property to its specifier, or with the more specific claim by Rizzi (2015a: 22–3) that SUBJP serves the function of 'signaling to the interpretive systems that the argument in its Spec is the argument about which the event is presented'. Rizzi & Shlonsky (2007: 13) suggest that when the interpretive systems receive 'a representation in which no argument is expressed in the aboutness position' (i.e. in spec-SUBJP), they 'interpret the structure presentationally'. This would seem to be tantamount to claiming that a SUBJP containing no argument in spec-SUBJP is semantically vacuous, raising the question of why this does not cause the derivation to crash at LF.

[25] The claim that FIN is nominal in truncated clauses raises the question of why a FINP with a nominal head can't serve as the complement of a transitive head like the preposition *of* – e.g. in structures like (iii) and (iv) below:

(i)   He's guilty, you can be sure *of* it
(ii)  That he is guilty, you can be sure *of*
(iii) You can be sure (*of) [he is guilty]
(iv)  Who do you feel sure (*of) [is guilty]?

One answer might be that only [+V] heads like verbs and adjectives can select a truncated complement, not (e.g.) a preposition/case particle like *of* – though this begs the question of how to explain this stipulation. Another might be that a nominal FIN is an expletive which (like expletive *there* under some analyses) is case-resistant and hence cannot occur as the complement of a transitive head like *of* – though this runs into the problem that seemingly transitive bridge verbs like *think/say* select a nominal FINP complement.

feature'. In the light of this, consider what will happen in the case of a structure like the following if *that* raises from FIN to FORCE:

(57)   [$_{\text{FORCEP}}$ [$_{\text{FORCE}}$ that] [$_{\text{FINP}}$ [$_{\text{FIN}}$ ~~that~~] [$_{\text{SUBJP}}$ [$_{\text{SUBJ}}$ ø] [$_{\text{TP}}$ [$_{\text{T}}$ will] come who]]]]

If *that* originates in FIN but cannot lexicalise a nominal FIN, it follows that FIN here is not nominal and so cannot satisfy the Subject Criterion. This means that the only way of satisfying the criterion is for *who* to move to spec-SUBJP; but if this happens, *who* will be frozen in place, and thus be unable to be extracted and move to the front of the main clause – so accounting for the ungrammaticality of

(53b)   *Who do you think that will come?[26]

As for varieties which allow *that*-trace violations in sentences like (53b),[27] Rizzi & Shlonsky propose that in such varieties, *that* is directly merged in FORCE, and can c-command a nominal FIN with agreement features in the lower edge of the periphery of the same clause. *Who* can then move to

---

[26]   Rizzi & Shlonsky (2007: 33) offer the following account:

> Under the natural assumption that expletive and argument functions cannot be performed by the same element, *that* ... cannot simultaneously be the head of a declarative – a clausal argument – and function as an expletive-like surrogate to formally satisfy the Subject Criterion

Rizzi (2015a: 30) suggests that movement of *that* from FIN to FORCE 'makes *that* unsuitable as an expletive satisfier of the Subject Criterion; if it did while in Fin, its movement to Force would violate criterial freezing.'

A rather different analysis would be to take *that* to be a non-nominal complementiser which is generated in FORCE and cannot occur in a clause periphery containing a nominal FIN (perhaps because of an agreement relation between FORCE and FIN, or equivalently because of features percolating down from FORCE to FIN).

[27]   My data contain the following examples of *that*-trace structures:

(i)   Michael Owen, I'm sure [**that** — will be touted round many clubs] (Stan Collymore, Talksport Radio)

(ii)   Who did you feel [**that** — ran the dressing room]? (Michael Vaughan, BBC Radio 5)

(iii)   What are we hoping [**that** — can come from this]? (Johnny Gould, Talksport Radio)

(iv)   It's another aspect of his game that I've always thought [**that** — needs improvement] (Andy Townsend, ITV)

(v)   It was an extraordinary world that we should both be glad [**that** —'s no longer part of our everyday life in Britain] (Danny Kelly, Talksport Radio)

(vi)   What it seems [**that** — happened] is that there was a break in play (Tom Vickery, BBC Radio 5)

An alternative account of such structures would be to take each bracketed clause be a truncated FINP with a nominal head as in (54), and to suppose that in the relevant varieties, *that* can lexicalise a nominal FIN.

spec-FINP to value the agreement features on FIN, and thereafter move into the matrix clause, transiting through spec-FORCEP as below:

(58)    *Who* do you think [$_{FORCEP}$ ~~who~~ [$_{FORCE}$ that] [$_{FINP}$ ~~who~~ [$_{FIN}$ ø] [$_{SUBJP}$ [$_{SUBJ}$ ø] [$_{TP}$ [$_T$ will] come ~~who~~]]]]

FIN (being a nominal expletive here) can satisfy the Subject Criterion requirement for SUBJ to be locally c-commanded by a nominal constituent.

Rizzi (2015a) extends the truncation account of subject extraction to deal with more complex cases like the following (where — represents a gap/trace left behind by movement of the subject *who*):

(59)    a. *This is the man who I think **that** — will sell his house next year
       b. This is the man who I think **that**, *next year*, — will sell his house
       c. *This is the man who I think **that**, *his house*, — will sell next year

He observes that use of the overt complementiser *that* blocks extraction of the subject *who* in a sentence like (59a), giving rise to a *that*-trace effect; however, the effect is alleviated by the presence of an intervening (italicised) peripheral adverbial in sentences like (59b), though not by the presence of an intervening topic in sentences like (59c). He proposes a FINP recursion analysis of sentences like (59b), under which the SUBJP projection serves as the complement of a nominal FINP, the relevant FINP serves as the complement of a MODP housing the adverbial adjunct *next year*, and MOD in turn serves as the complement of a non-nominal FIN containing *that*, so that (prior to movement of *who*) the embedded clause has a FINP structure which includes the peripheral projections bracketed below:

(60)    [$_{FINP}$ [$_{FIN}$ that] [$_{MODP}$ next year [$_{MOD}$ ø] [$_{FINP}$ [$_{FIN}$ ø] [$_{SUBJP}$ [$_{SUBJ}$ ø] will who sell his house]]]]

The lower (null) FIN head is nominal in nature (thereby satisfying the Subject Criterion in the manner discussed in relation to (54) above), and also carries agreement features which attract the subject *who* to move to spec-FINP, from where it can subsequently move (in successive-cyclic fashion) to the front of the relative clause containing it. By contrast, the *that*-clause in the ungrammatical topic structure in (59c) has the (simplified) pre-extraction structure below:

(61)    [$_{FINP}$ [$_{FIN}$ that] [$_{TOPP}$ his house [$_{TOP}$ ø] [$_{FINP}$ [$_{FIN}$ ø] [$_{SUBJP}$ [$_{SUBJ}$ ø] will who sell next year]]]]

Rizzi maintains that extracting *who* out of the *that*-clause in (61) is ruled out by selectional constraints, since (by hypothesis) only a nominal FIN allows subject extraction, and the only peripheral head which can select a nominal FINP as its complement is MOD (not TOP). The wh-subject *who* cannot move directly to the edge of the higher FINP in (61) because any such direct movement skipping over a lower FINP to move to the edge of a higher FINP would involve a locality/minimality violation.

However, opening up the possibility of FINP recursion raises the question of what would rule out a structure like that in (62) below, where the lower FIN is nominal and the higher FIN is not, and *who* transits through the edge of each FINP:

(62)    Who do you think [$_{FINP}$ ~~who~~ [$_{FIN}$ that] [$_{FINP}$ ~~who~~ [$_{FIN}$ ø] [$_{SUBJP}$ [$_{SUBJ}$ ø] will come ~~who~~]]]

Rizzi (2015a: 31) rules out double-FIN structures like (62) by appealing to a constraint 'blocking head reduplication' which he formulates as follows (ibid.):[28]

---

[28] If MOD is the only peripheral head that can select a nominal FINP complement, this in itself could be argued to rule out (62), without any need to appeal to the Head Reduplication Constraint/HRC. At any rate, the formulation of HRC in (63) appears to be too general, since it would seemingly (wrongly) rule out structures like those below, which appear to involve iteration of PP:

    (i)   The noise came *from inside the house*
    (ii)  *Out from under the bed* crawled James Bond

Moreover, it would also seemingly rule out recursive modification of NPs in structures like (iii) below, if each adjective is the specifier of a separate MODP projection (as in Radford 2016):

    (iii)  She dreamed of meeting a *tall, dark, handsome* stranger

This is because the head MOD of the MODP containing *tall* will select a MODP complement containing *dark*, and the head MOD of the MODP containing *dark* will select a MODP complement containing *handsome*. In addition, topic recursion structures like that below also provide a challenge for HRC:

    (iv)  *My supervisor*, **a man like that**, she would never hire (Emonds 2004: 107)

Rizzi (2015a: 32, fn. 2) suggests that such problems can be overcome if each stacked head is distinct in kind. For example, the italicised topic in (iv) is dislocated whereas the bold-printed topic is fronted, and it is reasonable to suppose that they are housed in projections with different kinds of topic heads. However, this 'get-out' is problematic for two reasons. The first is that if HRC allows recursion of two distinct types of TOP head, we would expect it also to allow recursion of two distinct types of FIN head in a structure like (62), containing a FINP headed by a non-nominal FIN spelled out as *that* stacked on top of a FINP headed by a nominal FIN with a silent spellout. The second problem is that (as we will see in Chapter 2), there do appear to be cases of topic iteration which involve two topics of the same kind – e.g. two dislocated topics.

(63)     **Head Reduplication Constraint**
          A head cannot select a categorically nondistinct head

(63) rules out (62) because it involves iteration of FINP. Since (55), (57) and (62) all fail to yield a convergent outcome, (53b) is correctly specified to be ungrammatical in standard varieties of English.[29]

The upshot of our discussion here is that bare complement clauses have a truncated periphery which projects only as far as FINP, albeit (as we have seen) FIN can itself have a MODP complement which in turn selects another FINP as its complement, thereby giving rise to FINP recursion.

## 1.6     Summary

This chapter has provided a brief introduction to approaches to the syntax of the clause periphery in work over the past seven decades. In §1.2, we saw how peripheral material was treated in the S-analysis of clause structure in work in the 1950s and 1960s, before turning to examine S'- and S''-analyses in work in the 1970s. In §1.3, I went on to outline the CP analysis of the periphery in work in the 1980s, and the use of CP recursion to handle structures containing multiple peripheral constituents. In §1.4 I discussed the rationale for positing a more articulated structure for the periphery in cartographic work from the 1990s on, examining the special status of truncated clauses in §1.5.

Having given a broad sketch of approaches to the syntax of the clause periphery in this chapter, in the remaining chapters of the book I turn to look at the syntax of the clause periphery in three different types of structure found in colloquial English. Wherever possible, I use authentic examples sourced from my own recordings of live unscripted broadcasts or from internet data, in an attempt to avoid the potential pitfalls of artificially constructed examples.

---

[29] A potential problem for Rizzi's account of *that*-trace effects is that (as observed by Ackema 2010: 228) *that*-trace effects can be alleviated by intervening parentheticals like that underlined below:

(i)   Who did you say that, as the FBI discovered recently, — was a spy?

If parentheticals are not constituents of the structure containing them (as argued by Espinal 1991), this poses problems for syntactic accounts like Rizzi's. See Ackema & Neeleman (2003) and Llinàs-Grau & Fernández-Sánchez (2013) for an alternative prosodic account of *that*-trace effects. However, it is not obvious to me how a prosodic account can handle the distinction between (59b) and (59c). I note in passing that there are varieties of English which allow *that*-trace structures (as reported in Pesetsky 1982b: 328; Engdahl 1984; White 1986: 13; Sobin 1987, 2002); Rizzi (2014a) discusses ways of handling these in his analysis.

# 2 Topics

## 2.1 Introduction

This chapter looks at the syntax of peripheral topics in colloquial English. I shall argue that colloquial English differs from more formal styles of English in making less use of fronted topics, and more use of dislocated and orphaned topics. I begin by looking at three different types of topic structure in §2.2. before turning to look at the derivation of topics in §2.3 and of multiple topic structures in §2.4. I then turn to examine the position of topics in clauses containing complementisers in §2.5, the position of topics in relation to other peripheral non-wh constituents in §2.6, the position of topics in interrogative and exclamative wh-clauses in §2.7, and the position of topics in relative clauses in §2.8. I summarise my main findings in §2.9. My overall goal in this chapter is to explore the range of positions which topics can occupy within the clause periphery, to examine how they get there, and to explore the range of clause types they can occur in: to this end, I present (and refine) a number of existing analyses.

## 2.2 Three Types of Topic in Colloquial English

In this section, I look at the types of topic structure found in colloquial English, and discuss ways in which topics differ from focused constituents.

In colloquial English, we find three superficially distinct types of structure containing a peripheral topic followed by a comment clause. One type involves an italicised topic associated with a gap (—) in the comment clause, as illustrated by the following examples from my broadcast English data:

(1)   a. *Those kind of things* I love —, I really do (Andy Dillon, Talksport Radio)
      b. The referee's let two or three bad tackles go, but *that one*, he wasn't happy with — (Gerry Armstrong, Sky Sports TV)
      c. He will not start at the weekend. *That*, I'm sure of — (Alan Brazil, Talksport Radio)
      d. You two aren't going to argue about that. *That much*, I do know — (David Gower, Sky Sports TV)

The topic is interpreted as originating in the gap position, so that (e.g.) *those kind of things* is interpreted as the complement of *love* in (1a). The gap is traditionally taken to arise through movement of the topic phrase from the gap position into the italicised position in the clause periphery via a displacement operation called Topicalisation.[1]

A second type of peripheral topic structure involves an (italicised) topic associated with an (underlined) resumptive constituent:

(2)     a. *This guy*, it was only a few hours ago that <u>he</u> had a speech that was a mile long (Peter Allen, BBC Radio 5)
        b. *These footballers*, there's a level of education that <u>they</u> require (Sean Udall, BBC Radio 5)
        c. *That kind of thing*, if they could stop <u>it</u>, they certainly would (Simon Mayo, BBC Radio 5)
        d. *Lee*, I've been following <u>his</u> progress very much over the last month (Colin Montgomerie, BBC Radio 5)

In structures like (2), the topic is said to be dislocated in the sense that it is in a separate intonation group from the comment clause, this being marked in the written language by the use of a comma (the relevant intonation contour being referred to informally as 'comma intonation'). The dislocated topic is linked to an (underlined) resumptive constituent interpreted as referring back to the topic: such structures are traditionally said to be instances of (Hanging Topic) Left Dislocation.

A third type of topic structure is that illustrated below:

---

[1]  Further potential cases of topic fronting in my broadcast English data are the following:

        (i)    He will try. *Of that*, I am certain — (Character in the channel 5 TV series *Gotham*)
        (ii)   They're chronically short of a couple of defensive players. *Of that*, there is no doubt (Michael Owen, BT Sport TV)
        (iii)  He's just a captivating personality. *Of that*, there is no doubt (Jonathan Edwards, BBC Radio 5)
        (iv)   As a team, *to bowl India out like that*, we're delighted with — (Stuart Broad, Talksport Radio)

In such cases, it might seem as if the topicalised demonstrative pronoun *that* pied-pipes the italicised material along with it when it moves. However, what is puzzling in the case of (ii)–(iv) is that the potential sources *There is no doubt about/\*of that* and *We're delighted (\*with) to bowl India out like that* are ungrammatical (for me, at least). The sentences in (ii) and (iii) may involve a processing error – perhaps a blend with a structure like *Of that, you can be sure*. As for (iv), the potential source is ungrammatical because it violates a constraint termed the Presentential Preposition Constraint in Radford (1979), barring a preposition in English from having an immediately following (non-wh) finite or infinitival clausal complement at PF. The constraint is obviated in (iv) because the *to*-clause is fronted via Topicalisation.

(3)    a. *Defoe*, even I could have scored that goal (Alan Green, BBC Radio 5)
       b. *Bale*, I thought that was an absolutely super cross (Jimmy Armfield, BBC Radio 5)
       c. *Cars like this*, the performance is not about the figures (James May, BBC2 TV)
       d. *The defending for the time being*, there's good movement and no slack (Jon Driscoll, Sky Sports TV)

The topic is once again dislocated, and hence in a separate intonation group from the comment. However, the dislocated topic in structures like (3) is orphaned, in the sense that there is no apparent syntactic or lexical link between the topic and the comment clause (e.g. there is no gap or resumptive in the comment clause linked to the topic): for this reason, Lambrecht (1994: 193) refers to this type of constituent as an 'unlinked topic'. The lack of any syntactic link between the topic and comment clause leads to such sentences being stigmatised by prescriptive grammarians as examples of the kind of sloppiness (i.e. lack of morphosyntactic marking of grammatical relations/ functions) supposedly characteristic of colloquial English.

However, in order for sentences like (3) to be felicitous, the comment must be interpretable as relevant (and hence linked) to the comment. Thus, in structures like (3), it is not that there is no link between topic and comment: rather, the link is pragmatic in nature. For example, in (3a), via a chain of pragmatic inferencing the hearer is intended to infer that Defoe had just missed a goal which was so easy to score that even the sexagenarian commentator could have scored it.

The discussion above suggests that there are three different ways in which a peripheral topic can be linked to the comment clause in spoken English. Structures like (1) contain a gap-linked (or *G-linked*) topic; structures like (2) contain a resumptive-linked (or *R-linked*) topic; and structures like (3) contain a pragmatically linked (or *P-linked*) topic. My broadcast English data on topics contain 130 examples of clauses with R-linked (left-dislocated) topics, 63 examples of clauses with P-linked (orphaned) topics, and just 13 examples of clauses with G-linked (fronted) topics: this underlines the point made by Frey (2005, fn. 4) that gap-linked (fronted) topics are 'rather uncommon in British English'. I shall not attempt to explore potential semantic and pragmatic differences between the three types of topic here,[2] but rather focus on aspects of their syntax.

---

[2] For discussion of the semantic and pragmatic properties of different kinds of topic, see Gundel (1975, 1985, 1988), Keenan & Schieffelin (1976a, 1976b), Prince (1981a, 1981b, 1984, 1985, 1997), Reinhart (1981), Ward & Prince (1991), Geluykens (1992), Lambrecht (1994), Ziv

Alongside peripheral topic structures, English also has clauses containing a peripheral focused constituent which serves to introduce new information (i.e. information not previously mentioned in the discourse and assumed to be unfamiliar to the hearer). Because focusing introduces new information and questions are often used to elicit new information, focusing can be used in replies to questions. By way of illustration, consider the following dialogue:

(4)     SPEAKER A: How many goals did Alfredo di Stéfano score for Real Madrid?
        SPEAKER B: 308 *goals* he scored — in 396 games. Amazing!

Here, the italicised phrase produced by speaker B originates in the gap position as the complement of the verb *scored*, and is then moved to the periphery of the bracketed clause in order to focus it (i.e. mark it as conveying new information). My data contain 67 examples of focus structures like (4B), including the following (where the focused constituent is italicised):

(5)     a. We told you there were going to be goals, and *goals* there were (Jake Humphreys, BT Sport TV)
        b. *A certain twitchiness* there was nearly all day (Nick Robinson, BBC1 TV)
        c. *Excellent football* that was (Ray Wilkins, Sky Sports TV)
        d. *Very relaxed* they were in the interview, as far as I could see (Sir Ming Campbell, BBC Radio 5)
        e. *Straight up the other end*, Crusaders went (Ian Abrahams, Talksport Radio)
        f. *Stay here* he must for a few more days, under observation (Reporter, BBC1 TV)

As these examples illustrate, a wide range of different types of constituent can undergo focusing.

An interesting question arising from the above discussion is what differences there are between topicalised and focused constituents. One important difference lies in their semantic properties: topics represent old/familiar information and tell us what a sentence is about, and are often paraphraseable by 'as for ... '; by contrast, focused constituents represent new/unfamiliar information, and are often paraphraseable by a cleft or pseudo-cleft sentence. Consequently, (3a) is paraphraseable in the following terms: 'As for Defoe, even I could have scored that goal'. Topicalised and focused constituents also differ in that there is typically a slight pause immediately after a topic (marked by the comma in 3), but not after a focused constituent – although it should be noted that the pause after a topic is sometimes imperceptible. Furthermore (as we will see in the next

(1994), Büring (1997, 1999, 2003), Birner & Ward (1998a, 1998b), Portner & Yabushita (1998), Gregory & Michaelis (2001), Casielles-Suárez (2004), Frey (2004, 2005), Shaer & Frey (2004), Manetta (2007), Bianchi & Frascarelli (2010), Miyagawa (2017).

section), a topic can be positioned on the edge of a clause either by Move or by Merge, whereas a focused constituent can only get into the clause periphery by Move (and so is always associated with a gap internally within the main body of the clause).

A further difference between topicalised and focused constituents is that topics (by virtue of referring to a specific entity assumed to be familiar to the hearer) are referential expressions, and consequently non-referential/non-specific pronouns like *something/someone/somebody, anything/anyone/any-body*, or *everything/everyone/everybody* can only be focused, not topicalised – as we see from the ungrammaticality which results from using the kind of (underlined) referential resumptive pronoun associated with a dislocated topic to reprise a fronted non-specific pronoun in sentences such as:

(6)  a. *Everything*, the tanks destroyed (*<u>it</u>)
     b. *Something*, I think (*<u>it</u>) must have upset him
     c. *Anything*, people are willing to confess to (*<u>it</u>) under torture

If the italicised constituents in (6) were topics, it ought to be possible for them to be reprised by a (bold-printed) resumptive pronoun; the fact that this is not possible suggests that non-specific expressions are not possible topics (and hence that the italicised constituents in (6) are focused).

An additional difference between focused and topicalised constituents is that clauses can contain more than one peripheral topic (as we will see in more detail in §2.4), but cannot contain more than one peripheral focused constituent. This is illustrated by the contrast between the grammatical double-topic structure in (7a) below, and the ungrammatical double-focus structure in (8b):

(7)  a. **My supervisor**, *a man like that*, <u>she</u> would never hire (Emonds 2004: 107)
     b. *\*Something, everyone* he gave — to — (cf. He gave something to everyone)

(7a) contains two peripheral topics (a bold-printed dislocated topic and an italicised fronted topic), whereas (7b) contains two (italicised) peripheral focused constituents. Rizzi (1997: 297) argues that the clause periphery cannot contain more than one focused constituent because the complement of a focus head is a presupposition, and focus recursion would lead to an 'interpretive clash' (Rizzi 1997: 297). See Rizzi (1997) for more detailed discussion of differences between topic and focus.

Having briefly looked at the types of topic structures found in English and some of the ways in which topics differ from focused constituents, in the next section I turn to look at the derivation of topic structures.

## 2.3    The Derivation of Topics

In this section, I explore the question of whether topics are directly merged in situ, or whether they are moved into their superficial position in the clause periphery from some lower position. I will explore a range of analyses presented in earlier work, and ultimately conclude that gap-linked topics involve movement, but that dislocated and orphaned topics are directly merged in situ in their superficial positions.

Ross (1967: 209) claims that gap-linked topics undergo a movement operation called Topicalisation by which a constituent like that bold-printed in (8a) below is moved into the italicised position in the clause periphery in (8b) in order to mark it as a topic; likewise Ross (1967: 422) claims that resumptive-linked topics are also moved to the clause periphery via a copy-movement operation termed Left Dislocation, which yields the outcome that the fronted topic 'is not deleted but remains behind in a pronominal form, as a kind of place-marker' (Ross 1967: 421) – the relevant resumptive pronoun being underlined in (8c):

(8)    a. I'm going to ask Bill to make the old geezer take up **these points** later
          (Ross 1967: 209, ex. 4.186a)
       b. *These points* I'm going to ask Bill to make the old geezer take up later
          (Ross 1967: 209, ex. 4.186b)
       c. *These points*, I'm going to ask Bill to make the old geezer take <u>them</u> up
          later

However, Ross has nothing to say about structures like (3) containing orphaned topics.

There was widespread subsequent acceptance of the claim that Topicalisation structures like (8b) involve movement (including by Lakoff 1969; Neubauer 1970; Emonds 1970, 1976; Postal 1971, 1972; Ross 1973; Hirschbühler 1973, 1974, 1975), but much less widespread acceptance of the claim that Left Dislocation structures like (8c) also involve movement (although a movement analysis was adopted by Emonds 1970, 1976; Neubauer 1970; and Contreras 1976). Boeckx (2003, 2012) and Boeckx & Grohmann (2005) offer a more recent implementation of the movement analysis of left-dislocated constituents in which the resumptive pronoun is treated as the head D of a DP which has the dislocated NP as its complement, and Left Dislocation is taken to involve movement of the relevant NP to the clause periphery, thereby stranding the resumptive pronoun/RP and resulting in the structure below (where <angle brackets> indicate that the lower copy of the relevant NP has a null spellout at PF):

(9)      NP$_i$ ... [$_{TP}$ ... [$_{DP}$ RP [<NP$_i$>]] ... ] (Boeckx & Grohmann 2005: 13, ex. 23)

They claim that the dislocated NP and the resumptive do not agree in case, but instead the dislocated NP at the front of the sentence receives default case (accusative in English, nominative in German).[3]

However, many researchers have argued that Left Dislocation does not involve movement,[4] but rather requires the topic to be merged in situ and associated with a resumptive separately generated in a position below the topic (Gruber 1967; Postal 1971; Hirschbühler 1973, 1974, 1975; Rodman 1974, 1997; van Riemsdijk & Zwartz 1974, 1997; Gundel 1975; Rivero 1980; Vat 1981; van Haaften et al. 1983; Grohmann 1997, 2000, 2003). A wide variety of evidence has been adduced in support of this analysis and I will review some of it below.

Rodman (1974, 1997) argues that certain types of left-dislocated topic cannot plausibly be analysed as derived by movement. One such are coordinate topics reprised by multiple resumptive pronouns in structures such as those below (from Rodman 1997: 36, 30):

(10)     a. *Me and Lenny,* <u>he</u>'s gonna pet some bunnies and <u>I</u>'m gonna go get my six
            shooter
         b. *Bill, Sue and that damn snake,* <u>he</u> told <u>her</u> to get <u>it</u> out of their sleeping bag

It is implausible to suppose that a single (italicised) coordinate topic could be moved from two or more distinct (underlined) resumptive positions in such cases. Rather, such structures seem to require a derivation in which the topic is directly merged in situ in the clause periphery and associated with one or more independently generated resumptives in the comment clause.

A second argument offered by Rodman against a movement analysis of left-dislocated topics comes from a constraint proposed by Emonds (1970) to the effect that no two preposing root transformations can apply within the same clause. Rodman notes that this constraint is incompatible with a movement derivation for the (italicised) left-dislocated topic in a sentence like:

---

[3] See Grewendorf (2002) for an alternative implementation of the movement analysis.

[4] Note that the discussion here concerns Hanging Topic Left Dislocation, and this is not to be confused with Clitic Left Dislocation structures like the Italian example below, in which an (italicised) dislocated topic is reprised by a (bold-printed) clitic:

(i) La propria$_i$ identità, Piero$_i$ non l'ha   ancora persa (Cinque 1977: 401, ex. 16)
    The own      identity, Piero not it'has yet   lost
    'His identity, Piero has not yet lost'

Cinque (1977) argues that Clitic Left Dislocation does indeed involve movement, while maintaining (1977: 406) that Hanging Topic Left Dislocation does not.

(11)    *Those petunias*, **what** did Joanne do — with <u>them</u>? (after Rodman 1997: 38, ex. 10)

The pronoun *what* undergoes Wh-Movement from the gap position into the bold-printed peripheral question operator position in (11): this means that if the topic *those petunias* underwent movement from the position occupied by the underlined resumptive pronoun to the italicised topic position, there would be a violation of Emonds' constraint, and sentences like (12) would wrongly be predicted to be ungrammatical. By contrast, if the left-dislocated topic *those petunias* is directly merged in situ, there will be no constraint violation, and the sentence will correctly be predicted to be grammatical. This argument can be given a more recent formulation in terms of the Intervention Constraint, which (as noted in §1.4) was given the following informal characterisation by Abels (2012: 247):

(12)    **Intervention Constraint**
        Likes cannot cross likes

If left-dislocated topics involved movement, we should expect sentences like (11) above to result in an intervention violation parallel to that found in the corresponding Topicalisation (i.e. topic-fronting) structure below:

(13)    *\*Those petunias*, **what** did Joanne do — with —?

The fact that Topicalisation gives rise to intervention effects but Left Dislocation does not suggests that Topicalisation involves the operation Move whereas Dislocation involves Merge.

A third argument offered by Rodman against a movement analysis of left-dislocated topics is that there are dislocated topic structures like those below in which the topic could not plausibly be taken to originate inside the comment clause:

(14)    a. *The flat tyre*, John explained that there had been nails on the ground (after Rodman 1997: 38, ex. 37)
        b. *Restaurants*, the situation's hopeless in Chapel Hill (Rodman 1997: 39, ex. 39)

The italicised topic in each case is dislocated by virtue of showing so-called 'comma intonation' (marked in the written language by the presence of the comma after the topic). Sentences like (14) involve an orphaned dislocated topic which is not syntactically linked to the comment clause, but rather pragmatically linked. The topic cannot plausibly be taken to have moved out of the comment clause (because there seems to be nowhere in the comment clause that it could have originated), so must instead have been directly merged in situ. This makes it plausible to suppose that dislocated topics which are linked to a resumptive are also directly merged in situ (in the appropriate topic position in the clause periphery).

Further evidence against a movement analysis of resumptive-linked topics is presented by van Riemsdijk & Zwarts (1974, 1997): their evidence is drawn from Dutch, but I present English counterparts below. They note that reflexives and reciprocals can appear as topics if associated with a gap, but not if associated with a resumptive:

(15)    a. *Himself*, he would never pass (\*him) over
        b. *Each other*, John and Mary always blame (\*them) for everything[5]

In addition, idiom chunks can serve as topics if associated with a gap, but not if associated with a resumptive – as examples like those below illustrate:

(16)    a. *The wool*, you're certainly not going to pull (\*it) over my eyes
        b. *The ice*, we can break (\*it) with a couple of drinks
        c. *The cat*, he is sure to let (\*it) out of the bag sooner or later
        d. *The music*, you're going to have to face (\*it) on your own
        e. *A dead horse*, there is no point in flogging (\*it)
        f. *A blind eye*, we should never turn (\*it) to tax evasion
        g. *Liberties*, you should never take (\*them) with strangers
        h. *Significant headway*, we expect to make (\*it) by the end of the week

Furthermore, imperatives and yes-no questions allow resumptive-linked but not gap-linked topics:[6]

(17)    a. Your appointment with the dentist, don't forget \*(it)!
        b. Your appointment with the dentist, have you forgotten \*(it)?

If imperatives are introduced by a null imperative operator (Han 1998, 2001) and yes-no questions by a null interrogative operator (Katz & Postal 1964;

---

[5] At first sight, this claim might appear to be falsified by structures like the following:

> (i) *This picture of himself*, John took (it) while on holiday in South Africa

However, this is not the case, since the dislocated constituent in (i) is not the reflexive pronoun *himself* but rather the DP *this picture of himself*. Moreover, picture-noun reflexives are exempt anaphors (i.e. exempt from the requirement of being locally A-bound), as we see from sentences like:

> (ii) Physicists like myself were never too happy with the parity principle (Ross 1970: 230)

[6] The key point here is that the Topicalisation examples are more degraded than the Dislocation examples, even if some speakers may find them unidiomatic rather than ungrammatical.

Bresnan 1970; Larson 1985; Grimshaw 1993; Roberts 1993; den Dikken 2006; Haegeman 2012), we can suppose that a gap-linked topic which moves across the operator (or vice versa) will induce an intervention effect, but a resumptive-linked topic which is generated in situ will not. Overall, data like (15–17) are consistent with the view that Topicalisation involves movement, but Left Dislocation does not.

In addition, van Riemsdijk & Zwarts note that Topicalisation is sensitive to island constraints, but Left Dislocation is not – as illustrated by the examples below (adapted from corresponding Dutch examples in van Riemsdijk & Zwarts 1974: 100):

(18)   a. *Equi-NP Deletion*, I found Brame's arguments against *(it) very convincing
       b. *The authorities*, it seems unlikely to me that *(they) will do anything about it

These examples show that a resumptive (but not a gap) linked to a topic can be a constituent of a complex nominal with a subject (= *Brame*) as in (18a), or the subject of a clause introduced by an overt complementiser as in (18b), in violation of constraints barring extraction out of the relevant types of structure. This follows if gap-linked topics involve movement, but resumptive-linked topics do not.

Vat (1981) argues that further evidence that Topicalisation involves movement but Left Dislocation does not comes from their behaviour with respect to reconstruction effects for Binding Principle C in sentences such as:

(19)   a. *Ann*'s brother, I think she really likes him/*— (adapted from Vat 1981: 87, ex. 18)
       b. *John*, his mother loves him/*— (Demirdache 1991: 173, ex. 13)
       c. The friend who helped *Martin*, he thanked him/* — (adapted from Boeckx & Grohmann 2005: 9, ex. 16)

Here, the underlined pronoun can be coreferential to the italicised noun in the topic phrase if the topic is associated with a resumptive pronoun, but not if it is associated with a gap. This follows if the topic in gap-linked structures undergoes movement and is reconstructed back into the gap position (so that the italicised R-expression is prevented by Principle C of Binding Theory from being coreferential to the c-commanding underlined pronoun), and if the topic is directly merged in situ (and so does not show reconstruction effects) in the resumptive structure.

In much the same vein, Vat (1981), Zaenen (1997), Grohmann (2000) and Frey (2004) note that fronted and dislocated topics have different binding properties in sentences such as the following:

(20)    a. *His supervisor*, every student admires —/*<u>him</u>
        b. *The new article by Peter$_i$*, he$_i$ wants to publish <u>it</u>/*— in LI (Frey 2004: 5, ex. 9)

(20a) shows that an operator can bind a pronoun inside a fronted topic (with the pronoun being interpreted as a variable), but not inside a dislocated topic; (20b) shows that Principle C effects can be induced by an R-expression (like *Peter*) inside a fronted topic, but not by one inside a dislocated topic. These outcomes are expected if dislocated topics are directly merged in situ.[7]

Vat (1981) makes a similar point in relation to quantifier scope in sentences such as:

(21)    a. *Three articles by Chomsky*, all the students had problems with <u>them</u>/—
        b. *A Hollywood filmstar*, every man sometimes has fantasies about <u>her</u>/—

When the italicised topic is reprised by a resumptive pronoun, the topic obligatorily has wide scope with respect to the *all/every*-phrase (so that all the students have problems with the same three articles, and every man fantasises about the same filmstar), and this suggests that the topic is merged in situ. By contrast, when the topic is associated with a gap, it can have either wide or narrow scope, consistent with the view that it has undergone movement.

A further argument leading to the same conclusion can be formulated in relation to parasitic gaps, As noted by Ott (2012, 2014, 2015), a gap-linked topic licenses a parasitic gap (= *pg*) in a sentence like (22a) below, but a resumptive-linked topic in a sentence like (22b) does not:

(22)    a. *The escaped convict*, the police pursued — for months without ever catching *pg*
        b. **The escaped convict*, the police pursued <u>him</u> for months without ever catching *pg*

If parasitic gaps are licensed by traces of A-bar moved constituents, such data can be accounted for straightforwardly if gap-linked topics undergo A-bar movement, but resumptive-linked topics do not.

A number of linguists (including Rodman 1974; Gundel 1975; Cinque 1977, 1983; Vat 1981; Boeckx & Grohmann 2005) have argued that further evidence

---

[7] However, Shaer & Frey (2004) report that the relevant contrasts are not robust for all speakers.

against a movement analysis of resumptive-linked topics comes from case-marking. In this respect, consider the two alternative replies given by speaker B in the dialogue below (where capitals marks contrastive stress):

(23)    SPEAKER A: After hearing the evidence against them, what do you think about John and Mary?
        SPEAKER B: (i) HE, I think —— is guilty but SHE, I don't think —— is
                   (ii) HIM, I suspect that he is guilty but HER, I doubt whether she is

(23Bi) involves two TOPIC+GAP structures in which the capitalised topics move from the relevant gap position to the front of the clause containing them. Since a constituent moving to the clause periphery generally retains the case that it was assigned before it moved, the fact that the topicalised pronouns *he* and *she* in (23Bi) carry nominative case suggests that they were assigned nominative case by the finite copula *is* before moving to become the specifier of a topic phrase projection in the clause periphery. By contrast, in the TOPIC+RESUMPTIVE structures in (23Bii), the topicalised pronouns *him* and *her* carry a different (accusative) case from that carried by the italicised nominative resumptive pronoun. Since dislocated topics are generally accusative (as noted by Ross 1967: 430), this means that an (italicised) dislocated topic and the corresponding (underlined) resumptive can differ in case – as illustrated by the following examples from my broadcast English data:

(24)    a. *Me personally*, I'm not really bothered about what they do in their personal life (Adrian Durham, Talksport Radio)
        b. *Him and a couple of mates*, they went to a casino at 4 in the morning (Tim Vickery, BBC Radio 5)
        c. *Lee*, I've been following his progress very much over the last month (Colin Montgomerie, BBC Radio 5)
        d. *The memorial*, I was there a few hours ago (Peter Bowles, BBC Radio 5)

In all four sentences, an italicised topic which would seem to be accusative (even though it has a syncretic nominative/accusative form in 24c, d) is reprised by an underlined pronoun carrying a different case – namely by a nominative pronoun in (24a, b), a genitive pronoun in (24c), and a locative pronoun in (24d). The more general point to note is that dislocated topic structures in which there are case differences between topic and resumptive provide evidence against a movement analysis, and in favour of treating dislocated topics as directly merged in situ. In such cases, the in situ topic would appear to be assigned accusative case independently of the resumptive, perhaps by an abstract transitive topic-introducing preposition which assigns it accusative case (e.g. an abstract counterpart of *as for*), or via an abstract specifier–head agreement relation with a topic head, or by default (i.e. by virtue of not falling within the domain of any case-assigner: see Schütze 2001 on default case). Whatever the exact mechanism by which dislocated topics are assigned accusative case in English, the fact that a dislocated topic is assigned a case independent of that of the resumptive favours a Merge rather than a Move analysis.[8]

Further evidence against a movement analysis of resumptive-linked topics is presented by Hirschbühler (1973, 1974, 1975), who notes that the resumptive expression can be a nominal (e.g. a name or epithet) which is not a copy of the topic. Although his evidence comes from French, the same point can be illustrated in relation to English by the following sentences from my broadcast English data:

---

[8] I note, however, that the particular movement analysis of Left Dislocation proposed by Boeckx & Grohmann (2005) sketched in (9) above offers an account of case mismatches between dislocated topic and resumptive. I would also note structures like those below (the first two from my broadcast data and the others from the internet) where the topic (italicised) and resumptive (underlined) appear to match in (nominative) case:

>  (i)    And *he*, well <u>he</u>'s already taken a stage win (Carlton Kirby, Eurosport TV)
>  (ii)   *We in the Labour Party*, <u>we</u>'re not being seen in the forefront of this kind of action (Politician, BBC Radio 4)
>  (iii)  *We politicians*, <u>we</u> also have our own free time (facebook.com)
>  (iv)   Did you know that *we Brits*, <u>we</u> throw an estimated 7.2 million tonnes of food and drink in the bin each year? (moralfibres.co.uk)
>  (v)    But *he too*, <u>he</u>'s been playing delay tactics (naaoyooquartey.com)

The apparent case-matching between topic and resumptive here might at first sight seem to support a movement analysis of case-matched topic structures. However, there are alternative interpretations of such data which would allow for an in situ analysis of the topic. One possibility is that some speakers may allow in situ topics to be assigned nominative case (as in German or Arabic, for example); this is plausible for speakers (like me) who accept structures such as:

>  (vi)   *We in the Labour Party*, nobody considers *us* ready for government

Another possibility is that complex nominals introduced by nominative or accusative personal pronouns are syncretic nominative/accusative forms which can occupy both nominative and accusative positions – so allowing (e.g.) *we politicians* to be treated as an accusative topic in (iii). The following examples illustrate structures in which a phrase beginning with what appears to be a nominative pronoun is used in an accusative position (as the object of a preposition), suggesting that *we* can be used to spell out accusative case in such structures:

>  (vii)   But it is left to *we politicians* (web)
>  (viii)  Tito got no luck against *we Brits, Irish and Scots* (sonichu.com)
>  (ix)    As for *we Brits*, we've always been able to travel, live and work overseas (web)

The example in (ix) is particularly interesting, as it involves a *we*-topic after the complex prepositional topic-introducer *as for*.

(25)   a. *Gareth Bale*, I wouldn't be surprised if Man City were in for <u>Bale</u> (Robbie Savage, BBC Radio 5)
      b. *The pressure that you were under today*, your players are going to have to face <u>that kind of pressure</u> throughout the season (Connor MacNamara, BBC Radio 5)
      c. *The history*, they've had <u>a fantastic history</u> (Chris Waddle, BBC1 TV)
      d. *Many of them*, I have no idea where <u>these teams</u> are (Danny Kelly, Talksport Radio)
      e. *The championship*, one of the greatest things about <u>that league</u> is that it's the most unpredictable league around (Listener, BBC Radio 5)
      f. *Hamilton*, the pendulum swings back into <u>the Englishman's</u> favour (David Croft, Sky Sports TV)
      g. *What Mr Cameron has started*, the EU need to continue <u>that process</u> (Listener, BBC Radio 5)

In (25a–c) the resumptive bears only partial resemblance to the topic (by virtue of sharing a noun in common), while in (25d–g) the topic and the resumptive are completely distinct expressions, sharing no items in common. Cinque (1983) and Demirdache (1991) note that the resumptive can be a nominal that refers to the kind of entity denoted by the dislocated constituent – as in the examples below:

(26)   a. *John*, Mary doesn't like <u>that kind of person</u> (Cinque 1983: 17, ex. 19)
      b. *The shirt that John is wearing*, I really hate <u>that kind of shirt</u> (Demirdache 1991: 176, ex. 16c)

In structures like (25) and (26), the (underlined) resumptive clearly cannot be taken to be a copy of the (italicised) topic. Instead, the two must be merged in separate positions.

Reasoning along similar lines, van Riemsdijk & Zwarts (1974) argue that even in cases where the resumptive is pronominal, there are structures where it cannot be taken to be a copy arising via movement, since some such structures involve the use of a sloppy pronoun which does not agree in one or more phi-features with the pronoun. This point can be illustrated in relation to the following examples from my broadcast English data:

(27)   a. *Full details and latest transfer news*, <u>it</u>'s all on the website (Ian Abrahams, Talksport Radio)
      b. *All those sorts of things*, <u>it</u> does make going away quite stressful (Jonathan Agnew, BBC Radio 5)
      c. *High speed corners with a dry line*, <u>that</u>'ll burn your tyres out (Martin Brundle, BBC1 TV)
      d. *Their strikers*, <u>that</u>'s really all that's let them down (Danny Mills, BBC Radio 5)

e. *The person that I mentioned the name of*, the police know who <u>they</u> were (Listener, BBC Radio 5)

f. I think *Arsenal*, <u>they</u>'re gonna improve again (Alan Brazil, Talksport Radio)

g. *The squad of players that finished the season so strongly*, he wants to give <u>them</u> new contracts (Andy Dunn, BBC Radio 5)

h. I think that *Red Bull*, one of <u>their</u> spotters actually got arrested (David Coulthard, BBC1 TV)

In (27a–d), a plural topic is resumed by a singular pronoun, while conversely in (27e–h) a singular topic is resumed by a plural pronoun. The number mismatch between topic and resumptive in such cases argues against a movement derivation for the resumptive: for instance, treating the resumptive as a determiner stranded by movement of its complement would be problematic because a plural determiner does not allow a singular complement and vice versa.

Further problems arise in relation to the specific implementation of the movement analysis of left-dislocated topics proposed in Boeckx & Grohmann (2005), under which the resumptive is a determiner stranded under movement of its NP complement, so resulting in a structure with the schematic form in (9) above, repeated as (28) below:

(28)    $NP_i \ldots [_{TP} \ldots [_{DP} RP [<NP_i>]] \ldots ]$ (Boeckx & Grohmann 2005: 13, ex. 23)

Such an analysis has seeming plausibility for structures such as the following:

(29)    a. *Ryan Taylor*, it looks as if <u>he</u> will take the free kick (Alan Green, BBC Radio 5)

b. *People in Benghazi*, are <u>they</u> really still afraid? (Stephen Nolan, BBC Radio 5)

c. *For a Dutchman to be relying on Germany*, <u>it</u>'s not the perfect scenario (Clive Tyldesley, ITV)

d. *Balls in the box*, we didn't think there would be <u>too many</u> tonight (Gareth Southgate, ITV)

e. *Olympic events*, are you going to <u>any</u>? (Ronnie Irani, Talksport Radio)

f. *Hotels*, is there <u>enough</u>? (Alan Brazil, Talksport Radio)

g. *Chances in this half*, the best <u>ones</u> have gone to Ipswich (Commentator, Sky Sports TV)

Thus, in (29a, b) we could (in accordance with the DP Hypothesis of Abney 1987, whereby all referring expressions are DPs) take *he/they* to be determiners modifying the NPs *Ryan Taylor/people in Benghazi*, albeit we would need to devise a story about why *he/they* cannot be used as prenominal determiners (e.g. in structures like *\*he Ryan Taylor* and *\*they people in Benghazi*). Similarly, in (29c) we could posit that *it* is a determiner which has a CP headed by infinitival *for* as its complement – much as was assumed in early accounts of Extraposition structures like *It's embarrassing for a Dutchman to be relying on Germany.* If we suppose that QPs also allow topical NPs to be extracted out of them, we can extend the analysis in (28) to sentences like those in (29d–f), with the underlined quantifiers being stranded by movement of the italicised NPs to a peripheral topic position: this analysis could even be extended to (29g), if we take *ones* to be a stranded numeral quantifier.

However, there are also topic structures like those in (30) below where it seems implausible to analyse the resumptive as a determiner or quantifier stranded by movement of an NP complement:

(30)    a. *Me personally,* I'm not really bothered about what they do in their personal life (Adrian Durham, Talksport Radio)
        b. *This guy,* it was only a few hours ago that he had a speech that was a mile long (Peter Allen, BBC Radio 5)
        c. *The person that I mentioned the name of,* the police know who they were (Listener, BBC Radio 5)
        d. *That failure to persevere with European football,* that I think puts a huge question mark against his character (Tim Vickery, BBC Radio 5)
        e. *Their strikers,* that's really all that's let them down (Danny Mills, BBC Radio 5)
        f. *The memorial,* I was there a few hours ago (Peter Bowles, BBC Radio 5)

The D-stranding analysis of resumptive pronouns would require us to treat the dislocated constituent and resumptive as forming a DP recursion structure. Thus, *I* in (30a) would function as a determiner whose complement is the DP *me personally,* so requiring a DP recursion structure of the form [$_{DP}$ I [$_{DP}$ me personally]]: however, such a structure in which a DP headed by a first person pronoun takes another DP headed by another first person pronoun as its complement is both syntactically implausible (since DPs don't allow a DP complement) and semantically incoherent (since it is not clear what interpretation a double DP containing two first person pronouns would have). Likewise, it is implausible to treat *he* as a D taking the DP *this guy* as its complement in (30b), or *they* as a D taking the DP *the person that I mentioned the name of* as its complement in (30c), or *that* as a D taking the DP complement *that failure to persevere with European football* in (30d), or the singular D *that* as taking the plural DP *their strikers* as its complement in (30e), or the (locative) D *there* as taking the DP complement *the memorial* in (30f). Such DP recursion structures are problematic from both a syntactic and a semantic perspective, for the reasons noted earlier.

Other types of structure in which it is implausible to take the resumptive to be a determiner stranded by movement of an NP topic are illustrated below:

(31)    a. *All those sorts of things*, <u>it</u> does make going away quite stressful (Jonathan Agnew, BBC Radio 5)
        b. He's so full of confidence that he thinks *every ball*, he can score off <u>it</u> (Geoff Boycott, BBC Radio 5 Live Sports Extra)
        c. *Some of the circuits*, he has never driven <u>them</u> before (Graham Courtney, Talksport Radio)
        d. I think *a spin bowler*, what <u>you</u> want to do is make the batsman play (Shane Warne, Sky Sports TV)

Under the stranding analysis of resumptives, the singular pronoun *it* in (31a) will originate as the head D of a DP which takes the plural QP *all those sorts of things* as its complement: in (31b), *it* will be a D which takes the QP *every ball* as its complement; in (31c), *them* will be a D taking the QP *some of the circuits* as its complement; and in (31d), *you* will be a D taking an (indefinite) ARTP/ article phrase *a spin bowler* as its complement. Such analyses are implausible from both a syntactic point of view (e.g. there is a number mismatch between singular *it* and the plural QP *all those sorts of things* in 31a), and from a semantic point of view (e.g. *a spin bowler* has a predicative interpretation in 31d paraphraseable as 'if you are a spin bowler' or 'as a spin bowler').

The D-stranding analysis of resumptives is equally problematic in cases like:

(32)    a. *One of these riders in the 125 GP*, I've got <u>his</u> dad alongside me now (Matt Roberts, BBC2 TV)
        b. *Everybody who supports the club and is linked with the club*, <u>nobody</u> wants this game to happen at all (Listener, BBC Radio 5)

If *his* is a determiner which has *one of these riders* as its complement in (32a) and if the whole DP *his one of these riders* functions as the specifier of a null possessive D which has *dad* as its complement, extraction of the *one*-phrase will yield a violation of a constraint dating back to work by Cattell (1976), Cinque (1978) and Huang (1982), which can be characterised informally as follows:

(33)    **Constraint on Extraction Domains/CED**
        Extraction is only possible out of complements, not out of adjuncts or specifiers

The CED violation would arise from extracting the *one*-phrase out of a specifier: the stranding analysis would thus wrongly predict that sentences like (32a) are ungrammatical. And in the case of (32b), it seems implausible that the QP *everybody who supports the club and is linked with the club* could originate as the complement of the quantifier *no*, since this quantifier has its complement *body* incorporated into it (and in any case, negative quantifiers do not take QP complements).[9, 10]

A final remark to make in relation to the derivation of dislocated topics is the following. Boeckx & Grohmann (2005: 11) argue that conceptual considerations favour a 'unified approach' under which both Topicalisation and Left Dislocation involve movement. However, since UG allows for both Merge and Move operations, I would argue that a no less conceptually coherent approach is one which posits that topics can either be merged in situ, or moved to their superficial position in the clause periphery. Furthermore, since it is clear that orphaned topics (which are pragmatically linked to the comment clause) are merged in situ, treating dislocated topics as also merged in situ has independent motivation.

The overall conclusion we reach from our discussion in this section and the previous one is the following. English has three types of peripheral topic constituent: gap-linked topics, resumptive-linked dislocated topics, and orphaned (= unlinked/pragmatically linked) dislocated topics. While gap-linked topics can be argued to involve movement of a topic to the clause periphery, dislocated topics (whether resumptive-linked topics, or orphaned topics) are directly merged in situ in the appropriate position in the periphery. Having established this, in the next section I turn to look at the much debated

---

[9] One could perhaps imagine a rather more complex source paraphraseable as 'no person out of the set of all the people who support the club and who are linked to the club', but it is unclear what precisely that source structure would be (perhaps something akin to *nobody of everybody who . . .*, with *of* having a silent spellout).

[10] Villa-García (2015: 176–80) presents a further argument for treating dislocated topics as generated in situ and fronted topics as undergoing movement, arguing that dislocated topics allow subextraction, but fronted topics do not (because extraction out of a moved constituent is barred by the Freezing Principle of Wexler & Culicover 1980: 119). His data are from Spanish, but corresponding contrasts in English (like those below) seem murky:

(i) *You can just imagine [**which footballer**, *the recent scandal about*, the press had a field day with —]

(ii) *You can just imagine [**which footballer**, *the recent scandal about*, the press had a field day with it]

Each of the bracketed clauses involves a bold-printed wh-constituent extracted out of an italicised peripheral topic. The topic is fronted and associated with a gap in (i) and so should induce a freezing violation, but is dislocated and associated with a resumptive in (ii) and so should not give rise to a freezing violation. It may be that both sentences are heavily degraded because both involve a CED violation (by virtue of extracting out of a specifier – and what is worse, a D-linked one at that), and that this masks expected freezing differences.

question of whether English allows topic recursion – i.e. whether it allows more than one topic projection to occur within the periphery of a given clause.

## 2.4   Multiple Topic Structures

A number of linguists (including Rodman 1974; Cinque 1983; Shaer & Frey 2004: 490) have claimed that topic recursion is barred, in the sense the periphery of a given clause cannot contain more than one topic of a given kind. I shall review earlier literature on this, but ultimately conclude that (contrary to many earlier claims), colloquial English does indeed allow multiple topic structures.

Rodman (1974) argues that the periphery of a given clause cannot contain more than one dislocated topic – a claim which Rodman (1997: 37, ex. 31) suggests draws empirical support from the ungrammaticality of sentences such as:

(34)    *\*Bill, Sue, that damn snake,* he told her to get it out of their sleeping bag

Likewise, it has been claimed (e.g. by Rizzi 2013a) that fronted topics are also unique, and thus cannot be recursively stacked in English – as we see from the contrasts below attributed to Rachel Nye and Ian Roberts in Rizzi (2013a: 214):[11]

(35)    a. *John,* I convinced — to buy your car
        b. *Your car,* I convinced John to buy —
        c. *\*John, your car,* I convinced — to buy —
        d. *\*Your car, John,* I convinced — to buy —

However, Emonds (2004: 107) claims (on the basis of contrasts like that below) that the clause periphery can contain two different types of topic (e.g. a fronted and a dislocated topic), but that when the two co-occur an (italicised) dislocated topic must always precede a (bold-printed) fronted topic:

(36)    a. *My supervisor,* **a man like that,** she would never hire
        b. **\*A man like that,** *my supervisor,* I don't think she would hire

---

[11] Sentences like (35c, d) could be ruled out for independent reasons, e.g. by virtue of containing a string of two successive DPs, thereby violating the Distinctness Condition of Richards (2010: 5) which bars certain structures containing a linear sequence of two like (more precisely: non-distinct) constituents. Richards' constraint also bars the italicised double-DP string in cases of ellipsis like:

(i)   *\*Every man admired every woman, even* John Mary

Under Emonds' analysis, this ordering follows from dislocated topics being housed in a discourse shell/projection which lies outside the sentence structure containing the fronted topic.

Evidence supporting the claim that dislocated and fronted topics occur in different segments of the clause periphery comes from an observation made by Greenberg (1984) about the relative positioning of the interjection *man* with respect to dislocated and fronted topics. In sentences like (37) below containing an (italicised) dislocated topic, the interjection *man* can either precede or follow the topic:

(37)    a. **Man**, *John*, Mary really loves <u>him</u> (Greenberg 1984: 285, fn. 1)
      b. *John*, **man**, Mary really loves <u>him</u> (Greenberg 1984: 285, ex. 18)

By contrast, in sentences like (38) below containing an (italicised) fronted topic, the interjection *man* can precede but not follow the topic:

(38)    a. **Man**, *John* Mary really loves — (Greenberg 1984: 285, ex. 21a)
      b. *\*John*, **man**, Mary really loves — (Greenberg 1984: 285, ex. 21b)

This contrast can be accounted for if dislocated constituents and interjections like *man* are contained within a discourse projection above CP, but fronted topics occupy a lower position in the CP segment of the periphery.

In a similar vein, Bianchi & Frascarelli (2010: 15) claim that dislocated and fronted topics occupy different (but unique) positions in the clause periphery, and that this reflects their different semantic and pragmatic properties. They argue that a dislocated topic in English serves to mark 'a shift with respect to the aboutness topic of the previous sentence' – i.e. a change in what is being talked about: they refer to this type of topic as an A-topic. By contrast, fronted topics in English generally have an implicit or explicit contrastive function; hence they refer to this type of topic as a C-topic. They maintain that the uniqueness of each type of topic is a direct consequence of its pragmatic function. They also claim that the two types of topic can co-occur, but an (italicised) dislocated A-topic always precedes a (bold-printed) fronted C-topic – as illustrated below:

(39)    [A-TOP *My son*] [C-TOP **beans**] he likes, but [C-TOP **peas**] he hates (Bianchi & Frascarelli 2010: 16, ex. 23)

The respective ordering of the two types of topic constituent is said to follow from their semantic and pragmatic properties: an A-topic is contained within a separate speech act projection which is positioned outside/above the assertion projection containing other constituents of the sentence, whereas a C-topic is positioned within the assertion projection.[12]

Thus, the key claims made in the research reported above are that English has two types of peripheral topic (dislocated aboutness-shift topics, and fronted contrastive topics), that each is non-recursive, and that the former always precedes the latter. However, the empirical basis of the claim that dislocated topics are unique is called into question by the apparent stacking of dislocated constituents in the following sentences from my broadcast English data:

(40)    a. **Manchester United**, *the way they play*, it's not pleasing on the eye (Danny Higginbotham, Talksport Radio)
        b. **A good friend of mine**, *his daughter*, I promised to go and say hello to her today (Alan Brazil, Talksport Radio)
        c. **Hillary Clinton**, *her husband Bill Clinton*, his adviser was a Ku Klux Klan member (Political commentator, BBC Radio 5)
        d. You just get the feeling that **Arsenal**, *the way they keep the ball*, it's particularly clever (Steve Claridge, BBC Radio 5)
        e. **Everton**, if it wasn't for their goalkeeper, *Arsenal*, they could have scored eight (Darren Gough, Talksport Radio)

Each of the sentences in (40a–d) contains a bold-printed dislocated topic, followed by an italicised dislocated topic containing an (underlined) resumptive pronoun referring back to the bold-printed topic, and a sentence containing a further (underlined) resumptive pronoun referring back to the second dislocated topic. And (40e) contains two distinct topics (one bold-printed, the other italicised), each reprised by an (underlined) resumptive pronoun. Such sentences provide a clear challenge to the claimed uniqueness of dislocated topics.

However, there are two potential ways of defending the claim that dislocated topics are unique. One possible approach would be to hypothesise that the two topics form a single DP constituent, perhaps involving one DP coordinated with another.[13] This is by no means implausible in principle, since my

---

[12] A number of other projections have been posited which are akin to Emonds' Discourse Projection constituent or the Speech Act Projection of Bianchi & Frascarelli. These include the HP projection of a discourse head posited in Cinque (2008) and Giorgi (2014), the ParP constituent of Griffiths & DeVries (2013), and the FrameP constituent of Haegeman & Greco (2016). For example, Haegeman & Greco (2016) argue that a topic-comment structure involves two separate speech acts, namely a speech act of frame-setting and an illocutionary speech act of assertion, questioning, etc., and they maintain that dislocated constituents are contained within a FrameP projection whose complement is Rizzi's ForceP.

[13] An alternative single DP story would be to follow Giusti (1996, 2006, 2012) in allowing DPs to have internal topics, raising the possibility that in (40a) *Manchester United, the way they play* is a single DP which has *Manchester United* as its topic.

broadcast English data also include structures like those below in which the bracketed strings could be taken to involve a similar complex DP structure:

(41)  a. There are sections of the press who don't like [**Capello**, *the way he handles things*] (Gabby Logan, BBC Radio 5)
      b. We're also talking about [**John Toshak**, *the rumours that he's about to resign*] (Adrian Durham, Talksport Radio)
      c. With [**Manchester City**, *the style that they play now*], I wonder how easily he would fit in (Reporter, Talksport Radio)
      d. Let's give credit to [**Atletico**, *how* they've played] (Ray Parlour, Talksport Radio)
      e. So many fans have been scathing about [**Arsène Wenger**, *his side*, the way it's set up] (Andy Goldstein, Talksport Radio)

On this view, the DP bracketed in (41a) would be a coordinate DP, and the sentence would have an interpretation paraphraseable as 'There are sections of the press who don't like Capello and the way he handles things.' If we extended this approach to sentences like those in (40), we could suppose that the bold-printed and italicised DPs form a single larger DP, and thus that there is only one topic DP in the sentence. On one implementation of this analysis, the clause periphery in (40a) would have a structure along the lines shown in simplified form below:

(42)

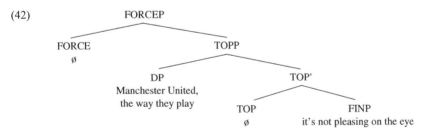

On this view, the corresponding sentence would contain a single dislocated topic, so allowing the restriction on clauses not containing more than one dislocated topic to be maintained.

A potential downside to the single topic analysis, however, is that the two dislocated constituents which supposedly form a single complex topic can be separated by other (underlined) intervening peripheral constituents, as we see from sentences like:

(43)  a. **Manchester United**, towards the end of the season, *the way they played*, it wasn't pleasing on the eye
      b. **Manchester United**, after Fergie left, *the way they played*, it wasn't pleasing on the eye

    c. **Manchester United**, <u>even though they kept grinding out wins</u>, *the way they played*, it wasn't pleasing on the eye

    d. **Manchester United**, <u>quite frankly</u>, *the way they played*, it wasn't pleasing on the eye

The fact that (underlined) constituents of various kinds can intervene between the bold-printed and italicised dislocated topics in (43) suggests that the two dislocated topic constituents in each of the sentences in (43) are contained in separate topic projections. In the case of (43a), for instance, the clause periphery will arguably contain the two distinct TOPP constituents shown in (44) below, separated by an intervening PP modifier which occupies the specifier position in a separate MODP projection:

(44)

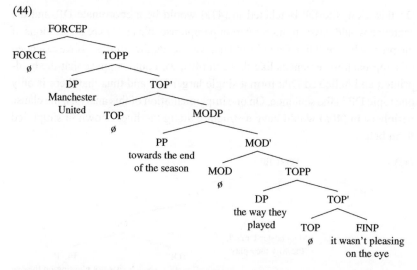

A structure like (44) would entail abandoning the Topic Uniqueness Constraint (allowing only one topic of a given kind in the periphery of any clause – e.g. only one dislocated topic) – at least in its strongest form. We might, however, envisage a revised version of the constraint whereby multiple topics are allowed only if each successive topic constituent is connected to (and refines) the topic immediately above it. On this view, the higher TOPP in (44) identifies Manchester United as the general A-topic, and the lower TOPP picks out the way they play as a more specific A-topic. On this view, multiple dislocated topics serve to successively refine and narrow down the A-topic.

    Thus far, I have examined resumptive-linked dislocated topics, setting aside orphaned dislocated topics. Although these are not discussed by Bianchi & Frascarelli (2010), in my broadcast data, (bold-printed) orphaned dislocated topics are found in conjunction with (italicised) resumptive-linked dislocated topics or with other orphaned topics in the following sentences:

(45)    a.  **FC United**, *the fans*, <u>they</u>'ve sold at least 3,200 tickets (Reporter, BBC Radio 5)

        b.  **The people on the street**, *the demands we are aware of*, <u>they</u> have a legitimacy (Alistair Burt, BBC Radio 5)

        c.  But **4–2–3–1**, *that lone striker*, <u>he</u> must be able to combine back to goal (Tim Vickery, BBC Radio 5)

        d.  **Everton**, *Saha*, <u>he</u> did look quite sharp (Danny Mills, BBC Radio 5)

        e.  **These kind of economy measures**, *this kind of reining in expenses*, is <u>that</u> related in any way to your poor start to the season? (Mark Clemett, BBC Radio 5)

        f.  *England*, **the condition of their units**, <u>they</u> are reasonably satisfied (Mike Hooper, BBC Radio 5)

        g.  **This pitch, that length**, it's just gonna disappear (Jonathan Agnew, BBC Radio 5 Sports Extra; *it* = the ball)

        h.  **Crystal Palace, Sam Allardyce**, what can you say? (Jamie Carragher, Sky Sports TV)

In (45a–e), an orphaned topic is followed by a resumptive-linked topic; in (45f) we find the converse order; and in (45g, h) we find two orphaned topics. In all cases, the two topics are linked in some way. Thus, pragmatic inferencing means that *the fans* in (45a) are construed as fans of *FC United*. Likewise, *the demands* in (45b) are construed as demands made by *the people on the street*. Similarly in (45c), *that lone striker* is construed as being the 1 in the *4–2–3–1* formation. In much the same way, *Saha* is construed as playing for the *Everton* team in (45d). In addition, in (45e), *this kind of reining in of expenses* is taken to be a specific implementation of *these kind of economy measures*. Similarly, in (45f), the second dislocated topic *the condition of their units* is linked to the first dislocated topic *England* by the resumptive pronoun *their*. And in (45g, h), the two topics are linked in such a way that (45g) is interpreted as meaning 'If you bowl that length on this pitch, the ball will just disappear', and (45h) as meaning 'As for Crystal Palace, when it comes to Sam Allardyce (i.e. their appointing him as their manager), what can you say?' Thus, in each case in (45) there is a pragmatic or syntactic link between the two topics, suggesting that in multiple dislocated topic structures, the two topics must be linked in some way.[14]

---

[14] Two further potential double dislocated topic structures are the following:

    (i)  **The first few minutes**, *Fernando Torres*, that was the only chance Liverpool had (Robbie Fowler, Sky Sports TV)

    (ii)  I think **Liverpool**, *if they were to qualify for the Champions League this year, that* would be success (Graeme Souness, Sky Sports TV)

A question which the discussion above raises is whether the linking requirement on multiple dislocated topics is a contingent property of the (limited) set of multiple topic structures found in my data, or whether it holds more generally. It certainly appears not to be universal, since Hirschbühler (1975) shows that French allows multiple dislocated constituents which are not linked to each other, e.g. in sentences such as the following (Hirschbühler 1975: 164, ex. 31a)

(46)    Jean, des  livres, je sais  bien qu'elle <u>lui</u>    en      a   volé  beaucoup
John, some books, I   know well that'she to.him of.them has stolen many
'John, books, I'm fully aware that she has stolen a lot of them from him'

It may therefore be that the topic linking found in sentences like (45) is simply a pragmatic effect: that is, hearers assume that multiple topics are linked where this yields a plausible or coherent interpretation of the relevant sentence – as it does in (45) but not in (46).

Thus far, we have seen that the periphery of a given clause can contain more than one dislocated topic. This raises the question of whether a dislocated topic can be combined with a gap-linked (fronted) topic. Given that (as noted in §2.2) gap-linked topic structures are comparatively rare in British English, it will come as no surprise to find that there is only one example of such a structure in my broadcast English data, namely:

(47)    **That failure to persevere with European football,** *that,* I think puts a huge question mark against his character (Tim Vickery, BBC Radio 5)

Here, we have a bold-printed dislocated A-topic which is resumed by an italicised demonstrative pronoun functioning as a C-topic which seemingly moves from being the subject of the *think* clause to a lower topic position in the periphery, leaving behind a gap. If so, (47) has a peripheral structure which includes the recursively stacked TOPP projections below:

---

However, if the expression *the first few minutes* in (i) is a temporal clausal modifier (e.g. a PP headed by a null counterpart of the preposition *in*) occupying the specifier of a MODP projection, (i) will not be a double-topic structure. Likewise, if topics are nominal constituents, it follows that *Liverpool* can be analysed as a dislocated topic in (ii), but the *if*-clause cannot: instead, the *if*-clause could be treated as a clausal modifier, perhaps occupying the specifier position in a separate MODP projection. However, an alternative possibility in (ii) would be to treat both *Liverpool* and the *if*-clause as resumptive-linked topics, and to regard the *if*-clause topic as narrowing down the particular aspect of Liverpool to be talked about, so that the two topics are equivalent to the single topic *Liverpool's qualifying for the Champions League this year.*

(48)     [TOPP *That failure to persevere with European football* [TOP-A ø] [TOPP **that**
         [TOP-C ø] I think — puts a huge question mark against his character]]

The relative ordering of the topics (with the dislocated topic preceding the
fronted topic) would then be in accordance with the ordering posited by
Emonds (2004) and Bianchi & Frascarelli (2010)

However, sentences such as (49) below (from Shaer & Frey 2004) cast doubt
on whether there are universal constraints on the relative ordering of fronted
and dislocated topics:

(49)     a. Now *my father*, **this junk**, he was always collecting. And *my mother*, **this
            same junk** she was always throwing away (Shaer & Frey 2004: 495,
            ex. 56b)
         b. Now, **this junk**, *my father* he was always collecting. And **this same junk**,
            *my mother*, she was always throwing away (Shaer & Frey 2004: 496,
            ex. 58)

In (49a), an italicised dislocated topic precedes a bold-printed fronted topic, as
expected; but the converse ordering (with the fronted topic preceding the
dislocated topic) also leads to a convergent outcome in (49b), thereby casting
doubt on the plausibility of the proposed ordering constraint. Sentences like
(49) are more consistent with the view that the relative ordering of different
peripheral constituents is in principle free, unless a specific ordering gives rise
to violation of some constraint. For example, in (48) independent factors
require *that* to be positioned after its antecedent, since a pronoun cannot
c-command its antecedent.

Another proposed constraint on topic structures which seems questionable is
the constraint (discussed earlier in relation to 35 above) that no clause can
contain more than one fronted topic. This cannot be an absolute prohibition,
since a double fronted topic structure like (50a) below is fine for me (in an
appropriate context, with the appropriate intonation), and Rizzi (2012: 216, fn.
7) reports an observation by Richie Kayne that sentences like (50b) are
relatively acceptable:

(50)     a. **An expensive diamond ring like this**, *a man like that*, I don't think would
            ever buy for his wife
         b. **That kind of book**, *that kind of student*, you'll never be able to convince to
            buy

What this suggests is that there is no rigid constraint against having more than
one gap-linked topic in the periphery of a given clause. Rather, restrictions on
multiple topic fronting are an artefact of independent constraints – including

the Intervention Constraint (12) preventing likes from crossing likes. Since intervention effects can be weakened (to the point of being almost imperceptible) in cases where a D-linked constituent (particularly one which is heavy) crosses some other intervening constituent, it follows that movement of the heavy D-linked fronted topic bold-printed in (50) across the italicised fronted topic does not induce a strong intervention effect.[15] A further factor may well be that (50) involves nested movement paths, and these induce less severe intervention violations than crossing movement paths (as observed by Pesetsky 1982a).

Another case where intervention effects can be alleviated in double fronted topic structures is illustrated by the following contrast:

(51)    a. ?**That man, liberty* we would never grant to
        b. **Liberty, that man*, we would never grant to

(52)    a. *To that man, liberty* we would never grant (Culicover 1996: 43, ex. 23a)
        b. *Liberty, to that man*, we would never grant (Culicover 1996: 43, ex. 24a)

In (51), we have two nominal arguments fronted, and this induces a relatively severe intervention violation (albeit the sentence is slightly less ill-formed when the first topic is D-linked, as in 51a).[16] By contrast, no strong intervention effect is found in (52), arguably because the two fronted arguments aren't 'likes' in terms of their categorial status (one being nominal and the other prepositional).

To summarise: in this section, we have seen that (contrary to claims made in much of the research literature), English does indeed allow more than one topic in the periphery of a given clause, and we have explored some of the factors which determine the relative ordering of different topic projections. In the next four sections, we turn to look at the position of topics with respect to other constituents in the clause periphery, beginning with a look at the relative positioning of topics and complementisers.

---

[15] See Haegeman et al. (2014) for discussion of the cumulative factors involved in constraint violations, and ways in which constraint violations can be alleviated. One such is D-linking, allowing a fronted D-linked topic to cross an intervening fronted interrogative operator without serious degradation in a sentence such as:

   (i) *That house that you were looking at*, how much did you say would cost per month?
       (Culicover 1996: 461)

[16] The sentences in (51) could also be argued to violate the the Distinctness Condition of Richards (2010: 5), which bars a linear sequence of two like constituents.

## 2.5     Topics and Complementisers

In this section, I explore the position of topics relative to complementisers in colloquial English. We shall see that topics generally follow the declarative complementiser *that*, but can precede or follow the interrogative complementisers *if/whether*. I note that only finite clauses (and adverbial gerunds) seem to license topics in English, and that infinitive clauses do not generally allow peripheral topics (albeit with some exceptions).

As we saw in §1.4, Rizzi (2015a) posits the following template describing the canonical ordering of heads in the clause periphery (where a star indicates potential iteration):

(53)     FORCE > TOP* > INT > TOP* > FOC > TOP* > MOD* > TOP* > FIN

Recall that Rizzi posits that there are two different types of clause: (i) complete clauses whose periphery comprises FORCEP as well as FINP projections, and may include one or more topics or other medial peripheral projections positioned between the two; and (ii) defective clauses whose periphery comprises only FINP constituents (and hence excludes topicalised or focused peripheral projections). More specifically, Rizzi (2014a: 30) claims that 'finite clauses with null complementisers in English involve truncation of the higher structure of the C-system, of Force (hence the absence of the declarative force marker *that*) and of the Topic-Focus system' and thus contain only 'a vestigial presence of the C-system' comprising a projection of 'the lowest head, Fin'. By contrast, complete clauses are FORCEP projections, with the FORCE head obligatorily lexicalised as *that* in embedded declarative clauses (cf. Rizzi's 1997: 35 remark that 'Complementisers such as *that, que* etc. are in Force°').

A claim embodied in (53) is that only complete clauses can contain peripheral topic constituents, not defective clauses. Given that Rizzi takes the complementiser *that* to obligatorily spell out declarative force in embedded clauses, and that topics occupy a lower position than FORCE in the template (53), this leads us to expect to find embedded declarative clauses containing the complementiser *that* followed by a topic. And indeed, my broadcast English data contain 27 examples of *that*+topic structures, including the clauses bracketed below (where the complementiser is bold-printed, and the topic is italicised):

(54)     a. What surprised me when I went on the field this morning is [**that** *the cracks*, they're big] (Michael Vaughan, BBC Radio 5 Sports Extra)
         b. I think [**that** *Red Bull*, one of their spotters actually got arrested] (David Coulthard, BBC1 TV)

c. It's just [**that** *Liverpool*, the game's passing too many players by] (Robbie Savage, BBC Radio 5)

d. Do you think [**that** *Chelsea*, there was too much change over the years]? (Interviewer, BBC1 TV)

Such sentences are consistent with the view that complete clauses can contain peripheral topics. If we suppose that clauses always contain a FINP constituent at the lower edge of the periphery, a clause like that bracketed in (54a) will have the peripheral structure below:[17]

(55)    [FORCEP [FORCE that] [TOPP the cracks [TOP ø] [FINP [FIN ø] they're big]]]

Such a structure is compatible with Rizzi's claim that a declarative FORCE head in an embedded clause is obligatorily spelled out as *that*. The FORCE > TOP > FIN ordering in (55) is consistent with the template in (53).[18]

But what of the position of topics with respect to the interrogative complementiser *if/whether*? Rizzi (2001) argues that interrogative complementisers occupy an INT(errogative) head position below FORCE in the periphery – as shown in the template in (53) above. One reason he gives for this is that in Spanish, the interrogative complementiser *se*$_{if}$ can be preceded by the Force head *que*$_{that}$ in sentences such as (56a) below – and indeed in Radford (2013) I reported similar structures like (56b) in my broadcast English data:[19]

(56)    a. Maria decía / preguntaba **que** *si* no debiéramos dejarlas en paz (Plann 1982: 300)
'Maria was saying/asking that if we shouldn't leave them in peace'

b. When you see Spain line up, do you sometimes wonder [**that** *whether* they need Xabi Alonso AND Busquets] (Mark Chapman, BBC Radio 5)

Another is that (according to Rizzi 2001) Italian allows an (italicised) topic to be positioned before or after an INT head like *si*$_{if}$, in structures like those below:

(57)    a. Mi domando, *questi problemi*, **se** potremo mai affrontarli
'I wonder, these problems, if we will ever be able to address them'

b. Mi domando, **se** *questi problemi*, potremo mai affrontarli
'I wonder, if these problems, we will ever be able to address them'

---

[17] In order to save space, I use labelled bracketings to represent structure here and subsequently.

[18] In Chapter 3, I will examine non-canonical structures which are potential examples of topic+*that* structures. I defer discussion of them until then in order to view them in the context of a wider discussion of non-canonical complementiser spellout in Chapter 3.

[19] However, an alternative possibility discussed in Chapter 3 is that *que/that* may be a REP(ortative) head in the kind of use illustrated in (56), and perhaps also in (59b) below.

By contrast, a topic can only follow a FORCE head like *che*_that in Italian. The different distributions of the FORCE heads *que/che* and the INT heads *si/se* are captured in the template in (53).

But what of the position of topics in clauses containing the interrogative complementisers *if/whether* in English (see Radford 2016 for evidence that these are indeed complementisers)? Van Gelderen (2009: 138) remarks that sentences containing an interrogative complementiser preceded or followed by a topic are 'judged very marked by native speakers (and a Google search did not find any)'. However, my broadcast English data contain the following three examples of structures in which an interrogative complementiser is followed by a dislocated topic reprised by a resumptive:

(58)    a. See **if** *David Silva*, you can then encourage <u>him</u> to be more in possession of the ball (Andy Townsend, ITV4)
        b. I wonder **if** *Jackson Bird*, that's why <u>he</u> tried the yorker (Shane Warne, Sky Sports TV)
        c. I don't know [**whether** *this high tempo*, we can sustain <u>it</u> for a full season] (Listener, Talksport Radio)

But what about the converse ordering of TOP > INT? Two potential candidates are the structures bracketed below:

(59)    a. I would love to talk about [*women's football*, **whether** you like it or **whether** you think it's awful] (Sean Wheelock, BBC Radio 5)
        b. It worries me now [<u>that</u> *Terry*, **does** he really want to play for England]? (Martin Keown, BBC Radio 5)

In (59a), the italicised topic precedes two coordinate clauses containing the interrogative complementiser *whether*, and so this may be an example of a TOPP+INTP structure (though another possibility is that it is an asyndetic coordinate structure, with an interpretation paraphraseable as 'I would love to talk about women's football and whether you like it or whether you think it's awful'). As for (59b), if yes-no questions contain an abstract interrogative operator functioning as the specifier of an INTP projection, this may involve a structure in which a FORCEP containing *that* is followed by a TOPP containing *Terry*, and this in turn is followed by an INTP containing a null yes-no question operator and the inverted auxiliary *does*.

Now let's turn to look at the question of whether clauses headed by the infinitival complementiser *for* can contain a peripheral topic. As we saw in §1.4, Rizzi (1997) argues that *for* is a non-finite head occupying the head FIN position of FINP. There are no examples of *for*-clauses containing a topic in my data, and constructed examples like those below are ungrammatical:

(60)    a. *He is keen [**for** *antisocial behaviour like that*, the authorities to clamp down on (it)]

   b. *He is keen [*antisocial behaviour like that*, **for** the authorities to clamp down on (it)]

One possible account of the ungrammaticality of clauses like those bracketed in (60) would be to suppose that *for*-infinitives are defective/truncated clauses which project only as far as FINP. This would predict that *for*-clauses won't allow any other constituent to be positioned in their periphery. However, any such claim seems to be too strong in the light of clauses like those bracketed below:

(61)    a. What's critical is, [*if people saw the helicopter*, **for** them to contact us] (Police spokeswoman, BBC Radio 5)

   b. SPEAKER A: What was the advice given by the police to the general public? SPEAKER B: [*Under no circumstances* **for** anyone to approach the escaped convicts] (Radford 2004a: 334)

   c. Al were it good [*no woman* **for** to touche] (Chaucer, 'Wife of Bath's Tale') 'Although it would be good to touch no woman'

   d. As Liverpool chase the game, there may be more room [*in which* **for** Manchester United to manoeuvre] (Commentator, Sky Sports TV)

   e. There should be six days [*on which* **for** men to work] and a day [*on which* **for** men to rest] (tombstone inscription, Jim McCloskey, pc)

   f. It's not clear [*how best* **for** us to proceed at this point] (Politician, BBC Radio 4)[20]

   g. They wanted to do something, but they weren't sure [*what* **for** to do] (Belfast English, Baltin 2010: 332, crediting the example to Alison Henry, pc)

In (61a), we find a subordinate clause (which can be taken to be a clausal modifier occupying the specifier position in a MODP projection) positioned in front of *for*. If we adopt the suggestion made in Rizzi (2014a) to allow FINP recursion structures of the form FINP+MODP+FINP, we could accommodate this structure within a FINP analysis of *for*-infinitives by supposing that *for* occupies the lower FIN position. However, this proposal can't be extended to structures like (61b, c) where there is a focused negative constituent in front of *for*, or to structures like (61d, e) where there is a relative constituent in front of *for*, or for structures like (61f, g) where there is an interrogative operator in front of *for*. It would seem, then, that *for*-clauses are not defective, but rather are complete clauses which can accommodate a wide range of peripheral

---

[20] Evidence that *how best* can serve as a fronted wh-phrase comes from sentences such as:

(i) How best can we deal with this problem?

constituents (albeit speakers who have some version of the Doubly Filled COMP Filter in their grammar will find some of the structures degraded).

However, if *for*-clauses are not defective, the question arises as to why peripheral topics cannot occur in *for*-clauses like those in (60). The ungrammaticality of (60a) is relatively straightforward to account for, if an accusative case-assigner has to be be immediately adjacent to the constituent it case-marks (as claimed in Chomsky 1980, 1981; Stowell 1981; but see fn. 17 in Chapter 1): this case-adjacency requirement would prevent *for* from assigning accusative case to the subject *the authorities* in (60a) across the intervening topic, so leaving the case feature on the subject unvalued. However, this still leaves us with the question of why a topic can't precede *for* in English, especially as Rizzi (1997: 309) reports structures like (62) below to be acceptable in Italian (where *di* is a prepositional infinitival complementiser which Rizzi argues to be in FIN):

(62)  Gianni  pensa,  *il*  *tuo*  *libro*,  **di**  conoscerlo  bene
      Gianni  thinks,  the  your  book,  of  know.it  well
      'Gianni thinks that your book, he knows it well'

A plausible answer might be that only finite clauses allow topics in English – perhaps because topics are licensed by (i.e. must be locally c-commanded by) a finite FORCE head. Such a constraint would appear to gain empirical support from the observation that neither gerund clauses like those bracketed in (63a, b) below nor infinitive clauses like those bracketed in (63c–g) allow topics:

(63)  a. *I hate [*that kind of tooth*, having (it) extracted]
      b. *I can't imagine [*that kind of contract*, Jim agreeing to sign (it)]
      c. *I am not keen [*the children*, to take (them) on holiday with me]
      d. *The children seem [*their holidays*, to want to spend (them) in Spain]
      e. *I am not sure [whether *the children*, to take (them) on holiday with me]
      f. *A serial killer is not the kind of prisoner [*liberty* to grant (it) to]
      g. *A TV studio is not the kind of place [in which *a stunt like that* to carry (it) out]

And yet, a blanket ban on non-finite clauses containing topics would appear to be too strong, at least for speakers like me who allow topics in non-finite clauses like those bracketed below:

(64)  a. [*That solution* Robin having already explored and rejected], she decided to see if she could mate in six moves with just the rook and the two pawns (Culicover & Levine 2001: 297, fn. 14, cited in Haegeman 2012: 152)
      b. I do love [*the Arsenal*, to watch them play] (Listener, Talksport Radio)

c. [*A policy like that* for conservatives to advocate] would previously have
   been unthinkable (Haegeman 2012: 152, fn. 2; citing a pc from me)
d. It's difficult to know [*death-threats like that*, whether to take them seriously or not]
e. It's difficult to know [*death threats like that*, how to deal with them]

(64a) suggests that gerunds which are subordinate adverbial clauses permit
topics, while (63a, b) suggest that gerund complement clauses do not: this may
be because adverbial gerund clauses are more independent of (and less integrated into) the matrix clause than complement clauses, and so have a more
articulated peripheral structure. (64b) could be an example of a control clause
in which *the Arsenal* is a topic in TOPP, and the control infinitive has a PRO
subject assigned null case by FIN: however, it could alternatively be an
asyndetic coordinate structure with an interpretation paraphraseable as 'I do
love the Arsenal, (and I do love) to watch them play', and so should probably be
discarded as being of indeterminate status. (64c) seems to involve a fronted
topic moved to the front of a *for*-clause subject: this is more likely than the topic
being moved to the front of the main clause and thereby being illicitly extracted
out of a subject clause, in violation of the Constraint on Extraction Domains
(33). (64d, e) involve a dislocated topic positioned in front of an interrogative
complementiser/adverb in an infinitival complement clause. It is difficult to
discern a clearcut pattern here (and judgements are murky), so I leave the
precise nature of this constraint as a topic for future research.

To summarise: in this section, we have seen that topics are positioned
internally within the periphery, and can occupy a range of positions between
the outermost FORCE head and the innermost FIN head. In declarative complement clauses, FORCE is spelled out as *that* and can be followed by one or
more topic constituents. In embedded interrogative clauses, the complementisers *if/whether* occupy an INT position between FORCE and FIN, and allow
a topic to be positioned before or after them. It would appear that only finite
clauses (and adverbial gerunds) license topics in English, and that infinitive
clauses (generally) do not allow peripheral topics.

## 2.6    Topics and Other Peripheral Non-wh Constituents

Having looked at the syntax of topics in clauses containing complementisers in
the two previous sections, in this section I look at the position occupied by
topics in relation to other non-wh constituents in the periphery, before going on
to explore the position occupied by topics in interrogative and exclamative wh-
clauses in §2.7 and relative clauses in §2.8.

To put our discussion on a concrete footing, let's begin by looking at sentences like the following, from my broadcast English data:

(65)  a. **Fernando Alonso**, *189 points* he'll have — (David Croft, BBC Radio 5)
      b. **Kevin Pietersen**, *five* he was out for — (George Reilly, BBC Radio 5)
      c. **The goal**, *none more important* he has scored — than that one (Gary Neville, Sky Sports TV)
      d. **Stuart Broad**, *a fantastic piece of bowling* that was — in the last test match (Elliot Cook, Talksport Radio)

These involve a dislocated or orphaned (bold-printed) topic preceding an (italicised) focused constituent. The bold-printed constituent is a dislocated topic in (65a–c), reprised by the underlined resumptive pronoun *he* within the main body of the clause in (65a, b) and by *that one* in (65c); in (65d), by contrast, the bold-printed constituent is an orphaned topic, and so is unreprised. The italicised constituent is focused by moving it to the clause periphery (leaving behind a gap at its extraction site) and conveys new information about the feat accomplished by the sporting superstar in question. Although TOP > FOC is the only order in my broadcast data, it seems to me that the converse order FOC > TOP is also possible, e.g. in (constructed) sentences such as:

(66)  a. *Five*, **Kevin Pietersen**, he was out for not fifty-five
      b. *Anything Messi can do*, **Ronaldo**, I feel sure he can do better
      c. *Southpaws*, **other boxers**, they often seem to struggle against

Sentences like (65) and (66) are in keeping with the claim made by Rizzi (1997: 291) that 'A focus and one or more topics can be combined in the same structure. In that case, the focal constituent can be both preceded and followed by topics' (1997: 291). Indeed, (66c) is ambiguous with respect to which highlighted constituent is the topic, and which is the focus.

Now consider the position of topics with respect to clausal adjuncts. Since such adjuncts are taken to serve as specifiers of MODP, the template in (53) above (repeated as 67 below) would lead us to expect that topics can either precede or follow one or more clausal adjuncts, since (67) allows for the sequence TOP* > MOD* > TOP*:

(67)  FORCE > TOP* > INT > TOP* > FOC > TOP* > MOD* > TOP * > FIN

And indeed clauses like those bracketed below are compatible with this claim:

(68)  a. I just felt [**that** *Roy Hodgson*, a few weeks ago, when Liverpool lost to Everton, he was in a minority of one] (John Motson, BBC Radio 5)

  b. I just felt [**that** a few weeks ago, when Liverpool lost to Everton, *Roy Hodgson*, he was in a minority of one]

Thus, (68a) shows an (italicised) topic followed by two (underlined) adjuncts, and (68b) shows a topic preceded by two underlined adjuncts.

   However, alongside (68) we can also have (69) below, with the order MOD > TOP > MOD, which is clearly not compatible with the claim in (67) that there is only one MODP projection, low in the periphery:

(69)    I just felt [**that** a few weeks ago, *Roy Hodgson*, when Liverpool lost to Everton, he was in a minority of one]

And indeed the template in (67) is further called into question by sentences such as the following:

(70)    a. I really felt [**that**, yesterday, *how* could anyone go and celebrate that?] (Ian Abrahams, Talksport Radio)
        b. I wonder, *if you were in a situation like that*, **whether** you would react differently
        c. At the top of the Eiffel Tower, *what a breathtaking view* there is!
        d. I have to say [**that**, despite what people think, *a situation like that*, in no way would I attempt to profit from it]

In (70a), the underlined adverbial adjunct is contained in a MODP positioned between the FORCEP constituent headed by *that* and the FOCP constituent housing the focused interrogative *how*. In (70b), we find an *if*-clause adjunct positioned in front of an INT head containing the interrogative complementiser *whether*. In (70c), the underlined PP adjunct is positioned in front of a fronted exclamative phrase which I argued in the previous section to serve as the specifier of an (exclamative) operator projection which may perhaps subsume Rizzi's INTP. And in (70d), the underlined PP adjunct is positioned below the FORCE head *that* but above the TOPP projection containing *a situation like that*, the FOCP projection containing the focused negative phrase *in no way*, and the FINP containing the inverted auxiliary *would*. Data like (69, 70) suggest that there is far more flexibility in respect of the position of clausal modifiers than claimed in (67). It seems likely that (just like topics), modifiers/adjuncts can occupy any position in the periphery between the highest FORCE head and the lowest FIN head in the periphery, perhaps with different types of modifier occupying different positions (e.g. higher MODP projections may house scene-setting adverbials, as suggested by Benincà & Poletto 2004 and Haegeman 2012).

   A further question of interest concerns the issue of what kinds of clause allow peripheral topics: I will only touch on this briefly here, and set aside numerous complications: see Haegeman (2012) for a detailed and insightful account. Ross (1967: 424–5) claimed that only root clauses can contain topics, and that both Topicalisation and Left Dislocation are root transformations – i.e. operations restricted to occurring in root clauses (like 71a/72a below) and in a restricted set of complement clauses (as illustrated in 71b/72b), but not permitted in subject clauses (like those in 71c/72c), or subordinate clauses (like those in 71d/72d, e), or relative clauses (like that in 71e):

(71)    a. *Informers*, they never use
        b. ?The Revenooers claim [that *informers*, they never use]
        c. *[That *informers* they never use] is claimed by the Revenooers
        d. *I'm going to write to the Game Warden [if *more than one deer* my neighbour brings back][21]
        e. *I don't know the boy [who *the flowers*, Mary gave to]

(72)    a. *My father*, he's Armenian, and *my mother*, she's Greek
        b. I said/?*acknowledged that *my father*, he was tight as a hoot owl[22]
        c. *That *my father*, he's lived here all his life is well known to those cops
        d. *If *my father*, he comes home late, my mother always grills him
        e. *It started to rain after *Jackie and me*, we had finally gotten to our seats

In a similar vein, Cinque (1983: 11) claimed that topics are restricted to occurring in root clauses, but (1983: 35, fn. 7) noted that English may 'marginally allow the topic to be embedded in the complement to some verbs'. Likewise (as noted in §1.4), Authier (1992) and Watanabe (1993a) claimed that topics are barred from occurring in factive clauses like that bracketed in (73a) below, noun complement clauses like (73b), subordinate clauses like (73c), and subject clauses like (73d) – the relevant examples being from Maki & Kaiser (1998: 291, ex. 2):

(73)    a. *John regrets [that *this book*, Mary wrote]
        b. *John believes the rumor [that *this book*, Mary wrote]
        c. *[Before *this book*, Mary wrote], John had been a student
        d. *[That *this book*, Mary wrote] is true

Bianchi & Frascarelli (2010: 3) claim that topics are restricted to 'root' or 'root-like' clauses which are (at least potentially) endowed with assertive force.

However, the relevant claims seem too strong in certain respects. Consider, for example, the claim that factive clauses don't allow topics (a claim made in

---

[21] Although presented by Ross as an example in which the italicised constituent is topicalised, this seems to be a case of focusing.
[22] This restriction could be stylistic in nature, if dislocation is characteristic of informal styles and hence incompatible with a verb like *acknowledge* which tends to be used in formal styles.

work ranging from Hooper & Thompson 1973 to Haegeman 2012). The empirical basis of this claim is called into question by factive clauses such as those bracketed below, which are fine for speakers like me:

(74)    a. Poirot noticed [that *the gun in the drawer*, someone had removed (it) several days earlier]
        b. It is true [that *the unemployment statistics*, the government has been massaging (them) for years]
        c. I am glad [that *the person responsible for the attacks*, the police have now caught (him)]
        d. He forgot [that *the intimate photos he had taken of her*, he had kept copies of (them) on his hard drive]

Nye (2013: 76) reports similar judgements. Moreover, exclamative clauses (which are factive) allow topics, as we will see in the next section.

Similarly, the claim that topics are not permitted in a range of subordinate clauses is also questionable. For example, we will see in §2.8 below that relative clauses permit topics. Moreover, the claim that topics cannot occur in subject clauses or in noun complement clauses is called into question by sentences such as the following:

(75)    a. [Whether *behavior like that*, we should simply turn a blind eye to (it)] is a moot point
        b. He made the point [that *the teams in blind football*, the style of play had an almost exact parallel in the style of play by the senior football team] (Tim Vickery, BBC Radio 5)
        c. People like Dale need to have confidence [that *the kind of policing they need*, that we can still deliver it] (Police spokesman, BBC Radio 5)
        d. This is probably the biggest problem, I think, for the 2014 World Cup, the fact [that *the cities of the South (Porto Alegre, Conchuba)*, you could even get temperatures down to freezing] (Tim Vickery, BBC Radio 5)

And as for the claim that topics cannot occur in subordinate clauses, this is called into question by the subordinate clauses such as those bracketed below (76b–k being from my broadcast English data):

(76)    a. Herbert will certainly be at this party, [because *his mother*, I talked to her this morning] (Hooper & Thompson 1973: 492)
        b. That's [because *Smalling and Jones*, neither of them have made it for this match] (John Murray, BBC Radio 5)
        c. I've gotta see what I can do moving forward, because *the past*, I can't change (Paul Stewart, Talksport Radio)
        d. I think this data is a little bit misleading, [because *London*, we know prices are going up] (David Buick, Talksport Radio)

    e. Davies hardly ever wastes a ball in the air, [whereas *Crouch*, you can't rely on him] (Alan Green, BBC Radio 5)

    f. This free kick is just within range, [although *Mata*, I'm not sure he's got the power to score one from there] (Michael Owen, BBC Sport TV)

    g. [If indeed *Joey Barton*, the rumours are true that they want him at the football club], do West Ham go ahead and sign him? (Adrian Durham, Talksport Radio)

    h. [If, *their role models*, they see them behaving in this manner], it's not sending out the right message (Local councillor, BBC Radio 5)

    i. [If *Luca Modric*, everything he's saying is correct], then Daniel Levy has to take a good look at himself (Adrian Durham, Talksport Radio)

    j. The competition really starts to come alive if you come to the last stage [when *both of those teams*, one of them has to lose] (Graham Taylor, BBC Radio 5)

    k. Does it somehow take a bit of pressure off [now that *the Heineken Cup*, you'll have to pull out of]? (Ian Robertson, BBC Radio 5)

A complication to be noted here is that Haegeman (2006a, 2006b, 2012) argues that while some types of adverbial clause allow fronted topics, others don't. For example, Haegeman (2012: ch. 5) argues that adverbial clauses introduced by a temporal subordinator like *when/before/after/until/since* contain a temporal operator which originates within TP and from there moves to the clause periphery, with the result that fronted topics give rise to an intervention violation (although in situ dislocated or orphaned topics do not). It would appear that (76k) is a potential counterexample to this claim if *now that* involves a structure paraphraseable as 'at a time in the present when', and if a null operator (in effect a null counterpart of *when*) originates within TP and moves to the periphery, inducing an intervention violation because the fronted topic intervenes in the movement path of the temporal operator. Still, it may be that in this case, the wh-operator is generated in situ in the periphery of the *now that* clause, so that fronting *the Heineken Cup* does not induce an intervention violation – and indeed it could be that relative *when* is also generated in situ in sentences like:

(77)    It was a time **when**, *the scandalous behaviour of certain presenters*, the BBC turned a blind eye to —

so that topic fronting does not cause an intervention violation in cases like (77) either.

    To summarise: contrary to some earlier claims, it would seem that most finite clauses allow topics. If finite clauses are canonically complete clauses which contain a FORCEP projection able to include a full range of peripheral constituents (including topics), we should indeed expect them to be able to contain topics. However, two exceptions should be noted. One is in cases where independent constraints rule out the relevant structures (e.g. the Intervention Constraint rules out a fronted topic which crosses or is crossed by another like constituent moving to the periphery). Another exception relates to defective/ truncated finite clauses whose periphery contains only a FINP projection: recall that according to Rizzi (2014a: 30), 'finite clauses with null complementisers in English involve truncation of the higher structure of the C-system, of Force (hence the absence of the declarative force marker *that*) and of the Topic-Focus system' and thus contain only 'a vestigial presence of the C-system' comprising a projection of 'the lowest head, Fin'. By contrast, English generally does not allow topics in non-finite clauses, albeit for some speakers there are interesting potential exceptions (e.g. 64).

Having looked at the position of topics with respect to a range of other types of peripheral non-wh constituent in this section, in the next two sections I turn to explore the position of topics with respect to peripheral wh-constituents.

## 2.7    Topics in Wh-interrogatives and Exclamatives

In this section, I turn to explore the syntax of topics in clauses containing peripheral interrogative or exclamative wh-constituents. I shall argue that topics can in principle either precede or follow interrogative and exclamative wh-constituents, although specific orderings will be ruled out by independent constraints in some cases.

Let's begin by looking at the position occupied by topics in wh-questions. Rizzi (1997, 2001) and Haegeman & Guéron (1999) argue that fronted interrogative operators move to spec-FOCP in questions involving auxiliary inversion, and the inverted auxiliary moves through FIN into FOC.[23, 24] Empirical

---

[23]   Rizzi (1997: 331, fn. 22) remarks that 'the auxiliary should reach Foc° in order to satisfy the Wh Criterion'. He posits that the focused wh-operator and the auxiliary carry a wh-feature, and movement of the operator to spec-FOCP and of the auxiliary to FOC satisfies the Wh-Criterion requirement for a wh-specifier to have a wh-head and vice versa. A variant of the same story is that the auxiliary and the interrogative operator both carry a focus feature, and movement of both to the edge of FOCP is required in order to satisfy the Focus Criterion of Rizzi (1996).

[24]   My broadcast English data include the examples in (i) and (ii), where the italicised interrogative phrase seems to function as a dislocated topic and does not trigger Auxiliary Inversion in the root clause (i):

> (i)   *Which of those two sides*, the way <u>they</u>'re set up suits the game best? (Matt Holland, Talksport Radio)
>
> (ii)   I'm trying to sort out *which modules* it's desirable <u>they</u> don't clash (Administrator, University of Essex)

evidence consistent with this claim is provided by sentences such as the following:

(78)  a. He protested [**that** *how* could he have known that his office was bugged?] (Radford 1988: 585)

b. *\*Which book* under no circumstances would you read? (Haegeman & Guéron 1999: 226)

(78a) suggests that *how* occupies a position below a FORCE head like *that*; (78b) suggests that a fronted interrogative is incompatible with a fronted negative constituent (as would be expected if both compete for the specifier position in FOCP). Rizzi (1997: 291) claims that 'a WH operator in main

On the other hand, examples like those below involve a resumptive interrogative structure which does indeed trigger Auxiliary Inversion in root clauses:

(iii) *Which guys* did you say that you didn't know whether their friends were gonna rat on them or not? (Kayne 1984: 191, fn. 20)

(iv) *Which of the linguists* do you think that if Mary marries him, then everyone will be happy? (Sells 1984)

(v) *Which picture of John* were you wondering [whether it was going to win a prize at the exposition]? (Pesetsky 1998: 28)

(vi) *Who* did the police say that finding his car took all morning? (Merchant 2004)

(vii) *Who* do you think that if the voters elect him, the country will go to ruin? (Merchant 2004)

(viii) *Who out of them* d'you instinctively say: SHE's got to go through? (Cheryl Cole, ITV)

(ix) *Which word* are they not sure how it's spelled? (adapted from McCloskey 2006)

(x) *Which exam question* does no professor ever wonder if it will be tough enough? (Beltrama 2013)

Maybe the italicised wh-constituent in such cases originates as a dislocated constituent in the embedded clause, and from there (by virtue of being interrogative) undergoes movement through the edge of FINP in the matrix clause into the edge of FOCP or WHP, thereby triggering inversion. Ackerman et al. (2014) report experimental evidence that a resumptive pronoun is preferred to a gap in sentences like:

(xi) *Which man* did Jane say that the parent who scolded him forgave the babysitter's mistake?

By contrast, Polinsky et al. (2013) report experimental evidence that wh-questions containing a resumptive are judged as particularly bad. My broadcast English data contain the following example of a dislocated wh-interrogative expression in an *if*-clause:

(xii) I wonder *how many other clubs*, if their entire first team is on that kind of money (Bob Beech, Talksport Radio)

The interrogative clause here appears to be a query about how many clubs there are whose first team players earn so much money. It looks like *how many other clubs* is a dislocated constituent here, reprised by the resumptive pronoun *their*.

questions is compatible with a Topic in a fixed order (Top Wh)'. And indeed, TOP > WH structures have been widely reported in the research literature, as the examples below illustrate:

(79)    a. *A book like this*, **to whom** would you give? (Delahunty 1983)
        b. *That kind of pen*, **what** can you use it for? (Radford 1988: 532)
        c. *Tom*, **why** would anyone want to meet? (Bianchi 1999: 179)
        d. *A book like this*, **why** should I buy? (Hudson 2003: 614)
        e. *That kind of behaviour*, **how** can we tolerate in a civilised society? (Radford 2009a: 329)
        f. *Such perfect symmetry*, **where else** would you find? (Haegeman 2012: 29, pc from me)

This claim (if generalised to inversion questions) would appear to be borne out by my broadcast English data, which contain 18 examples of TOP > WH ordering in auxiliary inversion questions (13 in root questions like 80a–e below and 5 in embedded questions like 80f), and no examples of the converse ordering:

(80)    a. *Tottenham*, **where** do they go from here? (Ronnie Irani, Talksport Radio)
        b. *This kind of performance*, **how** do you think the fans will react to it? (Mark Chapman, BBC Radio 5)
        c. *Agbonlahore*, **how sharp** was he? (Jason Cundy, Talksport Radio)
        d. *Danny*, *England*, **what sort of side** are we gonna see against Norway? (Alan Brazil, Talksport Radio, addressing Danny Higginbotham)
        e. I thought a draw would have been a fairer result, but *these things*, **how** do you judge fairness? (Graham Taylor, BBC Radio 5)
        f. Now it's just a case of *Middlesboro*, **how brave** can they be? (Danny Higginbotham, BBC Radio 5)

On the assumptions made by Rizzi, Haegeman and Guéron, the ordering WH > TOP is ruled out in inversion questions, irrespective of whether the topic precedes the inverted auxiliary as in (81a) below, or follows it as in (81b):

(81)    a. ***Where**, *Tottenham*, <u>do</u> they go from here?
        b. ***Where** <u>do</u> *Tottenham*, they go from here?

Structures like (81a) are ruled out because the inverted auxiliary moves only as far as FIN and does not move to FOC (leading to a violation of the Wh-Criterion/Focus Criterion: see fn. 23). Structures like (81b) are ruled out because in order to get from FIN to FOC, the inverted auxiliary has to move through the head TOP position of the TOPP housing *Tottenham* (in order to satisfy the Head Movement Constraint of Travis 1984 or the Relativised Minimality Condition of Rizzi 1990), but this is not possible because TOP is an inert head which cannot attract an auxiliary (as noted by Rizzi 1997: 303).

However, a potential problem with the account offered above of the ungrammaticality of structures like (81) is that it is dependent on the assumption that inverted auxiliaries move to FOC in cases of interrogative (or negative) inversion. This predicts that the fronted negative or interrogative constituent and the inverted auxiliary will be immediately adjacent. And yet the robustness of this assumption is called into question by a phenomenon observed by Ross (1967: 31) which Haegeman (2000a) terms non-adjacent inversion, and which (as shown below) has been reported in a number of studies:

(82)    a. **Why**, *after maintaining that you were sick*, <u>did</u> you get out of bed? (Ross 1967: 31)
        b. **What**, *although you've never been in one*, <u>would</u> you do in a typhoon? (ibid.)
        c. **How long**, *in the light of this promotion*, <u>will</u> you stay here? (ibid.)
        d. **What else**, *with no money to speak of*, <u>could</u> he possibly have done? (Kayne 1998: 155, fn. 66)
        e. **How often**, *that book*, <u>has</u> he praised it in public? (ibid.)
        f. **Under what circumstances** *during the holidays* <u>would</u> you go into the office? (Sobin 2003: 193)
        g. **On no account** *during the vacation* <u>would</u> I go into the office (Haegeman 2000a: 133)
        h. He prayed that **never again** *atrocities like these* <u>would</u> he witness (Haegeman 2012: 48, fn. 46)
        i. I can assure you that **no personal information** *to anyone I didn't know* <u>would</u> I ever divulge (Radford & Iwasaki 2015: 721)

In such examples, an (underlined) inverted auxiliary can be separated from the (italicised) phrase which licenses the relevant inversion by (one or more) intervening bold-printed constituents. Haegeman (2000a) claims that only some speakers allow such structures, but Sobin (2003) reports high acceptability scores for similar sentences in an experimental study. By contrast, an inverted auxiliary cannot be positioned above other peripheral material – we see from the ungrammaticality of sentences such as *Why do, in Scotland, they eat haggis?*

A plausible interpretation of the relevant data is that (in structures like 82), the inverted auxiliary raises to (and remains in) the head FIN position of FINP.[25] If the bold-printed fronted negative or interrogative constituent is in

---

[25] Further potential evidence in support of this claim comes from sentence fragments like that produced by speaker в below:

spec-FOCP (as claimed in Rizzi 1997 and Haegeman 2012), this suggests that circumstantial adjuncts like those italicised in (82a–d, f, g) or even dislocated/fronted topics like those italicised in (82e, h) can be positioned between FOCP and FINP. If inversion requires the inverted auxiliary and its negative/interrogative licenser to be in a local spec–head configuration at some stage of derivation, this further suggests that the fronted negative or interrogative expression transits through spec-FINP on its way to spec-FOCP (as argued by Haegeman 1996: 145 for related structures in Dutch). Given these assumptions, the *that*-clause in (82h) will have the peripheral structure shown below:

(83)   He prayed [$_{FORCEP}$ [$_{FORCE}$ that] [$_{FOCP}$ never again [$_{FOC}$ ø] [$_{TOPP}$ atrocities like these [$_{TOP}$ ø] [$_{FINP}$ ~~never again~~ [$_{FIN}$ would] he witness]]]]]

The FORCE > FOC > TOP > FIN ordering in (83) is compatible with the ordering of peripheral projections given in the template in (53/67).[26]

  (i)  SPEAKER A:  He's emigrating to Canada
  (ii) SPEAKER B:  Why?

If such fragments arise via movement of *why* into spec-FOCP and deletion of the FINP complement of the FOC head, and if the inverted auxiliary moves only as far as FIN, we can account for why there is no auxiliary left behind in FOC under ellipsis. On this type of ellipsis (termed *Why* Stripping), see Nakao et al. (2012), Ortega-Santos et al. (2014), Weir (2014a), and Yoshida et al. (2015). However, see Haegeman (2000a) for an alternative account of Interrogative Inversion under which the fronted negative/interrogative phrase first moves to spec-FOCP (and the inverted auxiliary to FOC) and then subsequently moves into a higher SCP/scene-setting projection positioned above a peripheral adjunct. See also Ross 1967: 31–2 for a proposal which is different in execution but similar in spirit.

[26] It may be that speakers who reject sentences like (82) do indeed require the inverted auxiliary to raise to FOC, so that sentences like (82) are ruled out because the auxiliary remains in FIN. I note in passing that the alternative ordering FORCEP > TOPP > FOCP > FINP is also possible, as illustrated by the following example from Radford (2004a: 329):

   (i)  He prayed [$_{FORCEP}$ that [$_{TOPP}$ atrocities like those, [$_{FOCP}$ never again [$_{FINP}$ would he witness]]]]

I further note that my broadcast data also contain examples of topics in inverted yes-no questions – 11 in root clauses like (ii) below, and 2 in embedded clauses like that bracketed in (iii):

   (ii)  Those Red Bulls, can they make the leap-frog against Maclaren? (David Croft, BBC Radio 5)
   (iii) It worries me now [that Terry, does he really want to play for England?] Martin Keown, BBC Radio 5)

On the structure of the topic clauses in (ii) and (iii), see the discussion of (59b) in the main text.

Now consider the position of topics in embedded wh-questions. Haegeman & Guéron (1999) and Haegeman (2000a) argue that wh-operators move to spec-FORCEP in uninverted embedded questions (i.e. questions without auxiliary inversion).[27] Since FORCEP is the highest projection in the clause periphery, this analysis predicts that topics will always follow wh-operators in embedded questions. At first sight, this prediction would appear to be borne out by the WH > TOP ordering in embedded clauses like those bracketed below:

(84)    a. My question is [**how** *other nations*, they see the England team currently] (Listener, BBC Radio 5)

       b. I was wondering [**to what kind of people** *books like these* you would actually have given if you had had the chance] (Culicover 1996: 460)

       c. I cannot see [**how** *this kind of behaviour*, we can tolerate in a civilised society] (Radford 2009a: 327)

       d. I don't know [**for what particular reason** *the medicines that the doctor prescribed*, he simply did not take (them)]

       e. I can't imagine [**why** *grossly offensive like that*, the police turn a blind eye to (it)]

However, there are two reasons for doubting whether wh-constituents really do move to the edge of FORCEP in embedded questions. One is that my broadcast English data contain 12 examples of structures like those below in which a wh-constituent in an uninverted embedded question is positioned after the complementiser *that*:

(85)    a. Do you think that they don't realise [**that** *how long* they're taking]? (Adam Hunt, Talksport Radio)

       b. Can you remember [**that** *when* he suddenly said he was going to go to the arch rivals]? (Danny Kelly, Talksport Radio)

       c. I spoke to him to say [**that** *what* had happened] (Brendan Rogers, Talksport Radio)

       d. You know [**that** *what* happened there] (Bob Wilson, Talksport Radio)

       e. I'm trying to understand [**that** *why* we don't see any French planes as part of the strike force] (Journalist, BBC Radio 5)

If *that* is a FORCE head, it follows that the italicised interrogative constituent following it must be housed in a lower projection than FORCEP.[28]

---

[27] To be precise, they claim that in embedded questions, wh-operators move to 'the highest specifier of the CP system'; and the template in (53/67) specifies that the highest peripheral projection is FORCEP.

[28] However, this argument is not particularly compelling, since (as argued in Chapter 3) *that* could be taken to be a REP/reportative head which has a FORCEP complement housing the italicised interrogative constituent.

A second problem with the claim that interrogative wh-constituents are positioned on the edge of FORCEP in uninverted embedded questions is that it is potentially undermined by embedded clauses which seemingly instantiate the order TOP > WH. Given the importance of these examples, below I cite all the examples of such structures in my broadcast English data:

(86)    a. I would assess [*their team*, **how good** I think it is] (Geoff Boycott, BBC Radio 5 Sports Extra)

b. I can sometimes understand [*people*, **why** they do that] (Alan Brazil, Talksport Radio)

c. I can't believe [*the last twelve months*, **how** it's been] (Lee Boardman, Talksport Radio)

d. Just describe [*the last three months*, **what** they've been like] (Aasmah Mir, BBC Radio 5)

e. It's interesting now to see [*Arsène Wenger*, **what** he's going to do] (Niall Quinn, Sky Sports TV)

f. You can see [*Fernando Torres*, **exactly what** he is going through right now] (Steve Froggatt, BBC Radio 5)

g. Everyone will get the chance to see [*all eight teams*, **what** they've been up to] (Karen Carney, BBC Radio 5)

h. Watch [*the players on either side*, **how** they accept the decision] (Geoff Boycott, BBC Radio 5 Sports Extra)

i. I wonder [*Wayne Rooney*, **what** his best position really is] (Jimmy Armfield, BBC Radio 5)

j. This comes down to Mark's point of Lampard and Gerard not necessarily knowing [*each other*, **what** they're going to do] (Pat Nevin, BBC Radio 5)

k. I think we're still waiting for [*the result*, **which way** it will go] (Alan Brazil, Talksport Radio)

l. We all know the history of [*Portsmouth*, **where** they overspent in recent times] (Reporter, Talksport Radio)

m. I'm very sceptical on [*Sven*, **where** he's been] (Robbie Savage, BBC Radio 5)

n. I'm delighted with [*the lads*, **what** they've done] (Football manager, BBC Radio 5)

o. I was still giggling after [*Roy Keane*, **what** he said] (Micky Quinn, Talksport Radio)

p. You have to fear for Blackpool because of [*Man United*, **where** they are] (Graeme Souness, Sky Sports TV)

q. I'm very disappointed in [*Aston Villa*, **how** they appear to have treated Steve McClaren] (Graham Taylor, BBC Radio 5)

r. Let's give credit to [*Atletico*, **how** they've played] (Ray Parlour, Talksport Radio)

s. Look at [*Murray*, **how** he played at Queens] (Chris Davis, Talksport Radio)

t. The big story will be [*Carlton Cole*, **where** he goes] (Reporter, Talksport Radio)

u. It's amazing [*these old-fashioned bunkers*, **how** they look] (Ken Brown, BBC2 TV)

If the structures bracketed in (86) are indeed clauses in which a peripheral topic precedes a fronted wh-constituent, it suggests that fronted wh-constituents in uninverted interrogatives (i.e. interrogatives without auxiliary inversion) move to a position below TOP.

However, we need to bear in mind that there are other interpretations of the relevant data. For example, (at least some of) the structures in (86) could involve asyndetic coordination, so that a sentence like (86a) could have a meaning loosely parahraseable as 'I would assess their team, and (I would assess) how good it is.' Indeed, in some cases, the structure beginning with the wh-constituent may be a free relative (hence nominal in nature), rather than an interrogative clause. And at least in the case of (86j), a coordination story seems more plausible than a topic story, since we saw from the ungrammaticality of (15a) '*Himself*, he would never pass <u>him</u> over' that an anaphor cannot serve as a dislocated topic.

Nevertheless, for at least some of the structures in (86), a topic analysis seems more plausible than a coordination story. For example, in (86i) *Wayne Rooney* can't be (a coordinate) complement of the verb *wonder*, since *wonder* does not select a nominal complement (cf. *I *wonder Wayne Rooney*): it is more likely that the complement of the verb *wonder* is a wh-question clause containing the topic *Wayne Rooney* followed by the wh-operator *what*. Thus I conclude that at least some of the sentences in (86) are TOP > WH structures, and that interrogative wh-operators in embedded questions in English (as in Italian) can occupy position lower than TOPP.

At the same time, however, an interrogative operator in an uninverted question can occupy a higher position than a focused phrase – as we see from (constructed) examples such as the following:[29]

---

[29] Rizzi (2001) argues that fronted interrogative operators in embedded questions in Italian occupy a position below a focused constituent in a sentence such as the following (where capitals mark a focused constituent which receives contrastive stress):

(i) Mi domando A GIANNI *che cosa* abbiano detto (non a Piero)
'I wonder TO GIANNI what they have said (not to Piero)'

However, the English counterparts of structures like (i) are unidiomatic.

(87)    a. I have no idea [**why** *at no point* did he apologise to her]
b. I can't understand [**how** *not a single trace of the killer's DNA* did the forensic team find]
c. The pharmacist will be able to tell you [**what kind of foods** *under no circumstances* should people allergic to peanuts eat]

If the italicised fronted negative phrase in sentences like (87) is focused and occupies spec-FOCP, it follows that interrogative wh-operators are positioned above focused constituents in embedded questions.[30]

Rizzi (2001) posits that interrogative wh-operators in embedded clauses move to the edge of a projection with a WH head whose specifier is the criterial position for an interrogative wh-operator. But what position does this WH head occupy in the clause periphery, in relation to the template in (53/67) above – repeated in (88) below?

(88)    FORCE > TOP* > INT > TOP* > FOC > TOP* > MOD* > TOP * > FIN

Since we have evidence from sentences like (85) that WH is positioned below FORCE, from sentences like (87) that WH is positioned above FOC, and from sentences like (84) and (86) that WH can be positioned either above or below TOP, the most plausible answer is that in English, WH occupies much the same position as INT. Indeed, it is even possible that in English, INT and WH should be conflated as a single OP(erator) head: in embedded yes-no questions, the OP head will be filled by *whether/if* and its specifier will be a null yes-no question operator; but in embedded wh-questions, the OP head will be null and its specifier position will be filled by an overt wh-operator.

Interestingly, sentences like those in (89) below raise the possibility that (at least some) English speakers allow interrogative operators to function as the specifier of an interrogative wh-projection in root clauses as well (and indeed Rizzi 2001 proposes that Italian *perchè* 'why' and *come mai* 'how come' occupy spec-INTP):

---

[30] An interesting question arises about the landing site of a phrase like that italicised below:

(i)  He travelled with the team, *no members of which* the customs officials detained at the airport
(ii) He travelled with the team, *no members of which* did the customs officials detain at the airport

It would seem that *no members of which* can either be treated as an interrogative wh-phrase which pied-pipes a superordinate negative constituent along with it and moves to spec-WHP without triggering inversion, or be treated as a focused negative phrase which moves to spec-NEGP and triggers inversion.

(89)   a. **Why** *at no point in the discussion* <u>did</u> you mention that setting up an APPG in return for payment or at the request of a paying client would be against the rules? (Commissioner for Standards, House of Lords, Committee for Privileges and Conduct, 10th report of session 2013–14, p. 177)

     b. **Why** *not once* did anyone stand up in that party and just say 'The Emperor has no clothes' (theguardian.com > politics > Liz Kendall)

     c. **Why**, *nowhere else in the Bible* is this statement made by Jesus? (R.L. Tegenkamp, *The Face of Jihad*, Google Books)

     d. What should Leo be allowed to eat, and **what**, *under no circumstances*, <u>should</u> he be allowed to touch? (P. Duncker, *Sophie and the Sibyl: A Victorian Romance*, Bloomsbury, London, 2015: 250)

     e. **Where** *under no circumstances* should you place a smoke alarm? (Duffield 2015: 61)

     f. **When** *under no circumstances* should you put your head above the parapet? (ibid.)

If no clause can contain more than one focused constituent (Rizzi 1997), it follows that (89) cannot involve FOCP recursion. It could instead be that the interrogative operator is on the edge of a wh-operator projection (WHP), the negative phrase on the edge of FOCP, and the inverted auxiliary on the edge of FINP.[31]

Having looked at the position of topics in interrogative wh-clauses, let's now take a look at the syntax of exclamative wh-clauses containing topics. Rizzi (1997: 283) takes a FORCE projection to serve the function of typing a clause as declarative/exclamative, etc. Accordingly, Radford (2004a: 332) suggested that 'exclamative wh-expressions … move into the specifier position within FORCEP'. Since (as we see from 88 above) FORCEP is the highest projection in the clause periphery, we should expect topics to follow exclamative constituents; and indeed Radford argues that this is the case, citing the following example in support of this claim:

(90)   **In how many countries**, *that kind of behaviour*, autocratic leaders would simply not tolerate!

Given this (and other) assumptions, a sentence like (90) would have a peripheral structure which includes a bold-printed exclamative phrase on the edge of FORCEP preceding an italicised topic on the edge of TOPP. The resulting WH > TOP order would be consistent with the template (88), if WHP occupies much the same position as INTP.

---

[31] Duffield (2015: 61) judges the NEG > WH > AUX ordering in sentences like that below to be marginal:

     (i)   ??Under no circumstances what should you give to a dog?

However, my broadcast English data show no examples of WH > TOP structures in exclamative clauses. By contrast, the data contain 15 examples of TOP > WH structures (8 in root clauses, 7 in embedded clauses), including those below:

(91)    a. *The young kid up front,* **what a week** he had! (Ray Parlour, Talksport Radio)
        b. *The United States,* **what a team** they've got! (Commentator, Eurosport TV)
        c. *City,* **what a game at Carrow Road** it was! (Ian Danter, Talksport Radio; *City* = Manchester City)
        d. I've got to say [*Alan Pardew,* **what a job** he's done!] (Stan Collymore, Talksport Radio)

Examples like those in (91) suggest that exclamative wh-constituents are not positioned on the edge of FORCEP, but rather occupy a lower position in the periphery. But what position, exactly?

Nye (2013: 316) reports internet-sourced examples such as the following, showing an (italicised) exclamative phrase positioned after the (bold-printed) complementiser *how*:

(92)    a. I forgot [**how** *what a simple thrill* it can be]
        b. He told me [**how** *what a wonderful girl* I was]
        c. I clearly remember this one woman coming up to me after the group was leaving and told me [**how** *what a wonderful waitress* I was] as she pressed a crisp bill into my hand

Nye takes *how* in (92) to be a factive complementiser occupying the head of a TYPEP projection which she takes to be the highest projection in the periphery. My broadcast English data contain 14 examples of clauses like those bracketed below in which an italicised exclamative wh-phrase follows the complementiser *that*:

(93)    a. He's proved in his career [**that** *what a very, very good manager* he is] (Peter Taylor, Talksport Radio)
        b. I'm gonna show you [**that** *what a good player* I am] (Graham Beecroft, Talksport Radio)
        c. We know [**that** *how good* he is, going forward] (Ray Parlour, Talksport Radio)
        d. I want people to be reminded [**that** *how important* football is to me] (David Beckham, Sky Sports TV)

If we follow Rizzi (2011, 2012, 2015a) in taking a peripheral exclamative phrase to serve as the specifier of an EXCL(amative) wh-operator projection, this suggests that the exclamative projection EXCLP is positioned below the highest FORCE/TYPE head containing the complementiser *that*.

Further evidence relating to the position of EXCLP comes from the following sentence (from Radford 2004a: 332):

(94)    **In how many countries of the world**, *such behaviour*, <u>under no circum-stances</u> would autocratic leaders tolerate!

(94) suggests that an exclamative constituent can occupy a position in the periphery above an (italicised) topic, a focused negative phrase, and an inverted auxiliary; however, sentences like those in (91) suggest that an exclamative constituent can also be positioned after a topic. These two sets of sentences taken together suggest that wh-exclamatives occupy essentially the same position as wh-interrogatives, leading to the conclusion that the criterial position for both is the specifier position of a wh-operator projection WHP.[32]

To summarise: in this section, I have argued that the criterial position for interrogative and exclamative wh-constituents is the specifier position within an (appropriate kind of) wh-operator projection WHP. I have further argued that topics can (in principle) either precede or follow WHP, albeit specific orderings are sometimes ruled out by independent constraints.

## 2.8    Topics in Relative Clauses

Having looked at where topics are positioned in interrogative and exclamative wh-clauses in the previous section, I now turn in this section to look at where they are positioned in relative clauses. I shall show that, contrary to what happens in interrogative and exclamative wh-clauses, topics always follow relativisers in relative clauses.

My broadcast English data contain the following examples of (bracketed) relative clauses containing a (bold-printed) wh-relativiser, an (italicised) dis-located topic, and an (underlined) resumptive pronoun:

(95)    a. There are a lot of very small ones [**which**, *the critics*, <u>they</u> might want to sneer at] (Political correspondent, BBC Radio 5)
        b. He crossed a ball [**which** *Sam Allardyce*, <u>he</u> wasn't too happy with his defenders] (Danny Mills, BBC Radio 5)
        c. This is the stage [**where** *big players*, <u>they</u> produce] (Steve McClaren, Sky Sports TV)

---

[32] If, as suggested earlier, WHP occupies the same position as INTP in English, the two can be conflated into a more general OPP/operator projection.

    d. Aquilani was a decent passer of the ball, [**where** *Xabi Alonso*, it was obvious how much Liverpool missed him] (Andy Brassell, BBC Radio 5)

    e. This may be the reason [**why** *England*, some of their passing went astray] (Mike Ingham, BBC Radio 5)

    f. It's one of them situations now [**where** *Harry*, what does he do?] (Ray Parlour, Talksport Radio)

    g. Joe Hart has come out to look at the wall, [**which**, *Negredo*, is he gonna join?] (Clive Tyldesley, Sky Sports TV)

In all cases, the topic follows the relative pronoun, and in (95f, g) the topic in turn precedes an interrogative structure containing an inverted auxiliary. But do clauses like those bracketed in (95) show the canonical ordering of peripheral projections specified in the template in (53) above, repeated as (96) below?

(96)    FORCE > TOP* > INT > TOP* > FOC > TOP* > MOD* > TOP * > FIN

The answer clearly depends on where relative pronouns are positioned.

    Rizzi (1997: 298) claims that 'Relative operators occupy the specifier of FORCE, the one position which cannot be preceded by topics.' He sees FORCEP as serving to mark clause type (1997: 283): consequently, since relative operators type a clause as a relative clause, it would seem plausible to take them to be positioned on the edge of FORCEP. Since FORCE is the highest peripheral head in the template in (96), it follows that topics will be positioned after relative operators, precisely as we find in (95). And indeed a similar REL > TOP ordering had been observed in earlier work, e.g. in relation to sentences such as:

(97)    He's a man [**to whom** *liberty* we could never grant] (Baltin 1982: 17)

Furthermore, Rizzi (1997: 289) observes that the same REL > TOP ordering is required in Italian.[33]

---

[33] Note that (97) involves a fronted topic, whereas all the examples of topic-containing relatives in my broadcast English data involve dislocated topics. The absence of relatives with fronted topics in my data is in part attributable to the very low frequency of topic fronting in colloquial English, and in part to the fact that topic fronting in relative clauses could (in appropriate structures) give rise to violations of the Intervention Constraint. It should be noted, however, that in cases like (97), *liberty* could be a focused constituent, in line with the claim made by Douglas (2016: 86) that 'argument fronting in RCs in English is focalisation rather than topicalisation' (RCs = relative clauses). However, Douglas' claim proves potentially problematic in relation to sentences like:

    (i)  *Serious diseases like that*, only rarely do people recover from

If fronted negatives like that underlined in (i) are focused (as claimed in Rizzi 1997) and if fronted arguments (like that italicised above) are focused (as Douglas would have us believe),

An interesting positional property illustrated in (95f, g) is that a topic within a relative clause can precede an interrogative wh-constituent and an inverted auxiliary. If, as argued by Rizzi (1997: 298, 325) and Haegeman & Guéron (1999: 345, 526), wh-questions with Auxiliary Inversion involve movement of the interrogative wh-constituent to spec-FOCP and concomitant movement of the inverted auxiliary through FIN into FOC, the relative clause bracketed in (95f) could seemingly be taken to have a peripheral structure along the lines shown below:

(98)      [$_{\text{FORCEP}}$ where [$_{\text{FORCE}}$ ø] [$_{\text{TOPP}}$ Harry [$_{\text{TOP}}$ ø] [$_{\text{FOC}}$ what [$_{\text{FOC}}$ does]
          [$_{\text{FINP}}$ [$_{\text{FIN}}$ ~~does~~] he do]]]]

(98) is compatible with the claim made by Rizzi (1997: 291) that 'Both TOP and FOC are compatible with a preceding relative operator', and with the template in (96). The relative clause in (95g) will have a slightly different derivation if yes-no questions contain a yes-no question operator in spec-INTP, and if the auxiliary moves into INT in order to ensure that the INTP is visible at PF.

However, a potential problem with the analysis in (98) is the following. A key assumption underlying Rizzi's work is that the FORCE head in a clause marks the (declarative, interrogative or imperative etc.) force of the clause: consequently in (98) it will mark the clause as interrogative. However, in (98) the FORCE head also serves to house the relative pronoun *where*, and so serves the function of typing the clause as relative. But if this is so, the FORCE head in (98) will carry two different interpretable features (an interrogative force feature and a relative type feature). The problem this poses is that it violates a featural uniqueness principle posited by Cinque & Rizzi (2008), which can be outlined informally as follows:[34]

(99)    **One Feature One Head Principle**
        Each functional head carries only one interpretable feature

It follows from (99) that if the FORCE head in (98) marks interrogative force, it cannot also mark relative type. So what is the peripheral structure of this kind of sentence?

---

the sentence in (i) contains two focused constituents, in violation of Rizzi's (1997) constraint that no clause can contain more than one focused constituent. Clearly, no such problem arises if the italicised fronted argument in (i) is a topic. Nevertheless, it should be acknowledged that Maekawa (2007) argues that not all fronted negative constituents are focused.

[34] Kayne (2016: 18) proposes a stronger version of (99) in which he drops the word 'interpretable', and hypothesises that 'There is no bundling of syntactic features into a single head.'

A plausible hypothesis is that on top of the FORCE head in (98) there is a separate clause-typing head marking the clause as relative in type (below denoted as REL); and indeed this is the assumption made by Rizzi in more recent work (2005, 2013a, 2015a). This RELP constituent will be the highest projection in the periphery of a relative clause, in order to type the clause as relative (and in order to be adjacent to the antecedent in non-extraposed restrictive relatives). If so, the relative adverb *where* in (95f) would not be on the edge of FORCEP, but rather on the edge of RELP – as shown in simplified form below:

(100)   [$_{\text{RELP}}$ where [$_{\text{REL}}$ ø] [$_{\text{FORCEP}}$ [$_{\text{FORCE}}$ ø] [$_{\text{TOPP}}$ Harry [$_{\text{TOP}}$ ø] [$_{\text{FOCP}}$ what [$_{\text{FOC}}$ ø] [$_{\text{FINP}}$ [$_{\text{FIN}}$ does] he do]]]]]

Such an assumption would be broadly consistent with work by Nye (2013) arguing for a TYPEP projection (REL being a specific kind of TYPE head).[35, 36] Under the

---

[35]  Bob Borsley (pc) points out that a potential drawback to this analysis is that type is a syntactic notion, and force a pragmatic notion (e.g. a question like *Could you close the window?* is interrogative in type but has the force of a request): see Huddleston (1994) for discussion of the force/type distinction. Bob notes that relative clauses are typically declarative in interpretation. He suggests that a clause like that bracketed in (95f) involves a question embedded inside a declarative relative clause, and thus has a fuller structure paraphraseble as (ii):

(i)  It's one of them situations [where the question is: Harry, what does he do]?

On the other hand, Cinque & Benincà (2014: 268) claim that while restrictives are inherently declarative, appositive and kind-defining relatives can have interrogative force. On kind-(defining) relatives, see Prince (1990, 1995), Benincà (2003, 2012b), and Cinque & Benincà (2014).

[36]  Douglas (2016: ch. 3) claims that different types of relative clause are of different sizes: e.g. *that*-relatives and finite wh-relatives are FORCEP constituents, infinitival wh-relatives are FOCP constituents, *for*-relatives and finite zero-relatives are FINP constituents, and infinitival zero-relatives contain no peripheral projections. However, I am sceptical about this for theoretical and empirical reasons. For example, the claim that relativisers like *who/which* move to spec-FORCEP in finite wh-relatives but to spec-FOCP in infinitival wh-relatives is undesirable from a theoretical perspective because it means we have no unitary account of the syntax of relativisers: an account under which relativisers are always positioned on the edge of RELP for clause-typing purposes seems to me to be preferable (albeit it is plausible that there is more structure below RELP in some relative clauses than in others – e.g that RELP has a FORCEP complement in finite relative clauses, but a FINP complement in infinitival *for*-relatives). A further problem with the claim that relative operators move to spec-FOCP in infinitival wh-relatives is that '*wh*-RCs do not obviously have a focus interpretation' (Douglas 2016: 88, fn. 19, attributing the observation to Luigi Rizzi). From an empirical perspective, the claim that finite zero-relatives do not project beyond FINP is undermined by the internet-sourced example of Negative Fronting in (i) below, and the constructed example in (ii):

(i)  I am growing chillies this year which is something [*never* have I grown before] . . . (luxury columnist.com)

analysis in (100), the relevant clause would be relative in type but interrogative in force.

Further evidence lending potential support for this view comes from exclamative relative clauses such as the following:

(101)    a. We were put up in a hotel [**where**, <u>when we arrived</u>, *what a nasty surprise* there was in store for us!]

        b. It was a war [**in which**, *what unspeakable acts of brutality* people committed in the name of freedom!]

        c. It was a time [**when**, *how happy people* were to lead a simple life!]

        d. He was the kind of politician [**who**, <u>if the need arose</u>, *how ready* he was to put personal advantage above principle!]

        e. It was an experience [**which**, *how desperately* he wanted to forget!]

Sentences like (101) are consistent with the view that the bold-printed relative constituent is positioned on the edge of the highest projection in the clause (= RELP in the case of relative clauses), and the italicised exclamative constituent is positioned on the edge of a lower wh-operator projection/WHP housing the exclamative operator (with a MODP constituent containing an underlined clausal modifier being able to be positioned between the two).[37] On the assumptions made here, the relative clause bracketed in (101a) will have the peripheral structure shown in highly simplified form below:

(102)    [$_{RELP}$ where [$_{FORCEP}$ ø [$_{MODP}$ when we arrived [$_{WHP}$ what a nasty surprise [$_{FINP}$ there was in store for us]]]]]

---

(ii) This is something [*under no circumstances* should you try to replicate at home]

Moreover, I personally allow a fronted interrogative phrase or an imperative in sentences such as those below, suggesting the presence of a FORCEP:

(iii) A mobile phone is something [*how* can you possibly live without?]

(iv) I'm going to say something [*please* don't be offended by]

I also allow a dislocated topic, e.g. in:

(v) A Jag is something [*ordinary people like us*, we'll never be able to afford]

Examples like (i–v) suggest that finite zero-relatives (for speakers like me, at any rate) have essentially the same structure as *that*-relatives. There are parallels here with the traditional claim that zero finite complement clauses (like that italicised in 'He said *he was tired*') have a reduced structure: I challenge this claim in §3.2, and argue instead that (for some speakers, at least) they can have essentially the same structure as *that*-clauses.

[37] (101d, e) are marginally less good for me than (101a–c), perhaps because relative *who/which* cross exclamative *how often/how desperately*, thereby leading to violation of the Intervention Constraint of Abels (2012: 247) specifying that 'Likes cannot cross likes.' There will be no such effect in (101a–c) if the relative wh-constituents are in situ circumstantial adjuncts.

The clause in (102) will thus be relative in type but exclamative in force, underlining the difference between type and force.

Interestingly, sentences like those below suggest that relative clauses can also be imperative in force (or perhaps hortative in 103f):

(103)   a. The top speed (**which** please don't try to reach) is 220 miles an hour (Ferrari test driver BBC Radio 5)
        b. You will please correct the false statement made last week in your next issue, **after which** *please don't* handle my name at all (Robin Sterling 2013, *Tales of Old Blount County, Alabama*, Google Books, p. 278)
        c. You will start with completing their application form, **which** please be careful to triple check ... (interviewarea.com)
        d. Next we went to see the beach, **which** please note is NOT A BEACH (tripadvisor.co.uk)
        e. He was at it again on last week's Desert Island Discs, still complaining that the world – **for which** read the music press – does not appreciate his genius. (*Observer*, 6 December 2000: 23, col. 3; Haegeman 2012: 64, fn. 13)
        f. But there is, despite the book's brevity, and the fact that it is enormously pleasurable to read (**at which point** let me salute the translation) much going on. (*Guardian*, 12 April 2010: 13, col. 5; Haegeman ibid.)

If imperatives contain a null imperative operator (Han 1998, 2001), it is plausible to suppose that this operator occupies a position analogous to the spec-INTP position occupied by the operator in yes-no questions. More generally, it may be (as suggested earlier) that English has an operator projection/ OPP whose specifier is the criterial position for interrogative, exclamative and imperative operators. By contrast, declarative relative clauses like that bracketed in (104a) below will contain no such operator and have a peripheral structure along the lines shown in simplified form in (104b) (if inverted auxiliaries move only as far as FIN):

(104)   a. Syntax is something [which rarely do students master easily]
        b. [$_{RELP}$ which [$_{FORCEP}$ ø [$_{FOCP}$ rarely [$_{FINP}$ do [$_{TP}$ students master easily]]]]]

The bracketed clause will be relative in type (by virtue of containing the relativiser *which* on the edge of RELP) and declarative in force (by virtue of containing a null declarative FORCE head).

Although I have argued here that relativisers and topics are contained in different peripheral projections (the criterial position for relativisers being the edge of RELP, and that of topics being the edge of TOPP), there are nonetheless significant parallels between the ways in which topics on the one hand and relativisers on the other are linked to their associated propositions. Recall that, at the beginning of this chapter, I argued that in colloquial English we find the three different types of topic structure illustrated below:

(105)  a. *Those kind of things* I love —, I really do (=1a)
       b. *These footballers*, there's a level of education that <u>they</u> require (=2b)
       c. *Defoe*, even I could have scored that goal (=3a)

I argued in §2.2 that the italicised topic is linked to the associated comment clause in one of three different ways in these structures. In sentences like (105a), the topic originates in the gap position and is moved to its criterial position in spec-TOPP via A-bar movement. In sentences like (105b), the topic is directly merged in situ in its criterial position in spec-TOPP, and is linked to the comment clause by an (underlined) resumptive constituent. In sentences like (105c), the topic is again directly merged in situ in spec-TOPP, but is orphaned (i.e. not syntactically or lexically linked to the comment clause), and instead the link between topic and comment is pragmatic in nature. Accordingly, we find three ways of linking topics to their associated comment clauses, namely via G(ap)-linking as in (105a), R(esumptive)-linking as in (105b), or P(ragmatic)-linking as in (105c).

Interestingly, it would appear that relativisers can be linked to their associated propositions in colloquial English in precisely the same three ways, as illustrated by the examples below:

(106)  a. He is someone [*who* I don't think — stands a cat in hell's chance of getting elected]
       b. Kevin Pietersen is the kind of player [*who*, <u>he</u> likes to send a message to the opposition] (Ian Chappell, BBC Radio 5)
       c. He's a fabulous player [*who*, given the right conditions and the right management, we could be talking about one of the best players in the world] (Sid Lowe, Talksport Radio)

In these examples, the italicised relativiser (*who*) is linked to its associated proposition by a gap in (106a), and by an underlined resumptive (*he*) in (106b). However, in (106c) the relativiser *who* is orphaned (in that the clause contains no gap or resumptive linked to the relativiser), and the link with the associated proposition is instead pragmatic in nature. Gap-relatives like (106a) are register-neutral (in the sense that they are used in all registers of English), whereas resumptive relatives like (106b) and orphaned relatives like (106c) are restricted to use in colloquial registers, and occur relatively frequently, in spite of being largely overlooked in descriptive grammars (and heavily stigmatised in prescriptive grammars). In spite of their supposedly non-standard status, my data contain 386 examples of resumptive relatives, and 294 examples of orphaned relatives, suggesting that both are in widespread use in colloquial English. Let's briefly take a closer look at these two types of non-standard relative clause, starting with resumptive relatives.[38]

As with topics, resumptives (like those underlined below) can occur in a wide range of positions, and so can be used to relativise a subject as in (107a) below, an object as in (107b), a prepositional object as in (107c), or a genitive as in (107d):[39]

(107)    a. We keep talking about Cesc Fabregas, [*who* we all love the way he plays]
(Gareth Southgate, ITV)
b. They're individual decisions [*which* I respect them] (Micky Quinn, Talksport Radio)
c. Joe Root, [*who* everything depends on him], has just edged one to the slips (Commentator, BBC Radio 5)
d. And then there's the likes of Iaquinta, [*who* I don't think his form justified inclusion] (Andy Brassell, BBC Radio 5)

As in the case of topics, the relativiser appears in the default form *who/which* (Merchant 2004), while the resumptive is assigned the case appropriate to the position it occupies (nominative in 107a, accusative in 107b, c, genitive in 107d).

Moreover, the range of resumptive expressions found in relatives mirrors that found in the topic structures discussed in §2.3. Thus, the resumptive can be a personal pronoun (as in the examples in 107 above), a demonstrative pronoun (as in 108 below), a pronominal quantifier or numeral (as in 109), or a noun expression which may contain a full or partial copy of the antecedent or be entirely distinct (as in 110):

(108)    a. He's a player who plays off instinct, [*which* there's nothing wrong with that] (Stuart Robson, Talksport Radio)
b. We have had about 750 bursts or leaks, [*which* we have repaired about 450 of those] (Plumber, BBC Radio 5)
c. It'll be too cold to stage matches there in July, [*which* it's unfortunate that they miss out on this] (Tim Vickery, BBC Radio 5)
d. Then you launched these podcasts, [*which* how many times have these been downloaded]? (Richard Bacon, BBC Radio 5)

---

[38] The discussion here relates solely to the kind of resumptive pronouns found in English, termed *intrusive* in Chao & Sells (1983) and Sells (1984). Resumptive pronouns in some other languages have different properties, but (since my focus is on English), I will not not explore these here. See McCloskey (2002, 2017b) and Asudeh (2004, 2011a, 2011b, 2011c, 2012) for a typology of resumptive relatives.

[39] As illustrated by examples such as (107a–c), resumptive pronouns in relative clauses in my data are not restricted to occurring inside islands. I discuss the distribution of resumptive relatives in colloquial English at length in Radford (2017).

(109)    a. Last week we spoke about their problems, particularly their flankers, [*who* they've got <u>so many</u> to choose from] (Mark Saggers, Talksport Radio)

        b. The players were playing with passion today, [*which* I haven't seen <u>much</u> this season] (Listener, BBC Radio 5)

        c. I would be with the Dutch and their army of fans, [*which* they've got <u>a few</u> here] (Ray Parlour, Talksport Radio)

        b. Reina made his mistake, [*which* he probably makes <u>one</u> every 5 years] (Perry Groves, BBC Radio 5)

(110)    a. Avram Grant is from Israel, [*which*, if you go to <u>Israel</u> during Yom Kippur], there are no cars on the road (Nick Cosgrove, BBC Radio 5)

        b. There is a big problem for the centre-left, [*which* Corbyn is trying to find a solution to <u>the problem</u>] (Lord Wood, BBC Radio 4)

        c. He also came out with things [*which*, when you've got sensitive owners like those in Italy, you can't say <u>the things that he said</u>] (Eleanor Oldroyd, BBC Radio 5)

        d. This information is asked for on the census form, [*which* they threaten to fine you up to a thousand pounds if you don't fill <u>the thing</u> in] (Civil Liberty spokesman, BBC Radio 5)

Thus, the parallels between resumptive topic clauses and resumptive relative clauses are compelling. In each case, the topic/relativiser is directly merged in situ in its criterial position on the edge of a TOPP/RELP projection in the periphery of the clause, and is reprised by a resumptive constituent in the proposition component of the clause.[40]

Now consider colloquial relative clauses like those below which contain an (italicised) orphaned relativiser:

(111)    a. They played great, especially the two guys at the back, [*who* I thought Nemanja Vidic was outstanding] (Roy Keane, ITV)

        b. The same can't be said for Kittel, [*who*, it was a bit messy in the final sprint] (Daniel Lloyd, Eurosport TV

---

[40] Resumptive relatives have been extensively discussed in the research literature, in work dating back more than half a century. See (among many others) Ross (1967, 1986), Morgan (1972), Perlmutter (1972), Bever et al. (1976), McCloskey (1979, 1990, 2002, 2017a, 2017b), Kroch (1981), Chao & Sells (1983), Sells (1984, 1987), Prince (1990, 1995), Contreras (1991), Demirdache (1991), Erteschik-Shir (1992), Shlonsky (1992), Harris (1993), Bondaruk (1995), Pérez-Leroux (1995), Suñer (1998), Varlokosta & Armon-Lotem (1998), Sharvit (1999), Aoun (2000), Aoun, et al. (2001), McKee & McDaniel (2001), Alexopoulou & Keller (2002, 2007), Cresswell (2002), Rouveret (2002, 2011), Boeckx (2003, 2007, 2012), Herrmann (2003, 2005), Asudeh (2004, 2011a, 2011b, 2011c, 2012), Merchant (2004), Cann et al. (2005), Ferreira & Swets (2005), Grolla (2005), Alexopoulou (2006, 2010), Miller & Fernandez-Vest (2006), Fiorentino (2007), Hornstein (2007), Bianchi (2008), Friedmann et al. (2008), Omaki & Nakao (2010), Heestand et al. (2011), Hofmeister & Norcliffe (2013), Polinsky et al. (2013), Sichel (2014), Blythe (2016), Morgan & Wagers (in press).

c. We had Wilshere up there, [*who*, nobody seemed to want to keep the ball] (Neil Warnock, Talksport Radio)

d. The main target was to finish ahead of Ferrari, [*which*, we've extended our lead by 4 points] (Christian Horner, BBC Radio 5)

e. She gained a half pound, [*which* they were predicting she'd gain five pounds] (unidentified American informant, Kuha 1994)

f. Edgar Davids had to fork out loose change for his ticket, [*which*, I can't believe Palace make players pay for their tickets] (Paul Hawksbee, Talksport Radio)

Clauses like those bracketed above are termed 'gapless relatives', since there is no gap (or resumptive) linking the clause to the relativiser. Because there is no apparent link between the relativiser and the rest of the clause, such structures are stigmatised as sloppy in prescriptive grammar.

However, if there were no link of any kind between the relativiser and the rest of the clause, we'd expect the resulting structure to crash, since it would violate the constraint posited by Kuno (1976: 420) that 'A relative clause must be a statement about its head noun' (this statement being mediated by the use of a relativiser to link the two).[41] Thus, instead of saying there is no link between the relativiser and the clause, it is more plausible to suppose that the link between the two in structures like (111) is pragmatic (rather than syntactic or lexical). Accordingly, in (111a), the pragmatic inference is drawn that Vidic was one of the two guys at the back, and in (111b), the inference is drawn that Kittel (a famous sprinter) was involved in a messy sprint at the end of the

---

[41] I am assuming here that all relative clauses contain a wh-relativiser, albeit (by hypothesis) the relativiser has a null spellout in relatives like that bracketed in (i) below:

(i) He is someone [(that) I know quite well]

On the assumptions made here, (i) will have the structure shown in highly simplified form below, where WH is a null relativiser (which can be thought of here as a null counterpart of *who*):

(ii) He is someone [$_{RELP}$ WH [$_{REL}$ that/ø] I know quite well]

I take relative *that* to be a complementiser for four main reasons. Firstly, like the interrogative complementiser *if* and the factive complementiser *how*, it is inherently finite (and so cannot occur in infinitival relatives). Secondly, unlike relative pronouns such as *which*, it does not allow preposition pied-piping. Thirdly, unlike the relative pronoun *who*, it does not inflect for case (e.g. we find genitive *whose* but not genitive *\*that's* in standard varieties of English), and can be used with any kind of antecedent (rather than being restricted to use with human/inanimate antecedents like the relative pronouns *who/which*). And fourthly, unlike relative pronouns (but like its complement-clause-introducing homonym) it generally has a reduced vowel. For an alternative view of *that* as a relative pronoun, see Kayne (2008). See Radford (2016: 394–477) for a detailed discussion and critique of a range of analyses of relative clauses.

race ... and so on. Such a claim has typological precedents in other languages, since Chinese, Japanese and Thai have gapless relative clauses which have been argued to involve a pragmatic link between relative clause and antecedent (see Tsai 1997 and Zhang 2008 on Chinese; Kitagawa 1982 and Matsumoto 1997 on Japanese; and Hoomchamlong 1991 on Thai).[42]

If (as claimed here) the relativiser in gapless relatives is pragmatically linked to the associated clause, it follows that relative clauses containing orphaned relativisers are parallel to topic clauses containing orphaned topics. Just as the requirement for a comment clause to say something about its associated topic means there must be a link between topic and comment, so too the requirement for a relative clause to say something about its antecedent means that there must be a link between (the relativiser referring back to the) antecedent and the proposition component of the clause. And in both topic and relative clauses, the relevant link can be established in one of three different ways: (i) syntactically via G(ap)-linking, (ii) lexically via R(esumptive)-linking, or (iii) pragmatically via P(ragmatic)-linking.

The potential parallels between topics and relativisers are strengthened by the observation that the relativiser in gapless relatives like those in (111) typically has much the same aboutness interpretation as a topic. Thus, the relativisers *who/which* in all the examples in (111) have an interpretation loosely paraphraseable as 'about whom I would comment that'. Indeed, the parallels between topics and relativisers extend further in that in (R-linked and P-linked) clauses where the topic/relativiser is directly merged in situ, the topic/relativiser is assigned default case (in the sense of Schütze 2001), and is often set off from the rest of the clause by an intonation boundary marked in the spelling by a comma – as in (111).[43] These similarities between relative and

---

[42] For completeness, I note that two main syntactic alternatives have been proposed to the pragmatic analysis of gapless relatives proposed here. One is to suppose that the relativiser has become reanalysed as a (subordinating or coordinating) conjunction, so that (e.g.) *which* can be substituted by *although* in (111f): see Ihalainen (1980), Kjellmer (1988), Miller (1988, 1993), Kuha (1994), Miller & Weinert (1998), and Loock (2005, 2007, 2010) for analyses of this ilk, and see Collins & Radford (2015: 193–9) for a critique of this approach. A second is to suppose that the relativiser in gapless relatives functions as the complement of a 'missing' preposition which is given a silent spellout as the result of an operation taken to involve *ellipsis* in Herrmann (2003), *pruning* in Radford (2010a, 2010b), Radford & Felser (2011) and Radford, Felser & Boxell (2012), and *ghosting* in Collins & Radford (2015): see Radford (2017) on potential problems with the 'missing preposition' approach. In much the same way, some work on gapless relatives in Japanese has argued that they involve relativisation of the complement of a missing postposition: for example, Kameshima (1989) argues this for gapless restrictive relatives in Japanese.

[43] See Douglas (2016: 149–51) on further similarities between relativisation and topicalisation.

topic structures raise the question of whether relativisers might actually be topics, positioned on the edge of a TOPP projection, in keeping with the suggestion made by Douglas (2016: 162) that 'Topicalisation and relativisation target the same structural positions in the C-domain.'

However, a topic analysis for relativisers is potentially problematic in certain respects. To see why, consider one implementation of the analysis, under which relativisers are positioned on the edge of a TOPP projection contained within a separate superordinate RELP-projection, so that in a sentence like (111e) above, the bracketed *which*-clause has the structure shown in highly simplified form in (112) below:

(112)   She gained a half pound, [$_{RELP}$ ø [$_{TOPP}$ *which* they were predicting she'd gain five pounds]]

If *which* is a topic occupying its criterial position on the edge of TOPP, it will be frozen in place there by the Criterial Freezing Condition. But this means that it will be unable to move from there to the criterial position for relative pronouns on the edge of RELP.[44] It might seem at first sight as if we can get around this by supposing that REL and TOP heads can be conflated into a single (syncretic) RELTOP 'relative topic' head, resulting in a structure like that below:

(113)   She gained a half pound, [$_{RELTOPP}$ *which* they were predicting she'd gain five pounds]

However, such a syncretic RELTOP head would arguably violate the One Feature One Head Principle (99), which stipulates that no head can carry more than one interpretable feature: the violation would be incurred because the RELTOP head would carry both an interpretable topic feature and an interpretable relative feature.[45] An analysis like (113) is made even less

---

[44] An analogous dilemma arises in the case of root wh-questions like:

(i)   Who were you talking to?

Since *who* is an interrogative wh-operator, its criterial position could plausibly be taken to be the edge of WHP (an interrogative wh-operator projection). However, by virtue of being focused, its criterial position could equally plausibly be taken to be the edge of FOCP.

[45] One might try and circumvent this objection by arguing that REL and TOP are initially merged as independent heads, but that subsequently TOP adjoins to REL in the syntax, so forming a syncretised TOP+REL head. However, such an approach is essentially ad hoc, since there is little point in merging two functional heads as distinct constituents if they are subsequently always going to be conflated into a single head. Moreover, the adjunction analysis in effect voids the *One Feature One Head Principle* of empirical content, since a technical device will always enable the constraint to be bypassed/nullified.

plausible by the observation that relative pronouns and topics have different distributions. Thus, an (italicised) topic is positioned below a (bold-printed) FORCE head like declarative *that*, as we saw in §1.4 for sentences such as:

(114)    a. John said **that** *this book*, Mary should have read (Watanabe 1993a: 127, ex. A16a)

        b. *John said *this book*, **that** Mary should have read (Watanabe 1993a: 127, ex. A16b)

By contrast, relative pronouns are positioned above FORCEP, as we can see from sentences like (108d) above, where the relativiser *which* is positioned above the interrogative FORCEP containing *how many times*, as shown in highly simplified form below:

(115)    Then you launched these podcasts, [RELP **which** [FORCEP *how many times* have these been downloaded]]

Consequently, relative pronouns always precede topics, as we see from sentences like (95a) above, where the relative clause has the (highly simplified) structure bracketed below:

(116)    There are a lot of very small ones [RELP **which**, [TOPP *the critics*, they might want to sneer at]]

These distributional differences argue in favour of relativisers being positioned on the edge of a RELP projection above TOPP, as in (116).

    Furthermore, there are three other differences between topics and relative pronouns which provide additional evidence against treating relative pronouns as topics. Firstly, while both topics and relative pronouns can occur in embedded clauses, only topics can occur in root clauses.[46] Secondly, topics have independent reference, whereas relative pronouns don't (but rather take

---

[46] However, in a review of the Pixel C tablet, I came across the following example of a *which*-clause seemingly treated as an independent sentence:

      (i)  It's better than the HTC-made Nexus 9 which was great but not exceptional. Which the 'C' most certainly is (techadvisor.co.uk)

Here we have two appositive *which*-clauses, with the antecedent of the first *which* being 'Nexus 9', and the antecedent of the second *which* being 'exceptional'. The use of a full-stop may simply be a punctuation device designed to avoid (incurring the wrath of prescriptive copy-editors who stigmatise) successive sequences of similar constituents (in this case, two *which*-clauses) internally within the same sentence.

their reference from their antecedent).[47] And thirdly, relative pronouns can have a null spellout in English, but topics can't.[48]

The conclusion that relative pronouns occupy a separate position from topics raises the question of why relative pronouns and topics should share a number of properties in common. I would venture to suggest that the essence of these common properties is that TOPP and RELP are both peripheral projections, and the specifier of a peripheral projection can (in principle) be linked to the propositional component of the clause in three different ways – either (i) syntactically (via a gap), or (ii) lexically (via a resumptive), or (iii) pragmatically (via a chain of inferencing).[49]

## 2.9    Summary

This chapter has looked at the types of topic found in colloquial English, the positions they occupy in the clause periphery, how they get there, and how they are linked to the associated comment clause. In §2.2, I argued there are three different types of topic in colloquial English – namely gap-linked, resumptive-linked and pragmatically linked topics. In §2.3, I argued that gap-linked topics involve movement from the gap position to a peripheral topic position, on the grounds that (inter alia) they are sensitive to movement (e.g. island and intervention) constraints, but that dislocated and orphaned topics are directly generated in situ in their peripheral position. In §2.4, I examined traditional claims that topic recursion is not permitted in English, and the weaker claim that no clause can contain more than one topic of a given type. However, I argued against these claims, adducing data which show that both fronted topics and in situ topics can be recursively stacked in appropriate contexts (as long as no strong constraint violation is thereby incurred). In §2.5, I explored the relative position of topics and complementisers.

---

[47] However, topics are linked to a discourse antecedent.

[48] This generalisation holds for English, but not universally. For example, as noted by Barbiers (2013), Dutch allows a fronted topic like that italicised below to optionally have a null spellout:

> (i) (*Dat*)    zag    ik    toen    niet
>     that     saw    I     then    not
>     'That I didn't see then'

[49] However, independent factors may rule out certain possibilities in certain cases. For example, if wh-questions canonically involve a wh-operator on the edge of a WHP projection binding a variable, and if resumptives are bound pronouns (not bound variables), it follows that we will only find gap-linked wh-questions, not resumptive-linked or pragmatically linked wh-questions – albeit it should be noted that we find sporadic examples of resumptive wh-questions in colloquial English, like those illustrated in fn. 24.

I noted (and illustrated) the traditional claim that declarative clauses only allow a topic if introduced by *that*, and that the topic must always follow *that*. I went on to show that in embedded finite interrogative clauses, the complementisers *if/whether* occupy an INT position between FORCE and FIN, and allow a topic to be positioned before or after them. I further noted that non-finite clauses generally do not license topics in English (though I observed that there are some potential exceptions). In §2.6, I looked at the position of topics with respect to focused constituents and clause-modifying adjuncts, and noted that topics can either precede or follow FOCP and MODP: more generally, I suggested that MODP can in principle occupy any medial position in the periphery (i.e. any position between the highest FORCE head and the lowest FIN head). I also looked at what kinds of clause can contain topics, arguing that most finite clauses allow topics and most non-finite clauses do not, but noting that there are puzzling exceptions to both generalisations. In §2.7, I looked at the syntax of topics in interrogative and exclamative wh-clauses. I noted that root wh-questions allow a topic in spec-TOPP to precede a fronted interrogative operator in spec-FOCP, and that some speakers allow a topic following the wh-operator: I accounted for this by positing that some speakers require an inverted auxiliary to raise to the head of the projection containing the operator, but others allow it to remain in FIN (and permit TOPP to be positioned between FOC and FIN). I went on to argue that in exclamatives and embedded questions, the fronted wh-constituent targets the specifier position of a wh-operator projection/WHP, which seems to occupy essentially the same position as the INTP constituent that houses interrogative complementisers, and may represent an OPP (operator projection) which has an (interrogative, exclamative or imperative) operator (either overt or null) as its specifier. In §2.8 I looked at where topics are positioned in relative clauses. I argued that relativisers occupy the highest position in the periphery (on the edge of RELP), and thus precede topics (and indeed all other constituents) in a relative clause. I went on to argue that relativisers can be linked to their associated clauses in the same three ways as topics can be linked to comment clauses – namely by G(ap)-linking, R(esumptive)-linking or P(ragmatic)-linking.

The conclusion that both topics and relativisers can be pragmatically linked to their associated clauses debunks the prescriptive myth that the grammar of spoken English is sloppy in that it often fails to mark syntactic links between constituents. The fallacy of this claim is that it is based on the misconception that syntax is the only way of linking constituents. However, as I have shown in relation to topic and relative clauses in this chapter, sometimes the links between constituents are pragmatic rather than syntactic in nature.

Having looked at the syntax of topics in this chapter, in the next chapter I turn to look at the syntax of complementisers, focusing mainly on variation in the range of peripheral heads that can be spelled out as *that* in colloquial English.

# 3 *Complementisers*

## 3.1 Introduction

This chapter looks at aspects of the syntax of complementisers, and more specifically at how a range of different peripheral heads come to be spelled out as the complementiser *that* in indicative clauses in colloquial English.[1] I will not look at subjunctive *that* for the simple reason that my broadcast English data contain too few examples to draw any firm conclusions about its use (which is scarcely surprising, given that its use is largely restricted to formal registers of written English).

Typical structures in which descriptive and pedagogical grammars of English claim that the indicative complementiser *that* is and isn't used in standard varieties of English are illustrated below:

(1)   a. (*That) he can't stand garlic
      b. I suspect [*(that) *garlic*, he can't stand (it)]
      c. *He says [*garlic*, **that** he can't stand (it)]
      d. I wonder [*why* (**\*that**) he doesn't like garlic]
      e. (You'd never believe) [*how much* (**\*that**) he hates garlic!]
      f. Garlic is something [(**\*which**) **that** he can't stand]
      g. He doesn't like gazpacho [*because* (**\*that**) he can't stand garlic]

---

[1] This chapter has its origins in material in Radford (2010a, 2010b, 2010c, 2011a, 2011b, 2013), and in presentations made at the annual meeting of the *Irish Network in Formal Linguistics* in Dublin in September 2011, at the University of Sevilla in October 2011, at the *Fifth Annual Conference on Formal Linguistics* in the Guangdong University of Foreign Studies in December 2011, and at the Autonomous University of Barcelona in May 2012. I am grateful to the audiences there and to Paolo Acquaviva, Enam Al Wer, Merete Anderssen, Martin Atkinson, Sjef Barbiers, Gavin Barry, Josef Bayer, Paola Benincà, Bob Borsley, Memo Cinque, Chris Collins, Stephen Crain, Silvio Cruschina, Claudia Felser, Ángel Gallego, Teresa Guasti, Liliane Haegeman, Maria Lluïsa Hernanz Carbó, Wolfram Hinzen, Alison Henry, Anders Holmberg, Georgios Ioannou, Ángel Jiménez-Fernández, Mike Jones, Marie Labelle, Richard Larson, Adam Ledgeway, Mireia Llinàs-Grau, Jim McCloskey, Jaume Mateu, Jamal Ouhalla, Susan Pintzuk, Gemma Rigau, Ian Roberts, Tom Roeper, Luigi Rizzi, Andrew Spencer, Julio Villa-García and two anonymous referees to Radford (2013) for helpful observations, suggestions, references, or data.

The contrast between (1a) and (1b) suggests that indicative *that* can only be used in a subordinate clause like that bracketed in (1b), not in a main clause like (1a); moreover, as (1b) illustrates, *that* is obligatory in complement clauses when followed by a peripheral constituent. The ungrammaticality of (1c) suggests *that* has to be the first overt constituent in its clause: this same requirement will also rule out clauses like those bracketed in (1d–g), in cases where *that* is preceded by an (interrogative, exclamative or relative) wh-constituent, or by a subordinating conjunction. Thus, the overall picture painted by sentences like (1) is that (in canonical uses in standard varieties of English), indicative *that* is a subordinate, declarative,[2] clause-initial complementiser.

However, this characterisation is based on the (sometimes disputed) introspective grammaticality judgements of linguists rather than recorded samples of spoken English. Although there is some experimental evidence suggesting that introspective judgements of experienced linguists can be relatively robust (Sprouse & Almeida 2011a, 2011b), there is also conflicting experimental evidence (Radford, Felser & Boxell 2012) that the judgements of educated native speakers can unwittingly be influenced by prescriptive education. This raises the question of whether the constraints noted above hold in *Real English* in the sense of Milroy & Milroy (1993) – i.e. in authentic spoken English. In this chapter, I will present evidence that complementiser spellout in indicative clauses in colloquial English can work very differently from what is claimed in much theoretical and descriptive work on 'standard' English. I begin in §3.2 by reporting on the primary use of *that* to introduce an embedded clause, then go on in §§3.3–3.5 to look at secondary uses of *that* in a range of structures where the complementiser is preceded by a number of different types of constituent, before offering wider syntactic and processing perspectives on initial and non-initial complementisers in §3.6. I go on to summarise my conclusions in §3.7. In an Appendix at the end of the chapter (in §3.8), I look at the syntax of adverbial clauses involving the use of *that* after a subordinating conjunction: this is dealt with in an appendix because of the perplexing proliferation of potential alternative analyses to be evaluated.

## 3.2    Primary Spellout

In this section, I shall examine what I shall take to be the primary use of the complementiser *that* (because it is variety- and register-neutral), namely to

---

[2] If we follow Bošković (1997), Roberts & Roussou (2002) and Franks (2005) in taking C to be interpreted as declarative by default when a clause is not marked in some way as being interrogative, exclamative or imperative, we could alternatively replace 'declarative' by 'finite'.

introduce an embedded finite clause (whether indicative or subjunctive – although, for the reasons noted at the beginning of the previous section, my primary focus will be on indicative clauses here). In this section, we shall see that the complementiser *that* can be used to spell out a range of different types of peripheral head in finite embedded clauses when it is the first overt constituent in its clause: more specifically, it can spell out a FORCE head, a REP(ort) head, a REL(ative) head, a SUB(ordinator) head, and even a FIN head in a truncated clause.

Perhaps the most familiar use of the complementiser *that* is to serve to introduce an embedded declarative clause. In this use (as has been widely reported in the research literature from the 1960s on) *that* can be followed by one or more peripheral constituents, like those italicised below:

(2)    a. I promised [**that** *around midnight* he would be there] (Ross 1967: 309)
       b. I said [**that** *my father*, he was tight as a hoot owl] (Ross 1967: 424)
       c. I am aware [**that** *unfortunately* Mary has no other home] (Emonds 1970: 260]
       d. I exclaimed [**that** *never in my life* had I see such a crowd] (Hooper & Thompson 1973: 474)
       e. Sally plans for Gary to marry her, and he vows [**that** *marry her* he will] (Hooper & Thompson 1973: 474)
       f. I believe [**that** *this book*, you should read] (Chomsky 1977b: 93)
       g. I told Mary [**that** *of the students in the class*, several will fail] (Chomsky 1977b: 113)
       h. Becky said [**that** *these books, only with great difficulty* can she carry] (Koizumi 1995: 140]
       i. They told me [**that** *liberty, to that man*, they would never grant] (Culicover 1996: 453)
       j. I stress [**that** *if you call, nothing that I find* will I keep] (Culicover 1996: 456)

Similar structures are found in my broadcast English data, as illustrated below:

(3)    a. I think [**that** *Red Bull*, one of their spotters actually got arrested] (David Coulthard, BBC1 TV)
       b. You have to say [**that** *Higuain, normally* he would have hit the target] (Jon Driscoll, Sky Sports TV)
       c. I just felt [**that** *Roy Hodgson, a few weeks ago, when Liverpool lost to Everton*, he was in a minority of one] (John Motson, BBC Radio 5)
       d. You just get the feeling [**that** *Arsenal, the way they keep the ball*, it's particularly clever] (Steve Claridge, BBC Radio 5)
       e. I have heard [**that** *Willian, the Brazilian midfielder who plays for Shakhtar Donetsk*, Liverpool are interested in him] (Listener, BBC Radio 5)
       f. And advance warning [**that** *from midnight tonight, the A3 in Surrey*, it's going to be closed] (Traffic reporter, BBC Radio 5)

In the bracketed clauses in (2) and (3), a (bold-printed) complementiser is positioned in front of one or more (italicised) peripheral constituents, including fronted topics, fronted VPs, fronted negative phrases, dislocated topics, and adjuncts which comprise PPs, adverbs or adverbial clauses. This is consistent with the claim made by (Rizzi 2014a) that clauses which can contain a full range of peripheral constituents have the status of FORCEP constituents, and that the head FORCE constituent of declarative complement clauses is spelled out as *that*. Adopting this (and other) assumptions will mean that the bracketed complement clause in (3a) has the peripheral structure shown below:[3]

(4)    I think [$_{FORCEP}$ [$_{FORCE}$ that] [$_{TOPP}$ Red Bull [$_{TOP}$ ø] [$_{FINP}$ [$_{FIN}$ ø] one of their spotters actually got arrested]]]

Since FORCEP is the highest projection in the clause periphery, the complementiser *that* will therefore precede all peripheral constituents in the clause. Thus, data such as (2) and (3) are consistent with the claim made by Rizzi (1997: 35) that 'Complementisers such as *that, que* etc. are in Force', and with his (2014a) claim that a declarative FORCE head is obligatorily spelled out as *that*.

As noted in §1.4, although Rizzi takes complete (i.e. non-defective) clauses to have the status of FORCEP projections able to house a full range of peripheral constituents (e.g. topics and/or focused constituents), he also posits that there are a class of defective clauses whose periphery is truncated in the sense that it projects only as far as FINP. These are declarative complement clauses which are 'bare' in the sense that they are not introduced by the complementiser *that*. Such clauses are extremely frequent in colloquial English: for example, Llinàs-Grau & Fernández-Sánchez (2013: 62) report corpus data showing 97% use of bare (*that*-less) complement clauses after the verbs *think/know/say* in spoken English; and in a similar vein, Biber et al. (1999) present evidence from a more extensive corpus showing that bare

---

[3] Here and throughout, I ignore the possibility that structural economy requirements could mean that FIN is syncretised with the head above it wherever possible (e.g. with TOP in 4). I do this for two reasons. Firstly, there is relatively little concrete discussion of the nature of syncretism in the cartographic literature. For example, it receives only a brief mention in a footnote in Rizzi (1997: 332, fn. 28), in relation to the possibility of FORCE and FIN being syncretised when no other projection intervenes between them. And secondly, positing a syncretic TOP+FIN head in (4) carrying both topichood and finiteness features is potentially at variance with the One Feature One Head Principle (Cinque & Rizzi 2008) which posits that no functional head can carry more than one interpretable feature.

complement clauses are favoured in conversational English, and *that*-clauses in more formal styles like academic prose.[4]

Rizzi (2014a: 30) posits that 'finite clauses with null complementisers in English involve truncation of the higher structure of the C system, of Force (hence the absence of the declarative force marker *that*) and of the Topic-Focus system' and thus contain only 'a vestigial presence of the C-system' comprising a projection of 'the lowest head, Fin'. This means that the complement clauses italicised in (5a/6a) below have the different peripheral structures shown in (5b/6b) respectively:

(5)    a. Pinocchio says *that he never lies*
        b. Pinocchio says [FORCEP [FORCE that] [FINP [FIN ø] he never lies]]

(6)    a. Pinocchio says *he never lies*
        b. Pinocchio says [FINP [FIN ø] he never lies]

On this view, the complement clause in (5) is a complete/non-defective clause whose periphery projects all the way up to FORCEP, whereas the bare complement clause in (6) is a truncated/defective clause whose periphery projects only as far as FINP. The declarative FORCE head in (5a) is spelled out as *that*, but the FIN heads in (5b) and (6b) both receive a null spellout.

Bare complement clauses differ from complete complement clauses not only in respect of having a more limited structure (and not containing the complementiser *that*), but also in respect of having a more limited distribution. Thus, bare complement clauses are traditionally said to be restricted to occurring in a position immediately adjacent to and immediately c-commanded by an appropriate selector. The selector has to be a so-called

---

[4] It is widely claimed that (unlike their indicative counterparts) subjunctive clauses cannot be bare, but rather require the use of the complementiser *that*: if so, one might conclude that they are unable to have a truncated FINP structure. For example, Llinàs-Grau & Fernández-Sánchez (2013: 67) maintain that omission of *that* is not possible in structures such as:

    (i) The Congress has **voted** [*(that) the present law be maintained]

However, it's by no means uncommon to find subjunctive clauses not introduced by *that*, as illustrated by the internet-sourced examples below (which are fully grammatical and idiomatic in my own English):

    (ii) Word of the incident reached Eisenhower, who reprimanded Patton and **insisted** [he apologise] (bygone.todays.com)
    (iii) His instincts **demanded** [he keep his distance from her] (S. Rowe, *Leopard's Kiss*, Google Books, 2016, ch. 13)
    (iv) I told her it wasn't **essential** [she be there] (D. Ambrose, *Coincidence*, Google Books 2013, ch. 1)

'bridge' predicate like *say*, and cannot be (e.g.) a non-bridge verb like *quip*, as we see from the observation that (in sentences like those below) *say* can have a complement with or without the complementiser *that* introducing it, whereas *quip* requires use of *that*:

(7)   a. Bob *said* [(**that**) Minimalists are so myopic that they can't see the wood for the trees]
      b. Bob *quipped* [\*(**that**) Minimalists are so myopic that they can't see the wood for the trees]

Furthermore, according to Bošković & Lasnik (2003), bare clauses cannot be used in structures in which an embedded clause is separated from its selecting predicate (or has none), as in topic structures like (8a), pseudo-clefts like (8b), extraposition structures like (8c), right node raising structures like (8d), and gapped clauses like (8e):[5]

(8)   a. \*(**That**) the situation will improve, they certainly do not believe
      b. What we believe is \*(**that**) the situation will improve
      c. It seemed back then \*(**that**) the situation could not improve
      d. John imagined but Peter knew \*(**that**) Mary had left
      e. John believed (that) Mary was ill and Peter \*(**that**) she had left

Thus, there are significant structural and distributional differences between complete and bare clauses.

At first sight, the claim that bare clauses are defective clauses which project only as far as FINP might seem to be called into question by bare clauses like those bracketed below, whose periphery includes an (italicised) circumstantial adjunct:

(9)   a. I hope [*next year* they have karaoke performances at the Grammys] (Serena Williams, Twitter)
      b. I believe [*in a few weeks time* there'll probably be a reality show called Celebrity Pick Your Nose] (digitalspy.com)
      c. It was inferred because I quoted a 'conspiracy theory', when I feel sure [*soon* it will be deemed a fact] (disqus.com)
      d. It appears to be water resistant, but I expect [*if it rains heavily* some water might get through] (Amazon, customer reviews)
      e. I suspect [*when he gets big*, I might need a larger bed] (C.J. Fisher, *When We Were Alive*, Google Books, 2016, ch. 13)
      f. He said [*when he got home* he would do the dishes] (McCloskey 2006: 121, fn. 9)

---

[5] However, this claim is somewhat too strong for speakers like me who accept sentences like (8b–d) without *that*.

Here, the bracketed bare complement clauses contain an italicised local adverbial or prepositional adjunct which can be taken to be positioned in MODP. Now, the template for clause structure posited in Rizzi (2015a) given below takes MOD to be positioned above FIN:

(10)      FORCE > TOP* > INT > TOP* > FOC > TOP* > MOD* > TOP * > FIN

This might seem at first sight to suggest that the bare clauses in (9) are truncated MODP rather that FINP constituents.

However, if the bracketed complement clauses in (9) are MODP constituents, this means that predicates like *hope/believe/sure/expect/say* can select for a MODP complement – even though Rizzi (1997) made the point that predicates do not select for FOCP or TOP complements (and MODP was then treated as a subtype of TOPP), and even though Rizzi (2014a) implicitly assumes that predicates can only select for FORCEP or FINP complements.[6] Given that (as we saw in §1.4) Rizzi (2014a) allows FINP recursion structures of the form FINP > MODP > FINP, this opens up the possibility of treating bare clauses like those bracketed in (9) above as truncated clauses which involve FINP recursion. If so, the bracketed clause in (9a) will have the peripheral structure shown below:

(11)      I hope [$_{FINP}$ [$_{FIN}$ ø] [$_{MOD}$ next year [$_{MOD}$ ø] [$_{FINP}$ [$_{FIN}$ ø] they have karaoke performances at the Grammys]]]

We could then continue to maintain that all bare clauses have the status of FINP constituents, and suppose that *hope* selects a FINP complement in (11).

However, the hypothesis that all bare clauses are FINPs is undermined by bare complement clauses like those bracketed in (12) below whose periphery contains an (italicised) topic:

(12)      a.  I'm sure [*the lecture by Kayne*, he wouldn't want to miss] (Watanabe 1993a: 145, fn. 23, attributing the example to Chomsky, pc).
          b.  'I think [*the general physics community*, they're a little bored with the equation]', he said (*New York Times* cited in Shaer & Frey 2004: 484)
          c.  I think [*Sunderland*, they're pulling a fast one] (Darren Lewis, Talksport Radio)
          d.  I think [*Middlesboro*, it is a tricky time for them] (Marcus Speller, Talksport Radio)

---

[6] If we take FORCEP to correspond to a CP phase, and if we follow Branigan (2005) in taking FINP to be a phase, it would then follow that a predicate can only select a phase as its complement.

    e. At this stage, you have to say [*Rooney*, he's won everything but the FA Cup and the Europa League at club level] (Rick Seymour, Talksport.com)

    f. Everybody knows as a football fan [*a winning side*, you shouldn't really change it] (Listener, BBC Radio 5)

    g. We hear [*West Brom*, Steve Clark could be in the running] (Alan Brazil, Talksport Radio)

    h. I'm sure [*Manchester United*, Ibrahimovic will be a great signing] (Ray Parlour, Talksport Radio)

It is further undermined by bare clauses like those bracketed in (13) below whose periphery includes a focused negative constituent:

(13)    a. We swore [*never again* **would** we do that]. We swore [*never again* **would** we allow it to happen] (Gen. Anthony Zinni, cited in B. Buley, *The New American Way of War*, Routledge, New York, 2007: 136)

    b. There had been times before following a drunken binge where George had awakened in the morning and vowed [*never again* *would* he have another drink], [*never again* **would** he have a night he would regret] (D. Terbush, *Shaker Days*, AuthorHouse, Bloomington, 2005: 125)

    c. The First Lady knew who she was dealing with and promised [*under no circumstances* **would** she ever repeat that conversation] (C. Vance Cast, *Puppet Master Divine*, Google Books, 2008: 232)

    d. Bilbow claimed [*at no point* **had** Apple ever asked for this footage back] (missingepisodes.proboards.com)

    e. He claims [*at no time* did he consent to being groped] (mirror.co.uk)

    f. I went to pick up the car, and ** was condescending, rude, and told me [*nowhere else* **would** I get such a 'great price' as he was offering me] (mythreecents.com)

The periphery of the bracketed clauses contains an italicised topic in (12) and an italicised focused negative phrase in (13): since these are not the kinds of constituent which can be housed in MODP, sentences like (12) and (13) cannot be handled in terms of FINP recursion. Rather, given the claim by Rizzi (1997) that only complete clauses which project all the way up to FORCEP can contain a topicalised or focused constituent, complement clauses like those in (12) and (13) must be FORCEP constituents. If we make this and other assumptions, the relevant bracketed clauses in (12a/13a) will have the respective peripheral structures in (14a/b) below:

(14)    a. I'm sure [$_{FORCEP}$ [$_{FORCE}$ ø] [$_{TOPP}$ the lecture by Kayne [$_{TOP}$ ø] [$_{FINP}$ [$_{FIN}$ ø] he wouldn't want to miss]]]

    b. We swore [$_{FORCEP}$ [$_{FORCE}$ ø] [$_{FOCP}$ never again [$_{FOC}$ ø] [$_{FINP}$ [$_{FIN}$ would] we do that]]]

This would entail that (at least some) bare complement clauses can be FORCEP constituents, and that FORCE can sometimes have a null spellout in embedded clauses. This in turn suggests that Rizzi's claim that a declarative FORCE head is obligatorily spelled out as *that* is too strong, and should be reformulated as saying that (for many speakers) it is optionally spelled out as *that*. Interestingly, in experimental research involving a speeded binary judgement task (in which subjects were asked to rate test sentences as acceptable or unacceptable), Radford, Boxell & Felser (2014) found that bare complement clauses containing a peripheral constituent received a relatively high mean acceptability rating of 69.23% (compared to a mean rating of 89.74% for similar clauses introduced by *that*).

In all the clauses we have looked at so far, the complementiser *that* has been used to spell out a declarative FORCE head. However, Radford (1988: 585) reports the (constructed) example in (15a) below in which *that* is used in a (bracketed) complement clause where it is followed by a wh-constituent, and in addition my broadcast English data contain numerous examples of *that+wh* clauses. Twenty-nine of these are interrogative clauses, like those bracketed below:

(15)   a. He protested [**that** *how* could he have known that his office was bugged?]
       b. I'd just like to find out [**that** *how* do people on the continent remember Paul Scholes?] (Listener, BBC Radio 5)
       c. Harry Redknapp makes a very good point [**that** *why on earth* is Villas Boas getting wound up by those comments?] (John Cross, Talksport Radio)
       d. The strange thing with Joe Cole going to Lille is [**that** *why* did nobody in the Premier League want him?] (Ian McGarry, BBC Radio 5)
       e. That's what that government's trying to resolve there, [**that** *who*'s going to pay for all of this?] (Industrialist, BBC Radio 5)
       f. And I can understand [**that** *why*] (Graham Taylor, BBC Radio 5, in response to 'Not too many people give Villa a chance of beating United')

In addition, there are 17 examples in my data of exclamative *that+wh* clauses like those bracketed below:

(16)   a. He's proved in his career [**that** *what a very, very good manager* he is] (Peter Taylor, Talksport Radio)
       b. They've handed letters to the players telling them [**that** *what a dire situation* the club's in] (Listener, Talksport Radio)
       c. Matty Fryatt showed us again [**that** *what a good player* he is] (Steve Bruce, Sky Sports TV)
       d. If I'm going to get stick, I'm gonna show you [**that** *what a good player* I am] (Graham Beecroft, Talksport Radio)

   e. The fact they had to beat Holland to get through as the best qualified second-place team I think shows you [**that** *how good* they can be] (Andy Brassell, BBC Radio 5)

   f. It's also interesting [**that** *how quickly* reputations change] (Danny Kelly, Talksport Radio)

   g. He realised, I think, [**that** *how big* this thing was] (Film critic, BBC Radio 5)

Counterparts of English *that+wh* clauses are widely reported to occur in other languages, including Spanish (Rivero 1978, 1980, 1994; Plann 1982; Suñer 1991, 1993; Brucart 1993; Demonte & Fernández Soriano 2009; de Cuba & MacDonald 2013a, 2013b; Villa-García 2015), Catalan (Rigau & Suïls 2010; González i Planas 2014), Portuguese (Mascarenhas 2007), Hungarian (Kenesei et al. 1998) and Japanese (Saito 2012).

However, an experimental study by Radford, Boxell & Felser (2014) found that (interrogative) *that+wh* clauses received low acceptability ratings. On an untimed scalar judgement task (on which subjects were asked to rate the acceptability of a range of sentence types on a 5-point scale where 5 is the most acceptable and 1 the least acceptable), sentences containing interrogative *that+wh* complement clauses were awarded a low mean score of 2.68. Similarly, in a speeded binary judgement task (in which subjects were asked to rate sentences as acceptable or unacceptable), similar structures received a low acceptability rating of 17.77%. Radford et al. concluded that *that+wh* clauses do not represent a syntactic structure generated by the grammar, but rather represent processing errors which come about as a result of syntactic blending.[7] On this view, a *that+wh* clause like that bracketed in (17a) below would arise from blending the *that*-clause bracketed in (17b) with the wh-clause bracketed in (17c):

(17)   a. I want people to be reminded [**that** *how important* football is to me] (David Beckham, Sky Sports TV)

     b. I want people to be reminded [**that** football is so important to me]

     c. I want people to be reminded [*how important* football is to me]

The claim that sentences like (17a) result from a processing error (involving blending) would account both for the low acceptability of such structures in experiments, and for their comparatively low frequency of occurrence in corpora.

---

[7] On blending, see Bolinger (1961), Fay (1981), Stemberger (1982), Cohen (1987), Cutting & Bock (1997), and Coppock (2006, 2010).

3.2 Primary Spellout 115

However, there are reasons to be sceptical about the blend story. For one thing, structures which may have originated as blends can sometimes become grammaticalised. In this regard, consider the sentence in (18a) below, which at first sight might appear to be a production error arising from blending the infinitival raising structure in (18b) with the impersonal finite structure in (18c):

(18)    a.  What is thought has happened to him? (Interviewer, BBC Radio 5; Radford 2004a: 429)
        b.  What is thought to have happened to him?
        c.  What is it thought has happened to him?

And yet, Danckaert et al. (2016) argue that the raising of wh-subjects out of finite clauses in structures like (18a) has become grammaticalised for some English speakers, and shows syntactic properties typical of truncated clauses (i.e. of clauses which project only as far as FINP, not up to FORCEP).

Moreover, some of the *that+wh* clauses in my broadcast English data cannot plausibly be taken to be blends, as can be illustrated in relation to sentences like the following:

(19)    a.  Meg, can I ask [**that** *how many police* would normally be on duty at any one time?] (Neil Ashton, Talksport Radio)
        b.  It just makes you wonder [**that**, if we haven't got this world cup, *whenever* will we get one?] (Alan Shearer, BBC Radio 5)
        c.  When you see Spain line up, do you sometimes wonder [**that** *whether* they need Xabi Alonso and Busquets]? (Mark Chapman, BBC Radio 5)

Given that neither *ask* nor *wonder* (in the relevant kind of use) selects a *that*-clause complement, it is hard to see how structures like those in (19) can be treated as blends. Furthermore, the claim that COMP+WH structures occur only sporadically seems questionable, given that overall my relatively small corpus of broadcast English data contains 46 *that+wh* clauses in interrogatives and exclamatives.

Given their relative productivity in English, and given that parallel structures are grammaticalised in other languages, I shall assume from this point on that COMP+WH clauses represent a type of structure licensed in the grammars of some speakers, and ask what kind of structure they have. In relation to analogous structures in Spanish, Plann (1982) suggests that the complementiser has a quotative function, in that it is used to introduce direct speech after quotative predicates (i.e. predicates which allow a direct quote as a complement). Such an analysis would account for the use of Auxiliary Inversion in the wh-questions in the bracketed clauses in (15), since Inversion is characteristic of direct speech. Furthermore, it would also account for 13 examples of *that* followed by a yes-no question with Auxilary Inversion found in my broadcast English data, including the following:

(20)    a. Umpires should be saying [**that** *is there* any reason why it should be given out?] (Chris Martin-Jenkins, BBC Radio 5 Sports Extra)
        b. What you're trying to ask is [**that** *are they* happy with the business they've done so far?] (Darren Gough, Talksport Radio)
        c. It worries me now [**that** Terry, *does he* really want to play for England?] (Martin Keown, BBC Radio 5)
        d. The key question is [**that** *will consumers* see a benefit?] (Dominic Laurie, BBC Radio 5)
        e. The reality is [**that** *does it* create business?] (Industrialist, BBC Radio 5)
        f. The question we have to ask is [**that** *was Mike Gatting* wearing a sleeveless sweater?] (Vic Marks, BBC Radio 5 Sports Extra)

In addition, it would account for examples such as the following, in which *that* is used to introduce an imperative complement, since imperatives are only used in direct speech:

(21)    a. I think his family will be saying to him [**that** yeah, get yourself out there!] (Matt Holland, Talksport Radio)
        b. The moment you have rain on the first day, it just becomes mandatory [**that** finish at 7 and walk off!] (Nasser Hussain, Sky Sports TV)
        c. He said [**that** don't be shy, you can tell us] (fanfiction.net)

On this view *that* in structures like those above is a quotative complementiser used to embed quoted speech into a matrix clause, with the quoted speech essentially being unmodified (e.g. the pronoun *yourself* is not transposed into *himself* in 21a, as it would be in reported speech.)[8]

However, treating *that* in *that+wh* structures as as a quotative complementiser used to embed direct speech proves to be too narrow a characterisation, in that my recordings also contain *that+wh* clauses like those bracketed below which show characteristics of embedded rather than root questions:

(22)    a. When you see Spain line up, do you sometimes wonder [**that** *whether* they need Xabi Alonso and Busquets?] (Mark Chapman, BBC Radio 5)
        b. What's going to be important is [**that** *whether* he can win the final stage of the Tour de France] (Gary Imlach, ITV4)
        c. Among the wider Greek community, is it understood [**that** *what* he has done and *why* he has done it]? (Suzanne Chislet, BBC Radio 5)

---

[8] Although they differ from quotative *that*, the items *like* and *go* have been gramaticalised as quotative markers in colloquial English: see e.g. Romaine & Lange (1991), Tagliamonte & Hudson (1999), Macaulay (2001), Cukor-Avila (2002), Buchstaller (2004), Haddican & Zweig (2012).

    d. I'm trying to understand [**that** *why* we don't see any French planes as part of the strike force] (American journalist, BBC Radio 5)

    e. Do you think that they don't realise [**that** *how long* they're taking]? (Adam Hunt, Talksport Radio)

    f. I spoke to him to say **that** [*what* had happened] (Brendan Rogers, Talksport Radio; = to say 'What has happened?')

The use of the embedded clause complementiser *whether* in (22a, b) together with the absence of Subject-Auxiliary Inversion in (22c–e) and the presence of tense transposition (*has > had*) in (22f) suggest that the bracketed structures are embedded rather than root clauses. This raises the possibility of treating *that* in cases like (22) as a reportative complementiser. We could then suppose that in a sentence like (22a), *whether* marks the bracketed clause as a yes-no question, and *that* marks the reported character of the question: see Rizzi (2012: 208) for a similar claim about the Spanish counterpart of structures like (22a). Quotative and reportative *that* differ in that there appears to be a greater degree of embedding/integration of the complement clause into the matrix clause in reportative than in quotative structures: for example, embedded questions show auxiliary inversion in quotatives, but not in reportatives.[9] Plann's (1982) claim that quotative/reportative *that* is only used after quotative predicates would seem to be too strong, since in many of the examples above, the complementiser *that* does not occur after a quotative predicate (e.g. predicates like *find out/understand/prove/show/remind/interesting/realise/resolve/mandatory* are not quotative).

    An interesting question arising from the analysis of *that* as serving a quotative or reportative function is what position it occupies in the clause periphery. One possibility would be to follow the analysis proposed for analogous structures in Spanish by de Cuba & Macdonald (2013a, 2013b) and take reportative/quotative *that* to be particular kinds of FORCE head. If so, a clause like that bracketed in (23a) below could be taken to have a peripheral structure along the lines shown in highly simplified form in (23b), if the fronted interrogative phrase is focused, and if the inverted auxiliary is in FIN:

(23)    a. He protested [that a weapon like that, what valid reason could anyone possibly have for owning it?]

        b. [$_{FORCEP}$ [$_{FORCE}$ that] [$_{TOPP}$ a weapon like that [$_{TOP}$ ø] [$_{FOCP}$ what valid reason [$_{FOC}$ ø] [$_{FINP}$ [$_{FIN}$ could] anyone possibly have for owning it]]]]

---

[9] See González i Planas (2014) for an insightful discussion of differences between quotative and reportative complementisers.

Under the analysis in (23b), quotative *that* would occupy the same (initial) FORCE position in the periphery as declarative *that*.[10]

An alternative possibility would be to suppose that the embedded clause represents an independent speech act (as is suggested by the use of the question mark *?* at the end of the embedded clauses in 20, for example) and therefore the material following *that* should be treated as an independent FORCEP projection in its own right. We could then take quotative/reportative *that* to be a superordinate REP head corresponding to the report head posited by Lahiri (1991) and Saito (2012). This would mean that (23a) above would not have the peripheral structure shown in (23b), but rather would have a more articulated structure along the lines shown in simplified form in (24) below, if we conflate quotative and reportative *that* into a single REP(ort) head:

(24)     He protested [$_{\text{REPP}}$ [$_{\text{REP}}$ that] [$_{\text{FORCEP}}$ [$_{\text{FORCE}}$ ø] [$_{\text{TOPP}}$ a weapon like that [$_{\text{TOP}}$ ø] [$_{\text{FOCP}}$ what valid reason [$_{\text{FOC}}$ ø] [$_{\text{FINP}}$ [$_{\text{FIN}}$ could] anyone possibly have for owning it]]]]]

Such an analysis would mean that the template in (10) above has to be expanded to allow for the possibility of a REP head above FORCE.

A class of structures which illustrate a further use of clause-initial *that* are interrogative relative clauses like those bracketed below (with capitals in 25b marking emphatic stress on locative *there*):

(25)     a. Klinsmann is someone [**that** *how can you* argue with what he did as a footballer?] (Sean Wheelock, BBC Radio 5)
         b. THERE's a man [**that** *is he* gonna get his first ever podium?] (Motor cycling commentator, BBC2 TV)
         c. It's one of those [**that** *do we* just push to one side?] (Brian Laws, BBC Radio 5)

One way of dealing with such structures would be to take *that* to lexicalise a REL(ative) head which has a FORCEP complement which in most relative clauses is declarative in force, but which is interrogative in force in the kind-defining relatives in (25), and which can alternatively be imperative in force (as we saw in §2.8) in kind-defining relatives such as that bracketed below:

---

[10] There could be potential parallels with use of an apparent counterpart of *that* preceding a focused interrogative constituent in sentences such as the following in Gungbe:

    (i)  Ùn kànbíɔ́ ɖɔ̀   ménù wὲ   wá? (Aboh & Pfau 2010: 93)
      1   ask   that who FOC come
      'I  asked  who came?'

Aboh & Pfau take the complementiser *ɖɔ̀* 'that' to occupy FORCE. Similar COMP+WH structures are found in Hungarian (Puskás 2000).

(26)     I'm going to say something [**that** *please don't* take the wrong way!]

If relative clauses are indeed RELP+FORCEP structures, the relative clause bracketed in (25a) will have a peripheral structure along the lines shown in simplified form below:

(27)     Klinsmann is someone [$_{REL}$ [$_{REL}$ that] [$_{FORCEP}$ [$_{FORCE}$ ø] [$_{FOCP}$ how [$_{FOC}$ ø] [$_{FINP}$ [$_{FIN}$ can] you argue with what he did as a footballer?]]]]

We could then take *that* to spell out a REL head in a finite relative clause in a structure like (27).[11]

Alongside the interrogative and exclamative *that*+*wh* structures mentioned above, my broadcast English data also contain the following six examples of *that*+*wh* relatives:

(28)     a. You need to buy a world class striker [**that** *who* you can put in up front] (Mark Saggers, Talksport Radio)
         b. It's the business of the state such as the one [**that** *in which* we live to say what the tax should be on alcohol] (Politician, BBC Radio 5)
         c. This is a country [**that** *whose leadership* has been our ally for over 30 years] (Harvard professor, BBC Radio 5)
         d. The speed [**that** *which* they go at these days leaves no margin for error] (Darren Gough, Talksport Radio)
         e. He's taken many by surprise with the speed [**that** *which* he's adapted] (Tim Vickery, BBC Radio 5)
         f. In a club [**that** *where* you have presidential electors and political currents going on], there's lots of jostling for position (Tim Vickery, BBC Radio 5)

In these structures, the complementiser *that* is followed by an italicised relative wh-constituent, and so *that* would appear to be the head of a separate projection positioned above that housing the italicised relative constituent. Memo Cinque (pc) suggests taking *that* in (28) to be the spellout of a SUB(ordinator) head positioned above the RELP projection housing the relative wh-constituent. This would be consistent with the postulation of a SUB head for other types of clause (such as adverbial clauses introduced by a subordinating conjunction), e.g. by Bhatt & Yoon (1992), Rizzi (1997: 328, fn. 6), Bennis (2000),

---

[11] An alternative possibility (suggested by Bob Borsley, pc) would be to suppose that relative clauses are always declarative in interpretation, and that (25a) has a more complex structure paraphraseable as 'Klinsmann is someone ABOUT WHOM ONE COULD SAY that how can you argue with what he did as a footballer?' If so, *that* can be taken to be quotative complementiser (used to introduce the complement of the quotative verb SAY), and the capitalised constituents all receive a null spellout at PF. However, it's hard to see what is gained by the additional abstraction in this analysis, and equally hard to see what evidence could be used to support the postulated presence of the capitalised constituents.

Roussou (2000), and Haegeman (2006a, 2012).[12] If so, and if relativisers are positioned on the edge of a RELP projection, a restrictive relative clause like that bracketed in (28a) above could have a peripheral structure along the lines shown in simplified form below:

(29)    You need to buy a world class striker [$_{SUBP}$ [$_{SUB}$ that] [$_{RELP}$ who [$_{REL}$ ø] [$_{FINP}$ [$_{FIN}$ ø] you can put up front]]]

It would then be the SUB head which is lexicalised as *that* in such structures.

However, the following caveat should be noted. Given their rarity and oddity, *that*+*wh* relative clauses like those in (28) could alternatively be taken to be sporadic production errors. On one such view, they could be the result of a blend between a *that*-relative and a *wh*-relative. On another view, they could be instances of self-correction in which a speaker starts out intending to produce a *that*-relative and then switches to a wh-relative. The switch may come about because of prescriptive pressures that broadcasters are under (e.g. to avoid using *that* with a human antecedent, or to avoid preposition stranding, or to use wh-relatives because they are perceived to have a higher status than *that*-relatives), or to avoid a syntactic crash (e.g. the kind of crash that ensues if you try and relativise a possessive structure with *that* in a sentence like 28c).

To summarise: in this section, we have seen that the complementiser *that* can be used to spell out a range of different types of peripheral head in finite clauses. More precisely, it can spell out a declarative FORCE head in structures like (30a) below, a REP(ort) head in structures like (30b), a REL(ative) head in structures like (30c), and (if we set aside the caveat in the preceding paragraph) a SUB(ordinator) head in a structure like (30d). Moreover, under the account of subject extraction in Rizzi (2014a), *that* can also lexicalise a FIN head in a truncated (FINP recursion) clause structure like that in (30e) below (as we saw in §1.5):

(30)    a.  I think [$_{FORCEP}$ [$_{FORCE}$ **that**] [$_{TOPP}$ Red Bull [$_{TOP}$ ø] [$_{FINP}$ [$_{FIN}$ ø] one of their spotters actually got arrested]]] (=4)

        b.  He protested [$_{REPP}$ [$_{REP}$ **that**] [$_{FORCEP}$ [$_{FORCE}$ ø] [$_{TOPP}$ a weapon like that [$_{TOP}$ ø] [$_{FOCP}$ what valid reason [$_{FOC}$ ø] [$_{FINP}$ [$_{FIN}$ could] anyone possibly have for owning it]]]]] (=23)

---

[12] Note, however, that subordinating conjunctions in adverbial clauses (like *because/although/if* etc.) cannot be spelled out as *that*: this is presumably for detectability/parsability reasons, because if they were, there would be no way of knowing what kind of adverbial clause they were (whether causal, or concessive, or conditional etc.).

c. Klinsmann is someone [REL [REL **that**] [FORCEP [FORCE ø] [FOCP how
   [FOC ø] [FINP [FIN can] you argue with what he did as a footballer?]]]] (=27)
d. You need to buy a world class striker [SUBP [SUB **that**] [RELP who [REL ø]
   [FORCEP [FORCE ø] [FINP [FIN ø] you can put up front]]]] (=29)
e. This is the man who I think [FINP [FIN **that**] [MODP next year [MOD ø]
   [FINP [FIN ø] will sell his house]]]

This raises the question of whether there is a broader generalisation which can provide us with a unified account of these five (seemingly very different) uses of *that*. One property which all five uses share in common is that each of the peripheral head positions occupied by *that* is non-verbal, in the sense that it is not a position which can be occupied by a verbal constituent like an inverted auxiliary. A second property is that in each of the five cases, *that* is the highest head/first overt word in the periphery of the clause containing it. This suggests that use of the complementiser *that* in English is subject to spellout conditions along the lines outlined informally below:

(31)    **Complementiser spellout**
        *That* can lexicalise a non-verbal head which is the first word in an embedded finite clause[13]

The spellout condition in (31) will account for the bold-printed uses of *that* in (30), since in each case *that* spells out the highest head/first word in the periphery of an embedded finite clause. It can also account for the ungrammaticality of the *\*that that* string which would result if both REL and FORCE were spelled out as *that* in (30c), without the need to appeal to the constraint against complementiser iteration proposed in McCloskey (1992, 2006). In addition (31) will prevent *that* from lexicalising one or more of the bold-printed heads in structures like those below:

(32)    This is something [REL which [REL ø/*that] [FORCEP [FORCE ø/*that]
        [FINP [FIN ø/*that] I like]]]

The reason is that none of the bold-printed occurrences of *that* is the first word in its containing clause. The condition that a peripheral head can only be spelled out as *that* if it is the first word in its clause is consistent with the claim made by

---

[13] It should be taken as implicit here that only an appropriate kind of peripheral head can be lexicalised as *that*. For example, a declarative or subjunctive FORCE head can be lexicalised as *that*, but not an interrogative FORCE head (even if clause-initial), as we see from the ungrammaticality of the following if *that* is used:

   (i) I'm not sure [FORCEP [FORCE ø/*that] [WHP where [WH ø] [FINP [FIN ø] he has gone]]]

Staum Casasanto & Sag (2008) that the complementiser *that* serves the parsing function of marking the beginning of an embedded finite clause.

### 3.3    Secondary Spellout

Having looked in the previous section at the primary use of *that* to spell out the highest head in the periphery of an embedded finite clause, in this section I turn to look at the secondary use of *that* to spell out lower peripheral heads. I shall ultimately argue that this happens in finite clauses where a lower peripheral head has a criterial specifier.

At the end of the previous section, we saw that English does not allow complementiser iteration (e.g. it does not allow *that that* structures in which one occurrence of *that* immediately follows another). However, this should not be taken to mean that English does not allow any form of complementiser recursion, since (as we will see in this section) English does allow *that* ... *that* structures in which there is material intervening between the two occurrences of *that*. This phenomenon of complementiser recursion (sometimes termed recomplementation) has been widely reported to occur in a number of Romance languages (Escribano 1991; Campos 1992; Fontana 1993; Uriagereka 1995; Barbosa 2000; Ledgeway 2000, 2004, 2005, 2006, 2009, 2010, 2012a, 2012b, 2013, 2015, 2016; Poletto 2000; Martín-González 2002; Rodríguez Ramalle 2003; Cocci & Poletto 2007; Fernández-Rubiera 2009; Etxepare 2010; González i Planas 2010, 2014; Gupton 2010; Ledgeway & Lombardi 2014; Villa-García 2015). It has also been reported to occur in English (Higgins 1988; McCloskey 1992, 2006; Iatridou & Kroch 1992; Rizzi 1997: 330, fn. 19; Haegeman 2012), and indeed my broadcast English data contain 78 examples of embedded clauses containing two different occurrences of *that* with one or more other peripheral constituents positioned between them. In 31 cases, the intervening constituent is a local prepositional or adverbial adjunct (i.e. one modifying the clause it is contained in), like those italicised below:

(33)    a. My hope is [**that** *by the time we meet* **that** we'll have made some progress] (President Obama, press conference, BBC Radio 5)
   b. I just wanted to say [**that** *despite all these short term problems* **that** they needed to keep in mind the needs of the poor] (Bill Gates, BBC Radio 4)
   c. It's something [**that** *off the pitch* **that** we've got to help the players deal with] (Football executive, BBC Radio 5)
   d. I put it to him [**that** *with such a huge event and with so many vessels on the water,* **that** safety should be the number one priority] (Phil Williams, BBC Radio 5)

e. It's understandable [**that** *this weekend* **that** there's a certain amount of pressure on Arsenal] (Neil Ashton, Talksport Radio)

f. I think [**that** *overall* **that** Germany were better value] (Stan Collymore, Talksport Radio)

In 26 cases, the intervener is a local subordinate adverbial clause, like those italicised below:

(34)  a. The party opposite said [**that** *if we cut 6 billion from the budget,* **that** it would end in catastrophe] (David Cameron, Prime Minister's Questions, BBC Radio 5)

b. D'you think [**that**, *when you represent your country,* **that** your club form is irrelevant]? (Andy Goldstein, Talksport Radio)

c. Most commentators feel [**that**, *while default is a little bit further down the line,* **that** the economic consequences will start to be felt] (Paul Adams, BBC Radio 5)

d. Would I be right in saying [**that**, *because we've got the Olympics next year,* **that** every British sportsman will feel more pressure]? (Andy Goldstein, Talksport Radio)

e. The FA have decided [**that**, *although they have stripped John Terry of the captaincy,* **that** they were not going to ban him from the squad] (John Anderton, Talksport Radio)

f. He saw [**that** *once Brazil had a back four in,* **that** there was a lot of space in midfield] (Tim Vickery, Talksport Radio)

In a further 7 cases, the intervener is an (italicised) dislocated constituent reprised by an (underlined) resumptive pronoun, as in the examples below:

(35)  a. People like Dale need to have confidence [**that** *the kind of policing they need,* **that** we can still deliver it] (Police spokesman, BBC Radio 5)

b. Do you believe [**that** *Arsenal,* **that** they're that far short that they need 8 players]? (Neil Ashton, Talksport Radio)

c. The most we can hope for is [**that** *those people who are blood donors,* **that** they continue to donate blood] (Health spokesman, BBC Radio 5)

d. I'm not sure [**that** *any of those,* **that** you would put them in the same bracket as Ferdinand and Terry] (Steve Claridge, BBC Radio 5)

e. I'm glad [**that**, *whoever talked Strauss into it,* **that** they did] (Geoff Boycott, BBC Radio 5 Sports Extra)

And in the example below, we find both an intervening (italicised) dislocated topic and an intervening (underlined) phrasal adjunct between the two (bold-printed) occurrences of *that*:

(36)  Do you think [**that** *Paris Saint Germain,* with the money they have behind them, **that** they're the new powerhouse in French football]? (Alan Brazil, Talksport Radio)

The question posed by such examples is how we can account for the dual position of the complementiser *that* in clauses like those bracketed in (33–6) above.[14]

In analyses within the CP framework, recomplementation was treated as a case of CP recursion (Escribano 1991; Iatridou & Kroch 1992; McCloskey 1992, 2006; Fontana 1993). On this view, the bracketed complement clause in (35a) would have a CP recursion structure like that bracketed below:

(37)   People like Dale need to have confidence
       [$_{CP1}$ [$_{C1}$ **that**] [$_{CP2}$ *the kind of policing they need* [$_{C2}$ that] we can still deliver it]]

However, such an analysis is potentially problematic from a conceptual point of view, in that (if *that* in such clauses marks declarative force), CP recursion would lead to the undesirable outcome that the declarative force of the clause ends up being multiply marked (on each occurrence of C). This problem can be circumvented if we suppose that the two different occurrences of *that* correspond to two different types of head with two different sets of properties: for example, the initial occurrence of *that* corresponds to *że* in Polish, and the second occurrence corresponds to the different item *to*.[15]

Moreover, an important difference between the two types of complementiser (noted by Villa-García 2010, 2012c, 2015 for Spanish and by Haegeman 2012: 26, 84 for English) is that a non-initial complementiser is a barrier to extraction (e.g. of a fronted argument like that italicised below) in a sentence like (38a), whereas an initial complementiser is not a barrier to extraction in a sentence like (38b):[16]

---

[14] For completeness, I note that there were also two cases involving an intervening parenthetical between the two occurrences of *that* in (i) and (ii) below, and one case involving an intervening vocative in (iii):

      (i) It just shows [**that**, *you know*, **that** they have to pass the time] (Iain Carter, BBC Radio 5)

      (ii) I think [**that**, *you know*, **that** it will stand them in good stead] (Gary Neville, Sky Sports

      (iii) Are you worried now though [**that**, *Gary*, **that** some people might categorise you a little bit, particularly in boardrooms]? (Pat Murphy, BBC Radio 5)

[15] This was kindly pointed out by an anonymous reviewer of Radford (2013).

[16] The facts may well be more murky than they appear at first sight, however. For example, for speakers like me, an (italicised) fronted argument can move across a (bold-printed) non-initial *that* in sentences such as:

      (i) I think that, *naked ambition*, in someone so young, **that** people often find presumptuous

If the italicised wh-DP in (38a) is a topic, it may be that some speakers don't allow a TOP(ic) head to be spelled out as *that*.

(38)    a. I hope (that) *what their parents did for them* (\*that) they will never
          forget —
        b. *What their parents did for them,* I hope **that** as long as they live, they will
          never forget —

A plausible way of capturing the different properties of the two occurrences of
*that* would be to adopt a cartographic approach to the syntax of the periphery
and suppose that the initial occurrence of *that* marks declarative force/clause
type, the second marks finiteness, and that the latter (but not the former) is
a barrier to movement.[17] This would be consistent with the treatment of cases
of recomplementation in Romance by Ledgeway (2000 et seq.), Brovetto
(2002), Demonte & Fernández Soriano (2009), Fernández-Rubiera (2009),
and López (2009); and for Celtic by Roberts (2004). One way of implementing
this idea would be to suppose that whereas conservative speakers only have the
primary *that*-spellout condition (31) in their grammar (allowing *that* to spell out
a peripheral head which is the first word in an embedded finite clause), some
speakers also have a secondary *that*-spellout condition allowing *that* to spell
out a FIN head in an embedded finite clause in which FORCE and FIN are
separated by one or more intervening projections.

If we were to treat *that* as able to spell out FORCE and FIN heads in English,
the clauses showing *that*-recomplementation in sentences such as (34a) and
(35a) above could be analysed as having the corresponding peripheral structures shown in simplified form below:

(39)    a. The party opposite said [$_{FORCEP}$ [$_{FORCE}$ **that**] [$_{MODP}$ *if we cut 6 billion from*
          *the budget* [$_{MOD}$ ø] [$_{FINP}$ [$_{FIN}$ that] it would end in catastrophe]]]
        b. People like Dale need to have confidence [$_{FORCEP}$ [$_{FORCE}$ **that**] [$_{TOPP}$ *the*
          *kind of policing we need* [$_{TOP}$ ø] [$_{FINP}$ [$_{FIN}$ that] we can still deliver it]]]

This would mean that the higher (bold-printed) occurrence of *that* is in FORCE
and the lower (underlined) occurrence is in FIN.

However, any claim that recomplementation gives rise to structures in which
the higher complementiser is in FORCE and the lower complementiser is in
FIN faces potential empirical problems in respect of recomplementation in

---

[17] One account of this restriction would be to suppose that a projection headed by an overt
complementiser is a barrier to movement (perhaps by virtue of being a phase) unless it has an
edge feature permitting its specifier to be used as an escape hatch: if a complementiser can only
carry an edge feature when the projection it heads is the complement/sister of a bridge predicate,
it follows that non-initial complementisers will be barriers to movement. For an alternative
(albeit somewhat baroque) account of this barrierhood property, see Villa-García (2015: ch. 5).
Note that data like (38) can be accommodated within a CP recursion analysis if we suppose that
a CP which is not the complement/sister of a bridge predicate is a barrier to extraction.

structures like those below in which (bold-printed) non-initial occurrences of *that* are followed by (italicised) peripheral constituents:

(40)    a.  I rang Newbury to say [that, when she was due to race, **that** *for some unapparent reason* she got very upset] (Racehorse owner, BBC Radio 5)

        b.  It's deeply embarrassing for the government [that after authorising this rescue **that** *now* it turns out that she was killed by an American grenade] (Reporter, BBC Radio 5)

        c.  I don't think [that for the sake of your own well-being **that** *if you are in a bilingual classroom* **that** *once you have completed the homework in one language* that you should have to do it all over again in the second one] (example which Eiichi Iwasaki tells me Jim McCloskey informed him that Chris Potts devised)

In these examples, unhighlighted occurrences of *that* are clause-initial and can be taken to lexicalise a FORCE head, and the underlined occurrence of *that* in (40c) is immediately followed by a subject and so could be taken to be in FIN. However, the bold-printed occurrences of *that* in all three examples in (40) are unlikely to be exponents of FIN, since FIN is the lowest head in the periphery and yet the bold-printed occurrences of *that* are followed by an italicised local adverbial or prepositional adjunct which can be taken to be positioned in MODP.

Nonetheless, cases like (40a–c) would be consistent with taking lower occurrences of *that* to lexicalise FIN if we were to follow Rizzi (2014a) in allowing FINP recursion structures of the form FINP+MODP+FINP (see §1.5). This would open up the possibility of taking the complement clause bracketed in (40a) to have the peripheral structure shown below:

(41)    I rang Newbury to say [$_{FORCEP}$ [$_{FORCE}$ *that*] [$_{MODP}$ when she was due to race [$_{MOD}$ ø] [$_{FINP}$ [$_{FIN}$ **that**] [$_{MODP}$ for some unapparent reason [$_{MOD}$ ø] [$_{FINP}$ [$_{FIN}$ ø] she got very upset]]]]]

Under the analysis in (41), the higher (italicised) occurrence of *that* would represent a FORCE head, and the lower (bold-printed) occurrence a FIN head. More generally, an analysis like (41) would allow us to maintain the view that the complementiser *that* can only lexicalise FORCE and FIN heads.

Indeed, if we countenance the possibility of having more than two FIN heads in the periphery of the same clause, we could potentially extend the FINP recursion analysis to more complex cases like (40c), and treat the bracketed clause in it as having the peripheral structure shown below:

(42)  I don't think [$_{FORCEP}$ [$_{FORCE}$ that] [$_{MODP}$ for the sake of your own well-being [$_{MOD}$ ø] [$_{FINP}$ [$_{FIN}$ that] [$_{MODP}$ if you are in a bilingual classroom [$_{MOD}$ ø] [$_{FINP}$ [$_{FIN}$ that] [$_{MODP}$ once you have completed the homework in one language [$_{MOD}$ ø] [$_{FINP}$ [$_{FIN}$ that] you should have to do it again in the second one]]]]]]]]

Moreover, if *think* is a bridge verb which can select a truncated clause (=FINP) as its complement, even the initial *that* in (42) could potentially be a FIN head.

However, a FINP recursion analysis like that in (42) is questionable on both syntactic and semantic grounds. From a syntactic perspective, the problem is that economy considerations (in particular, the 'Avoid structure' principle posited by Rizzi 1997: 314) would argue against the postulation of three separate FINP constituents in (42) which seemingly have no rationale other than to serve as place-holders for *that*. And from a semantic perspective, it is hard to see what coherent interpretation the semantic component could assign to each of the different FINP projections in (42): after all, we would not want the corresponding LF representation to redundantly mark finiteness three times.

In any case, a fatal blow is struck to any lingering hopes of maintaining that the complementiser *that* can spell out only FORCE or FIN by (constructed) sentences such as the following:

(43)  a. I hope [that when they are adults **that** *at no time will* they forget the work that their parents put into their education] (Haegeman 2012: 85)
      b. I must admit [that, during the Paralympics held in Rio, **that** *the courage which some athletes showed*, it filled me with admiration]

As we saw in §1.5, a key assumption in Rizzi's FINP recursion analysis is that only a MODP projection can intervene between two FIN heads – not a FOCP or TOPP projection. And yet, (43a) potentially involves a focused negative constituent positioned after the lower (bold-printed) occurrence of *that*, and (43b) involves a dislocated topic positioned after the lower *that*. Given Rizzi's assumption that only a MODP projection can intervene between two occurrences of FIN, it follows that the bold-printed complementiser in structures like these cannot be in FIN. So where is it?

A plausible answer is that in such cases, *that* is the head of the projection containing the constituent immediately preceding it. Consider what this means for a sentence such as the following:

(44)  It is clear [that, *high-profile footballers like him*, **that** if they go out clubbing till the early hours of the morning, they will face a backlash on social media]

In (44) the bold-printed complementiser is preceded by an italicised dislocated topic, raising the possibility that the bold-printed complementiser spells out the TOP head. If so, the complement clause in (44) could have the peripheral structure bracketed below:

(45)    It is clear [$_{FORCEP}$ [$_{FORCE}$ that] [$_{TOPP}$ *high-profile footballers like him*
        [$_{TOP}$ **that**] [$_{MODP}$ if they go out clubbing till the early hours of the morning
        [$_{MOD}$ ø] [$_{FINP}$ [$_{FIN}$ ø] they will face a backlash on social media]]]]

Such an analysis is in line with much research treating similar cases of recomplementation in other languages as involving spelling out a TOP head as the counterpart of *that*: see e.g. Rodríguez Ramalle (2003), Paoli (2007), Mascarenhas (2007), Demonte & Fernández Soriano (2009), Ribeiro (2010), Villa-García (2011b, 2012a, 2012b, 2012c, 2015) and Garrett (2013).[18]

Villa-García (2015) proposes a parallel analysis for structures in Spanish in which a (phrasal or clausal) circumstantial adjunct precedes the complementiser *que*$_{that}$. Following Rizzi (1997), he treats circumstantial adjuncts as topics, and the complementiser as the head of the TOPP projection which contains the adjunct as its specifier. If we were to extend this analysis to English, the clause bracketed in (40a) would have the peripheral structure bracketed below:

(46)    I rang Newbury to say [$_{FORCEP}$ [$_{FORCE}$ *that*] [$_{TOPP}$ when she was due to race
        [$_{TOP}$ **that**] [$_{TOPP}$ for some unapparent reason [$_{TOP}$ ø] [$_{FINP}$ [$_{FIN}$ ø] she got very
        upset]]]]

However, a topic analysis of adverbial adjuncts is incompatible with the claim made by Cinque (1983) that hanging topics are canonically nominal in nature – and indeed with the similar claim made by Villa-García himself (2015: 164) that a 'hanging topic can only be a DP or NP'. In work since Rizzi (2004b), local peripheral adverbials have instead been treated as clausal modifiers housed in a MODP projection. This raises the possibility that (as claimed by Rizzi 2012: 125), a complementiser following a circumstantial adverbial clause spells out the head of the projection containing the adverbial clause. If so, in

---

[18]    A potential objection to analysing *that* as lexicalising the head of a projection which houses the immediately preceding peripheral constituent is that (as noted by Bayer & Dasgupta 2016: 3), there is often an intonation break between *that* and the constituent immediately preceding it, even though 'Elements in Spec,CP are normally prosodically integrated so that no prosodic break occurs between XP and C.' This might suggest that they are in separate projections – as indeed they would be (e.g.) under the FINP recursion analysis in (42). However, the local licensing relation between *that* and the XP immediately preceding it makes it plausible to posit that they are in a spec–head relation: for example, some speakers allow an adverbial but not a topic to license an immediately following *that*; similarly, some speakers allow a wh-constituent to license an immediately following *that* but others don't ... and so on.

place of (46) above we will have (47) below, with the lower (bold-printed) occurrence of *that* being positioned in MOD rather than in TOP:

(47)   I rang Newbury to say [FORCEP [FORCE *that*] [MODP when she was due to race [MOD **that**] [MODP for some unapparent reason [MOD ø] [FINP [FIN ø] she got very upset]]]]

An analysis along the lines of (47) would be consistent with the more general claim made by Villa-García (2015: 45) that in cases of recomplementation, a secondary complementiser 'can only occur where its specifier is filled'. We might then suppose that speakers who allow recomplementation have a disjunctive formulation of the *that*-spellout condition along the lines below:

(48)   **Complementiser spellout** (revised from 31 above)
       In an embedded finite clause, a non-verbal peripheral head can be spelled out as *that*
       (i) if it is the first word in the clause (= primary spellout condition)
       <u>or</u> (ii) if it has a criterial specifier (= secondary spellout condition)

The condition in (48) limiting *that* to spelling out a non-verbal head is a reflection of it not being able to occupy a verbal head position (e.g. one filled by an inverted auxiliary like the italicised position in 'He said under no circumstances *would* he apologise').[19] The assumption that only a constituent in a criterial specifier position can license secondary spellout of *that* embodied in (48ii) will preclude the possibility of (e.g.) FIN being licensed to be spelled out as *that* by the trace of some constituent which transits through spec-FINP on its way elsewhere. As will become apparent in the course of our discussion in this chapter, the question of what kinds of specifier can (or can't) license secondary use of *that* is subject to a great deal of inter-speaker variation.

To illustrate how the revised *that*-spellout rule in (48) works, let's consider how it can handle structures like those in (33–6) and (40) above. Under the assumptions made here, (34a/35a/36/40c) will have the respective peripheral structures shown in (49a/b/c/d) below:

(49)   a. The party opposite said [FORCEP [FORCE **that**] [MODP *if we cut 6 billion from the budget* [MOD <u>that</u>] [FINP [FIN ø] it would end in catastrophe]]]
       b. People like Dale need to have confidence [FORCEP [FORCE **that**] [TOPP *the kind of policing we need* [TOP <u>that</u>] [FINP [FIN ø] we can still deliver it]]]

---

[19] The condition barring *that* from spelling out a verbal peripheral head may be reducible to a more general property, e.g. if *that* lexicalises an inert head which does not trigger head movement, or if *that* is a free morpheme which does not allow another free morpheme (like an auxiliary) to adjoin to it.

c. Do you think [$_{\text{FORCEP}}$ [$_{\text{FORCE}}$ **that**] [$_{\text{TOPP}}$ Paris Saint Germain [$_{\text{TOP}}$ ø] [$_{\text{MODP}}$ *with the money they have behind them* [$_{\text{MOD}}$ that] [$_{\text{FINP}}$ [$_{\text{FIN}}$ ø] they're the new powerhouse in French football]]]]

d. I don't think [$_{\text{FORCEP}}$ [$_{\text{FORCE}}$ **that**] [$_{\text{MODP}}$ *for the sake of your own well-being* [$_{\text{MOD}}$ that] [$_{\text{MODP}}$ *if you are in a bilingual classroom* [$_{\text{MOD}}$ that] [$_{\text{MODP}}$ *once you have completed the homework in one language* [$_{\text{MOD}}$ that] [$_{\text{FINP}}$ [$_{\text{FIN}}$ ø] you should have to do it again in the second one]]]]]]

In each case, the bold-printed FORCE heads will be spelled out as *that* via the primary *that*-spellout condition (48i). In addition, the underlined MOD heads in (49a, c, d) and the underlined TOP head in (49b) will be lexicalised as *that* via the secondary *that*-spellout condition (48ii), because each has an italicised specifier in a criterial position. The spellout conditions in (48) will also handle a sentence like (50a) below containing both a peripheral dislocated topic and a peripheral adjunct, if (50a) has the structure in (50b):

(50)    a. It is clear [**that**, high-profile footballers like him, *that* if they go out clubbing till the early hours of the morning, that they may face a backlash on social media]

b. It is clear [$_{\text{FORCEP}}$ [$_{\text{FORCE}}$ **that**] [$_{\text{TOPP}}$ high-profile footballers like him [$_{\text{TOP}}$ that] [$_{\text{MODP}}$ if they go out clubbing till the early hours of the morning [$_{\text{MOD}}$ that] [$_{\text{FINP}}$ [$_{\text{FIN}}$ ø] they may face a backlash on social media]]]]

Thus, the FORCE head in (50b) will be spelled out as *that* via the primary *that*-spellout condition (48i); and the TOP and MOD heads will be spelled out as *that* via the secondary spellout condition (48ii), by virtue of having a specifier in a criterial position.

Although my focus here is on the use of indicative *that* (for the reasons set out at the beginning of this chapter), I note that the analysis outlined here can be extended to deal with cases of recomplementation in subjunctive clauses such as (51) below:

(51)    Please ensure [**that** if your faculty commit to permitting candidates to attend their classes, *that* there be sufficient diversity of courses and that syllabi permit visitors to attend] (Official university communication, Pennsylvania, Nov. 20, 2013, cited by Villa-García 2015: 96)

We can suppose that the bold-printed occurrence of *that* in (51) is a FORCE head which is spelled out as *that* via the primary *that*-spellout rule (48i), and that the italicised occurrence is a MOD head which is spelled out as *that* via the secondary *that*-spellout rule (48ii) in consequence of having the underlined adjunct clause as its specifier.

Thus far, I have examined use of secondary *that* in clauses which also involve primary use of *that* (i.e. in clauses introduced by *that*). However, my broadcast English data contain 29 examples of bare declarative complement clauses (i.e. declarative clauses not introduced by an initial complementiser) like those below which show secondary use of *that* after an (italicised) local phrasal or clausal circumstantial adjunct:

(52)    a.  And I'm hoping [*on Friday night* **that** we can turn up and get the points] (Dean Saunders, BBC Radio 5)

          b.  I'm sure [*behind the scenes* **that** he's got the backing] (Steve McClaren, BBC1 TV)

          c.  I think [*previously,* **that** *in trying to protect his off stump*] he flicked the ball to the on side (Ian Chappell, BBC Radio 5 Sports Extra)

          d.  Do you honestly think, though, [*if we created a global superleague* **that** there wouldn't be less bums on seats]? (Georgie Bingham, Talksport Radio)

          e.  Arsène Wenger said [*if a defensive midfield player becomes available,* **that** they will be in for him] (Mark Chapman, BBC Radio 5)

          f.  I'm not sure [*going into the Premier League* **that** their squad's that strong] (Jason Burt, Talksport Radio)

Experimental research by Radford, Boxell & Felser (2014) reported a relatively high mean acceptability rating of 67.94% for such structures on a speeded binary judgement task (a figure not significantly different from the 69.23% acceptability rating for corresponding structures in which no complementiser is used at all). But what is the structure of bare complement clauses like those bracketed in (52)?

Given the assumptions made by Rizzi (2014a) that bare clauses are FINP constituents, and that FINP can be recursively projected into a FINP+MODP+FINP structure, one possibility would be to take a bare clause like that bracketed in (52a) to have a peripheral structure along the lines shown below:

(53)    And I'm hoping [$_{FINP}$ [$_{FIN}$ ø] [$_{MODP}$ *on Friday night* [$_{MOD}$ **that**] [$_{FINP}$ [$_{FIN}$ ø] we can turn up and get the points]]]

The MOD head in (53) can be spelled out as *that* in accordance with the assumption embodied in the secondary *that*-spellout condition in (48ii) that the complementiser *that* in a finite clause can spell out a non-verbal peripheral head with an appropriate kind of specifier.

However, there are other bare clauses containing secondary *that* for which a FINP recursion analysis seems implausible. These include relative clauses like those in (54a–c) below, and predicative clauses like those in (54d, e):

(54)    a.  He's the kind of centreback [*if you're gonna play a back three*, **that** you wanna play in the middle] (Jamie Carragher, Sky Sports TV)
    b.  He's one of those guys [*in the past* **that** he's missed a few finals] (Steve Baxter, BBC Radio 5)
    c.  Sauber are the team [*by staying out all the while on intermediates*, **that** they have made massive gains] (David Croft, Sky Sports TV)
    d.  The problem we've got is [*in an ideal world* **that** all patients would be on single-sex wards] (Hospital spokesperson, BBC Radio 5)
    e.  Surely your aim is [*now that you're here* **that** you wanna stay here] (Stan Collymore, Talksport Radio)

If (as suggested in §§2.8 and 3.2), relative clauses are RELP constituents which contain a separate FORCE constituent which is generally declarative but can alternatively be interrogative, exclamative or imperative, the bracketed relative clause in (54a) above would have the peripheral structure in (55) below (if we analyse it as containing a null wh-relativiser/WH which originates in the gap position and ultimately ends up in spec-RELP):

(55)    He's the kind of centreback [$_{RELP}$ WH [$_{REL}$ ø] [$_{FORCEP}$ [$_{FORCE}$ ø] [$_{MODP}$ *if you're gonna play a back three* [$_{MOD}$ **that**] [$_{FINP}$ [$_{FIN}$ ø] you wanna play — in the middle]]]]

Since the MOD head has an (italicised) specifier, it can be lexicalised as *that* via the secondary *that*-spellout rule (48ii). If only complement clauses immediately adjacent to their selector can have a truncated FINP structure (as suggested in §3.2), it follows that predicative clauses like those in (54c–d) must be complete clauses which project as far as FORCEP, with the relevant FORCE head having a null spellout.

A further class of bare clauses which show secondary use of *that* are clauses which involve a dislocated constituent immediately followed by *that* (and reprised by an underlined resumptive pronoun). My broadcast English data contain the following four examples of such structures:[20]

---

[20]  The data also include the further three examples below which might also involve a bracketed clause containing a dislocated topic followed by the complementiser *that*:

> (i)  We trust [*Arsène Wenger*, **that** he'll find another Fabregas] (Martin Keown, BBC Radio 5)
> (ii)  Can I trust [*this man*, **that** he has the integrity to follow through what he has been promising]? (Stephen Nolan, BBC Radio 5)
> (iii) The family have complete confidence in [*the Pakistani authorities*, **that** he they will get to the bottom of this] (Lawyer, BBC R5)

However, I have not counted these as *topic+that* structures because they might alternatively involve asyndetic coordination – in which case, (i) would have an interpretation paraphraseable as 'We trust Arsène Wenger, and (we trust) that he'll find another Fabregas.' This seems less

(56)  a. I think [*Bayern Munich*, **that** <u>they</u> are a team to really watch in the final stages] (Andy Brassell, BBC Radio 5)

  b. You have to hope [*Zaragoza*, **that** <u>they</u> have a stronger wall than the one Ronaldo breached in the first 45] (Kevin Keatings, Sky Sports TV)

  c. They've been told [*eleven types of vegetables*, **that** they shouldn't eat <u>them</u> if they're locally produced] (Reporter, BBC Radio 5)

  d. I suggest [*anybody going today*, **that** <u>they</u> wrap up really well] (Sam Allardyce, Talksport Radio)

Given Rizzi's (1997) claim that only complete (FORCEP) clauses can contain a topic in their periphery, it follows from this (and other) assumptions that a sentence like (56a) above will have the peripheral structure below:

(57)  I think [$_{FORCEP}$ [$_{FORCE}$ ø] [$_{TOPP}$ *Bayern Munich* [$_{TOP}$ **that**] [$_{FINP}$ [$_{FIN}$ ø] they are a team to really watch in the final stages]]]

The TOP head can be spelled out as *that* via the secondary *that*-spellout rule (48ii) by virtue of having an (italicised) topic specifier; the FORCE and FIN heads will receive a null spellout by default. Although this is not the case in (56a), the FORCE head in (57) could alternatively be spelled out as *that* via the primary *that*-spellout condition (48i).

My data also contain the following examples of (bracketed) bare complement clauses containing both an (italicised) dislocated topic and and one or more (underlined) adverbial adjuncts:

(58)  a. I just think [*Arsenal*, <u>honestly</u>, **that** they are gonna fall behind if they don't sign a striker] (John Cross, Talksport Radio)

  b. Major League Soccer has a program in place (and they have for some time) saying [*any former Major League Soccer player*, <u>when he is finished with his playing career</u>, <u>if they wanna be a referee</u>, **that** there is money allocated so that they can be put on a fast-track system to become a referee in Major League Soccer] (Sean Wheelock, BBC Radio 5)

On the assumption that only complete (FORCEP) clauses can contain a topic, and given other assumptions made here, the bracketed complement clause in (58b) will have the peripheral structure shown below:

(59)  Major League Soccer has a program in place (and they have for some time) saying [$_{FORCEP}$ [$_{FORCE}$ ø] [$_{TOPP}$ any former Major League Soccer player [$_{TOP}$ ø] [$_{MODP}$ when he is finished with playing his career [$_{MOD}$ ø] [$_{MODP}$ if they wanna be a referee [$_{MOD}$ **that**] [$_{FINP}$ [$_{FIN}$ ø] there is money allocated so that they can be put on a fast-track system to become a referee in Major League Soccer]]]]]

likely in (iii), since a *that*-clause is not generally used as the complement of a transitive preposition, because *that* is case-resistant (Stowell 1981).

The lower MOD head can then be spelled out as *that* in accordance with the secondary *that*-spellout rule (48ii), by virtue of having a criterial specifier; and the remaining peripheral heads can receive a null spellout by default.

To summarise: in this section, we have seen that English has a secondary use of the complementiser *that* to lexicalise a peripheral head with a criterial specifier. As we have seen, this secondary spellout is found not only in clauses beginning with *that*, but also in bare complement clauses.[21] And in the next section, we will see that some speakers also extend the use of secondary *that* to wh-clauses.

## 3.4   Complementisers in Embedded Wh-clauses

Traditional descriptive and pedagogical grammars claim that embedded wh-clauses cannot contain an overt complementiser in standard varieties of English, whether in an interrogative clause like that bracketed in (60a) below, an exclamative like that in (60b), or a relative like that in (60c):

(60)    a. I have no idea [*in which hotel* (**\*that**) he is staying]
        b. You wouldn't believe [*what a great hotel* (**\*that**) he is staying in]
        c. This is the hotel [*in which* (**\*that**) he is staying]

---

[21] However, an anonymous referee remarks that they think they would only allow use of the (italicised) secondary complementiser *that* in a structure such as the following if the FORCE head is also spelled out as *that*:

(i) I think [$_{FORCEP}$ [$_{FORCE}$ **that/\*ø**] [$_{TOP}$ people like them [$_{TOP}$ *that*] they should be locked up]]

If this judgement is robust (e.g. if it is borne out by independent evidence from usage data or experimental results), there are at least two different ways of accounting for it. One is that some speakers obey the spellout rule devised by Rizzi (1997, 2014a) under which a declarative FORCE head in a complete (i.e. non-truncated) clause is obligatorily spelled out as *that*. This would predict that such speakers would still require the FORCE head to be spelled out as *that* even in a structure like (ii) below where the TOP head is null:

(ii) I think [$_{FORCEP}$ [$_{FORCE}$ **that/\*ø**] [$_{TOP}$ people like them [$_{TOP}$ ø] they should be locked up]]

However, if the referee allows the FORCE head to be null in (ii) but requires it to be overt in (i), it suggests that they impose an additional condition on the secondary spellout rule (48ii) to the effect that secondary spellout is contingent on primary spellout (e.g. a peripheral head with a criterial specifier can only be spelled out as *that* if the relevant clause is introduced by *that*). In the absence of more specific information about the referee's variety, it is difficult to say anything more definitive.

Use of an overt complementiser in wh-clauses is generally claimed to be restricted to specific regional varieties such as Belfast English (see e.g. Henry 1995: 90). For succinctness, I'll refer to clauses like those bracketed in (60) as WH+COMP structures.

A number of accounts have been developed of the ungrammaticality of WH+COMP structures in mainstream varieties of English. As noted in §1.3, Chomsky & Lasnik (1977) claimed that such structures are ruled out because they violate a PF filter which they characterise as in (61a) below, and to which Chomsky (1981) gives the more general formulation in (61b):[22]

(61)    Doubly Filled COMP Filter/DFCF
        a. *[$_{COMP}$ wh-phrase complementizer] (Chomsky & Lasnik 1977: 435)
        b. *[$_{COMP}$ α β] (Chomsky 1981: 243)

Given that (as we saw in §1.2) in earlier work all constituents in the clause periphery were taken to be in COMP, (61a) could be construed as amounting in more recent terms to a condition to the effect that the edge of a peripheral projection cannot contain an overt wh-phrase and an overt complementiser, and (61b) to the more general condition that the edge of a peripheral projection cannot contain more than one overt constituent. Either version of the filter will rule out clauses like those bracketed in (60) if their periphery contains an overt wh-phrase and an overt complementiser. The formulation in (61b) as it stands seems to be too strong, however, in that it (wrongly) rules out peripheral projections containing a fronted constituent and an inverted auxiliary (as in '*Which hotel* **are** you staying in?'). This could be overcome by reformulating the filter as barring PF structures of the form *[α β …] where α and β are overt constituents positioned on the edge of the same peripheral projection, and β is a complementiser.

Nonetheless, however formulated, the filter has the flavour of an ad hoc stipulation: after all, a reasonable question to ask is why such a filter should hold in English, and what its conceptual underpinnings are. Furthermore, any such filter is computationally inefficient (and will lead to crashes) since it envisages the grammar incorporating a set of syntactic operations which generate structures containing an overt complementiser with an overt specifier, and then ruling them out by an ad hoc PF filter like (61). This hardly seems to be an instance of the kind of efficient design which Minimalism takes to be a core property of natural language grammars. From this perspective, it would seem

---

[22] It should be taken as implicit in both formulations that the filter holds only where both constituents are overt, and not where either or both is null.

preferable to dispense with the filter entirely, or derive it from independently motivated LF or PF interface conditions.

One possibility along these lines would be to reduce the filter to a semantic interface condition ruling out structures that yield incoherent semantic interpretations. This is the position adopted by Rizzi (1990), who maintains that C and its specifier must not have conflicting feature specifications at LF. More specifically, he posits that an overt operator is specified as [+wh], the overt complementiser *that* as [−wh] and a null complementiser as either [+wh] or [−wh]. These assumptions will yield feature combinations including the following, under the CP analysis of the clause periphery adopted in Rizzi (1990):

(62)   a.   I wonder [$_{CP}$ what$_{+WH}$ [$_C$ ø$_{+WH}$] you saw]
       b.   *I wonder [$_{CP}$ what$_{+WH}$ [$_C$ that$_{-WH}$] you saw]
       c.   the thing [$_{CP}$ which$_{+WH}$ [$_C$ ø$_{+WH}$] you saw]
       d.   *the thing [$_{CP}$ which$_{+WH}$ [$_C$ that$_{-WH}$] you saw]

If structures involving a spec–head feature mismatch lead to a crash at LF, it follows that structures like (62b, d) which show a feature mismatch between a [−wh] head and a [+wh] specifier will give rise to an LF crash. This in turn means that the ad hoc filter in (61) can be dispensed with entirely (being simply an artefact of a requirement for syntactic structures to be mapped into coherent semantic interpretations). An alternative way of implementing Rizzi's idea of taking *that* to be a non-wh complementiser would be to suppose that it is inert in the sense that it cannot carry an edge feature triggering movement. This would then bar Wh-Movement from taking place in interrogative, exclamative or relative projections headed by *that*, like those bracketed in (62b, d).[23] In terms of our formulation of the complementiser spellout conditions in (48) above, this means that only a non-verbal, non-wh head can be spelled out as *that*.

---

[23] A question which I set aside here is how to deal with wh-less relative structures like that in (i) below:

(i)   [$_{DP}$ the [$_{NP}$ *thing* [$_{RELP}$ **that** you saw —]]]

If these involve Wh-Movement of a null wh-operator from the gap position to become the specifier of *that*, we clearly cannot treat *that* as an inert complementiser unable to trigger Wh-Movement. However, this problem does not arise if *that*-relatives involve Antecedent Raising rather than Wh-Movement – e.g. if the italicised antecedent *thing* in (i) raises from the gap position to the edge of the bracketed NP. See Radford (2016: 394–438) and the references cited there for discussion of the derivation of relative clauses.

An interesting prediction made by all the various accounts of the WH+COMP restriction outlined above is that speakers who treat *that* as a non-wh complementiser but have the secondary *that*-spellout condition (48ii) in their grammar will accept sentences like (63a) below, but not those like (63b):

(63)　　a.　I wonder [*how often*, <u>in times when money is in short supply</u>, *that* govern-
　　　　　　ments increase taxes on the poor]
　　　　b.　*I wonder [*how often* **that** <u>in times when money is in short supply</u>,
　　　　　　governments increase taxes on the poor]

Let us suppose that the embedded clauses in (63) have a structure along the following lines (in which the fronted interrogative operator is taken to move to the edge of a wh-operator projection, WHP):

(64)　　I wonder [$_{\text{FORCEP}}$ [$_{\text{FORCE}}$ ø] [$_{\text{WHP}}$ how often [$_{\text{WH}}$ **ø/*that**] [$_{\text{MODP}}$ <u>in times</u>
　　　　<u>when money is in short supply</u> [$_{\text{MOD}}$ *that/ø*] [$_{\text{FINP}}$ [$_{\text{FIN}}$ ø] governments raise
　　　　taxes on the poor]]]]

For speakers who have it in their grammar, the secondary *that*-spellout condition (48ii) will allow the MOD head in (64) to be spelled out as *that* by virtue of
having an (underlined) criterial specifier, so accounting for the grammaticality
of (63a). By contrast, the WH head in (64) cannot be spelled out as *that* for
speakers who treat *that* as a non-wh complementiser which does not allow
a wh-specifier, thereby accounting for the ungrammaticality of (63b) for such
speakers.

　　Received wisdom is that WH+COMP structures only occur in a small number
of regional varieties of English (like Irish English), and that they are acceptable
only to a minority of English speakers; and indeed independent support for this
comes from an experimental study by Radford, Boxell & Felser (2014)
which reported a low acceptability rate of 22.22% for embedded interrogative
*wh+that* clauses on a speeded binary judgement task. Nevertheless, careful
observation of spoken English reveals that a wide range of speakers from
a wide range of backgrounds produce such structures – as illustrated by the
examples below (examples 65a, b being from Radford 1988: 500, 65c from
Seppänen 1994, and 65d, e from Zwicky 2002):

(65)　　a.　I'm not sure *what kind of ban* **that** FIFA has in mind (Bert Millichip, BBC
　　　　　　Radio 4)
　　　　b.　We'll see *what kind of pace* **that** Daley Thompson's running at (Ron
　　　　　　Pickering, BBC1 TV)
　　　　c.　Definitions vary as to *which of these types of criteria* **that** are used
　　　　　　(Member of the English Department, University of Göteborg)

    d. I hadn't realised *just how many people* **that** were there (Maxx Faulkner on WCBE)

    e. I want to tell you *what experiences* **that** I've had here in my work (Columbus Stonewall presentation)

Zwicky makes the point (2002: 220) that such structures occur relatively frequently, and hence are not likely to be sporadic production errors, remarking that '*wh+that* clauses are not speech errors; one of my sources . . . seems to use these clauses fairly frequently in his radio broadcasts.' He also reports that Seppänen & Trotta (2000) collected 90 examples of *wh+that* structures like (65) from a corpus of 150 million words. Similar WH+COMP structures have been reported in other languages, including Bavarian and varieties of Italian (Bayer 1984a, 1984b), West Flemish (Haegeman 1983), and Norwegian (Taraldsen 1978).

If we look at the examples in (65), we see that they involve a nominal wh-phrase followed by *that*. One possibility which this raises is that such structures are 'instances of relative clauses of the headless type and not interrogative clauses' (Berizzi 2010: 74) – in other words, they are free relative nominals. On one implementation of this view, the *wh+that* structure in (65a) might have a structure along the lines shown in highly simplified form below:

(66)    [$_{DP}$ what [$_{NP}$ kind of ban [$_{CP}$ that [$_{TP}$ FIFA has in mind]]]]

However, there are reasons to be sceptical of the free relative nominal account. One (syntactic) reason is that it would mean that *wh+that* structures like those in (65) are nominal in nature, and this in turn would predict that they can only occur in case-marked positions: and yet, the *wh+that* structure in (65a) occurs in a caseless position as the complement of the intransitive adjective *sure*; by contrast (65a) is correctly predicted to be grammatical if *sure* selects an interrogative complement, and *what kind of ban* is interrogative. A second (lexical) reason for doubting the free relative analysis is that some of the wh-items which occur in *wh+that* clauses like those in (65) above (including *which* and *how many*) cannot be used in free relatives, as we see from the ungrammaticality of:

(67)    a. *I will choose *which (of them)* you choose
       b. *I will write to *how many (people)* you write to

Such considerations make it implausible to analyse all *wh+that* structures as free relatives (although nominals containing *what* or *wh-ever* items can indeed be used as free relatives – albeit not when occurring in caseless positions).

An alternative (related) way of analysing structures like (65) is to suppose that they arise as a blend (Bolinger 1961; Fay 1981; Stemberger 1982; Cohen 1987; Cutting & Bock 1997; Coppock 2006, 2010) or amalgam (Zwicky 2002) of relative and interrogative clauses. In more concrete terms, this would mean that a structure like (68a) below is a hybrid which comes about by blending the relative clause structure containing the overt complementiser *that* in (68b) with the interrogative clause containing a wh-phrase introduced by *what* in (68c) to form the WH+COMP structure in (68a):

(68)  a. We'll see *what kind of pace* **that** Daley Thompson's running at (=65b)
      b. We'll see *the kind of pace* **that** Daley Thompson's running at
      c. We'll see *what kind of pace* Daley Thompson's running at

However, such an account is undermined by the observation that the wh-phrase preceding *that* is not always nominal – as we see from examples like those below (69a–c being from Zwicky 2002, 69d–f from my broadcast English data, and 69g, h from the internet):[24]

(69)  a. Look at it as a tribute to *how deeply* **that** I feel about you (TV show 'Bob', Bob Newhart character speaking)
      b. I am pleased and frankly surprised at *how soon after the hearing* **that** the judge approved it (Mary Stowell, quoted in *New York Times*, p. B2, 20 August 1998)
      c. We don't know *to what degree* **that** the dialects are converging (Speaker at Ohio State University)
      d. This heat map shows *just how active* **that** Trippier was (Jermaine Jenas, BBC1 TV)
      e. It's amazing *how accurate* **that** you were at such a tender age (Rod Sharp, BBC Radio 5)
      f. It will be interesting to see *how seriously* **that** they will take these issues (Andy Jacobs, Talksport Radio)
      g. One of the biggest surprises about that night was *how cold* **that** it got (ournatureliesinmovement.wordpress.com)
      h. Melody spies on them to see *how badly* **that** they do without her (heydu dereviewed.wordpress.com)

---

[24] Examples like those in (69) also undermine the claim by Berizzi (2010) that *wh+ that* structures are predominantly free relatives, given the underlined expressions have no free relative use – as we see from the ungrammaticality of sentences like:

   (i)   *I feel about you *how deeply* **(that)** you feel about me
   (ii)  *He is not *how active* **(that)** you are
   (iii) *These dialects are not converging *to what degree* **(that)** the others are

On the basis of data like (65) and (69), Zwicky (2002) formulates the following generalisation about WH+COMP structures in standard varieties of present-day English:

(70)    **Zwicky's generalisation about WH+COMP structures**
  i. They occur only in subordinate clauses
  ii. They occur only in finite clauses
  iii. They occur only in interrogatives and exclamatives (not in relative clauses)
  iv. Only a wh-phrase (not a wh-word) can precede the complementiser[25]

He maintains that the seemingly idiosyncratic restrictions in (70) are best handled in terms of a construction-based grammar which recognises that present-day standard English has a wh-phrase+*that* construction used in embedded interrogative and exclamative (but not relative) clauses.

Nevertheless, Zwicky's implicit claim that the properties in (70) cannot be handled in a generative grammar seems too strong. The properties (70i, ii) can be attributed to it being a lexical property of overt complementisers (like *that*) that they are generally only used in non-root finite clauses. The property in (70iii) can again be treated as a lexical property of *that*, if it can have a Q-feature attracting a question operator to become its specifier, or an X-feature attracting an exclamative operator, but not an R-feature attracting a relative operator (see Radford 2016, ch. 7 on these features). Alternatively, if we take wh-relatives to involve Wh-Movement of a relative operator to the edge of the relative clause, and *that*-relatives to involve raising of the antecedent to a position on the edge of a nominal projection immediately above the relative clause, wh-relatives and *that*-relatives will have different derivations, and thus be expected not to co-occur. On this view, a *that*-relative like (71a) below would involve raising the antecedent *film* from the gap position to the italicised position on the edge of an NP above CP, while a wh-relative like (71b) would involve raising the wh-operator *which* from the gap position to italicised position on the edge of CP (with the antecedent being generated in situ):

---

[25] See the related remark by Henry (1995: 140, fn. 3) that 'There is a group of speakers for whom *that* can only occur if it does not directly follow a wh-word, so that (i) is grammatical but (ii) is not:

(i)   It depends *which story* **that** you believe
(ii)  *It depends *which* **that** you believe'

(NB: An inconsequential amendment has been made to the example numbering that Henry uses.)

(71)　　a. [DP the [NP *film* [CP that [TP we were watching —]]]]
　　　　b. [DP the [NP film [CP *which* [TP we were watching —]]]]

If Antecedent Raising and Wh-Movement are mutually incompatible, it follows that finite restrictive relatives can contain a complementiser or wh-operator, but not both.[26]

As for property (70iv) that only a wh-phrase (not a wh-word) can follow the complementiser, this seems unlikely to be an idiosyncratic property of a specific construction in English, since a similar restriction is found in Alemannic and Bavarian (Bayer & Brandner 2008), and in Lucernese and Swiss German (Schönenberger 2010). Far from being idiosyncratic, this property can be argued to be an artefact of the secondary *that*-spellout condition (48ii), if we suppose that (in relevant varieties) the head of a projection with a wh-specifier can be spelled out as *that*. To see how this might work, consider contrasts like that below, which Zwicky (2002) reports to hold in the grammars of many speakers (and which also holds in my own grammar):

(72)　　a. I'm not sure [*what kind of arrangement* **that** he has in mind]
　　　　b. I'm not sure [*what* (***that**) he has in mind]

If interrogative wh-phrases move to the specifier position in a wh-operator projection below FORCEP (Rizzi 2001), the complement clause in (72a) can be taken to have the peripheral structure below:

(73)　　I'm not sure [FORCEP [FORCE ø] [WHP *what kind of arrangement* [WH **that**] [FINP [FIN ø] he has in mind]]]

In varieties in which wh-phrases can license use of *that*, the secondary *that*-spellout condition (48ii) will allow the WH head to be spelled out as *that* because it is locally licensed by its italicised specifier. The grammar will thus correctly specify that (72a) is grammatical (except for speakers who treat *that* as a non-wh complementiser unable to spell out the head of a projection with a wh-specifier).[27]

---

[26] However, the derivations sketched in (71a, b) are far from unproblematic: see Radford (2016, ch. 7) for critical discussion of a range of accounts of the derivation of restrictive relative clauses.

[27] In (73), I take *that* to be in WH rather than in FIN. However, I note that Baltin (2010) claims that in WH+COMP clauses in Belfast English, the complementiser occupies the head FIN position of FINP and the wh-constituent serves as the specifier of a higher peripheral projection (a wh-operator projection, let us suppose). He bases his claim on the observation that the complementiser must be obligatorily deleted under Sluicing in sentences such as:

But now consider why (72b) is ungrammatical. If *what* behaves like *what kind of arrangement* in moving to the specifier position in the WH projection, (72b) will have the structure below:

(74)    I'm not sure [FORCEP [FORCE ∅] [WHP *what* [WH **that**] [FINP [FIN ∅] he has in mind]]]

However, we would then wrongly expect (72b) to be grammatical for speakers like me who accept (72a). To rule out the string *what that* under the analysis in (74) we would seemingly have to invoke some modified version of the Doubly Filled COMP Filter to the effect that the edge of a peripheral projection can't contain a wh-word which (asymmetrically) c-commands an immediately adjacent complementiser. The downside of this is that any such filter would be a purely ad hoc descriptive device with no explanatory power. Let's therefore explore an alternative solution.

Josef Bayer has argued that (for economy reasons[28]) wh-words move to C, whereas wh-phrases move to spec-CP (see Bayer & Brandner 2008, and Bayer

---

(i)    They discussed one of the models, but I can't remember [*which one* (**\*that**) ~~they discussed~~]

However, his argument is uncompelling. After all, if (as claimed by Lobeck 1990, and Saito & Murasugi 1990), functional heads can only license ellipsis of their complement when they agree with their specifier, it could be that English overt complementisers cannot carry agreement features (a key claim made in Rizzi's 1990: 52–3 account of the *that*-trace effect), and for this reason cannot license ellipsis of their complement. Alternatively, it could be that overt complementisers (like *that/if/whether*) do not license complement ellipsis in English, perhaps because the parsing function of a complementiser is to signal an upcoming (overt) clausal complement.

[28]    A key assumption of the economy claim is that a structure like (i) below where *who* moves to C is more economical than one like (ii) where *who* moves to spec-CP:

(i)    I wonder [CP [C who] she is meeting]
(ii)   I wonder [CP who [C' [C ∅] she is meeting]]

The reason is that (ii) creates an additional (C-bar) projection which is not present in (i). However, the economy claim is not entirely straightforward. This is because if *who* in (i) adjoins to a null complementiser, we will have the structure in (iii) below:

(iii)  I wonder [CP [C who+[C ∅]] she is meeting]

And the derivation in (iii) will create additional branching structure in C (unless movement of *who* to C can be treated as a case of remerger in the sense of Donati & Cecchetto 2011) – leaving us with the question of what the basis is for claiming that (iii) really is more economical than (ii). Bayer suggests that the relevant economy condition amounts to an 'Avoid specifier' principle which avoids the projection of a specifier wherever possible.

The Wh-Head-Movement analysis has potential implications for root questions like:

(iv)   Who is she meeting?

2014, 2015, 2016); likewise, Kathol (2001) argues that relative pronouns occupy the head C position of CP in German; and the same may be true of movement of wh-words in North Norwegian dialects in which movement of a verb into C is possible only when C attracts a wh-phrase, not when it attracts a wh-word (see Taraldsen 1978; Vangsnes 2005; Westergaard 2003, 2005; Westergaard & Vangsnes 2005). From a theoretical perspective, it is plausible to suppose that a null complementiser can attract a wh-head to adjoin to it, since a number of linguists (including Ormazabal 1995; Bošković & Lasnik 2003; and Epstein, Pires & Seely 2005) have argued that null complementisers behave like clitics in a variety of languages. Moreover, the claim that wh-words move to COMP is supported by empirical evidence from Bavarian that (like complementisers) fronted wh-words inflect for subject agreement and can host clitics. Such an analysis (if applied to English as in Radford 1997a: 332, and adapted to the framework used here) would mean that *what* moves to the head position of the wh-operator projection/WHP, so that the bracketed complement clause in (72b) has the structure in (75) below:

(75)   I'm not sure [FORCEP [FORCE ∅] [WHP [WH *what*] [FINP [FIN ∅] he has in mind]]]

Under this analysis, it is clear that the complementiser *that* could not occupy the head position of the wh-operator projection (since this is filled by *what*). Nor can *that* spell out the head of FINP, since the secondary *that*-spellout rule (48ii) specifies that only a head with a criterial specifier can be lexicalised as *that*, and FIN has no criterial specifier in (75). Thus, the analysis in (75) provides a principled account of Zwicky's observation (70iv) that the complementiser *that* can only occur after a wh-phrase, not after a wh-word.

To summarise the discussion so far in this section: we have looked at Zwicky's generalisation about constraints on the use of WH+COMP clauses, and the claim that these require a constructionist approach to grammar. Contrary to his claim, I have argued that the relevant restrictions can be handled in a principled fashion within a generative framework, and shown that they can be treated as lexical properties of complementisers, or as a consequence of the nature of the secondary spellout condition on the use of *that* (48ii). However, in the remainder of this section I will go on to argue that there is some doubt about the empirical robustness of Zwicky's claims. Since I will devote §3.5 to

---

If the head C position of CP is filled by the inverted auxiliary *is* here, *who* must seemingly move to the head position in a higher CP (or, in cartographic terms, perhaps *is* occupies the head of FINP and *who* the head of a higher wh-operator projection/WHP).

disputing his claim (70i) that complementisers do not occur in root clauses, I will begin here by casting a critical eye on his claim in (70ii) that WH+COMP structures are only found in finite clauses.

The empirical basis of this claim would appear to be undermined by infinitival relative clauses like those bracketed below:[29]

(76)  a. As Liverpool chase the game, there may be more room [*in which* **for** Manchester United to manoeuvre] (Commentator, Sky Sports TV)
      b. The physical habitat of the animal plays an important role in their welfare, meeting their physical requirements and providing a positive environment [*in which* **for** them to live] (blackpoolzoo.org.uk)
      c. So whether you have a Chameleon, Tree Python or an Emerald Tree Boa, we are sure to have the right equipment for you to replicate the perfect environment [*in which* **for** them to thrive] (reptiles.swelluk.com)
      d. Or do you create bigger headaches, more friction and one more thing [*about which* **for** them to worry]? (huffingtonpost.com)
      e. There should be six days [*on which* **for** men to work] and a day [*on which* **for** men to rest] (inscription on a tombstone in New Zealand, reported by Jim McCloskey, pc)
      f. The concept was to find musicians and porches [*on which* **for** them to play] (Porchfest, Wikipedia.org)
      g. But we also have a better basis [*from which* **for** them to get started] (cleverism.com)
      h. They took with them items that I had left there [*with which* **for** them to maintain the property] (propertyinvestmentproject.co.uk)

---

[29] *Wh+for* structures appear to be restricted to occurring in relative clauses in standard varieties of English, since interrogatives like *\*I wasn't sure which hotel for him to stay in* are ungrammatical. It would appear, however, that *wh+for* interrogatives are found in Belfast English, as illustrated below:

(i)   They wanted to do something, but they weren't sure *what* **for** to do (Alison Henry, cited as a pc in Baltin 2010: 332)

As for *wh+for* exclamatives like:

(ii)  *What a shame* **for** Steven Gerrard to miss the start of the season (John Cross, Talksport Radio)

the infinitive clause can be argued to be the wh-counterpart of the cleft sentence in (iii) below:

(iii) It is such a shame for Steven Gerrard to miss the start of the season

This is suggested by the observation that *it is* can occur between *what a shame* and *for* in (ii), and furthermore both (ii) and (iii) can be tagged by *isn't it?* Since exclamative clauses are factive (Grimshaw 1979; Abels 2010) and factive clauses are finite, we would not expect to find infinitival exclamatives (other than those in which the infinitive is a relative clause). On infinitival wh-exclamatives in English, see Radford (1980) and (2016: 447–50).

i. For me, advocating for that system as well as supporting individuals is the most meaningful way to create the best possible experience for patients and a place for them [*from which* **for** them to enjoy the best health possible] (jessicabean.com.au)

If relative operators move to the edge of a RELP/relative phrase projection and the complementiser *for* is in FIN, the infinitival relative in (76a) will have a peripheral structure which includes the projections shown below:[30]

(77)     As Liverpool chase the game, there may be more room [$_{RELP}$ *in which* [$_{REL}$ ø] [$_{FINP}$ [$_{FIN}$ **for**] Manchester United to manoeuvre]]

Such a structure would not violate the Doubly Filled COMP Filter because the wh-phrase and complementiser are contained in separate peripheral projections. However, if the wh-phrase transits through spec-FINP on its way to spec-RELP (perhaps because FINP is a phase, as argued by Branigan 2005), such structures will be ungrammatical for speakers who treat *for* as a non-wh complementiser which is unable to attract an overt wh-constituent to become its specifier.[31]

Consider now the empirical robustness of Zwicky's claim (70iii) that WH+COMP structures are only found in interrogatives and exclamatives, not in relatives. This claim appears not to hold for free relatives, as the following examples from my broadcast data illustrate:

(78)     a. The Court have said that she's well within her rights to choose [*whichever provider* **that** she wants] (Dotun Adebayo, BBC Radio 5)

---

[30] I have assumed here that *for*-infinitives lack force in standard varieties of English, and hence that there is no FORCEP projection between RELP and FINP: this is consistent with *for* not being used in clauses with interrogative force in standard varieties of English (as noted in fn. 29). However, in varieties like Belfast English where we find interrogative *for*-infinitives such as those below (from Henry 1995: 88):

(i) I don't know [*where* **for** to go]
(ii) He wasn't sure [*what* **for** to do]

it seems plausible to take the bracketed clauses to contain an interrogative FORCEP projection.

[31] However, it might be argued that *for* can attract a null relative operator to become its specifier in structures such as:

(i) There may be more room [for Manchester United to manoeuvre in]

But an alternative possibility would be that structures like (i) involve Antecedent Raising, not Operator Movement. Note that an alternative way of ruling out structures like (77) for speakers who don't accept them is to suppose that the relative clause-typing feature percolates down from the highest to the lowest head in the periphery, so that FIN carries a relative feature which bars it from being spelled as *for* for speakers who treat *for* as a non-relative complementiser. On percolation of features from higher to lower peripheral heads, see §3.6.

    b. Madrid is anxious that [*whatever funds* **that** are available] go directly to the banks (Gavin Hewitt, BBC1 TV)

    c. We want them to hire [*whatever company* **that** is out there] to clear up the mess (Florida resident, BBC Radio 5)

    d. We've taken [*what measures* **that** we can] (Meteorologist, BBC Radio 5)

    e. The club can take [*whatever action* **that** they wish to] (Listener, Talksport Radio)

    f. Everyone wants a bit more in the future, [*whichever club* **that** they support] (Mark Saggers, Talksport Radio)

Furthermore, a Google search revealed numerous other examples of WH+COMP free relatives, including those bracketed below:

(79)    a. The best tool for the job in my opinion is [*whichever one* **that** I am most comfortable in], [*whichever one* **that** I can code the fastest in], whichever one will get the product to the market sooner (MattKremer.com)

    b. But [*whichever way* **that** Angel swung], he was a sexy creature (Ruth Brandon, *Caravaggio's Angel*, Soho Press, New York)

    c. [*Whichever way* **that** you go] (Song by Rob Cole, YouTube)

    d. Now that I seem to know what lies beyond me, maybe I can reach out in [*whatever way* **that** I can] (Paul Ottley, *Prosperity: The Fruit of Challenge*, Google books, 2010: 187)

It thus seems that WH+COMP free relatives are acceptable to a wide range of speakers (me included) – even those who don't otherwise allow WH+COMP structures. How come?

A plausible answer is to suppose that free relatives are DPs in which the wh-phrase and complementiser are in separate projections, with the wh-phrase on the edge of DP and the complementiser on the edge of CP/RELP.[32] One implementation of this idea would be to suppose that the free relative in (78a) has a superficial structure along the lines shown in simplified form below:

(80)    ... she's well within her rights to choose [$_{DP}$ whichever [$_{NP}$ provider [$_{CP}$ that she wants]]]

---

[32] For a range of alternative views on the syntax of free relatives, see Hirschbühler (1976, 1978), Bresnan & Grimshaw (1978), Groos & van Riemsdijk (1981), Harbert (1983), Hirschbühler & Rivero (1983), Borsley (1984), Larson (1987), Battye (1989), Grosu (1989, 1996, 2003), Kayne (1994), Rooryck (1994), Jacobson (1995), Citko (2000, 2002, 2004, 2008, 2011), Izvorski (2000), Vogel (2001), Caponigro (2002), de Vries (2002), van Riemsdijk (2017), Donati (2006), Caponigro & Pearl (2008, 2009), Nakamura (2009), Donati & Cecchetto (2011), Ott (2011), Benincà (2012a), Caponigro, Torrence & Cisneros (2013), Radford (2016: 464–70) and Cinque (2017).

Under the analysis in (80), CP does not have an overt specifier, and so no Doubly Filled COMP violation will arise, even for speakers who do not otherwise allow WH+COMP structures. On this view, free relative structures like (78) and (79) do not challenge Zwicky's claim (70iii), if we interpret (70iii) as meaning that no relative clause CP can have a clause periphery containing a wh-operator and an overt complementiser.

However, a more substantial challenge to the claim in (70iii) comes from restrictive relative clauses.[33] Contrary to Zwicky's claim that they don't occur, *wh+that* restrictive relatives are indeed attested – as the following examples from my broadast English data illustrate:[34]

(81)   a. I'm aware of the speed [*with which* **that** they work] (Tim Vickery, BBC Radio 5)
       b. The manner [*in which* **that** Reina has been dispatched] just isn't the right way to do business (Nat Coombs, Talksport Radio)
       c. They slowed our build-up to a level [*at which* **that** we lost momentum] (Sir Alex Ferguson, Sky Sports TV)
       d. The reason [*why* **that** there is a buzz in here] is because Mark Webber is in pole position (Jake Humphreys, BBC1 TV)
       e. England put themselves in a position [*whereby* **that** they took a lot of credit for tonight's game] (Ron Greenwood, BBC Radio 4, reported in Radford 1988: 486)
       f. We could end up with one of these ping-pong scenarios [*where* **that** it keeps going backwards and forwards] (Reporter, BBC Radio 5)
       g. There was a long time [*when* **that** they didn't win the league] (Andy Brassell, BBC Radio 5)

Such structures can be treated as further cases of secondary *that*-spellout (48ii), whereby a finite peripheral head can be spelled out as *that* when it has a criterial

---

[33] And potentially from appositives as well, albeit my data only contain the following two examples of appositives containing a wh-constituent immediately followed by *that*:

(i)   This isn't like football, [*whereby* **that** the actual participants are nowhere to be seen] (Ian Abrahams, Talksport Radio)
(ii)  It was a criticism of the calendar of Brazilian football, [*where* **that** they play all the year round] (Tim Vickery, BBC Radio 5)

[34] Zwicky (2002: 223, fn. 1) dismisses such structures as production errors, remarking in relation to (81e) that 'The appearance of the formal *whereby* in this otherwise colloquial bit of sports reporting is suspicious, as is the fact that there are no relative clause examples in the RZ [Radford & Zwicky: AR] corpus, and no example there with a one-word wh-expression ... My guess is that this is a production error, an online blend of a formal "fancy" construction with *whereby* and a colloquial, everyday construction with *that* (... *a position that they took a lot of credit for tonight's game*, say).' However, the other data in (81) call Zwicky's claim into question.

specifier, if we suppose that in the relevant variety a relative wh-specifier can license secondary use of *that*.

At the same time, it should be acknowledged that WH+COMP structures appear to be less frequent in restrictive relative clauses than in interrogatives or exclamatives: for example, my broadcast data contain 94 examples of embedded interrogative WH+COMP clauses, 25 examples of embedded exclamative WH+COMP clauses and 14 examples of restrictive relative WH+COMP clauses (plus the two appositive relative examples noted in fn. 33). Unfortunately, we cannot legitimately infer from this that there are speakers who allow WH+COMP structures in interrogatives and exclamatives but not in restrictive relatives: this is because data sets (like my broadcast English data) which comprise a heterogeneous set of sentences produced by a heterogeneous set of individuals (sometimes of unknown origin) clearly don't provide a suitable basis from which to abstract generalisations about specific varieties or individuals. Moreover the frequency differences could be attributable to other factors: for example, interrogative clauses are used more frequently than exclamatives, there are fewer exclamative than interrogative wh-words (especially pronouns), and so on. For the minority of speakers who allow *wh+that* restrictives, we can assume that they allow *that* to carry an R-feature triggering movement of a relative operator to the edge of the projection headed by *that*, whereas most speakers do not.

Now let's turn to examine the robustness of Zwicky's claim in (70iv) that a wh-word cannot precede a complementiser. Earlier, I suggested that this may be because wh-words are the heads of the phrases containing them, and hence do not allow use of *that* because secondary complementiser spellout is only licensed by a specifier. At first sight, the claim that only wh-phrases (not wh-words) license secondary use of *that* might appear to be called into question by clauses such as those bracketed below:

(82)   a. Capello has to know [*who*, <u>when the chips are down</u>, **that** he can trust to do a job for the team] (Graham Taylor, BBC Radio 5)
       b. I'm just wondering [*why*, <u>at the end of the season</u>, **that** Lerner gave McLeish the job] (Listener, BBC Radio 5)
       c. Sometimes we lose sight of [*how*, <u>in the very recent past</u>, **that** this has come about] (John Cross, Talksport Radio)

However, given the assumptions made here, use of the bold-printed complementiser will be licensed by the immediately preceding (underlined) adjunct phrase, not by the (italicised) wh-word – as shown for (82a) above in (83) below, where *that* is licensed to occur in MOD by the underlined adverbial in spec-MODP:

(83)    Capello has to know [FORCEP [FORCE ø] [WHP [WH who] [MODP <u>when the chips</u> <u>are down</u> [MOD **that**] [FINP [FIN ø] he can trust to do a job for the team]]]]]

Thus sentences like (83) do not undermine Zwicky's claim that only a wh-phrase (not a wh-word) can license an immediately following complementiser, for the obvious reason that the complementiser here immediately follows the underlined adjunct phrase, not the wh-word.

However, my broadcast English data do contain 30 examples of clauses like those below in which a wh-adverb immediately precedes *that* (12 with *why*, 8 with *how*, 4 with *where*, 4 with *whereby*, and 1 each with *when* and *whenever*):

(84)    a. I never understood [*why* **that**, <u>particularly detectives</u>, they never locked their cars] (Ian Payne Radio, BBC Radio 5)
        b. A soldier I met told me [*how* **that** their orders were indiscriminate] (Sue Lloyd Roberts, BBC2 TV)
        c. We could end up with one of these ping-pong scenarios [*where* **that** it keeps going backwards and forwards] (Reporter, BBC Radio 5)
        d. It's a nominal veto [*whereby* **that** the UK government can veto certain options] (Reporter, BBC Radio 5)
        e. There was a long time [*when* **that** they didn't win the league] (Andy Brassell, BBC Radio 5)
        f. You've gotta make sure you're ready [*whenever* **that** you get the call] (Alex Oxlade Chamberlain, BBC Radio 5)

At first sight, the bracketed clauses would appear to be counterexamples to the claim that wh-heads don't license secondary complementisers. How are we to deal with such examples?

An interesting property of the wh-words preceding *that* in (84) is that they are adverbial pronouns. There is a substantial body of research dating back to the 1970s which argues for treating adverbial (pro)nominals as PPs headed by a null preposition: see e.g. Emonds (1976, 1987), McCawley (1988), Collins (2007), Caponigro & Pearl (2008, 2009), and Radford (2016: 231–3). On this view, *whenever* in (84f) would be a PP with the fuller form 'AT whenever TIME', where the capitalised items are present in the syntax but receive a null spellout in the phonology – and a parallel PP analysis could be devised for the other wh-adverbs in (84). If the wh-adverbs in (84) are indeed PPs, it follows that (by virtue of being phrases and not heads) they occupy the specifier position in the projection immediately containing them, and so allow the head of the relevant projection to be spelled out as *that* via the secondary *that*-spellout condition (48ii). Given these (and other) assumptions, the bracketed clause in (84a) will have the structure shown below:

(85)    I never understood [FORCEP [FORCE ø] [WHP *why* [WH **that**] [TOPP <u>particularly</u> <u>detectives</u> [TOP ø] [FINP [FIN ø] they never locked their cars]]]]

The wh-pronoun *why* will be a PP (headed by an abstract counterpart of the preposition *for*[35]) which serves as the specifier of an interrogative wh-operator projection whose head is lexicalised as *that* (via the secondary *that*-spellout condition 48ii), and thus precedes the dislocated topic *particularly detectives*. The overall conclusion we reach, therefore, is that WH-ADV+COMP structures like those in (84) are consistent with the claim that wh-heads do not license secondary complementisers in English.

A greater potential challenge to the claim that wh-heads can't be immediately followed by *that* comes from the clauses bracketed in (86) below, where an argumental pronoun (*what/who*) immediately precedes *that*:

(86)    a. Obviously they've got a better understanding of [*what* **that** he wants from them] (Ray Houghton, Talksport Radio)
        b. We'll have to see [*what* **that** happens] (Eddie Irvine, BBC1 TV)
        c. It will be all about [*who* **that** they get the money for] (Pete Jenson, Talksport Radio)

The fact that my broadcast data contain only the three examples listed in (86) above suggests that this is a relatively rare type of structure in English, perhaps restricted to a small number of regional varieties – and indeed two of the speakers have strong regional accents (Ray Houghton being from Glasgow in Scotland, and Eddie Irvine being from Newtownards in Northern Ireland); moreover, Henry (1995: 88, 89) reports *who that* structures occurring in Belfast English.[36] However, such structures are clearly not anomalous from a wider perspective, since they have counterparts in other languages, as clauses like those bracketed below illustrate:

---

[35] Potential evidence for treating *why* as a PP headed by an abstract counterpart of *for* comes from sentences like those below, where *for* shows up overtly:

    (i) I've had a change of heart in the last week and I'll tell you **for** *why* (www .trollishdelver.com)
    (ii) I can remember getting back to the White House, and Laura said '*Why* did you do that **for**?' (George Bush, www.cnn.com/2005/ALLPOLITICS/01/14/bush .regrets)
    (iii) How come and **for** *why* hasn't this extra solar planet burnt up? (allegrasloman .com)

[36] I have been unable to trace the origins of Pete Jenson. Interestingly, my Dublin-born dentist Gavin Barry tells me that he finds *who/what+that* structures unacceptable, while accepting wh-phrase+*that* examples, suggesting that by no means all Irish English speakers accept *who/ what+that* structures (as noted by Henry 1995: 140, fn. 3).

(87)  a. Ik   weten   niet   [*wien*   **dat**   Jan   gezeen   hat]
         I    know    not    who     that    Jan   seen    has
         'I don't know who Jan has seen' (West Flemish, Haegeman 1983: 83)
      b. Jeg   forfalte   Jan   [*hvem*   **som**   var   kommet]
         I     asked      Jan   who      that    had   come
         'I asked Jan who had come' (Norwegian, Taraldsen 1978: 631)
      c. a   dochter   [*which*   **that**   called   was   Sophie]
         a   daughter   which    that     called   was   Sophie
         'a daughter who was called Sophie' (Middle English, Traugott 1972: 156)

How are we to analyse structures like (86)?

One possibility is that *who/what+that* structures like those in (86) are not interrogative clauses but rather are free relative DPs, and thus nominal in nature. Such an analysis is plausible for the sentences in (86), given that they involve a *who/what+that* structure used as the object of a transitive preposition or verb. If the relevant structures are indeed free relatives, and if (as argued by Donati & Cecchetto 2011) the free relative pronoun occupies the head D position of DP and the complementiser the head C position of CP, (86a) will have the (partial) structure shown below:

(88)   Obviously they've got a better understanding of [$_{DP}$ [$_D$ *what*] [$_{CP}$ [$_C$ **that**] he wants from them]]

Since *what* and *that* occupy different head positions, there will be no problem accommodating both the wh-word and the complementiser in a structure like (88).

However, the problem posed by such an analysis is that it raises the question of why structures like (88) are ungrammatical in most varieties of English.[37] Moreover, while a free relative account might be appropriate for *who/ what+that* structures which occur in transitive contexts like (86), it would not be appropriate for (internet-sourced) cases like those below where they occur in intransitive contexts:

---

[37] We might in principle exclude clauses like those bracketed in (88) by supposing that most varieties of English have a PF filter ruling out structures in which a wh-word asymmetrically c-commands and immediately precedes an overt complementiser; but any such filter would clearly be ad hoc unless it could be derived from independent principles. An alternative approach might be to suppose that *what* has to transit through C in order to move from its original position as the complement of *want* to its superficial position as the head D of DP, and the complementiser *that* (for speakers who don't accept sentences like 88) is an inert head which cannot license such movement (e.g. by virtue of being a non-wh head or a non-affixal head).

(89)    a. Everyone needs to carry so that the terrorists are not <u>sure</u> [*who* **that** they are dealing with] (preparedgunowners.com)
        b. It's not <u>clear</u> [*who* **that** 'they' refers to] (pnreview.co.uk)

Since the bracketed *who+that* structures in (89) occur as the complement of the intransitive predicates *sure/clear*, a free relative analysis would be implausible for such cases, since a nominal cannot serve as the complement of an intransitive head.

It would therefore seem that structures like those in (89) are more likely to be interrogative complement clauses. If so, how are we to deal with them? One possibility is that (by virtue of their dual status as minimal or maximal projections), pronouns like *who/what* can in principle occupy either the head position or the specifier position in an interrogative wh-projection, with different varieties of English choosing different options. If *who/what* occupy the specifier position in an interrogative wh-operator projection/WHP, this will leave the head position available to be filled by *that* via secondary *that*-spellout, as below:

(90)    Everyone needs to carry so that the terrorists are not sure
        [$_{FORCEP}$ [$_{FORCE}$ ø] [$_{WHP}$ *who* [$_{WH}$ **that**] [$_{FINP}$ [$_{FIN}$ ø] they are dealing with]]]

Such an analysis implies that speakers who produce structures like (90) place a greater importance on structural uniformity (i.e. on all wh-operator expressions moving to the same specifier position in the projection housing them) than on structural economy (i.e. on avoiding projecting specifiers wherever possible). By contrast (let us suppose), speakers who don't allow *who/what+that* place more importance on economy than on uniformity, and move wh-phrases into spec-WHP and wh-heads into head-WHP, so that for them the only position that could be spelled out as *that* would be FIN, as below:

(91)    Everyone needs to carry so that the terrorists are not sure
        [$_{FORCEP}$ [$_{FORCE}$ ø] [$_{WHP}$ [$_{WH}$ *who*] [$_{FINP}$ [$_{FIN}$ **that**] they are dealing with]]]

However, FIN could not be spelled out as *that* via the primary spellout condition (48i) because it is not clause-initial, nor by the secondary spellout condition (48ii) because it has no specifier. On this view, the variation between speakers who do and don't accept *who/what+that* structures could then be handled in optimality-theoretic terms, as reflecting different relative rankings of the economy and uniformity constraints. Speakers who move wh-words like *who/what* into spec-WHP as in (90) will allow *who/what+that*, whereas speakers who move *who/what* into head-WHP as in (91) will not allow *who/*

*what+that* because they have no mechanism for licensing use of *that*. By contrast, both sets of speakers would be expected to allow structures like

(92)  Everyone needs to carry so that the terrorists are not sure
      [FORCEP [FORCE ø] [WHP *what kind of people* [WH **that**] [FINP [FIN ø] they are dealing with]]]

because for both sets of speakers, wh-phrases (like that italicised above) move to spec-WHP, so allowing the WH head to be spelled out as *that* via the secondary spellout condition (48ii) – at least, for speakers who allow secondary spellout, and who don't treat *that* as a non-wh complementiser.

However, the downside of the account in the previous paragraph is that it requires us to suppose that wh-heads have different landing sites in different varieties of English (in spec-WHP in some varieties, and in head-WHP in others), and that this reflects different optimality-theoretic rankings of the uniformity and economy constraints.[38] But if we discount this type of analysis as sub-optimal, what alternative is there?

One possibility would be to adopt the position that (universally) wh-phrases move to spec-WHP (as in 92 above) and wh-heads move to head-WHP (as in 91), so that *wh+that* structures can in principle arise in the two ways shown below:

(93)  Everyone needs to carry so that the terrorists are not sure
      a. [FORCEP [FORCE ø] [WHP *what kind of people* [WH ø/**that**] [FINP [FIN ø] they are dealing with]]]
      b. [FORCEP [FORCE ø] [WHP [WH *who*] [FINP [FIN ø/**that**] they are dealing with]]]

In both cases, *that* is asymmetrically c-commanded by and immediately adjacent to an (italicised) wh-constituent; the difference between the two structures is that in (93a), the wh-constituent and *that* are on the edge of the same projection (= WHP), whereas in (93b) they are on the edge of different projections (*who* being on the edge of WHP, and *that* on the edge of FINP). So, one way of accounting for why some speakers accept *wh-phrase+that* but not *wh-head+that* is to suppose that the relevant speakers impose a strict locality condition to the effect that secondary spellout is only possible when the wh-constituent and *that* are on the edge of the same projection: in other words (to coin a term created by analogy with the term *clausemate*), some

---

[38] On constraint ranking in Optimality Theory, see e.g. Grimshaw (1997), Pesetsky (1998), Dekkers et. al. (2000), Sells (2001), Legendre et al. (2001), Müller (2000, 2001), Vogel (2006), and Broekhuis (2008).

speakers only allow secondary spellout when *that* and the wh-constituent are *edgemates* (i.e. on the edge of the same projection). As for speakers who accept *who that*, it would seem that they allow the *head* of WHP to license the use of *that* to spell out the head of FINP via a local head–head relation.[39]

Bearing in mind also that (as noted earlier) some speakers treat *that* as a non-wh complementiser and so don't allow a wh-constituent to license secondary use of *that*, let's suppose that the secondary spellout of the complementiser *that* is parameterised along the lines shown below:

(94)    **Complementiser spellout** (revised from 48 above)
> In an embedded finite clause, a non-verbal peripheral head can be spelled out as *that*
>> (i) if it is the first word in the clause
>> or (ii) if it has an adjacent superordinate (%edge-mate) (%non-wh) licenser

The % signs in (94) are intended to indicate that many (but not all) speakers require the licenser and head to be on the edge of the same projection, and that many (but not all) speakers don't allow a wh-constituent to license use of *that*. Speakers who impose the edgemate condition (but not the non-wh condition) on secondary spellout will allow (93a) because *what kind of people* and *that* are on the edge of the same (WHP) projection, but will not allow (93b) because *who* is on the edge of WHP, and *that* is on the edge of FINP. By contrast, (the minority of) speakers who impose neither the edgemate condition nor the non-wh condition on secondary spellout will allow both (93a) and (93b), because in both cases the wh-constituent is superordinate to (i.e. asymmetrically c-commands) and (immediately) adjacent to *that*.

The parameterised spellout conditions in (94) also offer us an interesting perspective on double-complementiser clauses like those bracketed below (which are acceptable only to a minority of speakers[40]):

(95)    a. I just don't know [*whether* **that** they will have the same attitude] (Mark Saggers, Talksport Radio)
        b. It's just a question of [*whether* **that** Liverpool can get their money back] (John Cross, Talksport Radio)

---

[39] There are possible parallels here with the account of subject extraction and *that*-trace effects developed in Rizzi & Shlonsky (2007) and Rizzi (2014a), under which the Subject Criterion requirement for a SUBJ constituent to be locally c-commanded by a nominal can be satisfied (via a local head–head relation) by a nominal FIN head which locally c-commands SUBJ: see the relevant discussion in §1.5.

[40] An experimental study by Radford, Boxell & Felser (2014) reported a low acceptability rate of 27.77% for *whether+that* structures on a speeded binary judgement task.

   c. I'm not sure [*whether* **that** Spurs fans will accept him] (John Cross, Talksport Radio)

   d. I do wonder [*whether* **that** their squad lacks the depth of City's] (Dominic Fyfield, Talksport Radio)

   e. England have enforced the follow-on. [*Whether* **that** they could have done it had it not been raining], I'm not sure (Jack Bannister, Talksport Radio)

   f. I just wondered [*whether* **that** as a next step we might look to see why this seems to be the case] (van Gelderen 2009)

   g. It's not clear, though, [*if* **that** they're just infecting the microbes that make us sick] (Carl Zimmer, BBC Radio 5)

If *whether/if* are complementisers (as argued in Radford 2016: 89–95) and if their criterial position is the head INT position of INTP (as argued by Rizzi 2001 in relation to their Italian counterpart *se*), the complement clause in (95a) will have a peripheral structure along the following lines (where *Op* is a null yes-no question operator):

(96)   I just don't know [$_{FORCEP}$ [$_{FORCE}$ ø] [$_{INTP}$ *Op* [$_{INT}$ whether] [$_{FINP}$ [$_{FIN}$ that] they will have the same attitude]]]

The parameterised secondary *that*-spellout condition in (94ii) will then correctly predict that varieties which allow a wh-constituent to license secondary *that* but impose the edgemate condition will not allow FIN to be lexicalised as *that* in (96) because *whether* and *that* are on the edge of different projections; however, minority varieties which don't impose the edgemate condition will indeed allow FIN to be spelled out as *that* in such cases.[41]

---

[41] However, it seems that there are speakers who accept *who+that* while rejecting *whether+that*. For example, Henry (1995) reports the following judgements for Belfast English:

   (i)   The man on the door asked her [*who* **that** she had come to see] (Henry 1995: 89)

   (ii)  *I don't know [*whether* **that** he's going] (Henry 1995: 88)

It would appear that in the relevant variety, a wh-operator (but not a yes-no question complementiser) can license secondary *that* – or alternatively, that (ii) is ruled out by a constraint against complementiser iteration.

An interesting question arising in relation to (95f) is what peripheral head is lexicalised as *that*. If we take the adjunct *as a next step* to be the specifier of a MODP projection, and if we adopt the FINP recursion analysis of Rizzi (2014a) and suppose that there is a vacuous FINP below MODP, (95f) will have the structure in (iii) below:

   (iii)  [$_{FORCEP}$ [$_{FORCE}$ ø] [$_{INTP}$ *Op* [$_{INT}$ whether] [$_{FINP}$ [$_{FIN}$ that] [$_{MODP}$ as a next step [$_{MOD}$ ø] [$_{FINP}$ [$_{FIN}$ ø] [$_{TP}$ we [$_{T}$ might] look to see why this seems to be the case]]]]]]

An alternative possibility (which does without FINP recursion) would be to suppose that there is only one FINP projection in (iii), namely the higher one whose head is lexicalised as *that*.

To summarise: in this section, we have seen that there is widespread use of WH+COMP structures in embedded clauses, but that in most varieties of English this is subject to a constraint to the effect that the wh-constituent must be a wh-phrase, not a wh-word. I noted, nevertheless, that some minority varieties allow WH+COMP structures even where the wh-constituent is a word, and suggested that this may be because the secondary complementiser spellout rule in embedded clauses is parameterised with respect to whether or not *that* can only be used where it is on the edge of the same peripheral projection as the wh-constituent. In the next section, I go on to argue that there is also parametric variation with respect to the use of complementisers in root clauses.

### 3.5    Complementisers in Root Clauses

So far, all the structures we have looked at have involved the use of the complementiser *that* in embedded clauses. However, in this section, I will argue that there are (hitherto largely unreported) cases where complementisers occur in certain types of root clause in colloquial English: these include focus structures, topic structures, exclamatives, comparative correlatives and clauses beginning with an adverbial.

A case in point are the following structures from my broadcast English data, in which an italicised focused constituent precedes the complementiser *that* in what would appear to be a root clause:

(97)     a. He passes the ball back to Flanagan. *Three-nil* **that** his side lead (Darren Fletcher, BBC Radio 5)
         b. *Lap 38* **that** we're into (Martin Brundle, BBC1 TV)
         c. *10.45* **that** Talbot ran (Athletics commentator, BBC2 TV = 'Talbot ran 10.45 seconds')
         d. *Four and a half years* **that** you said he's been in charge (Jason Cundy, Talksport Radio)
         e. *All over the pitch* **that** Wigan have been doing that (Niall Quinn, Sky Sports TV)
         f. *18 consecutive podiums* **that** Casey Stoner has completed (Steve Parrish, Eurosport TV)
         g. *Another good chance* **that** he's let go (Jim Beglin, BT Sport TV)
         h. *Not a particularly great time* **that** I had in New Zealand (Mark Ramprakash, Talksport Radio)
         i. *Twice* **that** City have knocked United out (Russell Hargreaves, Talksport Radio)

Interestingly, my broadcast English data also contain the following examples of what appear to be root clauses in which a dislocated topic is followed by *that*:

(98)   a. *Santos, who've just won the Libertadores (South America's Champions League)*, **that** they've got a couple of players who are talent personified (Tim Vickery, BBC Radio 5)
       b. *These people who are gifted with those little bits of genius*, **that** they have that about them (Tim Vickery, BBC Radio 5)

Adam Ledgeway (pc) suggests that there could be potential parallels here with the use of a root clause finite complementiser in Gascon after an (italicised) topicalised constituent (as in 99a below) or after an (italicised) focalised constituent (as in 99b) – the relevant examples being from Ledgeway (2012b: 167):

(99)   a. *Ta      pay      **qu'**ey    arribat*
          Your    father   that's   arrived
          'Your dad's arrived'
       b. *Quaunque   trufandèr   **que**   vos   dirà . . .*
          Whatever   joker       that     you   will.say . . .
          'Any joker will tell you . . . '

A further potential parallel is with the use of a finite complementiser in root focus structures such as the following in French (100a) and Italian (100b):[42]

(100)  a. *Trois   heures   **qu'**elle   a      passé   chez   son   avocat*
          three   hours    that'she    has    spent   at     her   laywer
          'Three hours she spent at her lawyer's office.' (Authier & Haegeman 2016: 12)
       b. *Da    venti    anni    **che**   non    lo    vedevo*
          from  twenty   years   that     not    him   I.was.seeing
          'I hadn't seen him for twenty years' (produced by a character in an episode of *Inspector Montalbano* on BBC4 TV)

If sentences like (97) and (98) are indeed root focus/topic clauses, an analysis broadly consistent with the assumptions about secondary spellout made here would be to take (97a/98a) to have the respective structures in (101a/b) below:

(101)  a. [$_{FORCEP}$ [$_{FORCE}$ ø] [$_{FOCP}$ *three-nil* [$_{FOC}$ **that**] [$_{FINP}$ [$_{FIN}$ ø] his side lead]]]
       b. [$_{FORCEP}$ [$_{FORCE}$ ø] [$_{TOPP}$ *Santos, who . . .* [$_{TOP}$ **that**] [$_{FINP}$ [$_{FIN}$ ø] they've got a couple of players who are talent personified]]]

A question which then arises is how the FOC head in (101a) and the TOP head in (101b) come to be spelled out as *that* in a root clause. One possible answer

---

[42] I set aside here distinctions between different types of focus such as contrastive focus (Zubizaretta 1998), corrective focus (Ortega-Santos 2013), information focus (Cruschina 2012) and mirative focus (Jiménez-Fernández 2015).

would be that some speakers have a less restrictive version of secondary complementiser spellout which lacks the restriction on secondary spellout only occurring in embedded clauses and this allows them to use *that* after a peripheral specifier in a criterial position, even in main clause structures like those in (101).

However, while the analyses in (101) may seem plausible, it should be noted that there are alternative analyses which would call into question whether sentences like (97) and (98) are indeed root clauses. For example, the (convoluted) topic structures in (98) could be argued to be the result of a processing error, in which the speaker wrongly thinks that the clause in question is an embedded clause (used e.g. as the complement of 'I think ... '), because the topic is so long and convoluted that the speaker forgets how he started the sentence. As for the focus structures in (97), we should bear in mind that at least some of them have cleft sentence paraphrases – e.g. the focus clause in (97a) has the cleft sentence paraphrase in (102) below:

(102)   I̲t̲'̲s̲ *three-nil* **that** his side lead

This raises the possibility that a focus structure like that in (97a) could be a concealed cleft derived from a structure like (102) via a PF process of Truncation which deletes weak (unstressed) material at the beginning of a root clause, so giving rise to deletion of the underlined string *it's* in (102). The same process would give rise to truncation of the material marked by strikethrough in a sentence such as:

(103)   ~~It's a~~ nice day today, *isn't it*?

where the italicised tag provides empirical support for the presence of *it is* in the syntax. Evidence in support of a concealed cleft analysis for (some of) the focus sentences in (97) comes from the fact that at least some of them allow a copular tag – as we see from:

(104)   Not a particularly great time that I had in New Zealand, *was it*?

If we adopt a concealed cleft analysis of focus structures like those in (97), the *that*-clause will serve as the complement of *is* and we can continue to maintain that the complementiser *that* only occurs in embedded clauses. This in turn would mean that we could continue to assume that the secondary *that*-spellout rule applies only in embedded clauses (as assumed in 94).

However, the tag argument is far from compelling, since some of the sentences in (97) allow a 'personal' tag like that in (105) below:

(105)   Twice that City have knocked United out, *haven't they?*

The personal tag used here is consistent with the view that the clause being tagged in (105) is a root clause (and not a concealed cleft). If so, colloquial English does indeed have a class of focus structures which allow use of *that* in a root clause – i.e. at least some of the clauses in (97) are root clauses.

A second potential source of root complementiser structures are (what appear to be) root exclamative clauses containing the complementiser *that*. Radford (1988: 501) reported the exclamative clause in (106a) below to have been produced by a celebrated Irish radio and TV presenter, and my more recent recordings contain 18 similar examples, including those in (107b–k):

(106)   a. *What a mine of useless information* **that** I am! (Sir Terry Wogan, BBC Radio 2)
        b. Alonso, *what an amazing thing* **that** he did in his home race! (Eddie Jordan, BBC1 TV)
        c. *What a service* **that** that man's given this club! (Ally McCoist, BBC Radio 5)
        d. What an agile and strong and natural athlete **that** he is! (Colin Jackson, BBC3 TV)
        e. *What a legend* **that** Frank Lampard is! (John Cross, Talksport Radio)
        f. Aaron Ramsey, again, *what a season* **that** he's having! (Ray Parlour, Talksport Radio)
        g. *What a run* **that** they're having! (Mark Pougatch, BBC Radio 5)
        h. *What a job* **that** he's done so far! (Sam Matterface, Talksport Radio)
        i. *What an all South-American forward line* **that** Barcelona can now boast! (Tim Vickery, BBC Radio 5)
        j. *What an amazing record* **that** he has! (Sue Barker, BBC1 TV)
        k. *What a fantastic statement* **that** he made in the interview (Hugh Porter, ITV4)

Moreover, the internet-sourced examples below suggest that it isn't just nominal exclamative phrases that can be followed by *that* in root clauses (107a, f being cited in Radford 2016: 459):

(107)   a. *How quickly* **that** people forget! (web)[43]
        b. *How quickly* **that** people turned this into a totally different place! (naira land.com)

---

[43] I use '(web)' to indicate internet material of unknown origin. It is used to denote sentences which I googled when writing an earlier draft of the manuscript several years ago but was unable to find the exact source for when I re-googled it while preparing the final version of my manuscript. I apologise for this oversight on my part, which may have arisen because the material was taken down from the relevant website at some point.

   c. *How well* **that** they coexist together! (web)
   d. *How gorgeous* **that** you look! (abbieandeveline.com)
   e. *How cool* **that** she is! (forums.soompi.com)
   f. *How pretty* **that** she looks in this photo! (web)

On the face of it, exclamatives like (106) and (107) appear to involve root clauses in which the complementiser *that* has an exclamative wh-specifier. They would seem to call into question Zwicky's claim (70i) that wh+comp structures occur only in subordinate clauses.

However, Zwicky (2002: 227) makes two interesting claims about potential root exclamatives like (106a). The first is that they are restricted to use in regional varieties (such as Irish English); in the same vein, he claims that Terry Wogan is 'not only a speaker of Irish English, but a proud speaker of this variety, given to exaggerating his Irishness'. The second is that in Irish English, a sentence like (106a) is the exclamative counterpart of a cleft sentence like *It's a mine of useless information that I am*. If Zwicky is right, (106a) is a reduced variant of a cleft sentence structure such as 'What a mine of useless information *it is* that I am' with the (italicised) copula *is* and its (italicised) subject *it* being given a silent pronunciation in the PF component. If this cleft analysis is generalised to other *wh+that* exclamatives, it will then mean that the *that*-clauses in (106) will be embedded rather than root clauses, and there will be no need to lift the restriction in (94) that the complementiser *that* is only found in embedded clauses.

However, Zwicky's claims are questionable in two respects. Firstly, my broadcast English data suggest that this structure isn't restricted to a handful of non-standard varieties. While it is certainly true that Terry Wogan and Eddie Jordan are speakers of Irish English, the remaining speakers in (106) are not. More specifically, Ally McCoist is Scottish; Colin Jackson is Welsh; John Cross, Ray Parlour, Mark Pougatch, Sam Matterface and Tim Vickery are Londoners; Sue Barker was born in Paignton (England); and Hugh Porter was born in Wolverhampton (England). Since (e.g.) London varieties of English don't have clefts like *It's a mine of useless information that I am*, this casts doubt on Zwicky's cleft analysis.

Further evidence against the cleft analysis comes from the tags used with such sentences, illustrated below:

(108)   What a mine of useless information that I am, *aren't I/*isn't it?*

If (108) were a reduced cleft with the fuller structure 'What a mine of useless information *it is* that I am', we should expect to find the impersonal tag *isn't it?* The fact that *isn't it?* is ungrammatical and that the personal tag *aren't I?* is required means that (108) is a monoclausal root exclamative, not a biclausal cleft. If the criterial position for exclamative operators is on the edge of an exclamative wh-operator projection/EXCLP which is positioned below FORCEP, a sentence like (107a) could plausibly be taken to have the peripheral structure below:

(109)   [FORCEP [FORCE ø] [EXCLP *how quickly* [EXCL **that**] [FINP [FIN ø] people forget]]]

This would mean that some speakers can lexicalise the (bold-printed) head EXCL constituent of EXCLP as *that* by virtue of having an appropriate kind of licenser (italicised) as its specifier, even in a root clause structure like (109). What lends potential cross-linguistic plausibility to the analysis in (109) is that root WH+COMP exclamatives are also found in French (Radford 1989), Italian (Radford 1997c) and Spanish (Hernanz & Rigau 2006).

A third potential source of root clause complementisers found in my broadcast English data are (the second clauses in) comparative correlative structures like those in (110c–f) below, in which a (bold-printed) overt complementiser follows an (italicised) comparative correlative constituent:

(110)   a. *The more rubber* that goes down, the better the car should perform (David Croft, BBC Radio 5)
        b. *The more police* that there are, the more sour and aggressive the atmosphere is (Stan Collymore, Talksport Radio)
        c. The longer the game, *the less effective* **that** Michael Yardy becomes (Vic Marks, BBC Radio 5 Sports Extra)
        d. The more Huddersfield come at them, *the more* **that** Millwall will enjoy that (Alistair Bruce-Ball, BBC Radio 5)
        e. *The more people* that there are around, usually *the safer* **that** things are (Tim Vickery, BBC Radio 5)
        f. *The sooner* that you can get on the scoresheet, *the easier* **that** it will be (Sam Matterface, ITV4)

As these examples show, either or both clauses in this type of structure can contain *that*. It has been argued (e.g. by Culicover & Jackendoff 1999, and by den Dikken 2005) that the second clause in comparative correlatives is a main clause (the first being a subordinate clause). Evidence supporting this conclusion comes from the way in which comparative correlatives are tagged in sentences like the following (from Culicover & Jackendoff 1999: 548):

(111)   The more we eat, the angrier you get, *don't you/*don't we?*

The fact that only the second clause can be associated with a *do*-tag provides evidence that the second clause of a comparative correlative is the main clause.[44] But if the second clause is a main clause, this suggests that English comparative correlatives are a further class of structure in which we find root complementisers. If (as argued by Iwasaki & Radford 2009) the italicised comparative correlative phrase moves to the edge of a FOCP projection, this suggests that the head FOC constituent can optionally be lexicalised as *that* not only in the subordinate clause, but also (for some speakers, at least) in the main clause as well. If so, the main clause in (110c) will have the peripheral structure bracketed below:

(112)   The longer the game, [FORCEP [FORCE ø] [FOCP *the less effective* [FOC **that**] [FINP [FIN ø] Michael Yardy becomes]]]

On this view, comparative correlatives provide further evidence that some speakers allow secondary *that*-spellout in root as well as embedded clauses.[45]

A fourth potential source of root clause complementisers are structures in which *that* follows an adverbial phrase or clause: for succinctness, I will refer to these as 'adverbial root clauses'. My broadcast English data contain 124 such structures, 47 of which involve ADV+COMP structures in which an adverb is followed by *that* in what appear to be root clauses like those below:

(113)   a. *Obviously* **that** the Achilles was giving him a bit of a problem (Ian Chappell, BBC Radio 5)
        b. *Maybe* **that** he's afraid of buying big name players (Frank Warren, Talksport Radio)
        c. *Perhaps* **that** it is a draining season (Tim Vickery, BBC Radio 5)
        d. *Clearly* **that** people are on high alert (Neil Ashton, Talksport Radio)
        e. *Inevitably* **that** there'll be some temptation there for cricketers (Angus Fraser, BBC Radio 5 Sports Extra)

---

[44] Although there are obvious potential pitfalls in drawing comparisons between a particular structure in English and its apparent counterparts in other languages, Claudia Felser points out that in German comparative correlatives like (i) below, the first clause shows the verb-final word order characteristic of subordinate clauses (and in some varieties can contain the overt complementiser *dass* 'that'), whereas the second clause shows the verb-final word order characteristic of main clauses, and cannot be introduced by *dass* 'that':

> (i)  Je    mehr (%dass) du  isst, umso dicker (*dass) wirst du
>      PRT   more (%that) you eat,  PRT  fatter (*that) get   you
>      'The more (that) you eat, the fatter you get'

[45] One way of avoiding the conclusion that comparative correlatives instantiate root complementiser structures would be to treat the complementiser *that* found in comparative correlatives as a separate lexical item (a 'correlative particle'), restricted to occurring in (main or subordinate) comparative correlative clauses. Such an analysis could be argued to be extensionally equivalent to constructionist analyses of comparative correlatives such as those outlined by Abeillé & Borsley (2008), Sag (2010) and Borsley (2011). However, this leaves unexplained the question of why this 'correlative particle' is homophonous with the complementiser *that*.

f. *Allegedly* **that** Spurs were interested in Carroll (Ray Houghton, Talksport Radio)

g. *Hopefully* **that** England can qualify in two years' time (Alan Green, BBC Radio 5)

h. *Unfortunately* **that** they won't have all the players that they had in the Premier League (Neil Ashton, Talksport Radio)

i. *Interestingly* **that** 6 weeks after Martin O'Neill left, Lerner opened his cheque book (Chris Davis, Talksport Radio)

j. *Really* **that** he's at one of the top clubs in the world (Ed Rhodes, BBC Radio 5)

k. *Sadly* **that** he didn't win (Rupert Bell, Talksport Radio)

l. *Sometimes* **that** it rattles people (Tyson Gay, BBC2 TV)

These (and most of the other structures discussed in the remainder of this section) have no plausible concealed cleft source (cf. \**It is really that he's at one of the top clubs in the world*), so how does *that* come to be used in root clauses such as those in (113)?

If (as assumed here) sentences like those in (113) are root clauses, and if we take the adverb to be the specifier of a MODP projection, a sentence like (113l) can be taken to have a peripheral structure along the lines shown below, given the assumptions made here:

(114)   [$_{FORCEP}$ [$_{FORCE}$ ∅] [$_{MODP}$ *sometimes* [$_{MOD}$ **that**] [$_{FINP}$ [$_{FIN}$ ∅] it rattles people]]]

We could then suppose that some speakers will allow the MOD head in (114) to be lexicalised as *that* even in a root clause because it has an (italicised) specifier. On this view, sentences like (113) provide a further source of root clause complementisers.

Nonetheless, it should be acknowledged that there are other ways of analysing structures like those in (113) in such a way as to take the *that*-clause to be an embedded clause rather than a root clause. One suggestion along these lines made by Bob Borsley (pc) is that sentences like (113) are processing errors which result from 'speakers forgetting what they said, e.g. saying *obviously* and thinking they have said *it's obvious*, and saying *maybe* and thinking they have said *it may be*': in such a case, we could say that the speakers mistakenly took the *that*-clause to be an embedded clause. However, this seems unlikely, for the following reasons: (i) *that* is immediately adjacent to the adverb, so it is unlikely that speakers will forget the immediately preceding word; (ii) the speakers who produced such utterances are mostly professional broadcasters who are not prone to dysfluencies; (iii) not all the structures have subordinate clause paraphrases (cf. *It is obvious/\*perhaps that*); (iv) the relevant structures occur quite frequently;

and (v) similar ADVERB+COMP structures are found in other languages (e.g. French, Italian, Spanish and Romanian).

An alternative possibility (suggested by Mike Jones, pc) is to suppose that the complementiser functions as the complement of the adverb in sentences like (113): this suggestion gains potential plausibility from the observation that e.g. *obviously that* is paraphraseable as *it is obvious that* and *hopefully that* is paraphraseable as 'I am hopeful that'. On this view, a sentence like (113a) might have the structure shown in simplified form below (where CP corresponds to FORCEP in cartographic terms):[46]

(115)    [$_{AdvP}$ [$_{Adv}$ obviously] [$_{CP}$ [$_C$ that] the Achilles was giving him a bit of a problem]]

Under the analysis in (115), the complementiser *that* would not be a secondary complementiser in a root clause, but rather would be a primary (clause-initial) complementiser introducing a subordinate CP used as the complement of the adverb *obviously*.

However, there are a number of reasons for being sceptical about the adverbial head analysis in (115). For one thing, (115) makes the counter-intuitive claim that the overall structure is not a clause but rather an adverbial phrase. Secondly, adverbs are traditionally taken to have the property that they do not allow complements, and while this claim is too strong (since e.g. the adverb *independently* can have the complement *of me* in a sentence like 'She made up her mind **independently** *of me*'), it would seem to be the case that adverbs (unlike adjectives) don't generally allow clausal complements[47] – as we see from contrasts such as the following:

(116)    a. He looked at her, **hopeful** *that she would agree*
         b. He looked at her **hopefully** (\**that she would agree*)

Moreover, an even more intractable problem posed by an adverbial head analysis like (115) is that alongside structures like those in (113) where the

---

[46] A related proposal is made by Hill (2007) to the effect that a Romanian sentential adverb like *sigur* 'surely' is the head of a Speech Act Projection which has a null specifier denoting the speaker.

[47] An apparent exception is the following (internet-sourced) example:

> (i)    Why are there stains on my husband's underwear, *especially* **that** he showers right after intercourse? (visihow.com)

One possibility is that *especially that* is a contracted variant of *especially as that*, with deletion of either *as* or *that* required because most speakers do not allow a *that* to be used as the complement of a subordinating conjunction like *as*. If so, *that* is the complement of (a null counterpart of) the conjunction *as*, not of the adverb *especially*.

adverbial expression is a single word and so might be taken to be a head, my recordings also contain 36 structures like those below in which the (italicised) adverbial preceding the complementiser is phrasal in nature:

(117)　a. *Of course* **that** they could do it (Sir Alex Ferguson, BBC Radio 5)

　　　b. *No doubt* **that** in 10 years' time the draw is going to be full of Asian players (Jonathan Overend, BBC Radio 5)

　　　c. *Without doubt* **that** the first game is the most important game (Kevin Kilbane, BBC Radio 5)

　　　d. *Fortunately for them* **that** they were rescued by Chelsea (Neil Ashton, Talksport Radio)

　　　e. *Luckily for him* **that** Howard Webb didn't see it (Dermot Gallagher, Talksport Radio)

　　　f. *To my mind* **that** the qualifiers for the Euros and then the European section of the World Cup are exactly the same competition (Listener, BBC Radio 5)

　　　g. *To be fair* **that** we have to learn from our mistakes (Troy Deeney, Sky Sports TV)

　　　h. *From what I've seen at the start of the Premier League,* **that** Villa will be about 6th or 7th at Christmas (Stan Collymore, Talksport Radio)

　　　i. *With the amount of quality that City have,* **that** they should be in front in this game (Mark Lawrenson, BBC Radio 5)

　　　j. *One by one* **that** those players are being edged out of Spurs (Roy Hayes, Talksport Radio)

　　　k. *In a way,* **that** the style of Arsenal has changed over the years (Martin Kemp, BBC Radio 5)

　　　l. *In the end,* **that** Spurs could only win by two goals (Listener, BBC Radio 5)

　　　m. *Quite often* **that** new players come into a club after pre-season has happened (Andy Goldstein, Talksport Radio)

　　　n. *Last year,* **that** they said he would never be invited back (Peter Bowes, BBC Radio 5)

Since phrases and clauses cannot be heads, it is plausible to take the adverbial phrases/clauses italicised in (117) to be specifiers – an analysis which could equally be extended to structures like (113), since adverbs can function as maximal projections and hence be specifiers. But if so, what kind of head do they serve as specifiers of?

An intriguing answer to this question is suggested by Anders Holmberg (pc), who suggests that root declarative clauses may be embedded as the complement of an abstract truth predicate, and that the adverbial in sentences such as (113) and (117) serves to modify this predicate. More specifically, Holmberg observes that a sentence like (113a) has a meaning paraphraseable as 'It's obviously true/the case that the Achilles was giving him a bit of a problem', and accordingly proposes that we should treat the adverb *obviously* as 'a specifier/modifier of a head meaning "true" which takes the *that*-clause as argument'. On this view, (113a) would have a structure including the substructure in (118) below, if we take the truth head to be an abstract PRED(icate) heading a PREDP projection (with capitals used to mark abstract items with no overt phonetic spellout):

(118)   IT IS [$_{PREDP}$ obviously [$_{PRED}$ TRUE] [$_{CP}$ [$_C$ that] the Achilles was giving him a bit of a problem]]

An important consequence of the analysis in (118) is that the complementiser *that* would not be a root clause constituent, but rather would serve to introduce a subordinate clause which is embedded as the complement of an abstract truth predicate.[48]

However, if (as Holmberg suggests) every declarative sentence contains an abstract truth predicate, the question which would then arise is why declarative root clauses like *\*That it is raining again* which do not contain a modal adverbial are not introduced by *that*. To account for this, Holmberg (pc) suggests that 'when TRUE is modified by an adverb, lexicalised by the adverb as it were, it can be taken to be the main predicate, and the clause a regular clausal argument'. However, this would be essentially an ad hoc stipulation, so let's explore another approach.

Jaume Mateu (pc.) makes the alternative proposal that the null predicate is licensed by the adverbial specifier. This could be argued to satisfy the detectability requirement of Chomsky (2001: 2) requiring abstract structure to be detectable at PF (since the overt adverbial specifier would provide evidence of the presence of a projection housing it); see also related ideas on the licensing of phrase structure in Speas (1994). Jaume points out that this proposal is lent plausibility by the observation that colloquial Catalan allows a modal predicate in a root clause to be given a null spellout (under certain conditions), but only when it has an overt adverbial specifier, resulting in structures like *Finalment*$_{finally}$,

---

[48] As Claudia Felser points out, a related proposal is made by Fitzpatrick (2005), who proposes an abstract FACTIVITY head which carries the presupposition that its complement is true. It is interesting to note that many sentential adverbials can also be used in sentence fragments where they can optionally be followed by *so* or *not* (cf. 'Perhaps', 'Perhaps so', 'Perhaps not'), as in the following dialogue:

(i)   INTERVIEWER: Do you see the riots continuing? POLITICIAN: *Hopefully not* (BBC1 TV)

See Kramer & Rawlins (2011) for one account of this phenomenon, and Holmberg (2010) on responses to questions.

*dir*<sub>say-INF</sub> *que*<sub>that</sub> ... 'Finally, I must/would say that ... ' (where the verb *dir*<sub>say</sub> is in the infinitive form selected by a modal).[49] What lends plausibility to the abstract truth predicate analysis in (118) is that adverbials like *obviously* have been claimed to function as truth operators (see Etxepare 1997: 50; and Hernanz 2007: 26).

However, the abstract truth predicate analysis is problematic in a number of respects. For one thing, if root *that*-clauses with an adverbial specifier contain an abstract truth predicate (so that *Obviously, you don't trust me* has a fuller structure paraphraseable as 'It is obviously true that you don't trust me'), we would expect the relevant sentences to allow an impersonal *isn't it?* tag. And yet, they require personal rather than impersonal tags, as we see from:

(119)   a. *Obviously (that) you don't trust me, *isn't it?*
        b. Obviously (that) you don't trust me, *do you?*

The tag pattern found here is consistent with adverbial clauses of this kind being root clauses, not with them being embedded within an abstract 'IT IS obviously TRUE' structure.

A further complication which arises with the truth predicate analysis in (118) is that many of the adverbials followed by *that* are not the kinds of expression which can readily be used to modify a truth predicate – as we see from the anomaly of paraphrases such as:

(120)   a. !It is *interestingly* true that 6 weeks after Martin O'Neill left, Lerner opened his cheque book (cf. 113i)
        b. !It is *with the amount of quality that City have* true that they should be in front in this game (cf. 117i)
        c. !It is *one by one* true that those players are being edged out of Spurs (cf. 117j)

Furthermore, my recordings also contain 34 structures like those in (121) below in which the adverbial preceding *that* is a subordinate clause:

---

[49] Jaume (pc) makes the following two qualifying remarks in this regard:

> (i)  this construction is only found in non-standard Catalan (and in non-standard Spanish) and, typically, after sequencing words like *finalment* (finally), *en primer lloc* (lit. 'in first place', i.e. first of all) and the like.
> (ii) The infinitive in this construction is restricted to verbs like *dir* (say), *lamentar* (regret/lament), *recordar* (remind), and the like. For example, it is not possible at all to say *Finalment, treballar aquesta tarda* with the meaning 'Finally, I must work or I want to work this afternoon.'

(121)   a. *If it's using too much fuel,* **that** the engine management system will shut
            itself down (Steve Parrish, BBC2 TV)
        b. *When Villa won there two years ago at Old Trafford,* **that** Ashley
            Young and Stuart Downing were the wingers (Neil Ashton, Talksport
            Radio)
        c. *Once he got over his ankle problems,* **that** he came into the team and
            proved to be one of the best left backs in the world (Neil Ashton, Talksport
            Radio)
        d. *Although Thompson has made an apology,* **that** there isn't enough of
            a public statement of contrition (Neil Ashton, Talksport Radio)
        e. *As it stands at the moment,* **that** the Spanish are almost just relying on
            Iniesta (Danny Mills, BBC Radio 5)
        f. *Having lost the title last season to Milan,* **that** Inter Milan want to do
            something about it (Neil Ashton, Talksport Radio)
        g. *Having sold Carrick in the past,* **that** they are not a feeder club for
            Manchester United (Neil Ashton, Talksport Radio)

It is clear that subordinate clauses like those italicised in (121) cannot be
construed as modifying an abstract truth predicate – e.g. (121a) doesn't have
a meaning paraphraseable as 'It is *if it's using too much fuel* true that the
engine management system will shut itself down.'[50] In short, the abstract
truth predicate analysis is unable to handle the full range of cases discussed
here.

Having explored a number of unsuccessful attempts to analyse adverbial root
clauses as embedded clauses, we are led back to the conclusion that they are
more plausibly analysed as root clauses. If circumstantial adverbials (whether
phrasal or clausal) serve as specifiers of a MODP projection, sentences like
(117n/121a) can plausibly be taken to have the respective peripheral structures
shown below:

(122)   a. [FORCEP [FORCE ø] [MODP *last year* [MOD **that**] [FINP [FIN ø] they said he
            would never be invited back]]]
        b. [FORCEP [FORCE ø] [MODP *if it's using too much fuel* [MOD **that**]
            [FINP [FIN ø] the engine management system will shut itself down]]]

---

[50] It might seem that we could rescue the abstract truth predicate analysis by supposing that (121a)
    has a structure paraphraseable as:

    (i)  IT IS TRUE THAT, *if it's using too much fuel,* **that** the engine management
         system will shut itself down

    But given the assumption that a complementiser is licensed by a constituent immediately
    preceding it, the bold-printed occurrence of *that* would then be licensed by the italicised adjunct
    clause, not by the truth predicate. This would mean that the truth predicate has no role to play in
    licensing the bold-printed complementiser in such a case.

Speakers who allow secondary *that*-spellout in root clauses will allow the MOD head in (122a, b) to be lexicalised as *that* by virtue of having an (italicised) licenser on the edge of the same projection.

As would be expected under the account developed here, in root clauses which contain more than one adverbial, the complementiser *that* can be positioned either after the first adverbial (as in 123a) below, or after the second (as in 123b):

(123)   a.  *Clearly* **that**, <u>for whatever reason</u>, the information wasn't getting through on the ground (Transport spokesman, BBC Radio 5)

      b.  *Maybe*, <u>over time</u>, **that** it's getting a little off track (Russell Hargreaves, Talksport Radio)

Given the assumptions made here, the italicised and underlined adverbial adjuncts will be housed in separate MODP projections, so that (123a/b) above have the respective peripheral structures in (124a/b) below:

(124)   a.  [$_{FORCEP}$ [$_{FORCE}$ ø] [$_{MODP}$ *clearly* [$_{MOD}$ **that**] [$_{MODP}$ <u>for whatever reason</u> [$_{MOD}$ ø] [$_{FINP}$ [$_{FIN}$ ø] the information wasn't getting through on the ground]]]]

      b.  [$_{FORCEP}$ [$_{FORCE}$ ø] [$_{MODP}$ *maybe* [$_{MOD}$ ø] [$_{MODP}$ <u>over time</u> [$_{MOD}$ **that**] [$_{FINP}$ [$_{FIN}$ ø] it's getting a little off track]]]]

The higher MOD head in (124a) and the lower MOD head in (124b) could then be lexicalised as *that* by speakers who allow secondary *that*-spellout in root clauses, by virtue of each having an adjacent specifier to license the use of *that*.

To summarise: in this section, I have argued that there are a range of structures in which root clauses allow an overt complementiser to occur after some other constituent in the clause periphery. Potential candidates for this kind of root clause structure include focus structures like (125a) below, topic structures like (125b), exclamatives like (125c), comparative correlatives like (125d), and adverbial clauses like (125e):

(125)   a.  [$_{FORCEP}$ [$_{FORCE}$ ø] [$_{FOCP}$ *three-nil* [$_{FOC}$ **that**] [$_{FINP}$ [$_{FIN}$ ø] his side lead]]] (=101a)

      b.  [$_{FORCEP}$ [$_{FORCE}$ ø] [$_{TOPP}$ *Santos, who* . . . [$_{TOP}$ **that**] [$_{FINP}$ [$_{FIN}$ ø] they've got a couple of players who are talent personified]]] (=101b)

      c.  [$_{FORCEP}$ [$_{FORCE}$ ø] [$_{EXCLP}$ *how quickly* [$_{EXCL}$ **that**] [$_{FINP}$ [$_{FIN}$ ø] people forget]]] (=109)

      d.  The longer the game, [$_{FORCEP}$ [$_{FORCE}$ ø] [$_{FOCP}$ *the less effective* [$_{FOC}$ **that**] [$_{FINP}$ [$_{FIN}$ ø] Michael Yardy becomes]]] (=112)

      e.  [$_{FORCEP}$ [$_{FORCE}$ ø] [$_{MODP}$ *sometimes* [$_{MOD}$ **that**] [$_{FINP}$ [$_{FIN}$ ø] it rattles people]]] (=114)

I have shown in this section that such structures can plausibly be taken to involve cases in which (a minority of) speakers allow a peripheral head in a root clause to be spelled out as *that* when immediately preceded by an appropriate superordinate licenser. The types of root clause structure illustrated in (125) above are inconsistent with our earlier formulation of complementiser spellout in (94) above, repeated as (126) below:

(126)   **Complementiser spellout** (= 94 above)
In an embedded finite clause, a non-verbal peripheral head can be spelled out as *that*
(i) if it is the first word in the clause
or (ii) if it is has an adjacent superordinate (%edgemate) (%non-wh) licenser

This is because (126) specifies that a peripheral head can only be spelled out as *that* in an embedded clause, and so rules out structures like those in (125) where *that* spells out a peripheral head in a root clause. In order to accommodate structures like (125), we need to modify (126) along the lines shown below (where % indicates conditions which hold in most but not all varieties):

(127)   **Complementiser spellout** (final version, revised from 94/126 above)
In a finite clause, a non-verbal peripheral head can be spelled out as *that*
(i) if it is the first word in an embedded clause
or (ii) if it (% is in an embedded clause and) has an adjacent superordinate (%edgemate) (%non-wh) licenser

The conditions in (127ii) account for some speakers allowing structures like (125) in which a root FOC or TOP or EXCL or MOD head can be spelled out as *that* in a root clause if it has a local (italicised) licenser.[51]

### 3.6    The Nature of Complementiser Spellout

Thus far, I have argued that colloquial English can spell out a non-verbal peripheral head as *that* either if it is the first word in an embedded clause, or

---

[51] An anonymous reviewer asks whether parametric variation in complementiser spellout in English is restricted to the three choice points marked by (%) in (127). I think additional data (from experimental, introspective or usage-based studies) are required before we can give a definitive answer to this question. For example, further potential points of parametric variation are identified in fnn. 18, 21, 29, 30 and 41. And (for some speakers), there may be parameterisation in respect of the kind of peripheral heads that can be spelled out as *that*: for example, I myself find structures in which *that* lexicalises a MOD head more acceptable than structures in which a TOP head is spelled out as *that* (especially in root clauses); and I find use of *that* more acceptable after an exclamative or interrogative wh-constituent than after a (restrictive or appositive) relative wh-constituent.

if it is adjacent to an appropriate superordinate licenser, with parametric variation in respect of the licenser (e.g. whether or not it can be a wh-constituent, and whether or not it has to be on the edge of the same projection as the head) and what kind of domain allows secondary spellout (e.g. whether it occurs in embedded clauses only, or in root clauses as well). As we have seen in earlier sections of this chapter, these spellout conditions (encapsulated in 127 above) can account for clauses like those bracketed below (many of which are found only in certain varieties):

(128)   a. Klinsmann is someone [$_{REL}$ [$_{REL}$ **that**] [$_{FORCEP}$ [$_{FORCE}$ ø] [$_{FOCP}$ how [$_{FOC}$ ø] [$_{FINP}$ [$_{FIN}$ can] you argue with what he did as a footballer?]]]] (=27)

   b. It is clear [$_{FORCEP}$ [$_{FORCE}$ **that**] [$_{TOPP}$ high-profile footballers like him [$_{TOP}$ *that*] [$_{MODP}$ if they go out clubbing till the early hours of the morning [$_{MOD}$ *that*] [$_{FINP}$ [$_{FIN}$ ø] they may face a backlash on social media]]]] (=50b)

   c. I wonder [$_{FORCEP}$ [$_{FORCE}$ ø] [$_{WHP}$ how often [$_{WH}$ *that*] [$_{MODP}$ in times when money is in short supply [$_{MOD}$ *that*] [$_{FINP}$ [$_{FIN}$ ø] governments raise taxes on the poor]]]] (cf. 64)

   d. I just don't know [$_{FORCEP}$ [$_{FORCE}$ ø] [$_{INTP}$ *Op* [$_{INT}$ whether] [$_{FINP}$ [$_{FIN}$ *that*] they will have the same attitude]]] (=96)

In such structures, the primary *that*-spellout condition (127i) licenses the use of the bold-printed clause-initial complementisers, and the parameterised secondary *that*-spellout conditions in (127ii) license the use of the italicised non-initial complementisers (in relevant varieties).

An interesting assumption implicit in the formulation of the secondary *that*-spellout conditions in (127ii) is that use of *that* as a secondary (non-initial) complementiser is licensed locally, and not at a distance. To see what this means, consider the structure of the clauses bracketed below:

(129)   a. There's some unclarity as to [*whether*, if they go into administration, **that** they will get a 9-point penalty] (Simon Jordan, BBC Radio 5)

   b. I'm not sure [*whether*, if they go down that route, **that** they're gonna continue to do that] (Robbie Brady, Talksport Radio)

   c. I wonder [*if*, one Thursday, **that** you wouldn't mind coming into the studio] (Andy Goldstein, Talksport Radio)

Given the assumptions made here, the bracketed clause in (129a) above will have the structure below:

(130)   There's some unclarity as to [$_{FORCEP}$ [$_{FORCE}$ ø] [$_{INTP}$ *Op* [$_{INT}$ whether] [$_{MODP}$ if they go into administration [$_{MOD}$ **that**] [$_{FINP}$ [$_{FIN}$ ø] they will get a 9-point penalty]]]]

The secondary spellout conditions in (127ii) lead to the conclusion that the bold-printed occurrence of *that* in (130) is locally licensed by the immediately preceding *if*-clause. However, an alternative possibility is that use of *that* in (130) might instead be licensed at a distance by the complementiser *whether* (i.e. *that* might be licensed by *whether* even though *whether* does not immediately precede *that*): this could be the case, for example, if *whether* allows any peripheral head that it c-commands to be spelled out as *that* (perhaps via an appropriate form of selection, agreement or downward feature percolation). However, licensing at a distance is problematic for speakers like me who don't allow sentences like (95) in which *whether/if* immediately precedes *that* (suggesting that *whether/if* do not license use of a following *that*), but do allow sentences like (129) in which some (underlined) constituent intervenes between the two (suggesting that it is this intervening constituent which licenses use of *that*).

Indeed, it might be possible to go further and specify that all complementisers require local licensing – not just secondary ones, but also primary ones. To illustrate how this might work, consider a structure such as (50b/128b) above, repeated as (131) below:

(131)　It is clear [$_{FORCEP}$ [$_{FORCE}$ **that**] [$_{TOPP}$ high-profile footballers like him [$_{TOP}$ *that*] [$_{MODP}$ if they go out clubbing till the early hours of the morning [$_{MOD}$ *that*] [$_{FINP}$ [$_{FIN}$ ø] they may face a backlash on social media]]]]

Here, the bold-printed occurrence of *that* is externally licensed via a local (head–complement) selection relation between a predicate (*clear*) which is external to the periphery of the complement clause and its FORCEP complement. By contrast, the italicised occurrences are internally licensed by a local clause-internal relation between a TOP/MOD head and its specifier.[52] The assumption that a complementiser like *that* must be locally licensed by

---

[52] This might involve an abstract form of spec–head agreement between two constituents positioned internally within the periphery of the relevant clause. One problem with this spec–head agreement story, however, is posed by Sluicing (i.e. deletion of the material marked by strikethrough below) in a sentence such as the following:

　　(i)　I know he's devised a plan, but I've no idea *what kind of plan* (\*that) ~~he has devised~~

If relevant kinds of functional head can license ellipsis of their complement when they agree with their specifier (Lobeck 1990; Saito & Murasugi 1990), we would (wrongly) expect *that* to be able to license Sluicing in (i) if it agrees with its wh-specifier. One seeming way round this problem might be to posit a Stranding Constraint like that proposed in Radford (2016: 143) to the effect that an overt complementiser like *that* can't be stranded, whether by movement or ellipsis of its complement – perhaps because the parsing function of an overt complementiser is to signal an upcoming overt clausal projection.

a superordinate constituent would account for why (even in varieties which allow secondary complementisers in root clauses) the complementiser can't be the first word in a root clause like *That it is raining*, since in such a position it would have no superordinate licenser.[53]

The local licensing account could even be extended to restrictive relative clauses containing *that*, if these have the structure indicated below, where *e* is an empty category left behind by Antecedent Raising of the NP *picture of himself*, after it 'has raised to spec-CP' (Kayne 1994: 86):

(132)   [DP [D the] [CP *picture of himself* [C **that**] Bill saw *e*]]

On this account, the occurrence of *that* in C is locally licenced by its specifier *picture of himself*.[54]

---

[53] Sentences like the following (which might at first sight appear to be root clauses introduced by *that*) are apparent exceptions to the claim that the complementiser *that* can't be used in a root clause because it would have no local c-commanding licenser:

  (i)   That he should have done such a thing!
  (ii)  That I should apologise unreservedly (used in reply to 'What did he say?')

However, (i) may be an elliptical variant of a structure like (iii) below, and (ii) may be a reduced form of (iv), with the capitalised material in both cases being present in the syntax but having a null spellout at PF:

  (iii)  IT IS AMAZING that he should have done such a thing!
  (iv)   HE SAID that I should apologise unreservedly

If so, the structures in (i) and (ii) are embedded clauses, with the complementiser *that* licensed via a local selection relation with an abstract superordinate predicate (AMAZING/SAID). However, such an analysis would seemingly run into problems if we adopted the claim made by Ross (1970) that all declarative root clauses are embedded as the complement of an abstract predicate like SAY, since then we would expect a root clause like *That it is raining* to be grammatical (since, by hypothesis, it is the complement of a root clause like I HEREBY SAY TO YOU . . . ).

A further potential problem for the local licensing requirement is posed by dislocated topic clauses like that italicised below:

  (v)   *That 1% of the population owns 90% of the world's resources*, I heard (it) in a documentary

One way of defending the local licensing account of complementiser use in relation to (v) would be to suppose that the topic clause at some level is the complement of (and locally licensed by) the verb *hear*. Another would be to suppose that it is the complement of (and hence licensed by) a light noun such as FACT or PROPOSITION, so that the dislocated clause is a DP of the form THE FACT/PROPOSITION that . . . In such a case, it may be that the complementiser has to be overt in (v) because its licenser is null.

[54] A problem with the local licensing account is that some speakers don't allow secondary spellout, and yet all allow relative clauses like (132). A further potential problem is posed by sentences such as the following:

An intriguing question arising from the spellout conditions in (127) is how a single lexical item (*that*) can lexicalise a multiplicity of different heads in the periphery of a finite clause, and how clauses can contain multiple occurrences of *that*. An interesting attempt to provide a principled syntactic answer to this question is found in work on Southern Italian dialects by Adam Ledgeway (esp. Ledgeway 2000, 2005), and in parallel work on Greek by Roussou (2000). Ledgeway proposes that (the Southern Italian counterpart of) the complementiser *that* in a finite clause originates in FIN (by virtue of marking finiteness) and from there moves into the highest head in the periphery (e.g. the FORCE head marking declarative force in declarative complement clauses). He further supposes that (in consequence of the Head Movement Constraint of Travis 1984), movement of *that* from the lowest to the highest head in the periphery proceeds in a successive-cyclic fashion, transiting through any intervening peripheral heads, with each individual step in the movement being driven by the need to check a finiteness, topic, focus, or force (etc.) feature. He also supposes that more than one copy of a moved complementiser can be overtly spelled out in the relevant head-movement chain.

Rizzi & Shlonsky (2007: 32) extend the complementiser movement analysis to English, claiming that 'the normal derivation of a *that* clause is one in which *that* is first merged in Fin, to express finiteness, and then moves to Force to check the Force feature': see also the related claim by Rizzi (2014a: 30) that the complementiser '*that* is externally merged in Fin and then moved to Force'. We can illustrate how such an analysis would work by considering the derivation of complement clause in (131) above, which (under the Head Movement analysis) will involve the movement operation arrowed below:

---

(i)   It just shows **that**, *you know,* that they have to pass the time (Iain Carter, BBC Radio 5)
(ii)  I think **that**, *you know,* that it will stand them in good stead (Gary Neville, Sky Sports TV)
(iii) Are you worried now though **that**, *Gary,* that some people might categorise you a little bit, particularly in boardrooms? (Pat Murphy, BBC Radio 5)

On the local licensing account, the secondary (underlined) occurrences of *that* will be licensed by the intervening (italicised) parenthetical phrase in (i) and (ii) and by the intervening (italicised) vocative in (iii). But if (for example) vocatives can license secondary use of *that*, we would expect that speakers who allow secondary use of complementisers in root clauses will produce root clauses like:

(iv)  *\*John,* that you need to make an appointment with the dentist

However, I am aware of no attested examples of such structures. There are a number of ways of dealing with this problem (e.g. supposing that parentheticals are inserted late in the derivation or that they are transparent for selectional purposes), but I will keep an open mind on this issue.

(133)

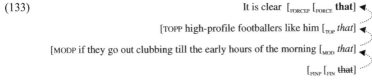

It is clear [FORCEP [FORCE **that**] ◄

[TOPP high-profile footballers like him [TOP *that*] ◄

[MODP if they go out clubbing till the early hours of the morning [MOD *that*] ◄

[FINP [FIN ~~that~~] 

[TP they [T may] face a backlash on social media]]]]]

The complementiser *that* will originate in FIN at the foot of the periphery, and from there move (in successive-cyclic steps) first from FIN into MOD, then from MOD into TOP, and finally from TOP into FORCE. To account for the data on colloquial English described here, we might suppose that each copy of the moved complementiser can (in principle) receive either an overt or a null spellout at PF, albeit independent factors will block certain spellout choices: for example, the FIN head in (133) cannot be spelled out as *that* if the MOD head is also spelled out as *that*, since this would result in a *that+that* string which would violate McCloskey's (1992) constraint against complementiser iteration – a constraint which may be a specific instance of a broader constraint 'blocking head reduplication' (Rizzi 2014a: 31), or of an even more general constraint blocking iteration of like constituents (Radford 1979).

The Head Movement analysis is potentially attractive in several respects. For one thing, it provides a principled account of why a range of different peripheral heads all come to be spelled out as *that*, rather than (e.g.) MOD being spelled out as one item, TOP as another, FORCE as yet another and so on. Furthermore, it accounts for the observation that each of the different heads through which the movement transits can be spelled out as *that* and not (e.g.) only the TOP head. Both of these properties can be given a principled account if Head Movement is a copying operation that applies in a successive-cyclic fashion.

Moreover, we have independent empirical support for the idea that Head Movement can involve copying from two sources. One involves clauses such as those bracketed below which potentially involve copying of other complementisers (interrogative *if/whether*, factive *how* and infinitival *for*):[55]

(134)  a. I wonder [**if**, given time, *if* Ramirez can fulfil that sort of role for the club] (Tim Vickery, BBC Radio 5)
   b. I wanted to know [**whether** in such a situation, *whether* it could adversely affect my LLM application . . .] (llm-guide.com)
   c. He remembered [**how** whenever he heard the slightest whimper from Gabriel's bed *how* he would be at his side in an instant] (fanfiction.net)

---

[55] I say such examples 'potentially' involve complementiser copying because (as I point out later), they could alternatively be taken to be sporadic production errors.

d. [**For** in any way, *for* any parts of Parks and Rec to be represented here would be really, really cool] (smithsonianmag.com)

A second piece of independent evidence for treating Head Movement as a copying operation is that (as observed by Guasti et al. 1995, and Hiramatsu 2003), Auxiliary Inversion can give rise to instances of auxiliary copying in Child English sentences like those below (from Guasti et al. 1995):

(135)   a. Why *could* Snoopy *could*n't fit in the boat? (Kathy 4;0)
        b. What *did* he *did*n't wanna bring to school? (Darrell 4;1)

Thus, at first sight, the Head Movement analysis sketched in (133) would appear to be both empirically and theoretically well grounded.

However, closer inspection reveals potential theoretical shortcomings in the copying analysis of multiple complementiser spellout. For example, if one of the functions of *that* in (133) is to serve as a topic particle, we might expect *that* to move from FIN to TOP, but thereafter to remain frozen in place in TOP (and not to move into FORCE) in consequence of the Criterial Freezing Condition (Rizzi (2005, 2014a; Rizzi & Shlonsky 2006, 2007), which specifies that a constituent is frozen in place once it reaches its criterial position. We would reach a similar conclusion if we adopted a related constraint proposed by Bošković (2008b) to the effect that a constituent is frozen in place after feature-checking.

Furthermore, if we take lower occurrences of *that* to be the overt spellout of intermediate copies left behind by movement of *that* from FIN to FORCE, we have to ask how these intermediate copies come to receive an overt spellout. After all, the general assumption about spellout is that only the highest copy of a moved constituent is overtly spelled out, and that lower copies obligatorily receive a null spellout unless an overt spellout is required for PF reasons.[56] For example, if the children who produced the auxiliary copying structures in (135) treat *n't* as a phonological clitic which attaches to an immediately preceding overt auxiliary at PF, the lower copy of the inverted auxiliary will require an overt spellout in order to provide an overt host for the clitic *n't*. However, it is not obvious what PF factors could plausibly be said to require the intermediate MOD and TOP heads in (133) to be spelled out as *that* – especially as they can alternatively receive a null spellout.[57]

---

[56] On why only the highest copy of a moved constituent is normally overtly spelled out, see Nunes (1995, 2001, 2004).

[57] One might conceivably devise a PF story to the effect that in structures like (133), MOD and TOP contain a null affixal head to which *that* adjoins, and an overt copy of *that* is required in order for the null affix to have an overt host. But since MOD and TOP can equally be null, we would then have to say that MOD and TOP can alternatively contain a non-affixal null head. This leads to the unwanted complication of positing two different types of MOD head and two

What casts even more doubt on the copy story is that it isn't always the case that the highest copy of the complementiser is overtly spelled out – as seen in (57) above, repeated as (136) below:

(136)  I think [$_{\text{FORCEP}}$ [$_{\text{FORCE}}$ ø] [$_{\text{TOPP}}$ *Bayern Munich* [$_{\text{TOP}}$ **that**] [$_{\text{FINP}}$ [$_{\text{FIN}}$ ø] they are a team to really watch in the final stages]]]

If the complementiser *that* originates in FIN and from there moves through TOP into FORCE, we should expect the highest copy of the complementiser in FORCE to require an overt spellout (given that the highest head in a movement chain generally receives an overt spellout); consequently, the movement analysis leaves us with no principled answer to the question of how the FORCE head comes to be null in (136).[58]

Moreover, the plausibility of the copy story is also weakened by the observation that sometimes the secondary complementiser is not a copy of the corresponding primary complementiser – as in the examples below:

(137)   a. It's just a question of [**whether** *that* Liverpool can get their money back] (John Cross, Talksport Radio) (=95b)
        b. There's some unclarity as to [**whether**, if they go into administration, *that* they will get a 9-point penalty] (Simon Jordan, BBC Radio 5) (=129a)
        c. It's not clear, though, [**if** *that* they're just infecting the microbes that make us sick] (Carl Zimmer, BBC Radio 5) (=95g)
        d. You wonder [**if** for some reason *that* you deserve what he is doing to you] (ehealthforum.com)
        e. I noticed [**how** after all the bad reviews on this complex *that* all of a sudden there was all these good reviews on the same day or the day after . . .] (apartmentratings.com)
        f. I remember [**how** when I was an Astros fan *that* no one took any of the Astros seriously, ever, even when Ryan was there] (joeposnanski.com)

In clauses like those bracketed in (137), the italicised secondary complementiser *that* cannot plausibly be taken to be a copy of the italicised primary complementiser (interrogative *whether/if*, factive *how*), since the primary and secondary complementisers are distinct items.

---

different kinds of TOP head – one affixal, and the other non-affixal. Moreover, even the non-affixal one has to be quasi-affixal in function, in order to allow a head transiting through the relevant position to adjoin to it on its way to a higher position in the periphery.

[58] We might devise a story whereby *that* is a topic particle in (136) and so raises only as far as TOP, and the null FORCE head is interpreted as declarative by default. However, this would be unworkable for clauses like that bracketed below, where the null FORCE head is interrogative:

(i)  I wonder [$_{\text{FORCEP}}$ [$_{\text{FORCE}}$ ø] [$_{\text{INTP}}$ *Op* [$_{\text{INT}}$ whether] [$_{\text{TOPP}}$ Bayern Munich [$_{\text{TOP}}$ **that**] [$_{\text{FINP}}$ [$_{\text{FIN}}$ ø] they are a team to really watch in the final stages]]]]]

Additional doubt is cast on the viability of the copying analysis by clauses such as those bracketed below, in which a complementiser is followed by a structure containing an inverted auxiliary:

(138)    a. I said [**that** never in my life *had* I seen a place like Bangor] (Roberts 2004: 303)
        b. He protested [**that** how *could* he have known that his office was bugged?] (Radford 1988: 585)
        c. John was asking me [**if**, when the house was sold, *would* they move back to Derry] (Irish English example attributed to Cathal Doherty in McCloskey 2006: 105)

Under the account of Subject-Auxiliary Inversion in Rizzi (1997), the auxiliary *had* in (138a) moves in a successive-cyclic fashion from the head T position of TP, through the head FIN position of FINP, into the head FOC position of a peripheral focus phrase projection housing the focused negative operator expression *never in my life*, thereby satisfying the Focus Criterion of Rizzi (1996) and forming the italicised Head-Movement chain in (139) below:[59]

(139)    I said [$_{FORCEP}$ [$_{FORCE}$ **that**] [$_{FOCP}$ never in my life [$_{FOC}$ *had*] [$_{FINP}$ [$_{FIN}$ *had*] [$_{TP}$ I [$_T$ *had*] seen a place like Bangor]]]]

Since FIN and FOC are occupied by copies of *had*, it is hard to see how the complementiser *that* could originate in FIN, and also undergo movement through FOC into FORCE in such structures. For one thing, *that* can only occupy a non-verbal head position, whereas conversely an inverted auxiliary can only occupy a verbal head position: this means that FOC and FIN have to be non-verbal in order for *that* to move into them, but at the same time must be verbal in order for the auxiliary to move into them – a contradiction which would lead to a feature conflict causing the derivation to crash.

Moreover, any such movement would violate a PF constraint which bars an inhospitable item like *that* (i.e. a free morpheme which does not serve as a host for other items to adjoin to in the syntax) from attracting a subjacent auxiliary to adjoin to it. Furthermore, even if *had* were to adjoin to *that* in FIN, we would expect the two to move together as a single unit thereafter (in much the same was as clitics in clusters do), not to move together as far as FOC and then for *that* to move into FORCE on its own – in violation of a constraint proposed by Chomsky (2001: 10) to the effect that 'Excorporation is disallowed.' Even if there were to be Excorporation (as

---

[59] I set aside here the tangential issue (discussed in §2.7) of whether the auxiliary does indeed raise as far as FOC, or only as far as FIN. This does not affect the point being made here.

pointed out by Adam Ledgeway, pc), it would be expected to involve extraction of the least embedded item (= the auxiliary *had*) and not the complementiser *that* to which *had* has adjoined (see Roberts 2010). For reasons such as these, it seems clear that in structures like (139), *that* must be directly merged in situ in the head FORCE position of FORCEP (a conclusion also reached by Roberts 2004: 303).

Moreover, taking *that* to be able to transit through a MOD head in a structure like (133) is problematic because MOD is an inert head which is resistant to movement. For example, an inverted auxiliary is not able to raise through MOD into a position in FOC above an (underlined) adjunct on the edge of MODP, e.g. in a sentence like (140a) below, with the peripheral structure in (140b):

(140)   a. *No work *did* while on holiday she do
        b. [FORCEP [FORCE ø] [FOCP no work [FOC *did*] [MODP while on holiday
           [MOD ~~did~~] [FINP [FIN ~~did~~] she do]]]]

Thus, positing that a complementiser can transit through MOD seems untenable.

The overall conclusion to be drawn from our discussion here is that it seems likely that each occurrence of the complementiser *that* in the periphery of a given clause is generated in situ. However, this still leaves the question of how *that* can occupy so many different positions in the clause periphery. In Radford (2010c, 2011a, 2011b, 2013) I argued that this can be accounted for by supposing that (for speakers who allow it to occupy any non-verbal head position in the periphery of a finite clause) *that* is a maximally underspecified complementiser which essentially serves to mark finiteness, and that (adapting the analysis of feature percolation outlined in Chomsky 2007, 2008) the finiteness feature (below shown as +FIN) originates on the highest head in the periphery and from there percolates down (one head at a time) onto the lowest head in the periphery,[60] in the manner shown by the arrows below:

(141)

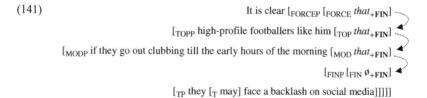

It is clear [FORCEP [FORCE *that*+FIN]
        [TOPP high-profile footballers like him [TOP *that*+FIN]
[MODP if they go out clubbing till the early hours of the morning [MOD *that*+FIN]
                [FINP [FIN ø+FIN]
        [TP they [T may] face a backlash on social media]]]]]

---

[60] And perhaps even further onto the head T of TP, although this is not shown in (141). One implementation of the percolation idea would be to suppose that the FORCE head enters the derivation with a valued [+FIN] feature, and that the lower peripheral heads enter with an unvalued [uFIN] feature which is valued via agreement with the [+FIN] feature on the FORCE head.

On this view, the FORCE head would enter the derivation carrying a finiteness feature, and a copy of this feature would percolate down from FORCE onto TOP, from TOP onto MOD, and from MOD onto FIN.[61] This would mean that each of the peripheral heads in a finite clause carries a finiteness feature, so that (in varieties where *that* is simply a finiteness marker), any one or more of the relevant peripheral heads can be spelled out as *that*.

Radford (2010c, 2011a, 2011b, 2013) further supposes that some of the outputs which percolation gives rise to are filtered out by independent constraints. So, for example, the possibility of spelling out the FIN head in (141) as *that* is ruled out by a constraint against iteration of identical complementisers, or identical heads or like constituents.[62] Likewise, the possibility of adjoining an inverted auxiliary to a peripheral head containing an overt complementiser like *that* is ruled out by the status of such items as free/inert/inhospitable morphemes which cannot serve as hosts that allow other heads to adjoin to them in the syntax.

However, the percolation story needs to be further refined in order to account for the range of inter-speaker variation that we find with respect to complementiser spellout. One plausible modification would be to suppose that not only finiteness but also other features (e.g. force and factivity) percolate from the highest to lowest leads in the periphery. There are potential parallels here with the suggestion made by Rizzi & Shlonsky (2007: 35) that FIN 'carries in some form the specification of its clausal type', so that (for example) FIN in an interrogative clause is characterised as 'Fin of a question'. This percolation story would help account for structures like those below in which a clause contains more than one complementiser of a given type:

(142)   a. I wonder [**if**, given time, *if* Ramirez can fulfil that sort of role for the club] (Tim Vickery, BBC Radio 5) (=134a)
        b. I just wonder, you know, [**whether** really *whether* Arsenal can get a result there] (Jimmy Armfield, BBC Radio 5)
        c. I wondered [**if**, given the same circumstances, *whether* a man such as Bird would have gone on a similar rampage 60 years ago] (*Observer*, 6 June 2010: 25, col. 3, cited in Haegeman 2012: 85)
        d. He remembered [**how** whenever he heard the slightest whimper from Gabriel's bed *how* he would be at his side in an instant] (=134c)

---

[61] An essentially equivalent analysis would be to suppose that there is some form of finiteness agreement between the FORCE head in (141) and all the lower peripheral heads within the same clause.

[62] See Radford (1979), McCloskey (1992, 2006), Bošković (2002), Demonte & Fernández Soriano (2009), Rizzi (2014a) for different formulations of this constraint. But see also Rigau & Suïls (2010: 162) and Villa-García (2015) for acceptable cases of complementiser iteration in Gascon Occitan and Spanish respectively.

e. [**For** in any way *for* parts of Parks and Rec to be represented here] would be really cool (=134d)

We could then suppose that in the case of (142a–c) both the INT head housing the bold-printed complementiser and the MOD head whose specifier is the underlined adjunct will carry an interrogative feature which has percolated down from the FORCE head. If so, both the INT and MOD heads can be spelled out as an interrogative complementiser – and not necessarily the same one, as (142c) shows. Likewise, the factivity/non-finiteness feature carried by the bold-printed complementiser at the outer edge of the periphery in (142d/e) will percolate down to the italicised head lower in the periphery.

The assumption that force as well as finiteness features percolate down from higher to lower peripheral heads offers us an interesting perspective on interspeaker variation in relation to the acceptability of clauses like those whose peripheral structure is bracketed below:

(143)    a. He admitted [$_{FORCEP}$ [$_{FORCE}$ that] [$_{TOPP}$ the comments he made in his interview [$_{TOP}$ that] [$_{FINP}$ [$_{FIN}$] they have upset a lot of people]]]

b. He asked [$_{FORCEP}$ [$_{FORCE}$ ø] [$_{INTP}$ *Op* [$_{INT}$ whether] [$_{TOPP}$ the comments he made in his interview [$_{TOP}$ that] [$_{FINP}$ [$_{FIN}$] they have upset a lot of people]]]]

If both force and finiteness features percolate down from the highest to all other peripheral heads, then speakers who treat *that* as only able to spell out a peripheral head marked as finite and declarative will be able to spell out the TOP head in (143a) as *that*, because TOP (via percolation) is marked as both finite and declarative; however, such speakers will not be able to spell out the TOP head in (143b) as *that*, since (via percolation) TOP will be marked as finite and interrogative, so speakers who restrict *that* to spelling out only heads carrying a declarative feature will not be able to spell out TOP as *that* in an interrogative clause. By contrast, speakers who allow *that* to spell out any peripheral head carrying a finiteness feature (irrespective of whatever force feature it inherits via percolation) will be able to lexicalise a topic head as *that* both in a declarative clause like that in (143a), and in an interrogative clause like that in (143b).

A plausible extension of this analysis would be to suppose that percolation can also transmit a feature giving information about the (non-)roothood of a clause (i.e. its status as a root or non-root structure) from the highest head to all other heads in the periphery of a clause. This has interesting implications for a root clause such as (117l) above, with the peripheral structure shown below:

(144)   [FORCEP [FORCE ø] [MODP in the end [MOD that] [FINP [FIN ø] Spurs could only win by two goals]]]

If the FORCE head carries a [+root] feature which percolates down to all other heads in the periphery, the MOD head in (144) will also carry a [+root] feature. It will then follow that (the majority of) speakers who only allow *that* to lexicalise a [–root] head will not allow *that* to be used to spell out the MOD head in (144). By contrast, the (minority of) speakers who have no such restriction on the use of *that* will allow *that* to spell out a MOD head in root and non-root clauses alike – hence in (144) also.

Thus, the essence of the percolation account outlined here is that finiteness, force, factivity and roothood features on the highest head in the clause periphery will percolate down onto all other heads in the periphery, and the question of what kinds of peripheral head *that* can spell out will be determined by the feature make-up of the complementiser *that*, which varies in a parametric fashion from one variety of English to another (e.g. speakers whose entry for *that* specifies that it lexicalises a non-verbal, non-wh, non-root finite head will not allow it to be used in embedded or root wh-exclamatives). I will not attempt to flesh out the details of this approach any further here, however, since (as already noted) my broadcast English data do not provide an adequate basis for developing an account of individual variation, because by their very nature they comprise a heterogeneous set of utterances produced by a heterogeneous set of speakers (whose background is often unknown). Nor will I attempt to look at possible complications which arise with the percolation story.[63] Instead, I will briefly turn to look at an alternative processing perspective on complementiser use.

There has been a substantial body of psycholinguistic research investigating possible processing factors affecting the use of complementisers. A number of different factors have been argued to play a role in this, including the presence/absence/length of material between the main verb and embedded subject (Elsness 1984; Rohdenburg 1998; Hawkins 2001), structural priming (Ferreira 2003), the complexity of the complement clause subject (Jaeger 2010), and phonological factors (Lee & Gibbons 2007; Jaeger 2012).

---

[63] One such is that while the secondary use of *that* occurs frequently in my data, the secondary use of other complementisers (like *if/whether/how/for* in sentences such as 142) seems rare. It would appear that a complementiser like *whether* is generally restricted to occurring in its criterial INT position (with secondary uses perhaps being the result of a processing error – as discussed in relation to 162–6 below), whereas *that* can spell out a multiplicity of peripheral heads in a finite clause (e.g. for some speakers it can spell out any peripheral head in an embedded clause which carries a finiteness feature and has an appropriate licenser).

However, here I will focus on research by Staum Casasanto & Sag (2008) and their discussion of recomplementation structures such as the following:

(145)   I truly wish [that if something like that were to happen **that** *my children* would do something like that for me] (Switchboard Corpus)

They argue that each use of *that* serves a different parsing function: more specifically, a primary (periphery-initial) complementiser like that underlined above signals the start of a (bracketed) embedded finite clause; whereas a secondary (periphery-final) complementiser like that bold-printed above signals an immediately upcoming (italicised) subject. However, structures which we looked at earlier in this chapter suggest that this account is too simplistic, in that it fails to account for the use of (bold-printed) periphery-medial complementisers in more complex sentences such as the following:

(146)   a. I rang Newbury to say [that, when she was due to race, **that** *for some unapparent reason* she got very upset] (Racehorse owner, BBC Radio 5) (=40a)

   b. I must admit [that, during the Paralympics, **that** *the courage that some athletes showed*, it filled me with admiration] (=43b)

   c. I hope [that when they are adults **that** *at no time will* they forget the work that their parents put into their education] (=43a)

While the underlined primary complementisers in (146) do indeed serve to signal the start of a (bracketed) embedded clause, the bold-printed secondary complementisers do not herald an immediately upcoming subject, but rather herald an immediately upcoming italicised adverbial adjunct in (146a), an italicised dislocated topic in (146b), and an italicised focused negative phrase in (146c).

   Since each of the constituents italicised in (146) is a specifier in its criterial position (in spec-MODP/spec-TOPP/spec-FOCP), a possibility which this suggests is that we could modify Staum Casasanto & Sag's account by supposing that a secondary complementiser serves not to signal an upcoming *subject*, but rather to signal an upcoming *criterial specifier*. Indeed it could be argued that the same is also true of the use of *that* as a primary complementiser, because this signals an upcoming specifier as well as signalling the start of an embedded clause. This would enable us to arrive at a unitary characterisation of both primary and secondary uses of *that*, as having the dual functions of (i) marking the structure immediately containing it as a peripheral projection in an embedded finite clause and (ii) signalling an immediately upcoming specifier in a criterial position. This would account for use of the complementisers in (145) and (146), since in both sets of sentences *that* signals that the structure immediately containing it is a peripheral projection in an embedded finite

184    *Complementisers*

clause. Likewise, in both sets of sentences, *that* signals an immediately upcoming specifier: more specifically the underlined primary complementiser in each case signals an immediately following phrasal or clausal adjunct in spec-MODP, and the bold-printed secondary complementiser signals an immediately upcoming italicised subject in spec-TP (or spec-SUBJP) in (145), an italicised adverbial adjunct in spec-MODP in (146a), an italicised dislocated topic in spec-TOPP in (146b) and an italicised focused negative phrase in spec-FOCP in (146c).

Moreover, the revised parsing account can also account for why (as observed by Browning 1996) intervening constituents ameliorate *that*-trace effects in *that*-clauses like those bracketed below:

(147)   a. *Robin met the man who Leslie said [**that** *t* was mayor of the city]
        b. Robin met the man who Leslie said [**that** <u>for all intents and purposes</u> *t* was mayor of the city]

Given the assumptions made here, (147a) is ungrammatical because the constituent immediately following *that* is the trace of an extracted subject/specifier, not a subject/specifier in its criterial position; by contrast, (147b) is fine because *that* is immediately followed by a specifier (namely, by an underlined adjunct phrase in its criterial position in spec-MODP).[64]

At first sight, the claim that the complementiser *that* can only be followed by a specifier (not by a head) would appear to be undermined by clauses like those below which contain a (bold-printed) complementiser immediately followed by an interrogative or imperative auxiliary (see 20–2 above for more extensive exemplification of these structures):

(148)   a. The key question is [**that** *will consumers* see a benefit?] (=20d)
        b. When you see Spain line up, do you sometimes wonder [**that** *whether* they need Xabi Alonso and Busquets?] (Mark Chapman, BBC Radio 5) (=22a)
        c. He said [**that** *don't* be shy, you can tell us] (fanfiction.net) (=21c)

These might at first sight appear to be structures in which a bold-printed complementiser is immediately followed by an italicised head (= an interrogative auxiliary in 148a, an interrogative complementiser in 148b and an imperative auxiliary in 148c), in apparent violation of the condition requiring *that* to be followed by a criterial specifier. However, if yes-no questions contain an interrogative operator (*Op*) in spec-INTP (Katz & Postal 1964; Bresnan 1970;

---

[64] However, the parsing account will need to be modified in some way in order to account for the observation made by Rizzi (2014a) that an intervening topic projection does not alleviate the *that*-trace effect in a sentence such as that below:

(i)   *This is the man who I think **that**, *his house*, – will sell next year

Larson 1985; Grimshaw 1993; Roberts 1993; den Dikken 2006; Haegeman 2012), a clause like that bracketed in (148a) could be taken to have a peripheral structure along the lines below, if the auxiliary moves through FIN into INT (thereby ensuring that the INT projection is detectable):

(149)   They key question is [FORCEP [FORCE that] [INTP *Op* [INT will] [FINP [FIN will] consumers see a benefit]]]

We can then take the complementiser *that* in (149) to signal an immediately upcoming specifier in a criterial position, the relevant specifier being the null yes-no question operator (*Op*) which occupies its criterial position in spec-INTP. A parallel analysis can be proposed for (148b) if *whether* is the head of an INTP projection with a null operator as its specifier, and for (148c) if *that* is immediately followed by a null imperative operator which serves as the specifier of an imperative projection/IMPP.

   The idea of taking *that* to signal an upcoming criterial specifier has important implications for how we analyse sentences like (35a) above, repeated as (150) below:

(150)   People like Dale need to have confidence [**that** *the kind of policing they need,* that we can still deliver it] (Police spokesman, BBC Radio 5)

Under the account of secondary spellout developed here, the underlined complementiser in (150) spells out the head of the TOPP projection housing the italicised topic, so that (150) has the structure below:

(151)   People like Dale need to have confidence [FORCEP [FORCE **that**] [TOPP *the kind of policing we need* [TOP that] [FINP [FIN ø] we can still deliver it]]] (=49b)

However, the analysis in (151) is incompatible with taking *that* to signal an upcoming specifier, since the underlined complementiser in (151) actually signals an upcoming FINP which has no specifier (and indeed no overt head either).[65] If we are to maintain the specifier-signalling analysis of *that*, we need instead to take *that* to occupy the head of FINP, as below:

(152)   People like Dale need to have confidence [FORCEP [FORCE **that**] [TOPP *the kind of policing we need* [TOP ø] [FINP [FIN that] we can still deliver it]]] (=39b)

We can then take the underlined *that* to signal the upcoming subject (*we*) in structures like (152); and indeed an analysis like (152) might seem to provide

---

[65] One way round this would be to suppose that the secondary complementisers in fact serve to signal that the constituent *preceding* them is a specifier. I will not pursue this possibility here, however, as it is clearly very different from the proposal made by Staum Casasanto & Sag.

a more straightforward account of the intonation boundary after the italicised topic. Thus, the specifier-signalling account offers a potentially promising parsing perspective on the use of *that*, albeit one which requires us to change some of our earlier assumptions.[66, 67]

Now let's turn to look at a second processing claim made by Staum Casasanto & Sag (2008), namely that secondary complementisers serve to facilitate the parsing of clauses which are hard to process. We can illustrate the general idea in relation to (145) above, repeated as (153) below:

(153)    I truly wish [*that* if something like that were to happen **that** my children would do something like that for me]

By the time we have finished processing the relatively long adjunct clause underlined in (153), we may have forgotten that it is a constituent of an embedded clause introduced by *that*; adding a second (bold-printed) occurrence of the complementiser serves as a reminder that the following material

---

[66] The account will need to be modified to handle non-standard varieties (e.g. those which allow *that* in root clauses, or those which allow *that*-trace violations). It may also need to be modified in the light of the theoretical assumptions we make – as can be illustrated in relation to:

(i)  He protested [**that** *what* could he have done?]

If *what* in (i) moves to the head (rather than specifier) position in a wh-operator projection, we clearly cannot maintain that the complementiser *that* signals an upcoming specifier, and will need to say instead (e.g.) that it signals an upcoming constituent in a criterial position. Even this claim is not straightforward, however, if *that* is a REP(ort) head and there is a vacuous FORCEP projection between *that* and the WH projection housing *that*, as in (ii) below:

(ii)  He protested [$_{\text{REPP}}$ [$_{\text{REP}}$ **that**] [$_{\text{FORCEP}}$ [$_{\text{FORCE}}$ ø] [$_{\text{WHP}}$ [$_{\text{WH}}$ *what*] [$_{\text{FINP}}$ [$_{\text{FIN}}$ could] he have done?]]]]]

This is because *that* is not adjacent to *what* in (ii), the two being separated by a FORCEP projection. I will not pursue such complications further here.

[67] The specifier-signalling analysis would also have implications for a clause like that bracketed below:

(i)  John denied [that he was drunk]

It would mean taking *that* to be in FIN as in (ii) below, rather than in FORCE as in (iii):

(ii)  John denied [$_{\text{FORCEP}}$ [$_{\text{FORCE}}$ ø] [$_{\text{FINP}}$ [$_{\text{FIN}}$ that] he was drunk]]
(iii) John denied [$_{\text{FORCEP}}$ [$_{\text{FORCE}}$ that] [$_{\text{FINP}}$ [$_{\text{FIN}}$ ø] he was drunk]]

This is because only in (ii) does *that* signal an immediately upcoming specifier. On the other hand, if we want to say that *deny* selects a *that*-clause complement, this would seemingly require us to suppose that *that* is in FORCE, if selection is a head–complement relation. This dilemma can be avoided if we suppose that FORCE and FIN are syncretised in such cases (as suggested in Rizzi 1997) – albeit syncretism appears to flout the One Feature One Head Principle of Cinque & Rizzi (2008), since it creates a syncretic head which marks both force and finiteness.

is still part of the same embedded clause. As Staum Casasanto & Sag put it (2008: 603):

> If the extra *that* serves the function of reactivating representations that were activated by the first *that*, these representations will have decayed more the farther apart the two complementizers are. Thus, the greater the distance between the two *that*s, the greater the functional utility of the second *that* should be.

They conducted an experiment designed to test subjects on the acceptability of sets of sentences like (154a) below where the material intervening between the two complementisers is short (and comprises only one word), and of sentences like (154b) where the intervening material is long (and comprises seven words):

(154)   a. John reminded Mary **that** <u>soon</u> (*that*) his brother would be ready to leave.
    b. John reminded Mary **that** <u>after he was finished with his meeting</u> (*that*) his brother would be ready to leave.

They found that use of a secondary complementiser was judged to be far more acceptable with a long intervener than with a short one, albeit in general subjects preferred sentences without a secondary complementiser. In a separate reading experiment, they found in relation to sentence pairs like (154) that 'the subjects of the complement clauses were read faster after an extra *that* than after a single *that* when the adverbial was long', but 'they were read non-significantly slower after an extra *that* when the adverbial was short' (2008: 604).

 However, Villa-García (2015: 9) argues that the generality of the length effect posited by Staum Casasanto & Sag is called into question by the observation that Spanish allows cases of recomplementation like that below, where a short (italicised) word intervenes between the two occurrences of the complementiser *que*<sub>that</sub>:

(155)   Ayer   le    dije  **que** *hoy* **que** no  vengo
    Yesterday to.him/her I.said that today that not I.come
    'Yesterday I told him that today that I'm not coming'

It might at first sight seem as if we can draw the same conclusion from recomplementation cases like the following in my broadcast English data, where the (italicised) intervener is a single word:

(156)   Now Alan Pardew accepts **that** *maybe* **that** the success they've had is going to come back and haunt them (Chris Davis, Talksport Radio)

But note that Staum Casasanto & Sag claim that recomplementation is *more likely to occur* in structures involving a long intervening constituent, not that it is *restricted to occurring* in such structures, and hence this claim cannot in principle be refuted by looking at individual examples like (155) and (156), but rather must be evaluated in respect of a much larger set of data.

In this connection, I note that in the overall set of recomplementation (*that. . .that*) sentences in my broadcast English data, the mean length of the constituents intervening between the two complementisers is 5.9 words, and 68% of the relevant structures contain 5 or more words between the two complementisers[68] – figures which might at first sight seem to be broadly consistent with the claimed length effect. However, when we look at bare complement clauses like that bracketed in (52b) 'I'm sure [*behind the scenes* **that** he's got the backing]', we find that the mean length of the constituent preceding the secondary complementiser falls to 4.3 words; and in the case of *wh+that* clauses, it falls even further to only 2.5 words. These figures raise the question of why the length effect should seemingly be stronger in *that. . .that* structures than in other clauses. One answer could be that the length constraint is (in part, at least) a reflex of a syntactic constraint against recursive embedding of like constituents (Radford 1979), with the constraint being stronger the closer together that the two like constituents are. This might also account for why Radford, Boxell & Felser (2014) reported that (on a speeded binary judgement task) subjects showed a much lower mean acceptability rate of 30.76% for *that+XP+that* structures compared to the 67.94% acceptance rate for corresponding bare complement clauses of the form *XP+that* (where XP in each case was a relatively short constituent with a mean length of 2.2 words).

A further claim made in Staum Casasanto & Sag's analysis is that only primary complementisers are generated by the syntax, and that secondary complementisers are 'extragrammatical' constituents added to facilitate parsing. Thus, they remark (2008a: 606) that secondary complementisers will 'not be generated by the grammar under a theory of performance that allows processing pressures to add structures to the set of possible sentences'. A potential generative counterpart of this claim would be to suppose that primary complementisers are contentful constituents generated in the syntax

---

[68] I followed Staum Casasanto & Sag in computing the length of a constituent in terms of the number of words it contains, although I acknowledge that (as pointed out by Stephen Crain pc), this is less satisfactory than computing length in terms of the number of syllables, segments, or seconds. I was relatively conservative in my word count, treating contracted forms like *we've*, compounds like *semi-final*, numerals like *1970* and acronyms like *UK* as single words.

(e.g. marking a clause as declarative in type), but secondary complementisers are expletive items added in the PF component, to facilitate parsing of PF structures by marking the boundary between adjacent peripheral projections.[69]

A related idea put forward by Franks (2000, 2005) is to take the complementiser *that* to be generated in the syntax when it is obligatory and blocks extraction (e.g. of *what* in the examples below) as in (157a), and inserted at PF when it is optional and introduces a clause which is a bridge for (i.e. allows) extraction, as in (157b):

(157)   a. *\*What* did Billy quip [**that** he saw —]?
        b. *What* did Billy say [(**that**) he saw —]?

Franks contemplates the possibility that complementiser insertion could be a morphological operation which creates new constituent structure at PF (e.g. an expletive projection of some kind). However, this seems undesirable both for economy reasons (by virtue of violating the 'Avoid structure' principle of Rizzi 1997: 314), and because it could be argued to violate the Inclusiveness Condition of Chomsky (1995, 2001) and the No Tampering Condition of Chomsky (2007, 2008, 2013) if these conditions bar introducing new structure in the PF component. So, a preferable implementation of the PF insertion idea would be to take *that* as an item inserted at PF to lexicalise one or more existing peripheral heads which do not already contain lexical material (e.g. which do not contain another complementiser like *whether*, or an inverted auxiliary).

A concrete illustration of what this means can be given in terms of a sentence such as the following:

(158)   He quipped *(**that**) the assignments you do in a bilingual class, (%*that*) if you do them in one language, (%*that*) you shouldn't be expected to rewrite them in the other

On the assumptions made in the previous paragraph, the bold-printed (obligatory) occurrence of *that* will be directly generated in the syntax, while the italicised (optional) occurrences will not, so that (158) has the syntactic structure below:

---

[69] See Law (1991a, 1991b) on expletive complementisers. The idea that complementisers are inserted at PF resonates to some extent with earlier work (Chomsky 1955; Lees 1960; Rosenbaum 1967) outlined in §1.2 suggesting that complementisers were not present in deep structure but rather were inserted at a later stage of derivation via a Complementiser Placement transformation.

(159)    He quipped [FORCEP [FORCE **that**] [TOPP *the assignments you do in a bilingual class* [TOP ø] [MODP <u>if you do them in one language</u> [MOD ø] [FINP [FIN ø] you shouldn't be expected to rewrite them in the other]]]]

When this structure is handed over to the PF component, speakers who have a secondary spellout rule in their grammar whereby a peripheral head in an embedded finite clause can optionally be spelled out as *that* if it has a criterial specifier will allow the TOP head to be optionally spelled out as *that* (because it has an italicised criterial specifier), and will likewise allow the MOD head to be optionally lexicalised as *that* (because it has an underlined criterial specifier); they will not, however, allow the FIN head to be lexicalised as *that* because it has no criterial specifier. The precise details of what peripheral heads do (or don't) allow secondary spellout in what contexts varies from speaker to speaker, as we have seen in earlier sections. The general approach sketched here would be consistent with view put forward by Barbiers (2009) that variation is restricted to lexical properties and PF spellout.

An interesting question which arises from the PF insertion analysis of secondary *that* is whether this analysis could be extended to primary uses of *that*, so that all occurrences of *that* (both secondary and primary) are treated as inserting expletive *that* at PF to spell out a peripheral head which would otherwise be empty. After all, a primary complementiser like *that* in:

(160)    He said [(**that**) he was leaving]

is optional, is not a barrier to movement, and is contentless if we follow Bošković (1997) and Roberts & Roussou (2002) in taking C to be interpreted as declarative by default. Even in cases where a primary complementiser is supposedly obligatory (e.g. after a manner-of-speaking verb like *quip*), it is easy enough to find examples of structures where it is not present, as the internet-sourced examples below illustrate:

(161)    a. McCoy can certainly identify with original Tampa Bay Buccaneers coach John McKay, who, when asked about his team's woeful execution, famously **quipped** *he* was 'all for it' (usatoday.com)
    b. Yup, one DU'er quipped they are the 'Green Tea-Baggers' (democraticun derground.com)
    c. GOOD Morning Britain fans **quipped** *they* would turn OFF the show . . . (thesun.co.uk)
    d. Kim Kardashian West has **quipped** *she* would be a better manager than her mother is (1newsnewzealand.com)

e. The Pussycat Doll quipped *she* wasn't on the show when Emily first appeared (thesun.co.uk)

Furthermore, the barrierhood property of manner-of-speaking verbs could be accounted for in other ways e.g. if *quip* is derived from MAKE THE QUIP, with the additional nominal structure creating a barrier to extraction. In any case, barrierhood is not a property limited to primary complementisers, if (as claimed by Villa-García 2010, 2012c, 2015 for Spanish and by Haegeman 2012: 26, 84 for English) secondary complementisers are also barriers to extraction (see the relevant discussion in §3.3).

Setting aside the issue raised in the preceding paragraph, a further question which arises from the PF insertion account of secondary spellout is whether it could be extended from *that* to other secondary complementisers (like secondary *whether/if/how/for* in 142 above). Consider what this might mean, for example, for a sentence like the following:

(162) I wondered [**if**, given the same circumstances, *whether* a man such as Bird would have gone on a similar rampage 60 years ago] (=142c)

Let us suppose that the periphery of the bracketed clause has the syntactic structure shown below:

(163) I wondered [$_{FORCEP}$ [$_{FORCE}$ ∅] [$_{INTP}$ *Op* [$_{INT}$ **if**] [$_{MODP}$ given the same circumstances [$_{MOD}$ ∅] [$_{FINP}$ [$_{FIN}$ ∅] a man such as Bird would have gone on a similar rampage 60 years ago]]]]

If the finiteness and interrogativeness features of *if* percolate down from higher onto lower peripheral heads (including MOD), we might then expect secondary spellout to allow MOD to be spelled out either as *whether/if* (because these can spell out a finite, interrogative, non-verbal head), or as *that* (because this can spell out a finite non-verbal head).

However, there are a number of reasons to be sceptical of the suggestion that sentences like (162) involve a productive secondary spellout operation. For one thing, these are not productive structures, but rather are highly sporadic (as we see from the observation they are not reported in most studies of recomplementation). Secondly, it is hard to see how items like interrogative *if/whether* could be considered to be contentless items. Rather, it seems more likely that structures like (162) are the result of sporadic production errors. For example, in a sentence like (162), the underlined adjunct can in principle either precede or follow the primary interrogative complementiser *if/whether*, as we see from the examples below:

(164)    a. I wondered [<u>given the same circumstances</u> **if/whether** a man such as Bird
         would have gone on a similar rampage 60 years ago]
         b. I wondered [**if/whether** <u>given the same circumstances</u> a man such as Bird
         would have gone on a similar rampage 60 years ago]

Thus, (162) could be the result of a blend between (164a) and (164b), which results when the speaker forgets having used *if/whether* before the adjunct, and (unintentionally) repeats it after the adjunct. This would mean that (162) is not a case of secondary spellout (in which a MOD head is given a secondary spellout as *whether*), but rather a case of reprojection of the INTP containing the yes-no question complementiser *if/whether*, so that (162) has the structure below:

(165)    I wondered [$_{FORCEP}$ [$_{FORCE}$ ø] [$_{INTP}$ *Op* [$_{INT}$ **if**] [$_{MODP}$ <u>given the same circum-</u>
         <u>stances</u> [$_{MOD}$ ø] [$_{INTP}$ *Op* [$_{INT}$ **whether**] [$_{FINP}$ [$_{FIN}$ ø] a man such as Bird would
         have gone on a similar rampage 60 years ago]]]]]

On this view, the (accidental) blend between (164a) and (164b) involves a sporadic production error which results in a structure like (165) which is ill-formed by virtue of containing two interrogative operator projections within the periphery of the same clause.

An interesting prediction made by the reprojection account of sporadic multiple complementiser structures in (165) is that we should expect reprojection sometimes to result in cases where a phrase/specifier is reprojected, rather than a head. And indeed examples such as those below seem to suggest that there are indeed sporadic projection errors of this kind:

(166)    a. Based on your reading about, and your understanding of, the pros and cons
         regarding inventor incentives or awards, **what measures**, <u>if any</u>, *what*
         would you propose to your client or your company that should be imple-
         mented? (Written class problem given to students on an Intellectual
         Property Management course; < web)
         b. It doesn't matter **how often**, <u>if at all</u>, *how much* you use such apps (web)
         c. **How many people**, when they have those meetings and vote on what
         movies get made, *how many people of color* are in those meetings?
         (thybackman.com)

In structures like (166), a bold printed WH projection containing an interrogative wh-constituent is projected to the left of an underlined adjunct, and then seemingly re-projected to the right of the adjunct (as the constituent shown in italics). The fact that the (italicised) repeated constituent is not an exact copy of the bold-printed consistent lends further plausibility to the claim that these are sporadic production errors.[70]

---

[70] However, one can also find examples of clauses (like those below) in which an (interrogative or relative) wh-word is reprojected in a structure where there is an (underlined) adverbial intervening between the two instances of the wh-word:

(i) I can't see **why**, and I've looked at this for years, *why* Lampard and Gerard can't play together (Alan Brazil, Talksport Radio)

(ii) Explain **why**, in the end, *why* he didn't get what he wanted (abramsbooks.com)

(iii) 'If we can put down boys by calling their behaviour puerile' speculated Maria, 'tell me **why** in all fairness *why* the reprehensible behaviour of ladettes and girlies shouldn't be described as puellile?' (Saif Rahman, *Archipelago*, Google Books, 2004: 28)

(iv) The reason **why**, perhaps, *why* we know so little of Shakespeare – compared with Donne or Ben Jonson or Milton – is that his grudges and spites and antipathies are hidden from us (W.A. Johnsen, *Violence and Modernism*, University Press of Florida, 2003: 119)

(v) He therefore could not understand **how**, under the circumstances, *how* he could think that he was not embarrassing the government (*London Daily News*, March 9, 1846, p. 6)

(vi) Even worse, for some of us, we don't know **when**, if ever, *when* we will get this upgrade (community.dell.com)

(vii) When I am on holiday in America, I always eat these pastry snacks called churros, but I am unsure **where**, if anywhere, *where* I can purchase them in the UK (answers.yahoo.com)

(viii) We'd want to find out **what**, if anything, *what* you've already done to help yourself in terms of your depression (resolvescotland.org.uk)

(ix) Schneider did not say **who**, if anyone, *who* he would vote for in the presidential election (inquisitr.com)

(x) I'm looking for someone **who**, of course, *who* has the same interests as me (match.com)

(xi) They implemented the security, they will know **how**, if at all, *how* to crack it (computing.net)

(xii) **Where**, for heaven's sake, *where* d'you want to go? (blesok.com.mk)

(xiii) It's what I need to hear at a time **when**, perhaps, *when* I feel down … (gurusfeet.com)

(xiv) And then she told us something **which** perhaps *which* may come as a disappointment to some of you, but which should not come as a surprise (bayernforum.com)

Such examples may involve some form of backtracking and appear to be different in kind from cases where both higher and lower copies of a moved constituent are spelled out overtly – as in the following example from Child English reported in Rizzi (2014b):

(xv) **When** do you think *when* the girl crossed the street? (Thornton 1995)

Rizzi conjectures that in cases like (xv) the lower copy serves the function of 'refreshing' the dependency. (Thanks to Yoshio Endo for pointing out this reference.)

A related question is whether complementiser recursion is related to preposition doubling in (internet-sourced) sentences like:

To summarise: in this section, we have looked at how complementiser spellout works. I began by outlining a movement account under which secondary complementisers are traces (i.e. overtly spelled out lower copies) left behind by successive-cyclic Head Movement of a primary complementiser (e.g. from FIN to FORCE): however, I argued against this on the grounds that (inter alia) a secondary complementiser is not always a copy of a primary complementiser (e.g. in *whether ... that* cases). Instead, I argued for an alternative feature percolation account, under which (finiteness, rootness, force, factivity etc.) features on the highest head in the periphery percolate down onto lower peripheral heads, with the result that (e.g.) speakers who allow *that* to spell out a finite peripheral head with a specifier can lexicalise (say) a TOP and/or MOD head as *that*. I then considered the plausibility of the parsing account of secondary complementation offered by Staum Casasanto & Sag (2008), under which *that* serves to signal the beginning of an embedded clause, and/or an upcoming subject. I noted, however, that the complementiser *that* can also be used to signal an upcoming topic, focus or adjunct, and suggested we could account for this by supposing that the complementiser *that* serves to signal the beginning of an embedded clause and/or an upcoming criterial specifier. I also looked briefly at a second processing claim made by Staum Casasanto & Sag (2008), namely that secondary complementisers serve to facilitate the parsing of clauses which are hard to process: I noted that my broadcast English data on *that ... that* structures seem to be broadly consistent with this claim. Finally, I considered their claim that secondary occurrences of *that* are 'extragrammatical', and I noted that a generative counterpart of such a claim would be to treat secondary complementisers as inserted at PF, and used to lexicalise (e.g.) a TOP, FOC or MOD head. I argued that such an account was plausible for the secondary use of *that*, but much less plausible for the

---

(xvi)   Edwin Landseer, a famous painter known **for** <u>above all</u> *for* his dogs, and horses, was asked to design the lions in 1858 (natm.wikia.com)

(xvii)  We'll hope **for** <u>sometime soon</u> *for* some new creative problems in life to write about (insipidlitany.blogspot.com)

(xviii) I think I get the boobie-prize **for** <u>stupidly</u> *for* running my lights all that time without having the engine running (st-owers.com)

(ixx)   Any non-US citizen can be deported **for** <u>at any time</u> *for* committing a crime (Google)

It is conceivable that such examples could be handled in syntactic terms (by positing a split projection structure for PPs with the underlined intervening adverbial 'sandwiched' between the upper and lower prepositional projections, or a split FINP+MODP+FINP structure with both FIN heads spelled out as *for*), but it may be that such structures can be better accounted for in processing terms (e.g. as instances of backtracking or sporadic processing errors). I leave these issues open here.

secondary use of other complementisers (e.g. in *if ... whether* structures), which I argued to involve sporadic production errors involving reprojection (e.g. of INTP).

## 3.7     Summary

This chapter has been concerned with accounting for the wide range of peripheral heads that can be spelled out as the complementiser *that* in collo-quial English. In §3.2, we saw that the primary use of the complementiser *that* (in all varieties) is as a clause-initial complementiser marking the beginning of an embedded finite clause, where it can have a declarative, quotative/reporta-tive, relative or subordinative function. In §3.3, I argued that we find a secondary use of the complementiser *that* to spell out a lower peripheral head with a criterial specifier (such as MOD or TOP), and that this is found not only in recomplementation structures introduced by *that*, but also in bare complement clauses whose FORCE head has a null spellout. In §3.4, I observed that there are speakers who allow use of *that* after a wh-phrase in embedded interrogative/exclamative/relative clauses. I also reported that some minority varieties allow WH+COMP structures even where the wh-constituent is a word, and suggested that this may be because secondary spellout of *that* is parameterised with respect to whether or not *that* can only be used only where it is an edgemate of (i.e. positioned on the edge of the same maximal projection as) the wh-constituent. In §3.5, I presented evidence that there are speakers who allow use of an overt complementiser in a root clause after a focused, excla-mative, comparative correlative, or adverbial specifier. I concluded from this that secondary spellout is parameterised not only in respect of the choice of licenser (e.g. whether or not secondary use of *that* is licensed by a wh-constituent or not) and in respect of the degree of structural adjacency required (e.g. whether or not licenser and complementiser have to be on the edge of the same projection), but also in respect of its domain of application (e.g. whether or not it can apply in root clauses). In §3.6, I discussed a number of alternative accounts of the use of the complementiser *that* in contemporary English. I began by suggesting that use of *that* has to be locally licensed either via a head–complement relation, or by a specifier–head relation. I went on to consider whether the multiplicity of positions which *that* occupies can be accounted for under a Head-Movement analysis, whereby *that* originates in FIN and from there moves (one head at a time) into the highest head position in the periphery, with one or more of the links in the movement chain being spelled out as *that*. However, I argued against the movement analysis, on the grounds that this would prove unworkable (inter alia) for cases where *that* occurs in a clause containing a different complementiser (like *whether*), or for cases in which *that* is followed by an inverted auxiliary which occupies (or transits through) FIN. I went on to consider an alternative account under which the (force, finiteness and rootness) features on the highest head in the periphery percolate down to all other peripheral heads, and *that* can be used to spell out a peripheral head carrying a set of features matching those in the lexical entry for *that*: I noted that this would enable us to reduce inter-speaker variation in the use of *that* to lexical differences in individual grammars in respect of the set of features on peripheral heads which *that* can spell out – e.g. with *that* lexicalising a [+finite] head for some speakers, a [+finite, +declarative] head for others, and a [+finite, +declarative, –root] head for yet others, and so on. I then turned to look at an alternative parsing account developed by Staum Casasanto & Sag (2008), under which *that* serves to signal the beginning of an embedded finite clause, and/or to signal an immediately upcoming subject. I noted, however, that this account runs into problems in respect of structures in which *that* is followed by (e.g.) a focused or topicalised constituent, or a peripheral adjunct, and suggested the alternative possibility of taking *that* to signal an immediately upcoming criterial specifier. I also noted Staum Casasanto & Sag's claim that use of a secondary complementiser in recomplementation structures serves to facilitate parsing (by reactivating earlier representations) in cases where a complementiser is followed by a relatively long peripheral constituent, but I noted that the length effect could alternatively be accounted for in terms of an economy constraint against redundant iteration of complementisers (or, more generally, of like forms), with the constraint being stronger the closer together the two like items are. I went on to consider Staum Casasanto & Sag's claim that secondary occurrences of *that* are 'extragrammatical', and I noted that a generative counterpart of such a claim would be to treat secondary complementisers as inserted at PF, and used to lexicalise (e.g.) a TOP, FOC or MOD head. I argued that such an account was plausible for the secondary (and perhaps even primary) use of *that*, but not for the secondary use of other complementisers, which I argued to involve sporadic production errors involving reprojection.

Before concluding this chapter, in the next section I include an Appendix discussing the use of *that* in adverbial clauses introduced by a subordinating conjunction. This material is included in the form of an appendix because there are a bewildering variety of alternative analyses to consider, and this could have led to confusion on the part of the reader if the relevant material had been included in the main body of the chapter.

## 3.8    Appendix: Complementisers in Adverbial Clauses

Adverbial clauses can be introduced by a wide range of subordinating conjunctions, including *after/although/as/because/before/if/like/once/since/unless/until/when/while*. In mainstream varieties of English, a subordinating conjunction (like those italicised below) cannot be immediately followed by the complementiser *that* – as we see from the ungrammaticality of sentences such as the following for speakers like me:[71]

(167)     a. *If* (\*that) vitamin C has no effect on colds, what should we take?
          b. The prisoners escaped *while* (\*that) the guards were asleep
          c. He apologised *because* (\*that) he had inadvertently offended her
          d. She arrived home *before* (\*that) I did
          e. He eventually signed the contract, *although* (\*that) he had misgivings about some of it

However, my broadcast English data include 65 examples of adverbial clauses (including those bracketed below) in which an (italicised) subordinating conjunction is immediately followed by the complementiser *that*:

(168)     a. The reason that England won't win the world cup is [*because* **that** the younger players coming through are too spoiled] (Andy Goldstein, Talksport Radio)
          b. It's important that they have support networks there [*if* **that** they have mental health issues] (Sports psychologist, BBC Radio 5)
          c. Some people were talking about it as some sort of race riot, [*as if* **that** the Dutch team was split along racial lines] (Andy Brassell, BBC Radio 5)
          d. [*Although* **that** they won the title], they finished on something of a low (John Cross, Talksport Radio)
          e. [*Even though* **that** we lost], I'd still put that down as one of my favourite games (Brett Lee, BBC Radio 5)
          f. It looks [*as though* **that** Juergen Klopp has signed a goalkeeper] (Graham Beecroft, Talksport Radio)
          g. It does look [*like* **that** they've admitted defeat] (Matt Scott, Talksport Radio)

[71] An important distinction which I will set aside here is that between central adverbial clauses (which follow the matrix clause containing them, are closely integrated with it, and have a reduced periphery) and peripheral adverbial clauses (which are more loosely integrated with the matrix clause, are often set off from it by a comma, can precede or follow the matrix clause, and have a full periphery). My primary concern here will be with peripheral adverbial clauses, although it could be argued that sentences like (168f, g) represent central adverbial clauses, or even complement clauses. I also overlook the possibility that adverbial clauses may contain a null operator: e.g. *before he gets back* may have a structure paraphraseable as 'before WHEN he gets back', where WHEN is a null relative operator. See Haegeman (2012) and the references cited there for discussion of these and related issues.

    h. And [*when* **that** we were 71 for none], there was a chance to sort of close the game out (Peter Moores, BBC Radio 5)

    i. For many it was inevitable, [*once* **that** David Hay walked into the room] (Mike Costello, BBC Radio 5)

    j. That's been the dominant philosophy in Brazil, [ever *since* **that** they lost to Holland] (Tim Vickery, Talksport Radio)

    k. It wasn't [*till* **that** we arrived at Great Ormond Street] that we realised what had happened (Interviewee, BBC Radio 4)

    l. They're not going to give up [*until* **that** they are sure that nobody else is missing] (Reporter, BBC Radio 5)

For convenience, I'll refer to subordinate adverbial clauses of this type as SUB+COMP structures.

Adverbial clauses with *that* date back centuries. For example, Chaucer uses complementisers in adverbial clauses after subordinating conjunctions, as the following examples from *Troilus and Criseyde* illustrate (where, to save space, I have run different lines of verse together, and quoted only relevant parts of sentences in some cases):

(169)    a. And therfore, *er* **that** age the devoure, go love

        b. An *if* **that** I be giltif, do me deyde!

        c. What mende ye, *though* **that** we booth appaire?

        d. And I afer gan romen to and fro, *til* **that** I herde, *as* **that** I welk alone, how he bigan ful woefully to grone

        e. Now am I glad, *syn* **that** yow list to dwelle

        f. On other thing his look som tyme he caste and eft on hire, *while* **that** the servyse laste

        g. And *whan* **that** he in chambre was allone, he doun upon his beddes feet hym sette

Similar SUB+COMP structures were found in Old English as well (Susan Pintzuk, pc). As suggested independently by Richard Larson, Jamal Ouhalla and Ian Roberts (pc), such structures may be an archaic feature which has gradually been dying out over the centuries, and which is widely assumed to have survived only in some fringe varieties of English like Irish English, where we find examples such as the following (kindly provided by Alison Henry, pc):

(170)    a. They got wet *because* **that** it was raining

        b. I will take an umbrella *if* **that** it's raining

However, my recordings show speakers from a much wider range of backgrounds producing similar structures: for instance, in relation to the people producing the examples in (168) above, I note that Andy Brassell, John Cross, Andy Goldstein, Matt Scott and Tim Vickery are Londoners, Mike Costello was born in Bromley, Peter Moores was born in Macclesfield, Graham Beecroft comes from Merseyside, and Brett Lee was born in Wollongong (Australia). This suggests that rather than surviving only in isolated varieties like Irish English, they have survived more widely and are still in use today by speakers from a wide range of backgrounds. However, my concern here is not with the sociolinguistic variables determining the use of *that* in adverbial clauses, but rather with the question of what syntactic differences (if any) there are between adverbial clauses with and without *that*.

An answer given within the traditional CP+TP analysis of clause structure (variants of which can be found in Huang 1982; Lasnik & Saito 1992: 91, 113–15; McCloskey 2006: 96–8; van Gelderen 2009: 187–8) is that the use or non-use of *that* reflects a difference in the structure of the adverbial clauses. On one implementation of this view, the bracketed subordinate clause in a sentence like (171a) below has the structure (171b) in varieties which allow use of *that*, and the reduced structure (171c) in varieties which do not allow the use of *that*:

(171)  a. He closed the door [*before* (%**that**) he left]
       b. [$_{PP}$ [$_P$ before] [$_{CP}$ [$_C$ that] [$_{TP}$ he [$_T$ ø] left]]]
       c. [$_{CP}$ [$_C$ before] [$_{TP}$ he [$_T$ ø] left]]

This structural difference may reflect a diachronic change from an earlier stage like (171b) (found inter alia in Chaucer) in which *before* was a preposition positioned outside the clause to a later stage in which *before* was reanalysed as a complementiser positioned inside the clause, with the concomitant difference that *before* had a CP-complement in the older structure in (171b), but has a TP complement in the newer structure in (171c). This would be consistent with a wider pattern of diachronic development described by van Gelderen (2009) whereby over a period of time, constituents often move from an earlier position external to the clause periphery to a later position internally within it. Under the analysis in (171), the head C position of CP in (171b) would be filled by *that*, but C in (171c) would be filled by the conjunction *before* (leaving no place for *that*).

A potential cartographic variant of the analysis in (171) would be to posit that a subordinate clause like *before that he left* above has a structure along the lines of (172a) below (where *before* is a preposition positioned outside the clause periphery), whereas a subordinate clause like *before he left* has a structure like (172b) (where *before* is a SUB/subordinating conjunction occupying a position inside the periphery, above FORCE):

(172)    a. [PP [P before] [FORCEP [FORCE that] [FINP [FIN ø] he left]]]
         b. [SUBP [SUB before] [FORCEP [FORCE ø] [FINP [FIN ø] he left]]]

Since the spellout condition in (127i) allows *that* to spell out a peripheral head which is the first word in an embedded finite clause, it follows that the FORCE head can be lexicalised as *that* in (172a) because it is the first word in the clause periphery, but not in (172b) where SUB *before* is the first word in the periphery.

The analysis of SUB+*that* structures in (172a) could be argued to gain plausibility from *preposition*+*that* structures such as the following, found in my broadcast English data:

(173)    a. He talks *about* [**that** making the move from South Africa to England was so hard for him] (Dominic Cork, Talksport Radio)
         b. Moyes seemed to be completely in the dark *about* [**that** this could happen] (Tony Evans, Talksport Radio)
         c. I knew nothing *about* [**that** bats can carry it] (American teenager, BBC Radio 5; *it* = rabies)
         d. We got wind *of* [**that** there was gonna be a big announcement tomorrow] (Dwight Yorke, Talksport Radio)
         e. I think he blotted his copybook a little bit, *in terms of* [**that** whether there was money he was prepared to give up in order to join Corinthians] (Tim Vickery, BBC Radio 5)
         f. Everything is pointing *to* [**that** we have found them] (Interviewee, BBC1 TV)

In these examples, we find a declarative *that*-clause serving as the complement of an (italicised) preposition: this lends plausibility to the idea that *before* is a preposition with a *that*-clause complement in adverbial clauses, precisely as (172a) suggests. Indeed, my data also contain 57 examples of bare clauses used after prepositions, in structures like those below:

(174)    a. People can be quite snobbish **about** [they only like test cricket] (Andy Jacobs, Talksport Radio)
         b. There's a lot of talk **of** [we might run the wets as long as we can] (Martin Brundle, BBC1 TV)
         c. I don't understand this obsession **with** [we've got to have an English manager] (Listener, Talksport Radio)
         d. It just comes back **to** [they've got to explain why they've done it] (Andy Dunn, BBC Radio 5)
         e. Has anything changed, apart **from** [people have kept their mouths shut]? (John Barnes, BBC Radio 5)
         f. I believe **in** [you can choose the country that you're committed to] (Paddy Barclay, BBC Radio 5)
         g. It's just been proven **by** [they've had one good test match in Perth] (Mike Gatting, BBC Radio 5)

h. I think you can make an argument **for** [they'd be top of the table] (Jamie Carragher, Sky Sports TV)

i. We've got to get **over** [we should beat the world at footie] (Listener, Talksport Radio)

j. It's now focused **on** [we have to go after the people who watch the Premier League] (Sean Wheelock, BBC Radio 5)

k. I don't know whether that's the reason **behind** [that's how the clubs have voted] (Nigel Pearson, Talksport Radio)

Data like (174) might be seen as providing additional support for an analysis like (172a) which posits that prepositions can have clausal complements.[72]

And yet, the analysis in (172) proves potentially problematic in a number of ways. For example, if the conjunction *before* is a preposition in (172a), we need to explain why (unlike other prepositions), it can't be stranded by movement of its complement, e.g. in a sentence such as the following:[73]

(175) *(*That*) *the concert took place*, he was taken ill a couple of hours [**before** —]

---

[72] An interesting question which arises is whether the bracketed clauses in (174) have a truncated periphery which projects only as far as FINP.

[73] It might be thought that the ungrammaticality of sentences like (175) is attributable to violation of a constraint noted by Ross (1967: 193) to the effect that extraction out of adjunct clauses in sentences like that below in ungrammatical:

(i) *The deed *which* I want to peruse that contract [**before** filing away —] is probably a forgery

However, it has been reported by Starke (2001: 40, fn. 10), Truswell (2007, 2009, 2011), Chaves (2012), and Fábregas & Jiménez-Fernández (2012) that extraction out of certain types of adjunct is acceptable in German, Spanish, Swedish and (as below) English:

(ii) This is something *which* you should think twice [**before** doing —]

Moreover, it is marginally possible to strand *before* when it has a (pro)nominal complement, as in:

(iii) ?It was a concert which he'd been looking forward to, but *which* he had been taken ill a couple of hours [**before** —]

However, stranding is completely unacceptable where *before* has a clausal complement, as illustrated in (175). Interestingly, my broadcast English data contain the following example of a bare clause which is the complement of a (non-adjunct) preposition being preposed:

(iv) *Carrick might play at the back*, I was reading one or two reports **of** (Ronnie Irani, Talksport Radio)

Moreover, if *before* is a transitive preposition, we have to explain why it allows *that* after it in varieties that have structures like (172a), even though *that* is a case-resistant complementiser (Stowell 1981).[74] Nor do the examples in (173) provide particularly strong support for the preposition analysis in (172a), because there are only seven such examples in my data involving only three prepositions (and indeed they could be concealed nominal structures containing a light noun, so that *got wind of that* ... has the fuller structure *got wind of THE FACT that* ...). Furthermore, it is unlikely that conjunctions like *although/if/when/once* etc. are prepositions, so they would have to be treated differently – raising the question of how.

Let's therefore explore the possibility of developing an alternative structural analysis which is loosely based on work by Danckaert (2011, 2012) on the syntax of the clause periphery in Latin. Danckaert argues that in adverbial clauses, there is parametric variation in respect of the position of conjunctions within the clause periphery. Just as Rizzi (1997) argued that some complementisers occupy a high position in the periphery (e.g. *that* occupies FORCE in declarative clauses) and others occupy a low position (e.g. *for* occupies FIN in infinitives), so too Danckaert argues that some subordinating conjunctions occupy a high position in the periphery, and others a low position. Let's see whether an analysis in the spirit of Danckaert's work can shed light on the difference between *that* and *that*-less adverbial clauses in English.

Building on earlier proposals made in Bhatt & Yoon (1992), Bennis (2000), Rizzi (1997: 328, fn. 6), Roussou (2000) and others, Haegeman (2006a, 2012) suggests that high subordinating conjunctions typically occupy a SUB(ordinator) position in the periphery above FORCE – a position which is generally projected only in subordinate adverbial clauses (complement clauses being FORCEP or FINP constituents). This raises the possibility that the adverbial clause in a sentence like (170a) above could have a peripheral structure along the lines shown below:

(176)  They got wet [$_{SUBP}$ [$_{SUB}$ because] [$_{FORCEP}$ [$_{FORCE}$ that] [$_{FINP}$ [$_{FIN}$ ø] it was raining]]]

Let us suppose that *because* can select a complement headed by *that* in the relevant varieties. If so, the complementiser *that* will be in FORCE in (176)

---

[74] One way round this would be to posit that prepositions with bare or *that*-complements are intransitive, in the sense that they do not case-mark their clausal complement.

rather than in FIN, given that selection canonically involves a local head–complement relation. Potential empirical support for taking *that* to be in FORCE comes from structures like (177a) below, where additional (underlined) peripheral material follows *that*, and this is consistent with taking *that* to be in FORCE as in (177b):

(177)  a. I don't see it making a big difference to my life, [purely *because* **that**, having lived for so long, the muscles have deteriorated] (Hospital patient, BBC Radio 5)

   b. [SUBP purely [SUB because] [FORCEP [FORCE that] [MODP having lived for so long [MOD ø] [FINP [FIN ø] the muscles have deteriorated]]]]

On this view, *because* would be a SUB constituent (perhaps with the adverb *purely* as its specifier), and *because* would have a FORCEP complement whose FORCE head is lexicalised as *that*.

By contrast, we might suppose that in mainstream varieties of present-day English, the subordinating conjunction occupies a lower position in the periphery – perhaps in FIN, as in (178) below:[75]

(178)  They got wet [SUBP [SUB ø] [FORCEP [FORCE ø] [FINP [FIN because] it was raining]]]

This would mean that there is no peripheral head position after *because* for *that* to occupy, so accounting for why mainstream varieties don't allow *that* to be used after conjunctions like *because*.

However, there are arguments against analysing conjunctions like *because* as FIN constituents. For one thing, a key defining property of low subordinating conjunctions identified by Danckaert (2011, 2012) is that they allow fronted constituents to precede them within the periphery of the adverbial clause containing them. For example, the Latin conjunction *cum*<sub>when</sub> allows an (italicised) fronted argument to precede it in an adverbial clause such as that bracketed below:

---

[75] A variant of this analysis would be to suppose that the adverbial clause projects only as far as FORCEP. The alternative possibility of the adverbial clause having a peripheral structure which comprises or includes the double-FINP structure below:

   (i)  [FINP [FIN *because*] [FINP [FIN **that**] [it was raining]]]

would be ruled out by a constraint proposed by Rizzi (2014a: 31) to the effect that 'A head cannot select a categorially nondistinct head' – a constraint which rules out iteration of FIN (i.e. it prevents a FIN head from selecting a FINP complement).

(179)  [*Eum*      **cum**      videro],           Arpinum              pergam.
       [Him-ACC    when        see.FUT.1.SG],    Arpinum-ACC          proceed-FUT.1.SG
       'When I have seen him, I'll move on to Arpinum.' (Cicero, from Danckaert,
       2012: 108)

However, *as* and *though* seem to be the only two subordinating conjunctions which potentially allow this kind of fronting in English, e.g. in structures such as the following:[76]

(180)    a. [*Hard* **though** he tried —], he could not open the door
         b. [*Try* **as** he might —], he could not open the door

By contrast, other subordinating conjunctions don't allow periphery-internal fronting – as we see from the ungrammaticality of the adverbial clauses bracketed below:

(181)    a. *[*His passport* **because** he had forgotten —], he had to return home
         b. *[*Harder* **if** you try —], you will surely succeed
         c. *[*Hot* **when** you feel —], you should take off your jacket

---

[76] On preposing in concessive clauses, see Ross (1967: 406), Radford (1981: 95), Culicover (1982), Meier (1989), Stuurman (1990: 235–47), and Kayne (2016: 2, fn. 2). An interesting possibility which arises if features percolate from the highest to the lowest head in the periphery (as suggested in §3.6) is that the SUB head may enter the derivation carrying a concessive feature which percolates down to FIN, so allowing the concessive conjunction *though* to be lexicalised in FIN. As Liliane Haegeman (pc) points out, the claim that *as*-clauses like (180b) involve fronting of the material preceding *as* is potentially problematic in the light of examples such as:

(i)   *Coming* as it does from a discredited politician, this comment isn't worth much

This is because if *coming* originated as the complement of *does*, it would be expected to be in the infinitive form *come*. Further evidence that *coming* is unlikely to originate as the complement of *does* comes from the observation that speakers like me can use the infinitive forms *do* or *come* as the complement of *does*:

(ii)  *Coming* as it does **come/do** from a discredited politician, the comment isn't worth much

A further type of structure which might seem to be a potential source of fronting within an adverbial clause is that illustrated below:

(iii)  [*Wily fox* **that** he is], Donald deftly ducked demands to publish his tax returns

However, as noted by Danckaert (2012: 103, fn. 9) the only type of constituent which can precede *that* in (iii) is an NP, suggesting that the bracketed constituent may be a predicative NP modified by a relative clause rather than an adverbial clause. If relative wh-pronouns require a referential or quantified antecedent, the ungrammaticality which results from substituting *that* by *who/which* in (iii) could be attributed to its antecedent being an unquantified, non-referential, predicative NP.

Thus it seems clear that while (some variant of) the analysis in (178) might be appropriate for *though* (and perhaps *as*[77]), it would not be appropriate for other subordinating conjunctions (like *because*, for example), since they do not allow this kind of fronting.

Still, one way of modifying the analysis in (178) in such a way as to account for *because*-type conjunctions not allowing fronting might be to suppose that they have a reduced periphery which contains only FINP. On this alternative view, in place of (178) above we would have (182) below:

(182)   They got wet [FINP [FIN because] it was raining]

An analysis along the lines of (182) would account both for the absence of fronting in *because*-clauses (since there is no position in the periphery above *because* to house the fronted constituent), and for absence of *that* in mainstream varieties (since there is no position in the periphery below FIN to accommodate *that* – at least, if we rule out FINP iteration).

---

[77] A first sight, sentences like (i) below might seem to call into question the assumption that *though* is in FIN:

> (i)   [Difficult to deal with **though** *at times* Jose can be], he is nonetheless a great manager

However, if we follow Rizzi (2014a) in allowing FINP recursion structures of the form FINP+MODP+FINP, *though* could be the head of a higher FINP which has a MODP complement housing the adjunct *at times*, with MOD in turn having a vacuous FINP complement. Analysing *though* as a FIN constituent would correctly predict that no other type of peripheral constituent can be positioned after *though*, and this claim is borne out by the ungrammaticality of sentences such as:

> (ii)   *[Disappointed **though** *in no way was* he with the result], Jose still whined about the officials
> (iii)  *[Difficult to deal with **though** *trainers like him*, people consider them to be], nonetheless they can sometimes be inspirational

It should be noted, however, that *though* seems to occupy a relatively high position in the periphery in structures where it does not show fronting – e.g. in sentences like (168e, f) where it is followed by *that*, or in sentences like those below, where *though* is followed by an (italicised) fronted peripheral constituent:

> (iv)   He reconciled himself with the past, **though** *never ever* would he forget what had happened
> (v)    I am generally an easy-going person, **though** *cruelty to animals*, I will not tolerate
> (vi)   We don't look to his paintings for common place truths, **though** *truths* they contain none the less (*Guardian*, G2, 18 February 2003, p. 8, col 1; Haegeman 2010: 642)

However, the claim embodied in analyses like (178) and (182) that the subordinating conjunction is positioned in FIN in adverbial clauses which don't contain *that*[78] is undermined by the observation that subordinating conjunctions used without *that* can be followed by a range of peripheral constituents which are typically found in clauses containing FORCEP, including (as in the examples below) dislocated topics, and fronted exclamative, interrogative and negative constituents:

(183)    a. Herbert will certainly be at this party, [**because** *his mother*, I talked to her this morning] (Hooper & Thompson 1973: 492)
         b. It's easy to forget about Everton, [**because** *what a good run* they're having] (John Cross, Talksport Radio)
         c. We puzzle over it a bit, and then brush it off and go on with our daily lives [**because** *what can* we do?] (steamcommunity.com)
         d. That is why I want a united Europe [**because** *never again should* we have wars amongst ourselves. . .] (otib.co.uk)

Given the assumption made in Rizzi (1997) that only FORCEP constituents can contain topicalised, focused or fronted constituents, it follows that subordinate adverbial clauses without *that* must contain a FORCEP projection.[79] Does this mean that we have to abandon the idea that there is a structural difference between adverbial clauses which do or don't contain *that*?

Not necessarily. One way of translating this idea into a cartographic analysis which recognises the presence of FORCEP in both types of structure would be to take conjunctions which can be followed by *that* to be SUB heads selecting a FORCEP complement (as in 184a below), and conjunctions which can't be followed by *that* to be FORCE heads (as in 184b):

(184)    a. They got wet [$_{SUBP}$ [$_{SUB}$ because] [$_{FORCEP}$ [$_{FORCE}$ that] [$_{FINP}$ [$_{FIN}$ ø] it was raining]]]
         b. They got wet [$_{FORCEP}$ [$_{FORCE}$ because] [$_{FINP}$ [$_{FIN}$ ø] it was raining]]

If we further suppose that FORCE (but not FIN) can be lexicalised as *that*, it follows that only the type of structure in (184a) will give rise to a *because that* structure. (184) would be a possible cartographic counterpart of the CP analysis in (171).

---

[78] It should be understood that the discussion hereafter relates to what I have called *because*-type conjuctions, and excludes conjunctions like *as/though* which allow fronting internally within the adverbial clause.

[79] As noted earlier, I set aside here what Haegeman (2012, ch. 4) calls 'central adverbial clauses', which she argues to be closely integrated into the matrix clause, and to have a reduced peripheral structure.

Nevertheless, treating subordinating conjunctions as FORCE heads in structures like (184b) is problematic. For one thing, it raises (but does not answer) the following question: if a SUB constituent containing *because* can select a FORCEP complement headed by *that* in (184a), why can't a FORCE head containing *because* select a FINP complement headed by *that* in (184b)? After all, in his account of the absence of *that*-trace effects in sentences such as:

(185)   This is the man who I think [**that**, *next year*, — will sell his house]

Rizzi (2014a: 32–5) takes *that* to spell out a FIN head in the bracketed complement clause (as we saw in §1.5), so we clearly cannot exclude the possibility of FIN being spelled out as *that*.

In addition, the analysis in (184b) runs into problems in relation to adverbial clauses like those bracketed below:

(186)   a. I did it [because what else could I do?]
        b. You should keep quiet, [because don't think the Mafia won't find out if you talk!]
        c. I was ashamed [because what a fool I made of myself!]
        d. I went home [because (%that) I was tired]

If *because* is a FORCE head here, the bracketed subordinate clause in (186a) will have a structure along the lines shown below:[80]

(187)   [$_{FORCEP}$ [$_{FORCE}$ because] [$_{FOCP}$ what else [$_{FOC}$ ø] [$_{FINP}$ [$_{FIN}$ could] I do]]]

But an analysis like (187) can be argued to violate a principle posited by Cinque & Rizzi (2008) which was outlined informally in §2.8 as follows:

(188)   **One Feature One Head Principle**
        Each functional head carries only one interpretable feature

The violation arises from the FORCE head carrying both an interpretable causality feature (marking it as a causal subordinating conjunction) and an interpretable interrogative force feature. Or, to put it another way, the analysis in (187) claims that *because* is an interrogative complementiser in (186a), an imperative complementiser in (186b), an exclamative complementiser in (186c), and a declarative complementiser in (186d). To claim that *because* shows a four-way ambiguity stretches credulity to breaking point.

---

[80]   For the reasons noted in §2.7, I have assumed here that the inverted auxiliary can remain in FIN rather than moving to FOC – though, for present purposes, it makes no difference whether the auxiliary moves to FOC.

Moreover, if (as claimed by Rizzi 1997: 310) a predicate with a clausal argument 'selects for the specification of Force', analysing subordinating conjunctions as FORCE heads would lead us to expect to find that just as there are predicates like *quip* which select a FORCEP complement headed by *that*, so too there are predicates which select a FORCEP complement headed by subordinating conjunctions *because*, or *until*, or *unless* etc. However, this is not the case: subordinating conjunctions are generally[81] not selected for by predicates, and this suggests that they are not FORCE heads.

A more plausible analysis would be to claim that *because* is a causal subordinator which can have as its complement a clause which is interrogative, imperative, exclamative or declarative in force. A straightforward way of capturing this insight is to treat *because* as a SUB head which selects a FORCEP complement that can be interrogative, imperative, exclamative or declarative in type. On this view, the subordinate clause in (170a) above would have the peripheral structure shown below:

(189)    They got wet [$_{SUBP}$ [$_{SUB}$ because] [$_{FORCEP}$ [$_{FORCE}$ ø/%that] [$_{FINP}$ [$_{FIN}$ ø] it was raining]]]

In most varieties of English, the declarative FORCE head in a structure like (189) would receive a null spellout; but in some varieties (including Chaucerian English), it could be spelled out as *that*. However, this raises the question of why use of *that* in adverbial clauses should be allowed in some varieties but not in others.

One possible answer is that the use (or non-use) of *that* after a subordinating conjunction reflects a low-level difference in the PF spellout conditions for *that*. One implementation of this idea would be to suppose that minority varieties which allow SUB+COMP structures permit a declarative FORCE head to be spelled out as *that* in any kind of embedded clause (including in clauses introduced by a subordinating conjunction), whereas mainstream varieties which don't allow SUB+COMP structures only permit a FORCE head to be spelled out as *that* when it is the highest head/first word in its containing clause.

---

[81] A possible exception is *like* in structures such as the following, where the predicates *seem/look/ sound* (but not e.g. *appear*) seemingly select a complement headed by *like*:

(i)    It *looks/seems/sounds/*appears* **like** he is planning a take-over

Interestingly, my data contain 22 sentences like (ii) below in which *like* is immediately followed by *that*:

(ii)    It does look [*like* **that** they've admitted defeat] (=168g)

This would mean that most speakers will not allow the FORCE head in (189) to be spelled out as *that* because it is not the first word in the adverbial clause containing it (the first word being the SUB constituent *because*), but a minority of speakers will allow such structures.

An alternative answer would be to treat use or non-use of *that* as a matter of selection (or subcategorisation) and suppose that, in standard varieties, subordinating conjunctions select a FORCEP complement with a null head, whereas in some minority varieties they can select a FORCEP complement whose head can either be spelled out as *that*, or receive a null spellout. However, this would raise questions about the nature of the relevant selection restrictions.[82] One possible answer would be to posit that standard varieties of present-day English have a constraint along the following lines:

(190)   **Complementiser Licensing Condition/CLC**
        In standard varieties of English, the complementiser *that* cannot be licensed by a superordinate peripheral head[83]

---

[82] We might try to derive the relevant selectional properties from independent properties of the conjunction and/or the complementiser. For example, Haegeman (1992: 57) relates the obligatoriness of the complementiser $dat_{that}$ in adverbial clauses (and other embedded clauses) in West Flemish to the observation that the complementiser inflects for agreement with the clause subject, and suggests that the complementiser has to be overt in order to spell out the agreement features which it carries. However, as Haegeman (pc) notes, such an analysis would be difficult to extend to English, given that the complementiser *that* in English is generally optional and does not inflect for agreement. An alternative analysis of a similar ilk would be to take the complementiser *that* to be nominal in nature in Chaucerian English and thus active for case/agreement relations: if conjunctions like *before/after* were transitive prepositions, we would then expect to find adverbial clauses introduced by *before/after* to have a *that*-complement (with *that* being case-marked by *before/after*). By contrast, if conjunctions like *before/after* are intransitive in standard varieties of present-day English and the complementiser *that* is a nonnominal constituent (inert for case/agreement), we would not expect *that* to occur as the complement of conjunctions like *before/after*. While it is clearly desirable in principle to attempt to reduce selection to independent properties, this particular case-based story is problematic: for example, it's not obvious how it would account for *in that* structures still being used in present-day English in sentences like (192a), or for the fact that non-prepositional conjunctions such as *when/although* were followed by *that* in Chaucer but no longer are in most varieties of contemporary English.

[83] I am assuming that a structure such as that below does not violate CLC:

>     (i)   I think [FORCEP [FORCE ∅] [MODP if it rains tomorrow afternoon [MOD *that*]
>           [FINP [FIN ∅] we should cancel the planned picnic]]]

This is because *that* is not licensed via selection by the bold-printed FORCE head, but rather by a local spec–head relation with the underlined adjunct (an instance of the secondary complementation phenomenon discussed in §3.3). An alternative (more general) variant of CLC would be to suppose that the complementiser *that* cannot be licensed by a superordinate *functional* head.

CLC would allow superordinate lexical heads like the verb *think*, the adjective *sure* and the noun *claim* to select a *that*-complement, but would rule out use of *that* in structures such as those below:

(191)    a. She told me [$_{\text{FORCEP}}$ [$_{\text{FORCE}}$ *how*] [$_{\text{FINP}}$ [$_{\text{FIN}}$ ø/*that**] she hadn't been feeling well]]

    b. I wonder [$_{\text{FORCEP}}$ [$_{\text{FORCE}}$ ø] [$_{\text{INTP}}$ *Op* [$_{\text{INT}}$ *whether/if*] [$_{\text{FINP}}$ [$_{\text{FIN}}$ ø/*that**] it will rain]]]

    c. I don't know [$_{\text{FORCEP}}$ [$_{\text{FORCE}}$ ø] [$_{\text{WHP}}$ [$_{\text{WH}}$ *what*] [$_{\text{FINP}}$ [$_{\text{FIN}}$ ø/*that**] she has in mind]]]

CLC would mean that peripheral heads like the factive complementiser *how* in (191a), the interrogative complementisers *whether/if* in (191b), and the wh-head *what* in (191c)[84] cannot license the use of *that* in standard varieties of English. More relevant to our present discussion is the fact that CLC would also rule out the use of *that* in adverbial clauses like that in (189) in standard varieties of English, because *that* heads a FORCEP complement selected by *because*, and *because* is a peripheral SUB head.

At first sight, the robustness of CLC might seem to be called into question by the observation that there are a handful of (simple or compound) subordinating conjunctions (or conjunction-like expressions) which can (or must) be followed by *that* in standard varieties of present-day English, like those italicised below:

(192)    a. Margaret Thatcher is a rarity among international leaders *in* **that** she has a science background (British National Corpus AB6 345, cited by van Gelderen 2009: 182)

    b. *Provided* **that** the weather is fine, we'll have a picnic on Saturday (grammar-monster.com)

    c. It was surprising that the government was re-elected, *given* **that** they had raised taxes so much (*Oxford Advanced Learner's Dictionary*)

    d. *For all* **that** Tottenham are a really big club, this is only their second season in European competition (Darren Fletcher, BBC Radio 5)

    e. He is very much in touch, *albeit* **that** he is 6 seconds back (Steve Parrish, BBC2 TV)

    f. The second half gave me hope, *inasmuch as* **that** Wilshere virtually ran the show (Lee Dixon, BBC Radio 5)

    g. It's a real problem *insofar as* **that** we haven't got a replacement for Torres lined up (Listener, BBC Radio 5)

---

[84] I am assuming here (following work by Josef Bayer and others discussed in §3.4) that an argumental pronoun like *who/what* moves into the head (rather than specifier) position of its criterial projection.

h. The easiest thing is not to talk about them at all, *in case* **that** you inadvertently reveal their identity (Reporter, BBC Radio 5)

One way of seeking to overcome this problem would be to argue that the italicised expressions in adverbial clauses like those in (192) are positioned outside the clause periphery, in which case such sentences would not violate CLC. In this respect, it is interesting to note that (as pointed out by van Gelderen 2009) the *Oxford English Dictionary* treats *in that* as a shortened form of *in the fact that*, suggesting that there is hidden structure here, and that the complementiser *that* is the first word in the periphery of the subordinate clause, and that *in* is positioned outside the subordinate clause itself. This idea gains plausibility from sentences such as the following, where we do indeed find *in the fact that*:

(193)   a. The referee's got this right *in the fact that* it was an elbow in the face (Ian Abrahams, Talksport Radio)
  b. We are all equal *in the fact that* we are all different. We are all the same *in the fact that* we will never be the same (C. JoyBell C., goodreads.com)
  c. I totally agree with him *in the fact that* the good reviews are fake on this hotel (tripadvisor.co.uk)

If so, it could well be that *in that* has a structure along the lines shown below (where capitals mark light constituents which are present in the syntax but have a silent spellout at PF):

(194)   [PP [P in] [DP [D THE] [NP [N FACT] [FORCEP [FORCE that] . . .]]]]

If so, use of *that* to introduce the subordinate clause would be licensed by the light noun FACT (not by a peripheral head), and (194) would not violate CLC. The idea that there is hidden structure is potentially more transparent in cases like *inasmuch as, insofar as, for all, in case* and *albeit*. Generalising, we might then claim that exceptional subordinating conjunctions (and conjunction-like expressions) which can be followed by *that* in standard varieties of English occupy a position external to the clause periphery, whereas ordinary subordinating conjunctions which cannot be followed by *that* occupy a position internal to the periphery. If only an external constituent (i.e. one positioned outside the clause periphery) can license *that*, not an internal one (positioned inside the periphery), CLC would not bar adverbial clauses like those in (192) in standard varieties of English.[85]

---

[85] Clearly details of precisely what 'outside the clause' means in specific types of structure need to be worked out for this analysis to be viable. A potential problem with the 'hidden structure' story is that even subordinating conjunctions which aren't followed by *that* in standard varieties of contemporary English could be argued to have hidden structure (as noted in §2.6). For example, a temporal conjunction like *since* may have a more abstract structure paraphraseable as 'since (THE TIME) WHEN', where the capitalised constituents have a null spellout.

As for varieties which allow use of *that* in adverbial clauses, we could suppose that CLC is not operative in them. In this connection, it is interesting to note Chaucerian structures like those below (from *Troilus and Criseyde*, where, to save space, I have run on two consecutive lines of verse in some cases):

(195)    a. An [*if* **that** I be giltif], do me deyde! (=169b)
         b. But [*wheither* **that** she children hadde or noon], I rede it naught, therefore I late it goon
         c. They stoden for to se [*who* **that** ther come]
         d. And [*what* **that** was his mone] ne wist I nought

As these examples show, subordinating conjunctions like *if*, complementisers like *wheither*, and pronouns like *who/what* license use of secondary *that* in Chaucerian English, consistent with the view that peripheral heads can license use of *that* in Chaucer. We find a similar story in Belfast English, where not only a subordinating conjunction but also a wh-word can license use of *that*, as we see from examples like the following:[86]

(196)    a. They got wet *because* **that** it was raining (=170a, Alison Henry, pc)
         b. The man on the door asked her [*who* **that** she had come to see] (Henry 1995: 89)

This is consistent with the view that Belfast English is a variety in which CLC is inoperative.[87]

Our discussion in this section might seem to suggest that the complementiser *that* is never used in adverbial clauses in mainstream varieties of English. However, Staum Casasanto et al. (2008) claim that use of *that* becomes acceptable when some other constituent intervenes between conjunction and complementiser, and they cite the following (Google-sourced) example:

(197)    It seems *like*, <u>theoretically</u>, **that** it would be possible to travel along in the middle of a tornado and survive

---

[86] However, Henry (1995: 88) reports that she does not allow the complementiser *whether* to license use of *that*, e.g. in a sentence such as:

    (i)    *I don't know [*whether* **that** he's going]

It may be that sentences like (i) are ruled out by a constraint against complementiser iteration in her variety.

[87] By contrast, as noted in fn. 36, my Dublin-born dentist Gavin Barry tells me that while he accepts *wh-phrase+that* structures like (72a) 'I'm not sure [*what kind of arrangement* **that** he has in mind]', he does not accept *who/what/whether/if+that* structures, nor structures like *because that* in which a subordinating conjunction is followed by *that*: this is consistent with the view that CLC is operative in his variety.

And indeed my broadcast English data contain 19 examples of similar structures, including those below:

(198)   a. *If*, <u>as David and Brian have indicated</u>, **that** vitamin C has no effect on colds, what should we take? (Gabby Logan, BBC Radio 5)
        b. It looks *as if*, <u>possibly as early as this weekend</u>, **that** NATO will take over from the United States (News reporter, BBC1 TV)
        c. It looks *like*, <u>although it's not been confirmed yet</u>, **that** they've got their wish (Matthew Etherington, Talksport Radio)
        d. I'm not sure it's a good idea, even *though*, <u>at thirty-six</u>, **that** Beckham still thinks he can play in the Premier League (Neil Ashton, Talksport Radio)
        e. I think that's the route they'll go down *unless* <u>of course</u> **that** they change their recruitment policy (Mick Dennis, Talksport Radio)
        f. There will have to be an enquiry into how the spectators had been allowed to remain in the stand *when* <u>clearly</u> **that** they were admitting they had drunk 6 bottles (Jonathan Overend, BBC Radio 5)
        g. Just *before* <u>in actual fact</u> **that** he broke his leg, he was in wonderful form (Ray Wilkins, Sky Sports TV)
        h. Interesting, *because* <u>Didier Drogba (who came off with concussion last week)</u> **that** he won't play for another two weeks (Neil Ashton, Talksport Radio)

How can we account for the observation that speakers like me who categorically reject structures in which a subordinating conjunction is immediately followed by *that* nonetheless allow *that* to be used in structures like (197) and (198) where there is an intervening constituent?

A plausible answer is that use of *that* is licensed by the underlined adjunct, not by the italicised subordinating conjunction (consistent with the wider view that use of the complementiser *that* is locally licensed by the constituent immediately preceding it). If the underlined adjunct in (198a) occupies the specifier position in a MODP projection, the *if*-clauses in (167a/198a) will have the respective peripheral structures shown in (199a/b) below:

(199)   a. [$_{SUBP}$ [$_{SUB}$ *if*] [$_{FORCEP}$ [$_{FORCE}$ ∅] [$_{FINP}$ [$_{FIN}$ ∅] vitamin C has no effect on colds]]]
        b. [$_{SUBP}$ [$_{SUB}$ *if*] [$_{FORCEP}$ [$_{FORCE}$ ∅] [$_{MODP}$ <u>as David and Brian have indicated</u> [$_{MOD}$ **that**] [$_{FINP}$ [$_{FIN}$ ∅] vitamin C has no effect on colds]]]]

Given that (in mainstream varieties), CLC prevents a peripheral head from selecting a complement headed by *that*, it follows that neither the FORCE heads nor the FIN heads in (199a, b) can be spelled out as *that*. However, as discussed at length in §§3.3–3.6, speakers who allow secondary spellout in MODP constituents will allow the underlined adjunct to license secondary use of *that* in (199b), via a local spec–head relation. Indeed, it would appear from

(198h) that some speakers even allow an (underlined) topic to license secondary use of *that*.

A further context in which some speakers allow *that* in adverbial clauses is in the second conjunct of coordinate subordinate clauses like those below:[88]

(200)    a. There are great deals on offer, *if* you've got a decent credit score and **that** you behave in the right way (Martin Lewis, BBC Radio 5)

b. *If* we were sitting here talking about police officers and **that** they were blatantly breaking the law, you'd be rightly aggrieved (Peter Kirkham, BBC Radio 5)

c. Even clubs within the top 3, *if* they do worse in the League than they expect or **that** they miss the Champions League for a year or maybe two, they end up having to sell portions of players to agents or investment funds (Andy Brassell, BBC Radio 5)

d. That's *because* he looks so young and **that** you and I are in our mid-50s (Keith Vaz, Talksport Radio)

e. You guys are legendary, *'cause* you say it how it is and **that** you talk about the hairs on the back of your neck (Listener, BBC Radio 5)

f. I think Mayweather's going to cruise it, *even though* he's not fought for two years and **that** he's 40 (Adrian Clarke, Talksport Radio)

In such structures, *that* is used to introduce the second conjunct of a coordinate adverbial clause in which the subordinating conjunction is not repeated. One possibility is that such structures involve an (italicised) SUB constituent which has two coordinate FORCEP constituents as its complement, with the FORCEP in the second conjunct being able to be spelled out as *that* because it does not immediately follow the italicised SUB constituent (and so is not subject to the constraint that rules out SUB+*that* structures).[89]

Some speakers even seem to extend this to coordinate root clauses (just as some speakers also allow a range of peripheral heads to be spelled out as *that* in a root clause, as we saw in §2.6). In this respect, I note that my broadcast English data contain 25 examples of structures like those below in which *that* is used immediately after a coordinating conjunction in a root coordinate clause (12 of these cases involving *and that*, 12 involving *but that*, and 1 involving *or that*):

---

[88] A similar type of structure is found in French, as noted by Chevalier et al. (1991: 124) in the following terms (translated by me from French into English): 'When two circumstantial clauses of the same type are coordinated, either the conjunction is repeated ... or the second clause is introduced by *que*$_{that}$ on its own.'

[89] Another is that sentences like (200) involve coordination of two SUBP constituents, with the SUB head in the first conjunction being spelled out as *if/because/even though* and the SUB head in the second conjunct being spelled out as *that* (because its content can be identified from the first conjunction).

(201)  a. He clips it away *and* **that** Dravid fields it at mid-on (Chris Martin-Jenkins, BBC Radio 5 Sports Extra)
   b. They are tacky *and* **that** they are too obvious (Nina Carter, BBC2 TV)
   c. Space is infinite, *but* **that** the region round the earth is limited (Chris Smith, BBC Radio 5)
   d. He can't be short of a few quid anyway, *but* **that** this will completely set him (Andy Brassell, BBC Radio 5)
   e. Either I'm in for a good hiding, *or* **that** only Dotun has been abbreviated to dot.on or donut, whichever you prefer (Dotun Adebayo, BBC Radio 5)

If *that* requires a superordinate local licenser, it is plausible to take the italicised conjunction to be the licenser for *that* in such cases. If as argued by Ross (1967: 162–5), the conjunction is a constituent of the second clause, and if it occupies the highest position in the periphery of the second clause, it may well be that the coordinating conjunction licenses use of *that* in much the same way as subordinating conjunctions do in adverbial clauses in varieties in which CLC is inoperative. I will not speculate further on such structures here, however.

To summarise a somewhat convoluted discussion: in this appendix, we have seen that there are a minority of speakers who allow *that* to be used after a subordinating conjunction (like *because/if/before/when* etc.). I have suggested that two types of factor seem to be involved in this. One is structural in nature, and relates to whether the conjunction is internal or external to the subordinate clause, and (if internal) whether it occupies a high or low position in the periphery. A second relates to the selectional properties of conjunctions (in respect of whether they allow or require a complement with or without *that*), and I speculated on whether selectional requirements are a reflex of independent conditions (e.g. possible parametric variation in respect of whether or not use of *that* can be licensed by a superordinate peripheral head).

# 4  *How come?*

## 4.1  Introduction

*How come* . . . is used in colloquial English to ask for the reason for some event or state of affairs.[1] Duffield (2015: 61) notes that it differs from *why* in that *how come* is 'a more colloquial expression', noting that 'It is hard to to imagine, for instance, a prosecuting barrister asking a defendant "How come you rang Jane Price on four separate occasions, Mr. Fox?"' For speakers of standard varieties of English, *how come* seems to be acceptable when followed by a finite TP containing an overt subject (bold-printed below) – as in the following pop song lyrics:

(1)       a.  *How come* **you** never go there? (Feist)
          b.  *How come* **you** are always off your head, and yet you still end up in your bed? (Courteeners)
          c.  *How come* **you**'re not here? (Pink)
          d.  So *how come* **no-one** loves me? (Beatles)

     Some speakers also allow the use of the complementiser *that* after *how come*, as in the following (internet-sourced) examples:

(2)       a.  *How come* **that** an infinite universe will collapse under gravity? (physics .stackexchange.com)
          b.  *How come* **that** hi-tech companies still shun digital marketing? (vickie1 .wordpress.com)

---

[1]  This chapter has developed out of talks given at the University of Essex in December 2014, and at the University of Manchester in April 2017. I am grateful to Yoshio Endo for sending me several interesting papers of his on *how come* (Endo 2014, 2015a, 2015b, 2017), for helping administer a questionnaire, and for helpful collaboration and correspondence; I'd also like to thank Chris Collins, Peter Culicover and Liliane Haegeman for extensive observations on earlier drafts. Additional thanks go to Doug Arnold, Bob Borsley, Memo Cinque, Simone De Cia, Roger Hawkins, Wyn Johnson, Mike Jones, Louisa Sadler and Andrew Spencer for interesting observations and comments, and to the individuals who kindly provided the acceptability judgements reported in the Appendix in §4.10.

216

    c. *How come* **that** you don't believe in us? (lyrics to song *Believe in us* by
       Jay-Jay Johanson)
    d. *How come* **that** you can't see through windows during the day? (amp
       .reddit.com)

There are also speakers who allow (Interrogative Subject-Auxiliary)
Inversion after *how come*, as in the examples below (3a being attributed to
Diane Lillo-Martin in Ochi 2004, 3b, c being examples from a corpus cited
by Kim & Kim 2011, and 3d being sourced from the internet by me):

(3)    a. How come *won't you* be here tomorrow?
      b. How come *does iodine* get into the human system of dwellers along the
         coasts from sea water?
      c. Now, how come *did you* give those baby-sitters such a hard time?
      d. How come *is it* that even ugly women my age can get a boyfriend but I am
         still single? (web)[2]

In order to differentiate the three types of *how come* structure illustrated above,
I shall refer to examples like (1) as *how come+subject* structures, those like (2)
as *how come+complementiser* structures, and those like (3) as *how
come+auxiliary* structures.

    Yoshio Endo and I conducted an informal questionnaire survey in which 20
university teachers of Linguistics or English from the UK, the US, Canada,
Australia and New Zealand were asked to rate the acceptability of a set of *how
come* sentences on a 5-point scale (5 = OK, 4 = ?, 3 = ??, 2 = ?*, 1 = *). The results
(reported in the Appendix to this chapter in §4.10) show that all speakers gave very
high scores (mean = 4.9) for *how come+*subject questions, only one speaker gave
a score above 3 to *how come+*complementiser structures (mean = 2.0), and only
one speaker gave a score above 2 to *how come+*auxiliary structures (mean = 1.3).

    This chapter presents an outline and critique of a number of earlier analyses
of *how come* questions, before going on to present an alternative analysis.
I begin by outlining an early analysis of *how come+*subject structures proposed
by Zwicky & Zwicky (1973).

## 4.2    Zwicky & Zwicky's *Reduction* Analysis

Zwicky & Zwicky (1973: 927–8) argue that a sentence like (4a) below is
a reduced form of (4b), derived by a *How Come Reduction* transformation
that deletes the material marked by ~~strikethrough~~:

---

[2] Recall from fn. 43 in Chapter 3 that I use the notation '(web)' to denote an internet-sourced
  example of unknown origin.

(4)    a. How come [you were arrested]?
       b. How ~~did it~~ come ~~about~~ [~~that~~ you were arrested]?

Several properties of *how come* questions can be accounted for under their Reduction analysis. One is that *how come* can be followed by the complementiser *that* for some speakers, as illustrated in (2) above. This can be given a relatively straightforward account under the Reduction analysis in (4b), since the complement of *come about* is a *that*-clause in (4b).

A second property accounted for under their analysis is that *how come* does not allow (Subject-Auxiliary) Inversion for most speakers, e.g. in sentences like:

(5)    *How come *has she* read the book? (Zwicky & Zwicky 1973: 928, ex. 62)

This is because Interrogative Auxiliary Inversion generally only takes place in root clauses. Accordingly, in (5) it involves invisible Inversion of *did it* in the *come* clause (because this is a root interrogative clause), but not of *has she* in the *read* clause (because this is neither a root clause nor an interrogative clause, but rather is an embedded declarative clause whose head C-position is filled by the complementiser *that*, with the presence of *that* in C serving as a further impediment to movement of an auxiliary from T to C). This situation can be represented as follows:[3]

(6)    [$_{CP}$ How [$_C$ *did*] [$_{TP}$ it [$_T$ ~~did~~] come about [$_{CP}$ [$_C$ **that**] [$_{TP}$ she [$_T$ *has*] read the book]]]]

A third property captured by the Reduction analysis is that the verb COME is invariable, and is always spelled out in the infinitive form *come*. This is expected under the Reduction analysis in (4b), because *come* is the complement of the auxiliary *do*, and *do* requires an infinitive complement. In this respect, *how come* questions differ from archaic-sounding questions like those in (7) below, where the verb is finite and we find a present/past tense alternation (*comes/came*), and sometimes there is no overt expletive subject (as in the last two examples, sourced from the internet):

(7)    a. How *comes* it, that thou art then estranged from thyself? (Shakespeare, *The Comedy of Errors*, II.2)
       b. How *came* it that only one in four of the known brothels were disturbed? (Charles Mayo Ellis, 1863)

---

[3] For the minority of speakers who allow Inversion with *how come* in sentences like (3), it would seem necessary to suppose that these have a different structure, as discussed in subsequent sections.

c. How *comes* that you have so many singing parts in this new record? (herzsynapsen.wordpress.com)

d. How *came* you never watched Sailor Moon? (turbomun.tumblir.com)

Sentences like (7) appear to involve a different (archaic) V2/Verb-Second structure in which the italicised finite verb raises from V to C and in some cases is used without an overt expletive *it* subject.[4]

A fourth property that follows from the Reduction analysis is that *how come* clauses are factive (i.e. presupposed to be true). This follows from the Reduction analysis in (4b) because the complement of *come about* is itself factive.

A fifth property of *how come* questions which can be accounted for under the Reduction analysis concerns the observation that *how* always has local scope. For instance, in a complex sentence such as the following (adapted from Zwicky & Zwicky 1973: 927, ex. 45)

(8)    How come [(%that) Herman said Gwen ate the goldfish]?

*how* can only be construed as modifying the *come*-VP and hence associated with the gap (—) in (9a) below, and not (e.g.) as modifying the *ate*-VP and associated with the gap in (9b):

(9)    a. *How* ~~did it~~ come ~~about~~ — [~~that~~ Herman said Gwen ate the goldfish]?
       b. *How* ~~did it~~ come ~~about~~ [~~that~~ Herman said Gwen ate the goldfish —]

Since the bracketed *that*-clause in (9) is factive and factive clauses are islands and hence barriers to the extraction of adjuncts (Oshima 2006), it follows that *how* cannot move to the front of the overall sentence from some position internally within the bracketed clause in (9b). The islandhood property of factive clauses is illustrated in (10) below:

(10)   a. *How* do you think [$_{\text{NON-FACTIVE}}$ that he died —]?
       b. *\*How* do you regret [$_{\text{FACTIVE}}$ that he died —]?

While the adjunct *how* can be interpreted as extracted out of the bracketed non-factive clause in (10a), it cannot be interpreted as extracted out of the bracketed factive clause island in (10b).

Overall, then, we see that a number of syntactic and semantic properties of *how come*+subject questions can be captured under the Reduction analysis.

---

[4] The website proz.com reports 300,000 Google hits for *how comes* (mainly from British-related sources), compared to 3 million for *how come*. The absence of *-s* on *come* in *how come* questions makes it unlikely that *how come* derives from *how comes it that*, according to Bolinger (1970: 66).

However, there are a number of potential problems with the analysis (as noted e.g. by Collins 1991; Ochi 2004; Fitzpatrick 2005; Conroy 2006; Kim & Kim 2011). For example, an obvious theoretical weakness is that the How Come Reduction operation posited by Zwicky is ad hoc, in the sense that it is not found in other structures (e.g. not in questions like *'When come you were arrested?'), but rather is restricted to occurring in *how come* questions. Moreover, it is also unprincipled in that it seems to involve deletion of the discontinuous, non-constituent string (*did it ... about that*), in violation of a general principle to the effect that a string of words can only undergo syntactic operations like movement or deletion if it is continuous and consti- tutes a maximal projection (i.e. a complete phrase).[5]

Furthermore, there are also empirical problems with the Reduction analysis. For one thing, it fails to account for numerous differences between *how come* questions and *how did it come about* questions. One such difference is that *about* cannot be used in *how come* questions but (for speakers like me) is obligatory in *how did it come about* questions: cf.

(11)    a.  How come (\**about*) you were arrested?
        b.  How did it come \*(*about*) that you were arrested?

A second difference concerns *that* being obligatory in *how did it come about* questions, but being ungrammatical for most English speakers in *how come* questions:

---

[5] We could avoid positing deletion of the preposition *about* if we took the structure to involve the same use of *come* (with the sense of 'happen') as is found in examples like those below (and in 7 above):

   (i)   How does it come that bond and loyalty are often stronger at the bottom in the organisation than at the top? (stephenbusby.com)
   (ii)  How does it come that even the richest nations drown in debts? (economy4man kind.org)
   (iii) Hey, Pete, how'd it come that you didn't know all this? (*Los Angeles Herald*, 1906)

Indeed, this structure is even used without an overt complementiser after *come*, as in:

   (iv)  How does it come people rarely talk about how strong 'Fireball' actually is (reddit .com)
   (v)   So how did it come he was annoyed this morning? (fictionpress.com)
   (vi)  How's it come you go to town so often and I don't ever get to go, Nixy? (readings .com.au)

If we set aside the optional complementiser, this would mean that deletion in essence affects the auxiliary *does/did* and the expletive subject *it*, with the auxiliary reducible to *'s/'d* in colloquial use as in (iii) and (vi) above. Claridge (2012) examines a range of possible diachronic sources for *how come*, but concludes (2012: 182) that it is 'not possible to suggest a clear route of evolution'.

(12)     a. How come (*that*) you were arrested?
         b. How did it come about *(*that*) you were arrested?

In the survey reported in the Appendix in §4.10, only 1 of the 20 informants gave *how come that* a score of 5/OK, and the mean score for *how come that* was only 2.0.

A third difference (illustrated below) is that *how* can be substituted by another question word (e.g. by *however* as noted by Culicover 2013, or *when*) in *how did it come about* questions but not in *how come* questions:

(13)     a. *How/However/When* did it come about that he resigned?
         b. *How/*However/*When* come he resigned?

A fourth difference is that (according to Collins 1991), *how* can be postmodified by *else* (or indeed by *the devil*) in *how+Auxiliary+it come about* questions but not in *how come* questions, as illustrated below:

(14)     a. *How else* could it have come about that he resigned?
         b. **How else* come he resigned?

(15)     a. *How the devil* did it come about that he resigned?
         b. **How the devil* come he resigned?

A fifth difference is that other constituents can be positioned immediately after *how* in *how did it come about* questions, but not in *how come* questions – e.g. a parenthetical PP like that italicised in (16) below, or a vocative like that italicised in (17):

(16)     a. How, *in your view,* did it come about that he resigned?
         b. *How, *in your view,* come he resigned?

(17)     a. How, *my friend,* did it come about that he resigned?
         b. *How, *my friend,* come he resigned?

Differences such as those illustrated in (11–17) can't be accounted for in any straightforward fashion under the Reduction analysis.

However, one apparent way of dealing with problems posed by such sentences within the spirit of the Reduction analysis would be to take *how come* to be some sort of frozen lexical chunk/FLC (resembling an idiom or construction in certain respects). Reasoning along these lines, we might suppose that *how come*+ subject questions have a frozen structure along the lines shown informally in (18) below (where IND marks indicative mood, and ~~strikethrough~~ marks items obligatorily given a null spellout at PF):

(18)     [$_{CP}$ how [$_C$ ~~did~~] [$_{TP}$ ~~it~~ [$_T$ ~~did~~] [$_{VP}$ [$_V$ come ~~about~~] ~~how~~ [$_{CP}$ [$_C$ ~~that~~] [$_{TP}$ ... T$_{IND}$
         ...]]]]]]

To say that the structure in (18) is a frozen lexical chunk means that the form, spellout and relative position of each of the items in (18) is fixed (e.g. *how* must immediately precede a null copy of *did*, etc.). This assumption will account for why neither *about* nor (for most speakers) *that* appears in *how come* questions, why *how* cannot be substituted by *however/when*, why *how* cannot be post-modified by *else/the devil*, and why no (e.g. parenthetical or vocative) material can intrude between *how* and *come*. Specifying that the gap associated with *how* (~~how~~) occupies a position where it modifies a projection of *come* also accounts for why *how come* always has local scope.

However, there are both theoretical and empirical objections to the FLC analysis. From a theoretical perspective, one problem is that there don't seem to be clear precedents for the seemingly random deletion of a discontinuous string of items like those marked by strikethrough in (18). Moreover, the missing constituents are simply stipulated to be null, with no attempt made to explain their absence. While there are precedents for storage of large chunks of structure in constructional approaches to grammar, there are no precedents for storing chunks of structure which comprise a non-constituent string, nor (as pointed out by Peter Culicover, pc) for storing chunks containing deleted constituents: by contrast, the stored idiom chunk *kick the bucket* is a complete VP constituent containing no deleted material, and allowing both morphological variation (e.g. *kick/kicks/kicked/kicking the bucket*) and modification (e.g. *kick the bloody bucket*).

There are also descriptive problems posed by the FLC analysis. One such is that it doesn't account for *how come* being found not only in root clauses but also in embedded clauses like those bracketed in the examples below (sourced from the internet)[6]:

(19)    a. I don't know [*how come* I never saw it before] (trans4mind.com)
        b. She asked [*how come* I don't smile] (lyrics to a song by Eric B & Rakim)
        c. I just found out [*how come* I can't keep a man] (lyrics to a song by Memphis Minnie)
        d. I have no idea [*how come* it has taken me so long to discover your writing] (markgimenez.com)

It is hard to see how an embedded *how come* clause like that in (19a) would be derived under the Reduction analysis – presumably either from an

---

[6] It should be noted, however, that Ochi (2004: 34, fn. 7) claims that 'Some speakers do not like to have *how come* in embedded questions', and Duffield (2015) claims that use of *how come* in embedded questions is marginal. On the other hand, Duffield (2015: 62) concedes that 'embedded examples with *how come* are attested', and Claridge (2012: 177) notes that *how come* occurs 'in both main and subordinate clauses'.

inverted structure like (20a) below, or from its uninverted counterpart in (20b):

(20)    a.  I don't know [how *did it* come about that I never saw it before]
        b.  I don't know [how it *came* about that I never saw it before]

However, (20a) is implausible as a source for (19a) because Auxiliary Inversion is ungrammatical in embedded questions in standard varieties of English (especially in factive/resolutive structures like 19c). Nor would an (inversion-less) source like (20b) be any better, since COME would then be spelled out as the past tense form *came*, and yet what we find in (19) is the default/infinitive form *come*.

A further problem with the FLC analysis (and indeed with the Reduction analysis) is that it would fail to account for contrasts such as:

(21)    a.  How did it come about that she lost her job – or did(n't) it?
        b.  *How come she lost her job – or didn't it?

As we see from (21a), a *how did it come about* question can have a *did(n't) it?* tag which questions whether it really did come about that she lost her job: the subject and auxiliary in the tag are copies of *did* and *it* in the main clause. However, no *did(n't) it?* tag is possible in a *how come* question like (21b), suggesting that (21b) is not a reduced form of (21a).

As a final piece of evidence against the FLC analysis (and the Reduction analysis), I note the observation by Collins (1991) that there are subtle semantic differences between *how come* questions and *how did/does it come about* questions. For example, Collins claims, (22b) below is not an appropriate paraphrase of (22a):

(22)    a.  How come two plus two is equal to four?
        b.  ??How did/does it come about that two plus two is equal to four?

Overall, then, it seems clear that the Reduction analysis is untenable, either in the original form proposed by Zwicky & Zwicky (1973), or in the revised Frozen Lexical Chunk variant suggested in (18).

Still, it might seem as if we can avoid some of the pitfalls of the Reduction analysis while retaining the intuition that *come* is a verb if we suppose that *how come* questions have a reduced clausal structure comprising a CP housing *how* and a verb phrase headed by *come*, as in (23) below:[7]

---

[7] If we assume a more articulated version of the structure of the verb phrase, VP might instead be analysed as a vP, or a VOICEP (in the sense of Collins 2005; Merchant 2013; Weir 2014a).

(23)        [$_{CP}$ how [$_C$ ø] [$_{VP}$ [$_V$ come] [$_{CP}$ [$_C$ ø] you don't like garlic]]]

Potential parallels might then be drawn with sentences like 'Why worry about it?' However, an analysis like (23) raises numerous questions, including whether CP can select a TP-less complement, why only *how* can occur in such a structure (and only when used with *come*) and why (for most speakers) *come* cannot select a *that*-clause complement in *how come* structures, even though it does in *how does it come* structures like the following:

(24)        a. How does it *come* **that** I can't see my pictures in EXPLORE? (flickr.com)
            b. How does it *come* **that** my ozeri pan sticks like crazy? (amazon.com)
            c. How does it *come* **that** when a girl wears guys' clothing nobody gives a crap, but when a guy wears girls' clothing everyone goes crazy? (answers .yahoo.com)
            d. How does it *come* **that** I have pictures in my phone stream I've never taken? (discussions.apple.com)

Moreover, if *come* is a verb in *how come* structures (as it is in 'Why come home tired?') we should expect it to be modifiable by an adverb like *constantly*: and yet, while we can say 'Why constantly come home tired?' we can't say *'How constantly come my phone dies on me?' And while *come* can be modified by *ever* in other uses as a verb (as in 'How did it ever come that I let myself be taken in by you?'), this is not the case with *how come* (cf. *'How ever come I let myself be taken in by you?').

Given such problems, I shall not pursue the analysis in (23) any further here. Instead, in the next section, I turn to look at an alternative analysis of *how come* as a complementiser proposed by Collins (1991).

### 4.3    Collins' Complementiser Analysis

Collins (1991) offers a monoclausal analysis of *how come*+subject structures under which *how come* is treated as a single word (which he writes as *how-come*) functioning as the head C/complementiser constituent of a CP/complementiser phrase. He claims that *how come* is directly merged/base-generated in the head C position of CP and selects an indicative TP complement – as in:

(25)        [$_{CP}$ [$_C$ how-come] [$_{TP}$ you [$_T$ were] arrested]]

The complementiser analysis in (25) can account for a number of characteristic properties of *how come* questions.

---

Indeed, it could even be that *how* is housed in an extended functional projection on the periphery of the verb phrase.

One such is that (as shown by the results of the survey reported in the Appendix in §4.10), most speakers don't allow the use of *that* in sentences like *How come (\*that) you were arrested?* Nor do most speakers allow Auxiliary Inversion in sentences like *\*How come were you arrested?* These properties follow from the analysis in (25) because the head C-position of CP is filled by *how-come* (so preventing *that* or an inverted auxiliary from occupying the same C-position).[8]

A second property of *how come*+subject structures which can be captured under the complementiser analysis in (25) is that *how come* always has scope over the clause it introduces, never over an embedded clause. Thus, in a sentence like:

(26)    How come John said Mary left?

*how come* questions the reason for John saying what he said, not the reason for Mary leaving. Collins argues that this follows if *how come* is generated in the head C-position of CP, and cannot undergo movement from the head C-position in the embedded CP into the head C-position of the main clause CP because this movement would be too long, in the sense that it would violate the locality requirement of the Head-Movement Constraint of Travis (1984).

A third property of *how come*+subject structures captured under the complementiser analysis is that *how come* always has wide scope with respect to quantifiers. In this respect, compare the following sentences:

(27)    a. Why does everybody hate John?
        b. How come everybody hates John?

In (27a), *why* can have wide or narrow scope with respect to *everybody*, but in (27b) *how come* only has wide scope. This is because *how come* is generated above *everybody* in the head C-position of CP, whereas *why* can originate in a position below *everybody* (as a VP adjunct, Collins claims).

A fourth property which Collins says can be captured under his analysis is that *how come* cannot be focused in cleft sentences such as:

(28)    *\*How come* it is that John quit his job?

---

[8] For this argument to go through, we also need to exclude the possibility of a CP recursion analysis under which a CP headed by *that* is embedded within a CP headed by *how-come*. One way of doing this is to follow Collins in stipulating that it is a lexical property of the putative complementiser *how-come* that it selects a TP complement, not a CP complement. Another is to appeal to some generalised version of the constraint against complementiser iteration proposed by McCloskey (2006: 107).

In this respect, it is interesting to note that wh-operators (like *why/when*) can be focused in clefts, but not a complementiser like *whether* – as we see from the contrast below:

(29)    I wonder [*why/when/\*whether* it was that John quit his job]

(28) is arguably ruled out because it would require *how come* to move to the edge of CP from the same position after *is* that is occupied by the *because*-phrase in 'It is *because of this* that John quit his job.' Accordingly, for (28) to be grammatical would require a Wh-Movement operation like that shown informally below:

(30)    *How come* it is how come that John quit his job?

But this kind of movement is not possible because *how come* originates as the head C of CP, and this is its criterial position, so it is frozen in place by the Criterial Freezing Condition of Rizzi (2005, 2006a, 2010, 2014a) and Rizzi & Shlonsky (2006, 2007), which was given the following informal characterisation in §1.4:

(31)    **Criterial Freezing Condition**
        A constituent which occupies its criterial position is frozen in place

Moreover, the constituents focused in clefts are maximal projections/phrases, and so cannot move into a head position like C, because this would violate the Chain Uniformity Condition of Chomsky (1995), which bars a specifier from moving into a head position (and conversely).

A fifth property of *how come* questions which can be accounted for in a straightforward fashion under the complementiser analysis is that *how come* doesn't appear in infinitive clauses like that bracketed below:

(32)    \*I don't know [how come to leave]

This restriction can be accounted for straightforwardly under the complementiser analysis by supposing that *how come* (like *if*) is a complementiser which selects a finite TP complement.[9] Indeed, if *how come* is a factive

---

[9] Mike Jones (pc) points out that the argument is not conclusive, because (for him) the adverb *why* is subject to the same restriction that it is not used in infinitives like \*'He couldn't understand why to apologise' (= why he should apologise). However, my broadcast English data include the following example of a *why . . . to* infinitive:

> (i) I don't see any reason why, at this late stage, to change that (Roy Hodgson, Sky Sports TV)

complementiser, this will follow from the more general requirement for a factive complementiser to select an indicative TP complement – like the factive complementiser *how* in:

(33)     They didn't tell me [*how* the tooth fairy doesn't really exist] (Legate 2010: 127, ex. 17a)

See Willis (2007), van Gelderen (2009), Legate (2010) and Nye (2013) on the use of *how* as a finite complementiser.

A sixth property of *how come* questions which Collins argues to follow from his complementiser analysis is that (unlike *why*), *how come* cannot occur in multiple wh-operator questions – as illustrated below:

(34)     a. *Why* did John eat *what*?
         b. **How come* John ate *what*?

This follows if only operators which bind a trace/variable can appear in multiple-operator questions, and if *why* is an operator which undergoes Wh-Movement and binds a trace that functions as a variable but *how come* is not (but rather is a complementiser directly merged in situ which does not bind any trace/variable).

A seventh property of *how come* questions which follows from the complementiser analysis is that *how* and *come* form an indivisible unit. For example, *how* cannot be substituted by another interrogative wh-word, as we saw in (13b) **'However/*When come he resigned?'* Moreover (as noted by Kim & Kim 2011), *come* cannot undergo an ellipsis operation like Sluicing on its own:

Moreover, Chris Collins (pc) notes that examples of *why to* can readily be found on the internet, citing the example below:

(ii)   So for the second half of today's lecture, Dustin Moskovitz is going to take over and talk about *why to* start a startup (startupclass.samaltman.com)

An informal internet search I undertook revealed that the phrase *how and why to* is particularly common, as illustrated by an internet article entitled 'How and why to improve your cursive penmanship.'

Yoshida et al. (2015, fn. 16) report that three out of ten informants they consulted accept (what they take to be) tenseless clauses with *how come* like (iii) below, in appropriate contexts:

(iii)   How come keep playing this game, if it is so boring?

They also report more than 300 Google hits for similar structures. However, given that (as we will see later) *how come* sentences allow subject drop for some speakers, it could be that the *keep* clause in (iii) is a finite clause with a null subject.

(35)    You're always grinning about something. *How \*(come)*? (Kim & Kim 2011: 4, ex. 13a)

In addition, *how* (according to Collins) cannot be postmodified in *how come* questions (as in 14b/15b *'How else come he resigned'/*'How the devil come he resigned?'), nor can any parenthetical constituent intrude between *how* and *come* (as in 16b *'How, in your view, come he resigned', and 17b *'How, my friend, come he resigned?')

The seven properties illustrated above can be given a straightforward account under Collins' analysis of *how come* as a single word functioning as a complementiser. Nevertheless, as we will see in the remainder of this section, there are considerations which call into question the viability of Collins' treatment of *how come*.[10] There are two separate but partly interrelated questions here: (i) Is *how come* one word or two?[11] And (ii) is it a complementiser or something else (e.g. an adverb like *why*)? If it is two words, it is hard to see how it can be a complementiser; if it is one word it could be a complementiser, but could equally be e.g. an adverb like *why*. Below, I present a number of arguments against treating *how come* as a single-word complementiser.[12]

Collins' analysis requires us to posit root/main clauses of the form (25) above, repeated as (36) below:

(36)    [$_{CP}$ [$_C$ how-come] [$_{TP}$ you [$_T$ were] arrested]]

One problem with (36) is that a root/main clause generally can't be introduced by an overt complementiser in English – as we see from the ungrammaticality of:

(37)    *[$_{CP}$ [$_C$ that/if/whether] [$_{TP}$ it [$_T$ is] raining]]

---

[10] The arguments outlined in this section also challenge any cartographic analysis which treats *how come* as a peripheral head – e.g. the analysis in Endo (2014) in which *how come* is taken to be the head of the interrogative projection INTP.

[11] An interesting issue which I set aside here is whether *how come* shows the stress pattern of a single word or of a phrase. *How* and *come* can both receive independent stress (suggesting they may be separate words); however (as noted by Wyn Johnson and Andy Spencer, pc) *come* can be more heavily stressed than *how*, and this is the kind of pattern found in a potential compound like *cream bun*.

[12] A note of caution which should be sounded at the outset is the following. Chris Collins points out that some of the counterarguments in this section can be subverted if we allow CP recursion, or adopt the split CP approach of Rizzi (1997) and much subsequent work – though it should be noted that in Collins' (1991) paper, he claims that the complementiser *how-come* selects a TP complement. Collins also points out that some of the counterarguments presented here are based on descriptive constructs (e.g. the Root Complementiser Filter and the Sluicing Constraint) whose theoretical underpinnings are unclear.

Chomsky & Lasnik (1977: 486, ex. 180) attribute the ill-formedness of structures like (37) to violation of a filter (= surface structure well-formedness condition = PF interface condition) ruling out root clauses containing an overt complementiser. The filter can be characterised for present purposes as follows:

(38)     **Root Complementiser Filter/RCF**
         No root clause can contain an overt complementiser in English at PF

However, the analysis of *how-come* as a complementiser in (36) violates (38), so wrongly predicting that sentences like (4a) 'How come you were arrested?' are ungrammatical. The filter (38) could be taken to reflect a parsing condition to the effect that an overt complementiser serves to signal embedding (in the spirit of Staum Casasanto & Sag 2008). Alternatively, if complementisers require a local superordinate licenser (as suggested in §3.6), RCF can be seen as an artefact of this requirement, since a sentence-initial complementiser will have no such licenser.[13]

It is interesting to note that *how come* differs markedly in this respect from the factive complementiser *how*. The complementiser *how* obeys RCF and so can only occur in an embedded clause like that bracketed in (39a) below, not in a root clause like (39b):

(39)     a. She told me [*how* she hadn't been feeling well for a while]
         b. **How* she hadn't been feeling well for a while

The fact that *how come* (but not the complementiser *how*) can occur in a root clause strengthens the case against *how come* being a complementiser.

A second property of *how come* which seems to militate against treating it as a complementiser is that (as noted by Shlonsky & Soare 2011), it allows Sluicing (i.e. ellipsis) of its complement – e.g. of *John left early* in:

(40)     They thought John left early, but they didn't tell me *how come* (Shlonsky & Soare 2011: 665, ex. 41b)

An important constraint on Sluicing (illustrated below) is that it is permitted after an interrogative wh-constituent in spec-CP (like the wh-words

---

[13] A potential challenge to the descriptive adequacy of RCF is posed by requestives like:

         (i) If you wouldn't mind passing the salt

Such a sentence might at first sight seem to involve the use of the interrogative complementiser *if* in a root clause. However, *if* is unlikely to be interrogative here, since it cannot be substituted by *whether*; rather, it is more likely that (i) is a conditional clause (hence a subordinate clause), associated with an abstract root clause (e.g. a null counterpart of *I'd be grateful*). On other apparent challenges to RCF, see Chapter 3, fn. 53.

italicised in 41a below), but not after an overt complementiser (like *if/whether* in 41b):

(41)   a. They thought John had been attacked, but they weren't sure *when/where/ how/why*
       b. *They thought John had been attacked, but they weren't sure *if/whether*

For concreteness, the relevant constraint can be outlined informally as follows:

(42)   **Sluicing Constraint**
       No overt complementiser allows Sluicing of its complement

The observation that *how come* allows its complement to be sluiced in sentences like (40) suggests that it behaves more like a typical wh-operator such as *when* in (41a) and unlike the complementisers *if/whether* in (41b). It may be that (42) is related to the more general Stranding Constraint proposed in Radford (2016: 143, ex. 86) which bars an overt complementiser from being stranded without an overt complement (irrespective of whether it is stranded by preposing or deletion of its complement). Alternatively, if functional heads can only license ellipsis of their complement when they agree with their specifier (as claimed by Lobeck 1990, and Saito & Murasugi 1990), it may be that English overt complementisers cannot carry agreement features (a key assumption in Rizzi's 1990: 52–3 account of the *that*-trace effect), and hence cannot license ellipsis of their complement. Yet a third possibility (in the spirit of Staum Casasanto & Sag 2008) is that the parsing function of an overt complementiser is to signal an upcoming overt clause.

Significantly, *how come* behaves differently from the wh-complementiser *how*, which (as observed by Nye 2013: 192) doesn't allow Sluicing in sentences like:

(43)   *I know he's a very successful author, but there's really no need for him to keep repeating **how** [~~he's a very successful author~~]

Moreover, we find further differences between *how come* and interrogative complementisers in respect of the following potentially related type of ellipsis (termed Stripping):

(44)   SPEAKER A: They are going to Arizona
       SPEAKER B: I wonder *why* Arizona/*how come* Arizona?

(45)   SPEAKER A: They are going somewhere
       SPEAKER B: *I wonder *if/whether* Arizona?

The fact that *how come* patterns like the adverb *why*,[14] and unlike the complementisers *if/whether* strengthens the case for treating *how come* as an adverbial rather than a complementiser.[15]

A third property of *how come* which seems to argue against it being a complementiser is that it can be modified by *exactly* – as in the internet-sourced examples below:[16]

(46)   a. The first step in getting your ex back is to see *how come* <u>exactly</u> the breakup happened (howdoyougetyourexback.doodlekit.com)
   b. But *how come* <u>exactly</u> you don't want to get it? (community.babycenter .com)
   c. So *how come* <u>exactly</u> you get to open your mouth to someone else doing the same thing? (andaplayertobenamedlater.com)
   d. *How come* <u>exactly</u> Lucas is the one with the 'heart of gold' and not Torres? (anfeels.tumblr.com)
   e. *How come* <u>exactly</u> they can't find Whitey Bulger? (nj.com)
   f. His DF is one of the best around. *How come exactly?* (orojacksom.com)

Merchant (2002) argues that *exactly* can postmodify a phrase (like *what kind of (a) doctor* in 47a below) but not a head (like *what* in 47b); consequently, *exactly*

---

[14] If *Arizona* moves to a focus position in the clause periphery below *why/how come*, such sentences can be taken to involve Sluicing of the rest of the clause. On this type of ellipsis (termed *Why/How Come* Stripping), see Nakao et al. (2012), Ortega-Santos et al. (2014), Weir (2014a), and Yoshida et al. (2015).

[15] Peter Culicover (pc) observes that this argument will be undermined if the constraint on Sluicing is a semantic one and *how come* has the appropriate meaning regardless of its category. He also points out the following difference between the behaviour of *why* and *how come* under ellipsis:

(i)   Why not/*How come not?

Merchant (2006) argues that *why not* involves adjunction of *not* to *why*. Since other wh-words don't allow ellipsis after *not* (cf. *When not? *Where not? *Who not?*), it may just be that this kind of adjunction is limited to *why* – so accounting for the the absence of *how come not*. However, I googled the following example:

(ii)   How come not? (J. Sandoval, quora.com)

Peter also notes the following contrast, which I have no account of at present:

(ii)   Tell me where you put the beer and *why/*how come*

In a different context, I googled the following examples of *and how come* in the title of an article/blog:

(iii)   The decline in CUNY applications: who and how come? (J.M. Farago & J. Weinman, 1978, *Research in Higher Education* 8: 193–203)
(iv)   Combatting obesity: How and how come? (blog, huffpost.com)

[16] However, Peter Culicover (pc) tells me that the string *how come exactly* isn't good in his own variety of New York English.

can postmodify a wh-phrase like *at what point* in (47c), but not a complementiser like *whether/if* in a sentence like (47d):

(47)   a. *What kind of (a) doctor* <u>exactly</u> is she?
        b. *\*What* <u>exactly</u> kind of (a) doctor is she?
        c. I don't know *at what point* <u>exactly</u> the whole building collapsed
        d. \*I don't know *whether* <u>exactly</u>/*if* <u>exactly</u> the whole building collapsed

Significantly, *how come* behaves like a wh-phrase in allowing modification by *exactly* in sentences like (46), but unlike a complementiser.

A fourth argument against categorising *how come* as a complementiser selecting a TP complement concerns the observation that such an analysis cannot be generalised to *how come that* clauses like the earlier examples in (2) above, repeated in (48) below:

(48)   a. *How come* **that** an infinite universe will collapse under gravity?
        b. *How come* **that** hi-tech companies still shun digital marketing?
        c. *How come* **that** you don't believe in us?
        d. *How come* **that** you can't see through windows during the day?

Such sentences would be expected to be ungrammatical if the head C-position of CP is already filled by the complementiser *how come* and if *how come* selects a TP complement, since (as we saw earlier) *how come* and *that* would be mutually exclusive by virtue of competing for the same C-position.

Moreover, many speakers who don't like sentences like (48) find the use of *that* more acceptable in sentences like those below, where an underlined constituent intervenes between *how come* and *that*:

(49)   a. *How come*, <u>after a long drawn-out conflict</u>, **that** the Israelis and Palestinians still haven't made peace?
        b. *How come*, <u>given that the sun's so near comparatively in your terms</u>, **that** we have any at all? (Melvyn Bragg, BBC Radio 4: example provided by Doug Arnold; *any* = 'any water')
        c. *How come* <u>if this is such a huge problem</u> **that** there isn't more useful and legit information on how to overcome it? (nextscientist.com)
        d. *How come* <u>all of a sudden</u> **that** the Federal Government has to stick their noses in this shit? (washingtonflyfishing.com)
        e. Well, in that case, *how come*, <u>in the USA</u>, **that** nuclear power gets both the same tax credit subsidies as wind power, but gets in addition loan subsidies from the Federal Government (realfeed-intariffs.blogspot.com)
        f. *How come*, <u>please</u>, **that** Bob Seger was inducted into the R&R hall of fame so much later than the Eagles? (segerbob.com)
        g. *How come*, <u>John</u>, **that** you received a birthday card signed Bright Eyes? (Chop Hooey, Google News)

    h. Alice Faye ... was becoming very upset about all this by now and demanded to know *how come* <u>last week</u> **that** they said it was standard operating procedure ... (mytripjournal.com)

In addition, in the informal questionnaire survey of 20 informants conducted by Yoshio Endo and me reported in the Appendix in §4.10, there were 5 who gave a relatively low (1/*, 2/?* or 3/??) acceptability rating to 'How come that I fell in love with someone like you?' but nonetheless gave a maximum (5/OK) rating to 'How come I fell in love with someone like you, and that you fell in love with someone like me?', where *that* does not immediately follow *come*. For speakers who allow the use of *that* in some or all of the sentences in (48–9), an analysis of *how come* as a complementiser selecting a TP complement is problematic.

    The argument against treating *how come* as a complementiser is strengthened by contrasts such as the following, for speakers like me who allow sentences like (50a) below, but not (50b):

(50)     a. She asked *how come* **that** I had apologised
        b. *She asked *whether/if* **that** I had apologised

If we generalise the double-*that* filter of McCloskey (2006a: 107) as a PF filter ruling out complementiser iteration in English, this filter will correctly rule out sentences like (50b). But if *how come* were a complementiser, sentences like (50a) would violate this filter and so would wrongly be expected to be ungrammatical for speakers such as me.

    A fifth observation which is difficult to account for if *how come* is a complementiser with a TP complement is that some speakers allow Auxiliary Inversion after *how come*, as in the examples in (3) above, repeated as (51) below:

(51)     a. How come *won't you* be here tomorrow?
        b. How come *does iodine* get into the human system of dwellers along the coasts from sea water?
        c. Now, how come *did you* give those baby-sitters such a hard time?
        d. How come *is it* that even ugly women my age can get a boyfriend but I am still single?

If Inversion involves an auxiliary moving into C, we'd expect it to be blocked if the head C-position of CP is filled by *how-come* – as shown in schematic form below:[17]

---

[17] The discussion here is simplified by setting aside possible syntactic differences between different varieties of English. For example, *how come*+complementiser or *how come*+auxiliary structures are only accepted by a minority of informants, and either or both of them could have a different structure from that of mainstream *how come*+subject structures.

(52)     $[_{CP} [_C$ **how-come**] $[_{TP}$ you $[_T$ *won't*] be here tomorrow]]

Thus, analysing *how-come* as a C with a TP complement leaves us with no account of data like (51).

A sixth argument against treating *how come* as a single-word complementiser is that some speakers use *why come* alongside *how come* – as in the internet-sourced examples below:

(53)     a. *Why come* you didn't call me last night? (urbandictionary.com)
         b. *Why come* you don't have a tattoo? (english.stackexchange.com)
         c. *Why come* you wanna know that? (m.facebook.com)
         d. *Why come* you don't love me? (title of song by Phil Lee)
         e. *Why come* you can't cancel till you talk to a manager? (tripadvisor.com)
         f. An if cabbage is so good, *why come* it don't say so? (reddit.com)
         g. *Why come* people only protest at abortion clinics? (twitter.com)

The fact that we find *why come* alongside *how come* potentially undermines the claim that *how come* is an indivisible complementiser (for people who use *why come*).

A further argument against treating *how come* as a single-word complementiser comes from the observation that *how* can be postmodified by an aggressive non-D-linker like *the hell* – as illustrated by the internet-sourced examples below:

(54)     a. *How the hell come* we stick these low-life bastards in these big-ass hotels anyway? (attributed to a soldier named Wooley in D. Roche, *Making and Remaking Horror in the 1970s and 2000s*, Mississipi University Press, 2014: 55)
         b. *How the heck come* I don't get my fair share? (readersupportednews.com)
         c. Then *how the fuck come* you were asking about me last night, huh? (H. Coben, *Back Spin*, Hachette, London, 2009)
         d. *How on earth come* they offer you some crap for 120p? (web)
         e. *How in the world come* you treat me this-a-way? (Lyrics to *Lorenzo Blues* by Skip James)

By contrast, the whole expression *how come* cannot be postmodified in the same way (cf. *'How come in the world you treat me this-a-way?'), according to Honegger (2004) and Kim & Kim (2011). Given the observation attributed to McCloskey in Merchant (2002) that a postmodifier like *the hell* can modify a wh-word (as in '*What the hell* kind of a doctor is she?') but not a wh-phrase (cf. *'What kind of a doctor the hell is she?'), this is consistent with the view that *how* is a separate word from *come* in sentences like (54), and that *how come* is a wh-phrase. If so, *how come* cannot be a complementiser.[18]

Moreover (contrary to the claim made by Collins 1991 in relation to sentences like 14b above), *how come* can be modified by *else* for some speakers, as the internet-sourced examples below illustrate:

(55)   a. *How else come* they're in diamond? (reddit.com)
   b. *How else come* the stock C172 in xplane 9 AND 10 flies and taxies so badly? (avsim.com)
   c. *How else come* that eighty percent of the juvenile delinquents in our prisons are Moroccans and Turkish? (salto-youth.net)

For speakers who accept them, sentences like (55) provide further potential evidence against treating *how come* as an indivisible single-word complementiser.

Having looked at the problems arising from analysing *how come* as a complementiser occupying the head C-position of CP, I now turn to look at an alternative analysis proposed by Ochi (2004) on which *how come* is treated as an adverbial which is directly merged in the specifier position of CP.

---

[18] However, Louisa Sadler (pc) points out that even a compound word like *however* seems to allow *how* and *ever* to split and a string like *the hell* to be inserted between them – as in the internet-sourced examples below:

   (i)   *How* the hell *ever* did you pick me?
   (ii)  *How* the fuck *ever* did you manage to respond to my blog so fast?
   (iii) *How* on earth *ever* did they compensate you?

In the internet-sourced example below, the whole string *how-the-hell-ever* is hyphenated, suggesting that it is treated as a compound word:

   (iv)  *How-the-hell-ever* did I forget about that GIF?!

On the other hand, in the internet example below, *ever* is separated from what precedes it by a comma, suggesting that it is treated as a separate word:

   (v)   *How* in the world, *ever*, did you make a connection in your mind from changing the 'none but natural born citizens can be president' to 'Jihadist gets elected president'?

Thus, the status of split *how* ... *ever* examples seems unclear. An interesting point noted by Culicover (2013: 234) is that *how come* has no *ever* derivative – as we see from the ungrammaticality of:

   (vi)  *How come ever you would do that?

whereas other wh-words do, e.g. *whyever/however/whenever/wherever/whoever/whatever*. This would follow if *how come* is a wh-phrase – though since the complementiser *whether* has no *ever*-derivative either, it could be argued to be equally consistent with Collins' claim that *how come* is a complementiser.

### 4.4      Ochi's Spec-CP Analysis

Ochi claims (2004: 51) that '*how come* is a wh-phrase' and that it is an in situ constituent which is 'merged as the spec of CP' (Ochi 2011: 27). If the CP housing *how come* selects a TP complement, a sentence like (4a) 'How come you were arrested?' would have the structure below:

(56)      [CP *How come* [C ø] [TP you [T were] arrested]]

Ochi does not say what kind of phrase *how come* is, or what kind of internal structure it has – but let's suppose that it is a causal adverbial of some kind. The assumption that it is directly merged in situ in spec-CP means that it does not bind a trace/variable, and hence is not an interrogative operator. As we will see below, such a spec-CP analysis can account for numerous properties of *how come* questions.

One such property is that *how come* never undergoes Wh-Movement. This is because *how come* is directly merged/base-generated in its criterial position as the specifier of an interrogative C, so is frozen in place by the Criterial Freezing Condition (31).

A second property of *how come* which can be accounted for under the specifier analysis is that it can't occur in clefts like (28) *'How come it is that John quit his job?' This is because interrogative clefts (like 'Why is it that he resigned?') involve Wh-Movement; and *how come* can't undergo the kind of movement operation arrowed in (30), because it is frozen in place by the Criterial Freezing Condition (31).

A third property of *how come* which can be accounted for under the specifier analysis is that it has wide scope with respect to quantifiers, as illustrated earlier in relation to (27b) 'How come everybody hates John?' This follows because *how come* is merged in situ in spec-CP, above the quantifier.

A fourth property which falls out from the specifier analysis is that *how come* doesn't appear in multiple operator questions like (34b) *'How come John ate what?' This is because *how come* isn't an operator (as noted earlier, it is generated in situ, so doesn't bind a trace/variable) and so cannot license other wh-operators.

A fifth property which can be accounted for under the specifier analysis is that *how come* doesn't trigger Auxiliary Inversion in standard varieties of English, as we see from the ungrammaticality (for most speakers) of sentences like that below:

(57)      *How come *were you* arrested?

This follows from the non-operator status of *how come*, if we suppose that *how come* is directly merged in situ, and that in questions '(English) subject-auxiliary inversion is triggered by interrogative operators linked to a syntactic variable (or trace)' (Shlonsky & Soare 2011: 666).

A sixth property which follows from the specifier analysis is that *how come* can't be followed by *that* for most speakers, e.g. in a sentence like *'How come that you were arrested?' Under the specifier analysis of *how come*, such a sentence would have a structure like the following (if the CP housing *how come* selects a TP complement):

(58)     [$_{CP}$ *How come* [$_C$ **that**] [$_{TP}$ you [$_T$ were] arrested]]

The resulting structure (58) would violate the Root Complementiser Filter (38), since *that* is the head of a root projection. Furthermore, for speakers who have the relevant filter in their grammar, (58) would also violate the Doubly Filled COMP Filter (Chomsky & Lasnik 1977; Chomsky 1981; see §1.3), which for present purposes can be formulated as follows:

(59)     **Doubly Filled COMP Filter/DFCF**
         No overt complementiser can have an overt specifier

DFCF is violated in (58) because the overt complementiser *that* has the overt specifier *how*.[19]

A seventh property which can be derived from the specifier analysis is that *how come* allows Sluicing of material following it, e.g. in a clause such as that bracketed below:

(60)     He is lying, and I wanna know [$_{CP}$ *how come* [$_C$ ø] ~~he is lying~~]

This does not induce violation of the Sluicing Constraint (42) because the head C of CP is null rather than overt.

An eighth property which can readily be accounted for under the specifier analysis is that *how come* (for most speakers) never appears in *to*-infinitives, as illustrated by the ungrammaticality of (32) above, repeated as (61) below:

---

[19] However, as Liliane Haegeman (pc) points out, the generality of the Doubly Filled COMP Filter/DFCF is unclear, since there are languages which appear to violate it. For example, Haegeman (1992: 51) notes that the West Flemish dialect of Lapscheure obligatorily violates DFCF, in the sense that whenever a phrase occupies spec-CP, the head C of CP has to be overtly spelled out; van Craenenbroek (2004: 44) makes a parallel claim about Frisian, and Bayer (2015, 2016) about Bavarian. Moreover, as we saw in Chapter 3, there are speakers of English who seemingly allow DFC structures (e.g. in which a peripheral projection headed by *that* has an adjunct, or topic, or wh-phrase as its specifier).

(61)      *I don't know [how come to leave]

One way of accounting for this is to attribute it to whatever constraint also blocks *'I don't know why to leave.'[20] An alternative is to suppose that *how come* can only be merged as the specifier of a finite C: this is arguably because *how come* questions are inherently factive, and factive clauses are finite.

Having shown how Ochi's spec-CP analysis can account for a range of properties of the *how come*+subject structures used by a majority of speakers, I will now go on to argue that it can also handle the *how come*+auxiliary structures used by some speakers. As noted in §4.1, there are a minority of speakers who accept Auxiliary Inversion after *how come*, although for most speakers this type of structure is strongly stigmatised – as we see from the fact that only 1 of the 20 speakers in the informal questionnaire survey reported in the Appendix in §4.10 gave a high (5/OK) acceptability rating to the sentence 'How come did I fall in love with someone like you?' and the mean score was just 1.3. Ochi (2004: 52, fn. 25) notes that Diane Lillo-Martin reported to him that there are some speakers who accept Inversion in sentences like (62) below, although she claims their numbers are 'quite limited':

(62)      How come *won't you* be here tomorrow?

Kim & Kim (2011, section 5) include a more extensive discussion of Inversion with *how come*, citing examples including the following (sourced from corpora):

(63)      a. How come *does iodine* get into the human system of dwellers along the coasts from sea water? (=3b)
          b. Now, how come *did you* give those baby-sitters such a hard time? (=3c)
          c. How come, if he's the Devil Incarnate, *does he* spend half the book down there in that poxy little room?

---

[20] However, this potential correlation seems to be an imperfect one, since (as noted in fn. 9) some speakers allow *why to* infinitives but not *how come to* infinitives. Moreover, Peter Culicover (pc) points out that he allows *why not to* infinitives (as in 'I don't know why not to leave') but not *how come not to* infinitives (as in *'I know how come not to do that') – although we find internet-sourced examples of *how come not to* like that below:

> (i) I do not use, or recommend using, any standard tire and/or rim without inner tubes. How come not to go tubless [*sic*]? (forums.mtbr.com)

Culicover also points out that *why* (but not *how come*) can be interpreted as originating within an ellipsed negative infinitive in sentences like 'He said for me to leave but I don't know why/how come.'

If Inversion in questions in English is 'triggered by interrogative operators linked to a syntactic variable (or trace)' (Shlonsky & Soare 2011: 666), this suggests that speakers who allow Inversion with *how come* treat it as a wh-operator like *why* that moves to spec-CP from a position below C. If so, a sentence like (57) 'How come were you arrested?' will have a structure along the lines of (64) below, with *how come* originating below C and undergoing Wh-Movement into spec-CP, as shown by the arrow:

(64)     [$_{CP}$ *How come* [$_C$ were] [$_{TP}$ you [$_T$ —] arrested —]]

Some evidence that *how come* in Inversion structures is treated as an operator comes from the observation that (like *why*) it can occur in cleft sentences – as the following internet-sourced examples illustrate:

(65)     a. How come *is it* that demand and supply of goods is always equal? (quora .com)
         b. How come *is it* that no-one can deliver on their promises? (m.facebook .com)
         c. How come *is it* that so many Americans find Hugh Laurie hot? (fanpop .com)
         d. How come *is it* that in the south people look at me like I'm crazy? (answers .yahoo.com)
         e. How come *is it* that when I tweet a celebrity, most of them never tweet back or RT? (web)
         f. How come *is it* that you don't have to pay to go into Wales but you have to pay to get out? (mobile.twitter.com)
         g. How come *is it* that even ugly women my age can get a boyfriend but I am still single? (=3d)

If such cleft wh-questions involve Wh-Movement of a wh-operator from a position after *is* in the cleft to the front of the relevant clause, it follows that *how come* must be an operator undergoing Wh-Movement, as in (64).

Further evidence in support of treating *how come* in Inversion structures as an adverbial wh-operator is that (as noted by Chris Collins, pc) it can be coordinated with other wh-operator constituents, like those underlined in the (internet-sourced) examples below:

(66)     a. And that in itself is something interesting as it makes me think and wonder *how come and for what reason* **would** so many different fashion houses produce such similar styles for this season (modelmanagement.com)
         b. Second, *how come and for how long* **has** Belhassen had Canadian residency? (alt-world-watch.blogspot.com)

    c. *How come and in what ways* **do** people co-operate in file-sharing net-
      works? (socio-informatics.org)
    d. *How come and for why* **hasn't** this extra solar planet burnt up? (allegraslo
      man.com)
    e. *Why and how come* **is** Fwb800 ALu stock only Euro399??????? (pimpmyair
      gun.com)

If the underlined expressions are wh-operators (as argued by Collins 1991 in
relation to *why*), this suggests that *how come* can have a similar operator
status.[21] Significantly, such sentences are unacceptable without Auxiliary
Inversion, suggesting that *how come* is not an operator in structures where it
does not trigger Inversion.

    In its operator use, *how come* (like *why*) can seemingly originate in
a relatively high position in the clause (perhaps in a Reason Phrase above
negation: Shlonsky & Soare 2011), since it doesn't give rise to intervention/
negative island violations in sentences like the following:

(67)    a. *How come* **didn't** I know Bruno performed COUNT ON ME in Jakarta?
       (web)
     b. May I ask, *how come* **couldn't** you get disability insurance? (benzobud
       dies.org)
     c. If Stephen Hawking is so flippin' smart, then *how come* **can't** he get out of
       his wheelchair? (reddit.com)
     d. *How come* **don't** young people care about 'selling out' anymore? (reddit
       .com)
     e. *How come* **won't** Siri work? (answers.yahoo.com)
     f. *How come* **wouldn't** one back this project (even after KD:M sucking
       almost all my $$$, hehe)? (kickstarter.com)

By contrast, the manner adverb *how* (which is generated in a lower position,
below negation) does indeed give rise to a negative island violation, as we see
from sentences like:

---

[21] Peter Culicover (pc) points out that although he does not generally allow Auxiliary Inversion
after *how come*, he accepts it in (i) below, though not in (ii):

    (i) Tell me, how come and for how long would you stay in a job that is as unrewarding
       as this one?
    (ii) *Tell me, for how long and how come would you stay in a job that is as unrewarding
       as this one?

It would appear that, for speakers like him, Inversion is only permitted when the wh-constituent
which ends up closest to the auxiliary is one that can trigger Inversion. An interesting question to
explore is whether there are potential parallels with closest conjunct agreement in coordinate
structures (see Bošković 2009b).

(68)    *How **didn't** Geraldine fix her bike? (Shlonsky & Soare 2011: 656, 14b)

But if (in varieties which allow Inversion) *how come* is a wh-operator under-going Wh-Movement, we'd expect it to be able to undergo long Wh-Movement (moving from a lower into a higher clause), and hence be able to be construed as an embedded clause constituent. In this respect, it is interesting to note that in a prepublication version of his (2004) paper presented at GLOW, Ochi (p. 39, fn. 18) includes the following remark attributed to Diane Lillo-Martin (where example numbering has been changed to fit in with that used here):

> Interestingly, she also informs us that there is a correlation between subject-aux inversion and the possibility of long-distance construal of *how come*. To the extent that (69b) is acceptable, it is ambiguous with respect to the interpretation of *how come*:
>
> (69)    a. How come you think that John is angry? (matrix only)
>         b. How come do you think that John is angry (ambiguous)

The possibility of construing *how come* in (69b) as questioning the reason for John's anger suggests that it has a derivation involving long-distance Wh-Movement of *how come*. If so, *how come* would appear to be able to function (in the relevant variety) as a wh-operator which undergoes Wh-Movement to spec-CP and triggers Auxiliary Inversion.[22]

Further potential evidence of *how come* being used as a wh-operator in some varieties comes from the observation that some speakers extend *how come* from use in interrogative clauses to use as a relative operator, as in the following internet-sourced examples:

---

[22] Memo Cinque (pc) points out that the Italian counterpart of *how come* (= *come mai*, literally 'how ever') can seemingly either have matrix or embedded scope in a sentence like:

(i)  Come    mai    pensi      che    si       sia      arrabbiata?
     How     ever   you.think  that   herself  she.be   angered
     'Why do you think she got angry?'

However, he notes that this only seems possible if *pensi* 'think' is present tense and has a second person subject. Thus, only matrix scope is possible in:

(ii)  Come   mai   Gianni  pensa    che   lei   si       sia    offesa?
      How    ever  Gianni  thinks   that  she   herself  be     offended
      'How come Gianni thinks she took offence?'
(iii) Come   mai   avevi   pensato  che   lei   si       fosse  offesa?
      How    ever  you.had thought  that  she   herself  were   offended
      'How come you had thought she had taken offence?'

I set aside here the issue of constraints on long-distance interpretation of *how come*.

(70)    a. Ok so now you see the reason *how come* he has taken four years just to put
           out an album beat (lyrics to the song Déjà Vu by Eminem)
        b. Probably also the reason *how come* most Americans are this close to
           snappin' (earlpittsamerican.com)
        c. The reason *how come* so many people are unsuccessful nowadays has
           NOTHING to do with them failing (manthesis.com)
        d. And you wanna know the reason *how come* I fired you? (ultraglis.com)
        e. Anyone here know the reason *how come* Javier Hernandez can play for two
           sides in each half? (nufcblog.org)

In this use, it seems to function in essentially the same way as the relative
pronoun *why* in a structure such as *the reason why I left him*. Shlonsky &
Soare (2011: 652) claim that *why* in such cases is a relative operator, and
that '*why* is moved to the position of relative operators from some lower
position, leaving a trace/copy that is interpreted as a semantic variable'.
It likely that *how come* in (70) has the same status as a relative operator,
and this lends further plausibility to the claim that *how come* functions as
an interrogative operator in questions in which it triggers Interrogative
Inversion.

Thus far in this section, I have outlined Ochi's analysis of *how come* as a wh-
phrase which is directly merged in spec-CP in structures not involving
Auxiliary Inversion, and have shown how it can be extended to *how come*
questions involving Inversion if some speakers treat *how come* as an operator
which originates in a position below T and from there moves to spec-CP. In the
remainder of this section, however, I will highlight problems which arise with
the spec-CP analysis.

One such arises in relation to the use of complementisers. As we saw in the
discussion of (58) above, the spec-CP analysis predicts that *how come* questions will not allow the use of a complementiser like *that* (because the Doubly
Filled COMP Filter 59 will bar the head C of CP from being filled by *that*, as
will the Root Complementiser Filter 38 in main clauses). However, the problem
this poses is that there are speakers (like me) who allow *that* to occur after *how
come* as in (71a) below, before *how come* (as in 71b) and both before and after
*how come* as in (71c):

(71)    a. *How come* **that** they searched his flat without a warrant?
        b. He protested [**that** *how come* they had searched his flat without
           a warrant?]
        c. He protested [**that** *how come* <u>that</u> they had searched his flat without
           a warrant?]

And indeed, I found numerous authentic examples of all three types of structure on the internet.[23] There is no immediately obvious way of accommodating structures like those in (71) within an analysis that takes the clause periphery to comprise a single CP in which *how come* is the specifier of a null C which selects a TP complement.

A second problem with the spec-CP analysis is this. If *how come* is the specifier of a null C with a TP complement, it will immediately precede the clause subject in spec-TP. But this raises the question of how to deal with structures in which other (underlined) peripheral constituents are positioned between *how come* and the (bold-printed) subject, like those in (72) below (the first two examples being internet-sourced, and the third being constructed):

(72)    a. *How come* <u>in the daylight</u> **we** can only see the sky but when it's night time you can see space? (helium.imascientist.org.au)
        b. *How come* <u>if you scratch an itch</u>, **more places** begin to itch? (quora.com)
        c. *How come* <u>at no point, even when asked to, did</u> **he** apologise?

A related problem arises in sentences like (73) below (where 73a is internet-sourced and 73b, c are constructed), which show that other (italicised) peripheral constituents can precede *how come* – even though, if the clause periphery comprises a single CP in which *how come* is the specifier of an interrogative C, we would expect *how come* to be the leftmost constituent of its clause):

---

[23] Below are some internet-sourced examples of *that how come that* structures:

(i)    My point is **that** *how come* <u>that</u> this combo happens so often?
(ii)   My schoolmate's comment was **that** *how come* <u>that</u> a boy like him dated such a girl ...
(iii)  But I just cannot comprehend **that** *how come* <u>that</u> enabling adversaries to deal with player fortifications was not top priority from day 1
(iv)   It has been puzzling me **that** *how come* <u>that</u> it is always drummed into riders, from being very young, to have heels down
(v)    If Hashemi is to be taken seriously on this, he should explain **that** *how come* <u>that</u> using the same 'paper Imam' has now become so bad?
(vi)   I was wondering **that** *how come* <u>that</u> payment processors such as STP and Payza don't do anything about it
(vii)  He indignantly posed the question **that** *how come* <u>that</u> the Hungarian counter-intelligence had not perceived anything at all
(viii) She lamented **that** *how come* <u>that</u> she could not come to her motherland Bangladesh ...
(ix)   One may well argue, as someone has, **that** *how come* <u>that</u> the Pakistan army, a legacy of the Raj, was not similarly labelled?
(x)    I thought **that** *how come* <u>that</u> a criminal like Chopper can speak like an angel/a devil, but our PM can't
(xi)   And I said **that** *how come* <u>that</u> this place is not following any of those tenets

(73)    a. <u>Given the property prices in London</u>, *how come* you still see so many apartments that seem to be inhabited by people with very limited funds? (quora.com)

   b. <u>Before you go to bed</u>, <u>after you've had a shower</u>, *how come* you check your email?

   c. <u>The mistakes we made when we were young</u>, *how come* we repeat them when we are old?

Sentences like (71–3) suggest we need to allow for other peripheral constituents to precede and follow *how come*. Indeed, if each underlined constituent preceding or following *how come* in (71–3) is contained in a separate peripheral projection, it is clear that we will have to recognise the existence of more than one peripheral projection above TP in such sentences.

One way of handling sentences like (71–3) is to adopt a CP recursion analysis, projecting one CP on top of another, with each CP containing a separate peripheral constituent. As we saw in §3.3, CP recursion seems to be independently required for structures like those below:

(74)    a. The party opposite said [$_{CP}$ [$_C$ **that**] if we cut 6 billion from the budget [$_{CP}$ [$_C$ *that*] it would end in catastrophe]] (David Cameron, Prime Minister's Questions; Radford 2013)

   b. John was asking me [$_{CP}$ [$_C$ **if**], when the house was sold, [$_{CP}$ [$_C$ *would*] they move back to Derry]] (McCloskey 2006)

Given the possibility of CP recursion, we might suppose that a *that+how come+that* clause like that bracketed in (71c) above has a CP recursion structure like that below:

(75)    He protested [$_{CP}$ [$_C$ that] [$_{CP}$ how come [$_C$ ø] [$_{CP}$ [$_C$ that] they had searched his flat without a warrant]]]

(75) would violate neither the Root Complementiser Constraint (38) nor the Doubly Filled COMP Filter (59). The CP recursion analysis could be extended to sentences like (72–3), if each of the underlined constituents is contained within a separate CP. On this view, (72c) would have the peripheral structure below:

(76)    [$_{CP}$ How come [$_C$ ø] [$_{CP}$ at no point [$_C$ ø] [$_{CP}$ even when asked to [$_C$ ø] [$_{CP}$ [$_C$ did] he apologise]]]]

Thus, it would seem at first sight as if the relevant data can be handled in terms of CP recursion.

However, a drawback of the CP recursion analysis is that all the bracketed peripheral constituents in a structure like (76) are said to be of the same categorial type (CP). But this categorisation fails to recognise that each of the different CPs in (76) has a very different function: the first houses the interrogative *how come*, the second houses the focused negative *at no point*, the third houses the clausal adjunct *even when asked to*, and the fourth houses the inverted auxiliary *did*. Moreover, the CP recursion analysis also fails to recognise that the different CPs are not interchangeable: for example, the CP housing *at no point* cannot be positioned above the CP containing *how come* (as we see from the ungrammaticality of 77a below), nor can the CP containing *even when asked to* be positioned below the CP containing *did* (as we see from the ungrammaticality of 77b):[24]

(77)   a. *At no point, how come, even when asked to, did he apologise?
       b. *How come, at no point did, even when asked to, he apologise?

In the next two sections, I show how work within the cartographic framework has sought to address such problems, and look at specific cartographic analyses of *how come* questions proposed by Shlonsky & Soare (2011) and Endo (2017).

## 4.5    Shlonsky & Soare's INTP Analysis

As we saw in §1.4, work within the cartographic framework developed by Rizzi (1997 et seq.) and others has argued that each constituent in the clause periphery is contained within a projection with a dedicated functional head (e.g. a focused constituent serves as the specifier of a focus projection with an overt or null focus particle as its head). Recall that Rizzi (2015a) posits the following template specifying the hierarchical ordering of heads in the clause periphery (where a star indicates that one or more heads of the relevant type can appear in the relevant position):

(78)   FORCE > TOP* > INT > TOP* > FOC > TOP* > MOD* > TOP * > FIN

---

[24] These problems could be overcome if the head C of each CP carried a feature identifying it as different from each of the other C heads in the structure: for example, Rizzi & Shlonsky (2007) use the notation $C_R$ to denote a relative complementiser, $C_Q$ to denote a question complementiser, and so on. Using this notation, the head C of the CP housing the focused negative *at no point* could carry a focus feature, and thus be a $C_{FOC}$ head. Ordering restrictions could then be formulated in terms of inter-relations between different types of C-head. However, this would be extensionally equivalent to the cartographic approach (e.g. of positing a FOC head corresponding to $C_{FOC}$) discussed in the next section. The CP recursion approach picks out the property of being a peripheral head as the reason for using the label C; the cartographic approach picks out the focus feature as the reason for using the label FOC. The two approaches can thus be argued to be notational variants.

Working within the cartographic framework and adopting an earlier analysis proposed by Rizzi (2001) for Italian *come mai* 'how come', Shlonsky & Soare (2011: 665) claim that '*how come* is a phrase, not a head' and that it is directly merged as the specifier of a null INT(errogative) head. On this view, a sentence like *How come he lied?* would have a structure along the lines below:

(79)     [FORCEP [FORCE ø] [INTP how come [INT ø] [FINP [FIN ø] he lied]]]

Their spec-INTP analysis can account for a wide range of properties of *how come* sentences, as we will see below.

One is that *how come* (for most speakers) does not trigger Auxiliary Inversion, e.g. in sentences such as (5) *'How come has she read the book?' Shlonsky & Soare (2011: 665) claim that this is because '(English) subject-auxiliary inversion is triggered by interrogative operators that are linked to a syntactic variable (or trace).' Because *how come* is directly merged in situ in spec-INTP, it does not undergo movement and therefore does not bind a variable/trace, with the result that it is not an operator and so does not trigger Inversion.

A slightly different account of the absence of Inversion is offered by Haegeman (2012), who posits that Negative Inversion and Interrogative Inversion involve movement of a focused negative or interrogative operator through spec-FINP into spec-FOCP, and that FIN attracts an auxiliary to move into FIN if an operator is in spec-FINP (or transits through spec-FINP, like *where* below):[25]

(80)     [FORCEP [FORCE ø] [FOCP *where* [FOC ø] [FINP ~~where~~ [FIN are] [TP you [T ~~are~~] going ~~where~~]]]]

In (80), *where* originates as the complement of *going*, and transits through spec-FINP (triggering Auxiliary Inversion, i.e. movement of *are* from T to FIN) before moving into spec-FOCP. By contrast, *how come* in (81) below is directly merged in spec-INTP, and (by virtue of not being in spec-FINP at any stage of derivation) does not trigger Inversion:

(81)     [FORCEP [FORCE ø] [INTP *how come* [INT ø] [FINP [FIN ø] [TP you [T are] going home]]]]

Thus, either Shlonsky & Soare's assumptions or Haegeman's can account for why most speakers don't allow Interrogative Inversion after *how come*

---

[25] I set aside the question of whether the auxiliary remains in FIN, or moves from there into FOC: see the discussion of non-adjacent Inversion in §2.7.

(although, as we will see in 83c below, they allow Negative Inversion after *how come*).[26]

In conjunction with the template in (78), the INTP analysis of *how come* makes a number of predictions about the relative ordering of *how come* with respect to other peripheral projections.[27] For example, it correctly predicts that *how come* can be preceded by a topic in a structure like (82a) below, or by a modifying adjunct in a structure like (82b) (if MODP can occupy any position between FORCEP and FINP, even though this is not shown in 78):

(82)    a.  $[_{\text{FORCEP}}$ $[_{\text{FORCE}}$ ø$]$ $[_{\text{TOPP}}$ the things you did last night $[_{\text{TOP}}$ ø$]$ $[_{\text{INTP}}$ *how come* $[_{\text{INT}}$ ø$]$ $[_{\text{FINP}}$ $[_{\text{FIN}}$ ø$]$ you can't remember (them)$]]]]$
    b.  $[_{\text{FORCEP}}$ $[_{\text{FORCE}}$ ø$]$ $[_{\text{MODP}}$ on Thursday $[_{\text{MOD}}$ ø$]$ $[_{\text{INTP}}$ *how come* $[_{\text{INT}}$ ø$]$ $[_{\text{FINP}}$ $[_{\text{FIN}}$ ø$]$ there were no lectures$]]]]$

Likewise, the INTP analysis (in conjunction with the template in 78) correctly predicts that *how come* can be followed by a modifying adjunct in (83a) below, a topic in (83b) or a focused negative in (83c):

(83)    a.  $[_{\text{FORCEP}}$ $[_{\text{FORCE}}$ ø$]$ $[_{\text{INTP}}$ *how come* $[_{\text{INT}}$ ø$]$ $[_{\text{MODP}}$ on Thursday $[_{\text{MOD}}$ ø$]$ $[_{\text{FINP}}$ $[_{\text{FIN}}$ ø$]$ there were no lectures$]]]]$
    b.  $[_{\text{FORCEP}}$ $[_{\text{FORCE}}$ ø$]$ $[_{\text{INTP}}$ *how come* $[_{\text{INT}}$ ø$]$ $[_{\text{TOPP}}$ the things you did last night $[_{\text{TOP}}$ ø$]$ $[_{\text{FINP}}$ $[_{\text{FIN}}$ ø$]$ you can't remember (them)$]]]]$
    c.  $[_{\text{FORCEP}}$ $[_{\text{FORCE}}$ ø$]$ $[_{\text{INTP}}$ *how come* $[_{\text{INT}}$ ø$]$ $[_{\text{FOCP}}$ nowhere in the Bible $[_{\text{FOC}}$ ø$]$ $[_{\text{FINP}}$ — $[_{\text{FIN}}$ does$]$ anyone mention the dinosaurs —$]]]]$

If the (underlined) focused negative phrase in (83c) transits through spec-FINP (before moving into spec-FOCP),[28] it will trigger Auxiliary Inversion. This means that although (for most speakers) *how come* does not allow Interrogative Inversion, it does allow Negative Inversion. Thus, overall, it would seem that

---

[26] Mike Jones (pc) points out that a potential problem arises with yes-no questions if they contain a null Question operator (*Op*) directly merged in spec-INTP which triggers Inversion in a structure like:

    (i)  $[_{\text{FORCEP}}$ $[_{\text{FORCE}}$ ø$]$ $[_{\text{INTP}}$ *Op* $[_{\text{INT}}$ ø$]$ $[_{\text{FINP}}$ $[_{\text{FIN}}$ are$]$ you going home$]]]$

    The analysis in (i) would raise the question of why *how come* does not trigger Inversion in the same way as *Op*. As noted by Haegeman (2012: 121), this problem can be overcome if yes-no questions are 'derived by moving a null operator through or to SpecFINP'.

[27] For the sake of clarity, I should point out that the claims made in relation to (82–9) below are made by me, not by Shlonsky & Soare.

[28] I set aside here the claim in Maekawa (2007) that not all fronted negative constituents are focused: for present purposes it would not matter if they moved through FINP into a superordinate NEGP projection (rather than through FINP into FOCP). I also set aside the possibility that the inverted auxiliary may raise further from FIN into FOC.

Shlonsky & Soare's INTP analysis can account for the position of *how come* relative to other peripheral constituents.[29]

In addition, the INTP analysis can also account for the pattern of ellipsis (termed *How Come* Stripping) found in sentences such as (84b) below (and likewise in 44 above), where capitals mark contrastive focus:

(84)    SPEAKER A: John spent Christmas in Paris
        SPEAKER B: How come PARIS?

Nakao et al. (2012) argue that in sentences like *Why Paris?* the constituent following *why* undergoes Focus Movement to spec-FOCP, and then the material following it undergoes ellipsis.[30] Assuming that this is also the case in the corresponding *how come* structure, (84b) will have the peripheral structure

---

[29] I note in passing that Endo (2014) proposes an alternative cartographic analysis taking *how come* to occupy the specifier position in a superordinate Speech Act Projection/SAP positioned above FORCEP, with *that* occupying the head FORCE position in FORCEP: see Haegeman & Hill (2014) and the references cited there for evidence of SAPs. On this view, a sentence like *How come that he is lying?* would have a structure which includes the peripheral projections bracketed in (i) below:

> (i)  [$_{SAP}$ how come [$_{SA}$ ø] [$_{FORCEP}$ [$_{FORCE}$ that] he is lying]]

However, the SAP analysis is problematic in several respects. For one thing, *that* is typically a declarative force marker, and yet *how come* sentences are interrogative (not declarative) in force. Secondly, since speech acts are properties of utterances and the syntactic counterpart of utterances are root clauses, the SAP analysis wrongly predicts that *how come* will only be used in root clauses, whereas as illustrated and discussed in relation to (19), they also occur in embedded clauses (though this objection would be undermined if we allow embedded speech acts). Secondly, if SAP is the highest projection in the clause, the analysis seemingly wrongly predicts that no other peripheral constituents can appear in front of *how come* – and yet this claim is challenged by structures like (82).

[30] An interesting question posed by the Focus Movement analysis is how to account for speaker B's reply in the dialogue below (where capitals mark contrastive stress):

> (i)  SPEAKER A: YOU should be the one who breaks the news to her
>       SPEAKER B: How come me/*I?

At first sight, it might seem unlikely that 'How come ME?' is a reduced form of (ii) below, because of the case mismatch between the default/accusative form *me* required in (i), and the nominative form *I* required in (ii):

> (ii)  How come I/*ME should be the one who breaks the news to her?

However, Yoshida et al. (2015, fn. 8) argue that this is because English has the possibility of assigning remnant nominals accusative case by default. An alternative possibility would be to derive 'How come ME?' from:

> (iii)  How come ME, I should be the one who breaks the news to her?

shown in simplified form below, with the material marked by strikethrough undergoing deletion in the PF component:

(85)    [FORCEP [FORCE ø] [INTP how come [INT ø] [FOCP PARIS [FOC ø] ~~John spent Christmas in~~]]]

The claim that *how come* can be immediately followed by a focused constituent is borne out by sentences such as (86) below (where capitals mark contrastive stress):

(86)    How come SYNTAX you don't like, but PHONOLOGY you do?

Thus, the INTP analysis can provide a principled account of Stripping in structures like (84b).[31] On the assumption that *how come* is generated in situ in structures like (85), it will not move across the fronted focused constituent *Paris*, and so will not induce the kind of intervention effect we find in sentences such as *\*'I wonder **how**, Mary, he behaved towards'*, where *how* crosses *Mary*.[32]

But can the INTP analysis also handle the *how come*+auxiliary questions found in some varieties? In §4.4, it was suggested that *how come* in Auxiliary Inversion questions functions as an interrogative operator, like *why*. Shlonsky & Soare (2011: 653) claim that *why* is 'externally merged as specifier of a dedicated functional projection – labeled *ReasonP* – configured above negation and adverbials and, most probably, above the canonical subject position'.[33] They further claim that *why* undergoes movement from its initial

---

and treat the remnant following *how come* as a dislocated constituent generated in situ. Yet another possibility (suggested by Weir 2014a) is that there is a concealed cleft structure, so that 'How come ME?' has a source paraphraseable as:

(iv)  How come ME ~~it is that should be the one who breaks the news to her~~

[31]  For Nakao et al. (2012), the constituent which serves as the complement of FOC is FINP, whereas for Weir (2014a) it is VOICEP: I set aside this issue here.

[32]  Note that *How Come* Stripping is not possible after the complementiser *that* (cf. *\*'How come that Paris?'*). This follows from a more general constraint to the effect that stripping operations are blocked by the presence of a complementiser, as illustrated below:

(i)  When I asked who did it, he said (\*that) you

See Wurmbrand (2017) on the nature of this constraint.

[33]  Chapman & Kučerová (2016) argue that *why* is ambiguous between a reason and a purpose interpretation. Thus, they claim that a sentence like *Why did she resign?* can have a reason reading on which an appropriate reply would be 'Because she got a pay cut', or a purpose reading on which an appropriate reply would be 'In order to earn more money'. They argue that purpose *why* is base-generated in a CAUSP projection within vP. *How come* differs from *why* in that it only has a reason interpretation.

position into its criterial position as the specifier of INTP in cases of short movement, but moves into the specifier position of a wh-operator projection/ WHP in cases of long movement.[34] If *how come* can function as an interrogative operator for some speakers, we might suppose that (in this use) it has essentially the same syntax as *why*. Consider what this might mean for sentences such as the following:

(87)   a. *How come*, if he's the Devil Incarnate, **does** he spend half the book down there in that poxy little room? (=63c, Kim & Kim 2011)
       b. *How come* when I try to make you laugh **does** it end up me who cries? (Lyrics to the song *How come?* by Otis Grand)
       c. My question is *how come* after not eating for 4 hours **does** my blood sugar go up? (diabeticconnect.com)

On the assumptions made here, (87a) could have a peripheral structure along the lines shown below below:

(88)   [$_{FORCEP}$ [$_{FORCE}$ ø] [$_{INTP}$ **how come** [$_{INT}$ ø] [$_{MODP}$ if he's the Devil Incarnate [$_{MOD}$ ø] [$_{FINP}$ ~~how come~~ [$_{FIN}$ *does*] [$_{REASONP}$ ~~how come~~ [$_{REASON}$ ø] he spend half the book down there in that poxy little room]]]]]]

This would mean that *how come* originates in spec-REASONP and transits through spec-FINP (thereby triggering Auxiliary Inversion) before moving on to its criterial position in spec-INTP. The fact that *does* is positioned after the underlined adjunct clause in (88) provides evidence that the auxiliary does not raise into INT in such sentences.[35]

The suggestion that *how come* is a wh-operator which undergoes Wh-Movement in *how come*+ auxiliary questions is consistent with the observation that such questions do not allow argument fronting, as we see from the ungrammaticality of sentences like those below:

---

[34] Their precise claim (2011: 663) is: 'short-moved *why* raises from Spec, Reason to Spec, Int and *cannot* target Spec, Wh, whereas long-moved *why* has exactly the opposite property, namely, it targets the matrix Wh and *not* the matrix Int.'

[35] I set aside the question of whether the inverted auxiliary *does* transits through the REASON head. Another question which arises is why the MOD head in (88) cannot be spelled out (via secondary spellout) as *that*:

   (i) How come, if he's the Devil Incarnate, (*that) does he spend half the book down there in that poxy little room?

The answer may well be that the complementiser *that* is non-verbal in nature and requires a peripheral head immediately below it to be non-verbal too. Consequently, it cannot occur in a clause where it is immediately followed by a FINP whose head is verbal and attracts an auxiliary to adjoin to it.

(89)    a. *\*How come* **Trump** are people put off by?
        b. *\*Trump*, *how come* are people put off by?

Here, the bold (-printed) argument *Trump* originates as the complement of the preposition *by* and (if topicalised) raises to a position on the edge of a TOPP projection; in addition, *how come* originates in a REASONP projection between FIN and the subject *people* and moves through the edge of FINP (thereby triggering Auxiliary Inversion) to the edge of an INTP projection above TOPP – as shown in diagrammatic form below (simplified, inter alia, by not showing the FORCEP projection on top of TOPP/INTP, to save space):

(90)

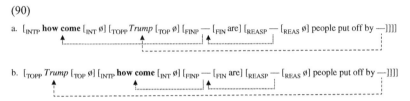

a. [$_{INTP}$ **how come** [$_{INT}$ ∅] [$_{TOPP}$ *Trump* [$_{TOP}$ ∅] [$_{FINP}$ — [$_{FIN}$ are] [$_{REASP}$ — [$_{REAS}$ ∅] people put off by —]]]]

b. [$_{TOPP}$ *Trump* [$_{TOP}$ ∅] [$_{INTP}$ **how come** [$_{INT}$ ∅] [$_{FINP}$ — [$_{FIN}$ are] [$_{REASP}$ — [$_{REAS}$ ∅] people put off by —]]]]

However, both derivations result in a structure in which one A-bar-moved constituent moves across another, thereby inducing a potential violation of the following constraint mentioned in §1.4:

(91)    **Intervention Constraint**
        Likes cannot cross likes (Abels 2012: 247)

The constraint is violated if we suppose that *how come* and *Trump* are 'likes' to the extent that both are constituents undergoing movement from a position below the periphery to an A-bar position within the periphery. Moreover, (90a) is somewhat worse than (90b) because (90a) also violates a constraint against crossing movement paths which was formulated by Pesetsky (1982a: 309) in the following terms:

(92)    **Path Containment Condition**
        If two paths overlap, one must contain the other.

This is because the two movement paths in (90a) are crossing, and neither path contains the other.[36]

---

[36] However, there may be additional factors at work here, since (89a) is awkward even if the constituent intervening between *how come* and the inverted auxiliary is a dislocated topic generated in situ, as below:

   (i) ?\*How come *Trump*, are people put off by <u>him</u>?

By contrast, an intervening in situ adverbial (in spec-MODP) positioned between *how come* and the inverted auxiliary yields much better results:

As noted at the beginning of this section, Shlonsky & Soare (2011: 665) claim that '*how come* is a phrase, not a head', and that it occupies the specifier position of INTP. This is consistent with it being able to be modified by a phrasal postmodifier like *exactly*, as we saw from the examples in (46) above, repeated as (93) below:

(93)    a. The first step in getting your ex back is to see *how come exactly* the breakup happened
        b. But *how come exactly* you don't want to get it?
        c. So *how come exactly* you get to open your mouth to someone else doing the same thing?
        d. *How come exactly* Lucas is the one with the 'heart of gold' and not Torres?
        e. *How come exactly* they can't find Whitey Bulger? (www.nj.com)
        f. His DF is one of the best around. *How come exactly?*

However, a potential problem for the claim that *how come* is a wh-phrase is posed by sentences like the following:

(94)    a. *How come the fuck* I don't have this one? (manlymovie.net)
        b. *How come the hell* that doesn't happen in real life? (itshardbeingmesome times.blogspot.com)
        c. *How come on earth* he has the power to beat the top players? (dragonsoul game.com)
        d. *How come in the world* they drop the ball like that in these 2 particular aspects? (web)
        e. *How come else* would she prefer that? (taneycrier.com)

The underlined expression in these examples is the kind of constituent that normally postmodifies a wh-word (not a wh-phrase), as we see from examples such as the following, where the underlined expression postmodifies the italicised wh-word, and is positioned internally within the bracketed wh-phrase:

---

(ii) How come, even though he was democratically elected, does Trump put people off?

It may be that the only kind of FINP which a TOP head allows as its complement is one with a non-verbal FIN as its head (i.e. a FIN that does not trigger Auxiliary Inversion) – but I will not pursue this issue further here.

Note that the relevant sentences are much better without Auxiliary Inversion, as below:

(iii) How come *Trump*, people are put off by?
(iv) *Trump*, how come people are put off by?

This is understandable if *how come* is generated in situ in such cases, since the fronted topic *Trump* will not cross *how come* at any stage of derivation in (iii), and in the case of (iv) *Trump* crosses *how come*, but *how come* is an in situ constituent, not an A-bar-moved operator.

(95)  a. [*What* the fuck kind of monstrosity] does Ryan Gosling pull out of the oven in *La La Land*? (jezebel.com)
      b. [*What* the hell kind of man] decides to dress up as a bat and run around the city? (brainyquote.com)
      c. [*What* on earth kind of bird] is this? (a-home-for-wild-birds.com)
      d. [*What* in the world kind of 'upgrade'] is this anyway? (community.logos .com)
      e. [*What* else kind of bowl] is there? (Anita Atkins, *The Seeker of Souls*, Google Books, 2015)

It could well be that speakers who produce sentences like (94–5) treat *how come* as a single word (as suggested by Collins 1991), raising the question of whether *how come* in this use is the specifier or head of INTP. Since a complementiser (or in cartographic terms, an INT head) like *if* doesn't allow this type of postmodifier, it seems more likely that *how come* in sentences like (94) is in spec-INTP, albeit it may well have the status of a single word for relevant speakers.

However, it is clear from examples like (96) below that there are other speakers (like me) who can position the relevant postmodifiers between *how* and *come*:

(96)  a. *How* the hell *come* you always know exactly what Harry Truman would have done? (cartoon in *The New Yorker*, 22 August 1988)
      b. *How* the heck *come* I don't get my fair share? (readersupportednews.com)
      c. *How* the fuck *come* I didn't follow you yet? (blameitonthesilence.tumbir .com)
      d. *How* on earth *come* you are using fahrenheit? (volcanocafe.wordpress .com)
      e. *How* in the world *come* you treat me this-a-way? (Lyrics to *Lorenzo Blues* by Skip James)
      f. *How* else *come* that eighty percent of the juvenile delinquents in our prisons are Moroccans and Turkish? (=55c)
      g. And *how* exactly *come* we sound exactly as BB? (gamefaqs.com)

An interesting question which this raises is whether there is parametric variation between speakers with respect to the status of *how come*. Speakers who produce *how come*+postmodifier structures like (93–4) above may treat *how come* as a wh-phrase/wh-word occupying spec-INTP as in (97a) below, whereas speakers who produce *how*+postmodifier+*come* structures like (96) may treat *how* (and any postmodifier it has) as occupying spec-INTP, and *come* as lexicalising the head of INTP as in (97b) below:

(97)  a. [$_{INTP}$ *how come* (postmodifier) [$_{INT}$ ø] ...]
      b. [$_{INTP}$ *how* (postmodifier) [$_{INT}$ *come*] ...]

In either case, *how come* would seem to be a lexical collocation/frozen chunk in such uses, in the sense that *come* can only be used in conjunction with *how* (except for a handful of speakers who produce *why come* sentences like those in 53 above): this might account for one writer hyphenating *how-the-hell-come* (criterionforum.org). The requirement for *come* to co-occur with *how* accounts for the obligatoriness of using *how* if *come* is used in the the italicised (second) conjunct of a coordinate sentence like that below:

(98)   How come you cheated on your wife with me and *(*how*) come you cheated on me with her?*

Both analyses in (97) will also account for why *come* is obligatorily stranded under Sluicing in sentences such as that below:

(99)   You're always grinning about something. *How* *(*come*)?* (=35)

If Sluicing involves deletion of the complement of the head of the projection housing the interrogative expression, then under either analysis in (97), Sluicing will involve deleting the complement of the INT head housing *come*, thereby leaving *how come* intact.[37]

Having seen that Shlonsky & Soare's cartographic analysis of *how come* can handle both *how come*+subject and *how come*+auxiliary structures (perhaps with minor modifications), in the next section I turn to look at work by Endo (2017) which offers a way of extending Shlonsky & Soare's analysis to deal with *how come*+*that* structures.

## 4.6   Endo's FINP Analysis

Building on Shlonsky & Soare's INTP analysis of *how come* as directly merged in spec-INTP, Endo (2017) examines the use of the complementiser *that* after *how come*, e.g. in sentences like (2a) above, repeated as (100) below:

(100)  *How come* **that** an infinite universe will collapse under gravity?

The complementiser *that* in indicative clauses generally marks declarative force (as in *We think* **that** *he did it*), but clearly *that* isn't declarative in (100) because *how come* clauses are questions, not statements; furthermore, FORCE

---

[37] A potential problem posed by Sluicing in (99) is that if *come* is an INT head for speakers who have the structure in (97b), it potentially violates the Sluicing Constraint (42) which specifies that complementisers don't allow Sluicing of their complements. However, this constraint appears not to be inviolable, since Villa-García (2015: 49–56, 73–81) reports cases in Spanish where an overt complementiser allows ellipsis of its complement.

is positioned above INT in the template (78), and this means that if *that* were a FORCE head, we'd wrongly expect it to be positioned above/before the INTP containing *how come*, whereas in (100) it is actually positioned below/after *how come*. Since *that* only occurs in finite clauses, Endo takes it to mark finiteness in *how come that* questions, and (more specifically) to spell out a FIN head: since FIN occupies a position below/after INT in the template in (78), this will account for *that* being positioned below/after *how come* in (100).

However, as noted in §4.1, 19 of the 20 informants in the survey reported in the Appendix in §4.10 gave a low acceptability score to *how come that* questions, raising the question of why this should be. Endo's answer is that *how come* obligatorily selects a FINP complement headed by a nominal FIN, so that *how come* questions have the peripheral structure shown below:

(101)   [FORCEP [FORCE ∅] [INTP how come [INT ∅] [FINP [FIN +N] ...]]]

Like Rizzi (2014a), Endo posits that a nominal FIN canonically has a null spellout; however, he claims that a small minority of speakers allow a nominal FIN to be spelled out as *that*. On this view, the use/non-use of *that* after *how come* is attributed to selectional properties (the head INT constituent of the INTP housing *how come* selects a nominal FINP complement), in combination with variable spellout conditions governing the use of the complementiser *that* (relating to whether or not a nominal FIN can be spelled out as *that*).

Endo reports the observation in Radford (2014) that some speakers who don't allow *that* immediately following *how come* nonetheless allow it to be used after an adverbial modifier following *how come* in sentences like those in (49) above, one of which is repeated as (102) below:

(102)   *How come*, after a long drawn-out conflict, **that** the Israelis and Palestinians still haven't made peace? (=49a)

Exploiting the device of FINP recursion utilised by Rizzi (2014a) to account for *that*-trace effects (see §1.5), Endo proposes that a sentence like (102) has the FINP recursion structure in (103) below (with one FIN above and another FIN below the underlined adjunct):

(103)   [FORCEP [FORCE ∅] [INTP *how come* [INT ∅] [FINP [FIN ∅] [MODP after a long drawn-out conflict [MOD ∅] [FINP [FIN **that**] the Israelis and Palestinians still haven't made peace]]]]]

He takes the two types of FIN constituent to be different in kind: by hypothesis, the higher FIN head is nominal [+N], but the lower FIN head is non-nominal [–N], as shown below:

(104)    [FORCEP [FORCE ∅] [INTP *how come* [INT ∅] [FINP [FIN +N] [MODP <u>after a long</u>
<u>drawn-out conflict</u> [MOD ∅] [FINP [FIN −N] the Israelis and Palestinians still
haven't made peace]]]]]

Speakers who allow a FIN which is non-nominal (and non-verbal[38]) to be spelled
out as *that* (but not a nominal FIN) will allow the lower FIN head to be spelled out
as *that* but not the higher one, and thus will accept sentences such as (102).

However, Endo notes that there are also speakers who do not accept sentences like (102). He conjectures that such speakers restrict the complementiser
*that* to spelling out a FORCE head, and do not allow it to spell out any kind of
FIN head. Hence, for such speakers, neither the higher (nominal) FIN nor the
lower (non-nominal) FIN can receive an overt spellout in a structure like
(104).[39]

By contrast, speakers who allow *that* to spell out either kind of non-verbal
FIN (whether nominal or non-nominal) would be expected to allow both FIN
constituents in (104) to be spelled out as *that* – as in (105) below:[40]

(105)    *How come* **that** <u>after a long drawn-out conflict,</u> **that** the Israelis and Palestinians
still haven't made peace?

---

[38] I add the phrase 'non-verbal' here, since a FIN housing an inverted auxiliary is clearly non-
nominal, but cannot be spelled out as *that* because it is also verbal. It would seem that, under
Endo's approach, a MOD head can select any kind of FIN as its complement. Thus, in addition
to MOD selecting a non-nominal, non-verbal FIN complement in a structure like (104), MOD
selects a nominal FIN in Rizzi's (2014a: 32–5) account of subject extraction in sentences like the
following, where *next year* is the specifier of an abstract MOD head (see §1.5 for further
details):

    (i)  This is the man who I think [that, *next year*, — will sell his house]

And in a structure like (ii) below, MOD selects a verbal FIN which triggers Auxiliary Inversion:

    (ii)  Why, *next year*, are you going to Cuba?

[39] A number of alternative accounts of this restriction could be envisaged. One is that such
speakers only allow MOD to select a nominal FIN, not a non-nominal FIN. Another is that
when *how come* selects a nominal FIN, all FIN constituents in the local domain of *how come*
have to be [+N], perhaps via some form of percolation or agreement. A third is that (as argued in
§3.6) the interrogative features on the FORCE head percolate down onto both FIN constituents,
and the complementiser *that* cannot spell out a peripheral head carrying an interrogative feature
for such speakers – and indeed Rizzi & Shlonsky (2007: 152) suggest that FIN in questions may
carry 'a formal *q*-feature which characterizes Fin as "Fin of a question"'. The relevant speakers
would then be predicted not to accept use of *that* in interrogative clauses like that below either:

    (i)  I wonder why, *next year*, **that** he is going to Cuba

[40] For speakers who allow a nominal FIN to be spelled out as *that*, it could equally be that the lower
FIN is also nominal (since MOD can select a nominal FIN as its complement, as noted in fn. 38).

And indeed such sentences are fine for speakers like me. However, given experimental evidence adduced by Staum Casasanto & Sag (2008) that double-*that* sentences are more acceptable the longer the material that intervenes between the two occurrences of *that*, such sentences become markedly less acceptable if the underlined adjunct is replaced by a much shorter adverbial (e.g. *still*).

Another property of *how come* questions which (following a suggestion I made to him) Endo claims his FINP analysis can account for is subject drop after *how come*. In response to a query from Liliane Haegeman asking whether *how come* allows subject drop, I googled numerous examples. I include a relatively extensive set of these below (where — is used to mark the missing subject) in order to establish this as a robust phenomenon, since use of subject drop after *how come* has not previously been reported, as far as I am aware:

(106)  a.  How come — can't get your balance when you dial 1745? (facebook.com)
      b.  How come — could not use WMP to listen to forum radio? (SgForums.com)
      c.  How come — couldn't see that? (E. Johnson, *Run to Win*, Google Books, 2014, Prologue, p. 1)
      d.  How come — am infected by genital warts yet am still a virgin? (steadyhealth.com)
      e.  How come — haven't heard of most of them? (audiotool.com)
      f.  How come — haven't updated your Faceook page? (facebook.com)
      g.  How come — wasn't stopped on the outward journey? (whatdotheyknow.com)
      h.  How come — didn't get a Super Galaxy Icon but got his El Tigre Icon? (leagueoflegends.com)
      i.  How come — wants to surprise me at this late hour, the prom will be starting in three hours (wattpad.com)
      j.  How come — had to bring J-J up single-handed? (grahamhurley.co.uk)
      k.  How come — heard much more about ReSpaces App, which is totally buggy? (macrumours.com)
      l.  How come — went back in time to help Thrall, Medivh and Arthas et al. fulfill their destinies? (eu.battle.net)
      m.  They went out to meet him and asked, 'How come — came back so soon, brother?' (J.E. Crist, *Before It's Too Late*, Xulon Press, Maitland, FL, 2012: 152)
      n.  Have written to hmrc to ask how come — get leter [*sic*] back saying i was not working between certain dates (forums.moneysavingexpert.com)
      o.  How come — felt so secure? (D. Broderick, *Transcension*, New York: Tor, 2002)
      p.  How come — gave up on the pump? (beersmith.com)
      q.  How come — forgot to tell you that? (forum.lowyat.net)
      r.  How come — missed out? (clubsnap.com)

Subject drop in such sentences can potentially be accommodated within Endo's analysis (as I pointed out to him) if *how come* selects a FINP complement with a nominal head, and if a nominal FIN can license an appropriate kind of null pronominal subject (below denoted as *pro*). To see how this might work, let us suppose that (106a) has the structure below (where the null *pro* subject is taken to be positioned on the edge of a subject projection/SUBP):

(107)   [$_{FORCEP}$ [$_{FORCE}$ ø] [$_{INTP}$ how come [$_{INT}$ ø] [$_{FINP}$ [$_{FIN}$ +N] [$_{SUBJP}$ *pro* [$_{SUBJ}$ ø] can't get your balance when you dial 1745]]]]]

If *how come* selects a FINP complement with a nominal head, if only a nominal FIN licenses a null subject in spec-SUBJP, and if a nominal FIN canonically has a null spellout, we can account for subject drop in *how come* questions like (106). Furthermore, such an analysis also predicts that subject drop will not be found in *how come that* sentences. This is because (under Endo's assumptions) *how come* selects a FINP with a nominal head as its complement, *that* can only canonically lexicalise a non-nominal FIN and a non-nominal FIN does not license subject drop. This means that we don't expect subject drop to occur after the complementiser *that* (i.e. we expect sentences like 'How come that — wasn't stopped on the outward journey?' to be ungrammatical); and indeed Endo reports that six English speakers he consulted at his own university were unanimous in accepting use of a null subject after *how come* (in an appropriate discourse setting), but not after *how come that*.

A further prediction made by the claim that only a nominal FIN licenses subject drop is that a verbal FIN (i.e. one that triggers Auxiliary Inversion) won't allow subject drop. This is borne out by the ungrammaticality of sentences such as the following:

(108)   a. So cold *was* *(it) that the mountaineers had to return to base
        b. Never again *will* *(I) tell anyone my innermost secrets
        c. How many times *has* *(he) been questioned by the police?

In (108), FIN must be verbal in order to attract the italicised inverted auxiliary to move into FIN: if only a nominal FIN licenses subject drop, it follows that subject drop will not be permitted in sentences like (108) with a verbal FIN. By contrast, other clauses containing fronted constituents which don't trigger Auxiliary Inversion appear to allow subject drop – e.g. exclamatives such as the following:

(109)   a. Wow, *what a great time* — am having @ Disney World (mobile.twitter .com)

b. Just can't say enough *how well* — am feeling!! (dundalkdesignstudio.com)

c. I can't tell you *how happy* — am that it got to you and resonated (jason connell.co)

Since wh-exclamatives don't trigger Inversion (and hence don't contain a verbal FIN), it might be supposed that sentences like those in (109) contain a nominal FIN which licenses subject drop.

An additional prediction made by the claim that subject drop is licensed by a local relation between a nominal FIN and a null subject in spec-SUBJP is that the licensing of a null subject by FIN should not be interrupted by A-bar movement. This appears to be borne out by subject drop in wh-exclamatives like those in (109) above, in wh-relatives like those bracketed in (110a, b) below, and in wh-interrogatives like those bracketed in (110c–e):

(110)    a. Give all clothes [*which* — have not worn for two years or more] to homeless (Fielding 1996: 3, cited in Haegeman & Ihsane 2001: 333)

b. Suddenly start thinking of former boyfriend Peter [*with whom* — had functional relationship for seven years] ... (Fielding 1996: 190, cited in Haegeman & Ihsane 2001: 333)

c. Not sure [*what* — can do with the concept yet] ... (styleanderror.co.uk)

d. Wonder [*how much* — paid for it too] (kerrydalestreet.co.uk)

e. Wonder [*where* — can go tomorrow] (imgrum.net)

In such cases, the italicised wh-constituent moves to the front of the bracketed clause, but this does not prevent the nominal FIN from locally licensing the immediately adjacent null subject, since at no point in the derivation does the wh-constituent intervene between FIN and the subject. Even if the italicised wh-constituent (below denoted as WH) transits through the specifier position in FINP, we end up with the substructure in (111) below:

(111)    ... [$_{FINP}$ WH [$_{FIN}$ +N] [$_{SUBJP}$ *pro* [$_{SUBJ}$ ø] ...]] ...

And since the WH constituent does not intervene between FIN and *pro*, the nominal FIN is immediately adjacent to (and so can license) the null *pro* subject in (111).

A further prediction made by Endo's claim that *how come* selects a nominal FINP as its complement is that *how come* clauses should permit subject extraction, since the assumption that a nominal FIN permits subject extraction is a key postulate of Rizzi's (2014a) account of the *that*-trace phenomenon (outlined in §1.5). Interestingly, I managed to google the following example of a sentence which seemingly involves extraction of the (bold-printed) subject of a *how come* clause (where — marks the gap left by Wh-Movement of *which*):

(112)    I must say this is one crappy article **which** I wonder *how come* — got published on a reputed newspaper site (blogs.tribune.com.pk)

Recall from the discussion in §1.5 that Rizzi posits that the subject can be extracted out of a clause which is the complement of a bridge verb (like *say*) in a sentence like that below:

(113)    This is an article **which** he said [— was published on a reputed newspaper site]

Rizzi maintains that the bracketed clause in a sentence like (113) is a FINP with a nominal FIN head carrying agreement features that attract the wh-subject *which* to move to the edge of FINP, from where it can be subsequently be extracted (in successive-cyclic fashion) out of the embedded clause into its criterial position in the matrix clause (as the specifier of a relative projection/ RELP). This raises the possibility that in sentences like (112), *how come* has a FINP complement with a nominal FIN head carrying agreement features that attract *which* to move from its thematic position as the complement of *published* to spec-FINP, with the result that it can thereafter move across *how come* in successive-cyclic fashion until it reaches its criterial position in the matrix clause (with the nominal FIN in turn acting as an expletive which serves to satisfy the Subject Criterion).

On the assumptions made above, *how come* serves as the specifier of an INT head which selects a FINP complement headed by a nominal FIN, and a nominal FIN can license both subject drop and subject extraction. Some potential support for this claim comes from the observation that (for some speakers, at least) other INT heads like *if* and *whether* likewise allow both subject drop in sentences like (114) below (where — marks the dropped subject), and subject extraction in sentences like (115) below (where — marks the position out of which the bold-printed subject is extracted):

(114)    a. I'm afraid, and I don't know *whether* — will get worse (scottishrecovery .net)
         b. Registered, but don't know *whether* — will vote (horizonpoll.co.nz)
         c. My 6 yr old asked *if* — was going to vote for Donald Trump (twitter.com)
         d. Doubt *if* — will go back (tripadvisor.com)

(115)    a. I probably played under 25 managers, **which** I'm not sure whether — is a good thing (Danny Mills, BBC Radio 5)
         b. I am permanently tired, and tearful most of the time, **which** I don't know *whether* — is because of my grief or due to the menopause (menopause matters.co.uk)
         c. I recently updated my iPhone to iOS.9.3.5, **which** I don't know *if* — is the cause of the matter (iphonepilot.wordpress.com)

    d. I always put it down to harvest mites in the grass at this time of year, **which** I don't know *if* — is the correct assumption or not (horseandhound.co.uk)

Sentences like (114) and (115) are compatible with the claim that an INT head can select a FINP complement headed by a nominal FIN which licenses both subject drop and subject extraction.[41]

Although (as we have seen), Endo's FINP recursion analysis (in conjunction with Shlonsky & Soare's INTP analysis) can seemingly handle a wide range of properties of *how come (that)* structures, it nevertheless faces potential theoretical and empirical problems. One theoretical problem (not specific to Endo's analysis of *how come* but rather associated more generally with Rizzi's FINP recursion analysis) is that it is not clear how the semantics interface can assign a coherent interpretation to a clause containing two FIN heads, if each FIN marks the same finiteness property: after all, clauses do not allow two FORCE or FOC or INT heads, so why should they allow two FIN heads? Moreover, as pointed out by Liliane Haegeman (pc) an important rationale for the cartographic approach was to eliminate recursion of peripheral projections (e.g. CP recursion), and allowing FINP recursion seems to be a retrograde step. If FINP recursion is to be utilised, there needs to be clear evidence that multiple FIN heads within the periphery of a single clause are distinct entitities with distinct formal and semantic properties.

Furthermore, there are also potential theoretical problems with Endo's claim that the complementiser *that* can spell out the lower FIN head in a structure like that in (103) above, repeated as (116) below:

(116)   [FORCEP [FORCE ∅] [INTP *how come* [INT ∅] [FINP [FIN ∅] [MODP after a long drawn-out conflict [MOD ∅] [FINP [FIN **that**] the Israelis and Palestinians still haven't made peace]]]]]

In Chapter 3, we saw that secondary use of *that* is licensed by an overt constituent which is immediately adjacent/superordinate to the complementiser. However, in (116), the constituent immediately adjacent/superordinate to *that* is a null MOD head – and this is not an appropriate kind of licenser for *that*. From this perspective, it is more likely that the complementiser spells out the

---

[41] It might be expected that movement of *which* across *how come* in (112) and across (a null operator which serves as the specifier of) *whether/if* in (115) would violate the Intervention Constraint (91) which bars likes from crossing likes. However, the resulting degradation is seemingly mild enough to be tolerated by the relevant speakers, perhaps because *which* is a fronted relative argument and *how come* (and the null operator serving as the specifier of) *whether/if* are in situ interrogative non-arguments, so that the two are at best partial likes (e.g. second cousins rather than identical twins).

MOD head in (116), and that it is licensed by the immediately superordinate underlined adjunct phrase in spec-MODP.[42]

There are also problems posed by the claim that that subject drop is licensed by a nominal FIN. From a theoretical perspective, it is not clear what the mechanism would be for a nominal FIN to license a null subject in spec-SUBJP. In Rizzi's (2014a) analysis of subject extraction in cases like (113), it is the nominal FIN itself which serves to satisfy the Subject Criterion, because 'a nominal Fin ... functions as an expletive formally satisfying the Subject Criterion' (Rizzi 2014a: 27). But if *how come* questions with subject drop have a null subject in spec-SUBJP as in (107) above, this null subject will satisfy the Subject Criterion entirely by itself, and the question then arises of why the FIN head immediately c-commanding the null subject should be required to be nominal.

One possible answer might be to suppose that a nominal FIN head carries agreement features (as claimed by Rizzi & Shlonsky 2007), and these can be valued in two alternative ways: (i) via a local spec–head relation with an A-bar moved subject which transits through spec-FINP in cases of subject extraction like (113); or (ii) via a local relation between FIN and the subject which serves as the specifier of the SUBJP complement of FIN in subject drop structures like (107). The idea that FIN has agreement features gains potential empirical support from wh-subject agreement in non-standard varieties of English (including that spoken in the East End of London) in which subject extraction can trigger wh-agreement on the complementiser *that*, with the result that the complementiser is spelled out as *what* in structures like that below:[43]

(117)    *Who* d'you reckon [**what** — done it]?

Accordingly, we might suppose that in cases of subject drop with *how come*, the agreement features on the nominal FIN serve to identify (the person/number properties of) the null subject.

However, the credibility of any such identification story is undermined by the observation that the putative phi-features of a nominal FIN are entirely abstract (i.e. invisible) and hence undetectable, so it is not clear in what sense they can 'identify' the null subject (and indeed classic accounts of null subjects claim that null subjects are canonically licensed by a head carrying rich overt

---

[42] It goes without saying, however, that this is a theory-specific objection which only holds if you buy into the story about secondary spellout developed in Chapter 3.

[43] See Berizzi (2010) and Berizzi & Rossi (2010) for arguments that *what* is a complementiser in this kind of use.

phi-feature agreement morphology[44]). It would therefore seem more likely that the null subject is discourse-identified in some way (i.e. interpreted as referring to some entity in the discourse context), consistent with the claim by Reiman (1994: 142) that subjects in English can only be null when 'predictable from the discourse context'.

Furthermore, if an agreeing FIN can license a null subject, we would expect an inverted agreeing auxiliary to license subject drop. However, this is not the case, as we see from the ungrammaticality of a structure such as:

(118)   I can assure you that no more concessions, even under duress, **am** *(*I*) going to make

Here, the inverted auxiliary *am* is in FIN, and yet (despite being inflected for person/number agreement) it does not allow the subject *I* to be dropped.

Another problem arising from Endo's claim that a nominal FIN can license a null subject is this. Endo claims that the minority of speakers who allow *how come that* have a non-canonical spellout rule which allows *that* to spell out a nominal FIN. Since he also claims that a nominal FIN can license a null subject, this predicts that the speakers in question should allow subject drop with *how come that*. And yet, he reports that none of his informants (not even those who allow *how come that*) accepted subject drop after *how come that*. This is unexpected under his analysis.[45]

Moreover, it is questionable on independent grounds whether subject drop can plausibly be taken to be syntactically licensed by FIN in *how come* sentences like (106). After all, subject drop after *how come* is not generally found in spoken English[46] but rather is restricted to cryptic registers of written English, much like the use of subject drop in note-taking (Janda 1985), telegrams and text messages (Barton 1998), newspaper headlines (Simon-Vandenbergen 1981), online blogs (Teddiman & Newman 2010) and emails/postcards (Nariyama 2006). The absence of subject drop after *how come* in

[44] See e.g. Platzack & Holmberg (1989), Roberts (1993), Vikner (1995), Rohrbacher (1999), Koeneman (2000) and Tamburelli (2007).
[45] One way of accounting for this while maintaining Endo's analysis would be to adopt a pragmatic approach and suppose that subject drop is found in cryptic styles, and in such styles functors with minimal/recoverable informational content are omitted wherever possible, in order to compress the message (e.g. to save time/money). We could then suppose that it would be anomalous to omit a subject while not omitting a complementiser like *that* which conveys minimal information in the sense that (in Endo's analysis of *how come that*) it serves merely to mark finiteness properties which are in any case independently encoded on the finite auxiliary/verb.
[46] Note, however, that the direct speech quotation in (106m) is an apparent exception, albeit it is a constructed sentence from a work of fiction.

spoken English would be puzzling if it were syntactically licensed by a nominal FIN, since it is not clear why a purely syntactic licensing mechanism should be restricted mostly to certain registers of the written language.

A further problem with Endo's FINP analysis of subject drop relates to the referential properties of the null subject. Haegeman (2015) notes that whereas *he* in a sentence like (119a) below can be interpreted as referring to Mourinho, the null subject of *became* in (119b) cannot:

(119)   a.   During Mourinho's first year in London, he became famous for his grey Armani coat
          b.   During Mourinho's first year in London, became famous for his grey Armani coat

She takes (119a) to be a complete clause with a full periphery in which the MODP containing the adjunct *during Mourinho's first year in London* is positioned above the SUBJP projection containing the subject *he*: since *he* does not cross *Mourinho* at any stage of derivation, there is no crossover violation and nothing therefore prevents *he* from being interpretable as referring to Mourinho. By contrast, Haegeman claims, subjectless clauses like (119b) are truncated at the SUBJP level, which means that the MODP constituent containing the *during*-phrase must be positioned below the SUBJP constituent containing the null subject (below denoted as *pro*). This is shown in simplified form below, where I follow Rizzi (2014a: 34) in supposing that MODP can be positioned below SUBJP, and where the null *pro* subject is assumed to move from some position within TP (say, spec-TP) to its canonical position as the specifier of SUBJP:

(120)   [$_{SUBJP}$ *pro* [$_{MODP}$ during Mourinho's first year in London [$_{TP}$ ~~pro~~ became famous for his grey Armani coat]]]

However, movement of the *pro* subject out of TP into spec-SUBJP crosses *Mourinho*, and thus induces a weak crossover violation if the null subject refers to Mourinho. The same weak crossover effect is also found in *how come* sentences like:

(121)   How come, during Luis van Gaal's time, didn't achieve much?

That is to say, the missing subject can be interpreted as referring (e.g.) to the speaker and/or addressee, and/or some third person/s (e.g. Wayne Rooney), but cannot readily be interpreted as referring to Luis van Gaal. Under Endo's FINP recursion analysis, (121) could have a derivation along the lines below:

(122)  [FORCEP [FORCE ∅] [INTP how come [INT ∅] [FINP [FIN ∅] [MODP during Luis van
       Gaal's time [MOD ∅] [SUBJP *pro* [SUBJ ∅] [FINP [FIN ∅] [TP ~~pro~~ [T didn't] achieve
       much]]]]]]]

Since movement of the null *pro* subject does not cross *Luis van Gaal* in (122),
there is no crossover violation and hence Endo's analysis wrongly predicts that
the null subject should be interpretable as referring to LvG. How can we
overcome this problem?

One possibility would be to adapt Haegeman's (2015) analysis of subject
drop in root clauses, which she argues to involve the relevant clauses being
truncated at (i.e. projecting up only as far as) SUBJP. If we were to adapt this
analysis to *how come* questions, we could suppose that *how come* has
a truncated complement which projects only as far as SUBJP. On this view,
(121) would have the structure shown below, where the null *pro* subject moves
from a position within TP (spec-TP, say) to its criterial position on the edge of
SUBJP, so resulting in the structure below:

(123)  [FORCEP [FORCE ∅] [INTP how come [INT ∅] [SUBJP *pro* [SUBJ ∅] [MODP during Luis
       van Gaal's time [MOD ∅] [FINP [FIN ∅] [TP ~~pro~~ [T didn't] achieve much]]]]]]

Since the null *pro* subject crosses *Luis van Gaal* in (123), this incurs a weak
crossover violation if the null subject refers to LvG, so correctly predicting that
the null subject in (121) cannot be interpreted as referring to LvG. On this view,
subject drop arises not because the sentence contains a nominal FIN licensing
subject drop, but rather because of truncation (i.e. non-projection) of the FINP
layer(s) of structure in the clause periphery. In other words, rather than being
present and licensing the null subject, FIN is actually *absent* in subject drop
clauses. We can extend this FINP truncation analysis of subject drop to
sentences like (109) and (110) which show subject drop in exclamative, relative
and interrogative wh-clauses if they contain an appropriate kind of (exclamative, relative or interrogative) wh-projection whose complement is SUBJP.

The assumption that subject drop sentences involve *how come* selecting
a SUBJP complement will account for contrasts like those below:

(124)   a. How come — said nothing?
        b. *How come nothing did — say?
        c. How come — can't stand garlic?
        d. *How come garlic, — can't stand the stuff?

Sentences like (124a, c) are consistent with the claim made here that (in subjectless clauses) *how come* selects a SUBJP complement housing a null subject, and
so are correctly specified to be grammatical. However, it is not the case that *how
come* has a SUBP complement in (124b), where the complement of *how come* is

a FOCP housing the fronted argument *nothing*, nor in (124d), where the complement of *how come* is a TOPP housing the dislocated topic *garlic*; thus, both (124b) and (124d) are correctly specified to be ungrammatical if (as claimed here) *how come* selects a SUBJP complement in subject drop sentences.[47]

The FINP truncation analysis of subject drop sketched above can also account for why subject drop after *how come* has a staccato feel to it – much more so than root subject drop in sentences like:

(125)   Can't find my mobile phone. Must have left it in the car

Under the truncation analysis, sentences like (125) in which a sentence-initial subject is omitted involve truncation (i.e. non-projection or non-pronunciation) of a continuous string of peripheral constituents at the <u>beginning</u> of a sentence: such sentences involving truncation of sentence-initial constituents feel perfectly natural and are commonplace in colloquial English. By contrast, subject drop in *how come* sentences involves truncation of a chunk of structure in the <u>middle</u> of the clause periphery (e.g. truncating the FINP between the INTP housing *how come* and SUBJP), and this leaves a 'hole' in the middle of the clause periphery which makes the sentence feel disjointed. Truncating FINP disrupts the canonical selectional relations between peripheral heads, and thus makes parsing the sentence more complex: this is arguably why truncating medial peripheral constituents (e.g. in *how come* sentences) is largely restricted to written registers (because when you have a written source in front of you, you can go back and re-read any material you have problems in parsing). It may be that FINP can be truncated because the edge of FINP is not a criterial position for any type of constituent, so that no essential (e.g. discourse or scope) information is lost by truncating FINP (and finiteness properties are not lost because they are spelled out on the relevant auxiliary/verb).

---

[47] However, this generalisation may not hold for all speakers, as I managed to google the following example of subject drop after *how come that*:

> (i)  How come that — can't do what they need to do to win a game? (twitter.com)

In addition, note that a question left unanswered by the SUBJP analysis is why an INTP projection housing *how come* can select a SUBJP complement housing a null subject, but (for example) a TOPP projection cannot select a SUBJP complement. It might seem as if subject drop is indeed possible after a dislocated topic, e.g. in a root clause like:

> (ii) Garlic, can't stand the stuff!

However, it may be that the topic *garlic* here is contained in a separate utterance, as the punctuation below is intended to show:

> (iii)  Garlic ... Can't stand the stuff

The FINP truncation analysis of subject drop outlined in the previous paragraph also offers an interesting account of why subject drop is not found in clauses with Auxiliary Inversion, like those in (108) above, repeated as (126) below:

(126)  a. So cold *was* *(it) that the mountaineers had to return to base
       b. Never again *will* *(I) tell anyone my innermost secrets
       c. How many times *has* *(he) been questioned by the police?

If inverted auxiliaries are in FIN (as argued in §2.7), and if subject drop involves truncation of the FINP projection, it follows that subject drop is incompatible with Auxiliary Inversion.

Moreover, the assumption that subject drop with *how come* involves *how come* directly selecting a SUBJP projection will account for why subject drop is not accepted after *how come that*. This is because if (as Endo claims) *that* is a FIN head, and if (as is suggested here) subject drop in *how come* sentences arises when FINP is truncated and *how come* has a SUBJP complement, there will be no place in a *how come*+SUBJP structure to accommodate a FIN head like *that*.[48]

To summarise: Endo claims that *how come* clauses with subject drop have a truncated structure in which *how come* selects a FINP complement. I have argued against this, and instead suggested that such clauses may have a more radically truncated structure in which *how come* directly selects a SUBJP complement, and the FINP layer between the INTP projection housing *how come* and SUBJP is truncated/absent, so giving the resulting sentence a somewhat disjointed feel. I have also suggested that the parsing problems

---

[48] But see fn. 47. Furthermore, a potential problem for this claim is seemingly posed by the following instance of subject drop after the complementiser *that* reported in Haegeman & Ihsane (2001: 332)

    (i)  Was worried *that* — might split (Fielding 1996: 227)

However, this is a different type of structure from *how come that* sentences, since *that* in (i) is a FORCE head marking the clause as declarative in type. It may be that this FORCE head lexicalised as *that* directly selects a SUBJP complement, as below:

    (ii)  [FORCEP [FORCE that] [SUBJP *pro* [SUBJ ø] might split]]

If so, the structure in (ii) could then also be taken to involve truncation of FINP, with the finiteness properties of the FORCE head percolating directly down onto the T head *might* (rather than onto FIN). Truncation of a medial peripheral constituent (e.g. the FINP between FORCEP and SUBJP) might then be expected to give the sentence a disjointed feel, for the reasons set out in the main text.

posed by truncating a periphery-medial constituent account for why this type of truncated structure is generally restricted to cryptic styles of written English.[49]

Having looked at subject drop, let's now examine other uses of *how come*. Recall that Endo claims that *how come* always selects a FINP complement headed by a nominal FIN, and that a nominal FIN requires a null spellout, for all but a minority of speakers. A nominal FIN (for Endo) can have a MODP complement which in turn can have a complement headed by a non-nominal FIN – as in (104) above, repeated as (127) below:

(127)   [$_{FORCEP}$ [$_{FORCE}$ ∅] [$_{INTP}$ how come [$_{INT}$ ∅] [$_{FINP}$ [$_{FIN}$ +N] [$_{MODP}$ after a long drawn-out conflict [$_{MOD}$ ∅] [$_{FINP}$ [$_{FIN}$ –N] the Israelis and Palestinians still haven't made peace]]]]]

In structures like (127), a nominal FIN is taken by Endo to select a MODP complement. However, this is seemingly at variance with Rizzi's (2014a) use of FINP recursion, in which (in all the cases discussed in his paper, at least) he treats a nominal FIN as selecting a SUBJP complement (and indeed this assumption is a key component of Rizzi's claim that a nominal FIN serves the function of satisfying the criterial feature on a SUBJ head via a local head–head relation).

A further selectional problem with Endo's FINP analysis is that his analysis predicts that the constituent following *how come that* is a clausal adverbial or the subject, and yet this is not always so. For example in sentences like those below, the (underlined) constituent is a fronted focused negative constituent which triggers inversion of an (italicised) auxiliary:

---

[49] It should be noted, however, that the FINP truncation analysis of the use of null subjects with *how come* leaves a number of questions in its wake. One concerns the case properties of the null subject (e.g. whether it is nominative, and if so how it is assigned case, and how it differs from the kind of null subject found in a pro-drop language like Italian). Another is whether subject drop is a specific instance of a more general phenomenon which involves omission of functors with low informational content in cryptic styles of written English, including not just subject pronouns but also auxiliaries and articles. For instance, as we see from the (constructed) example below, the material in angle brackets can be unpronounced in cryptic styles of written English (e.g. diary style):

(i)   How come <I've> gotta hand in <the> assignment before <the> vacation?

A syntactic account which deals with subject drop as a self-contained phenomenon has nothing to say about the omission of other functors in such sentences. From this perspective, it would seem preferable to adopt a pragmatic account in which omission of functors like those enclosed in angle brackets above results from a desire to compress the message conveyed as much as possible (in order to save time/money) by giving a null orthographic spellout to functors with relatively little informational content.

(128)   a. If you believe the Old Testament to be a factual account of the history of the world – as apparently you are now obliged to believe if you want to stand as a Republican and be endorsed by the Tea Party – then how come **that** nowhere in the Bible *does* anybody mention the dinosaurs? (Andy de la Tour, *Stand-Up or Die*, Oberon Books Ltd, London, 2013: 43)
   b. How come **that** nowhere in the paper *do* you explain what exactly, in your opinion, a nanobot is? (groups.google.com>sci.nanotech)
   c. How come **that** at no time *did* the police apologise for detaining him?
   d. How come **that** not once *did* he so much as glance at her?
   e. How come **that** not a shred of evidence did they adduce in support of the allegations?

And in sentences like those below, the constituent immediately following *that* is a fronted or dislocated topic:

(129)   a. How come **that** *the things you did last night*, you say you can't remember (them)?
   b. How come **that** *major issues like climate change*, politicians are reluctant to tackle (them)?
   c. How come **that** *whatever Apple does*, Samsung copies (it)? (adapted from gsmarena.com)

The significance of sentences like (128–9) is this. Endo takes *that* to be a FIN head in *how come that* structures and Rizzi (2014a: 31) claims that the only kind of peripheral constituent which can follow FIN is either a subject or a 'clausal adverbial' (and indeed this latter claim is central to Rizzi's analysis of *that*-trace effects, as we saw in §1.5). It follows from these two postulates that the complementiser *that* in sentences like (128–9) cannot be a FIN head.

  Note that sentences like (128–9) are also grammatical without *that*, and it is clear that in this use too they cannot involve *how come* having a FINP complement with a null nominal head. Rather, in such cases, *how come* has a TOPP or FOCP complement, as illustrated earlier in (83b, c) above, repeated as (130a, b) below:

(130)   a. [$_{\text{FORCEP}}$ [$_{\text{FORCE}}$ ∅] [$_{\text{INTP}}$ *how come* [$_{\text{INT}}$ ∅] [$_{\text{TOPP}}$ the things you did last night [$_{\text{TOP}}$ ∅] [$_{\text{FINP}}$ [$_{\text{FIN}}$ ∅] you can't remember (them)]]]]]
   b. [$_{\text{FORCEP}}$ [$_{\text{FORCE}}$ ∅] [$_{\text{INTP}}$ *how come* [$_{\text{INT}}$ ∅] [$_{\text{FOCP}}$ nowhere in the Bible [$_{\text{FOC}}$ ∅] [$_{\text{FINP}}$ — [$_{\text{FIN}}$ does] anyone mention the dinosaurs —]]]]]

Structures like (130) provide further evidence against Endo's claim that *how come* always selects a FINP complement.

  Considerations such as those outlined above undermine the idea of taking all occurrences of *that* after *how come* to be instances of FIN heads (and, more generally, of taking *how come* to always select a FINP complement). But if the *that* following *how come* is not a FIN head, what is it? In the next section, I argue that it is a FACT head – i.e. a peripheral head marking factivity.

## 4.7    A Factive Analysis of *how come that*

A clue to the identity of the *that* following *how come* may lie in the remark made by Collins (1991: 43) that '*how come* presupposes the truth of its complement' – a remark echoed in the observation by Fitzpatrick (2005) that *how come* clauses are factive. Conroy (2006: 7) builds on this by suggesting that *how come*+subject clauses contain a null factive complementiser (in the head C position of CP) and that *how come* serves as its specifier, so that a clause like (131a) below has the peripheral structure in (131b):

(131)    a. How come Stacey ordered pizza?
         b. [CP how come [C-FACT ø] Stacey ordered pizza]

This raises the possibility of treating the complementiser *that* in *how come that* structures as an overt spellout of the null factive complementiser in (131b).

At first sight, it might seem as if we can capture Conroy's insight in terms of the INTP analysis of *how come* outlined in the previous section by supposing that the factive complementiser *that* serves as the head of INTP, so that (131a) has a structure along the lines shown in simplified form below, with use of *that* being licensed by its specifier *how come*, as an instance of the secondary spellout phenomenon discussed in §3.3:

(132)    [FORCEP [FORCE ø] [INTP how come [INT that_FACT] [FINP [FIN ø] Stacey ordered pizza]]]

However, a structure along the lines of (132) runs into both empirical and theoretical problems. One empirical problem is posed by the claim made by Rizzi (2001: 296) 'other wh elements corresponding to higher adverbials can fill the position of Spec of INT (at least when construed locally).' If so, the analysis in (132) leads us to expect that we should be able to use *why* in place of *how come* in a clause like that bracketed below:

(133)    I wonder [*how come/*why* **that** Stacey ordered pizza]

However, for speakers like me, *how come that* is grammatical but *why that* is not, and the analysis in (132) seemingly offers no principled account of this contrast.

A second empirical problem relates to the suggestion made in §4.5 that some speakers may treat *how come* as comprising an INT head filled by *come* with an adverbial specifier *how* – as in (97b) above, repeated as (134) below:

(134)    [INTP *how* (postmodifier) [INT *come*] . . .]

It would seem plausible to suppose that speakers who treat *come* as a head may allow it to select the kind of *that*-complement which it has in *how does it come that* questions like those in (24), where *come* is a verbal head. But if *come* occupies the head INT position of INTP in structures like (134), it is clear that the complementiser *that* can't be in INT in *how come that* structures.

Furthermore the analysis of *that* as an INT head in (132) also runs into theoretical problems. For one thing (for speakers who have the relevant conditions in their grammar), it violates the Root Complementiser Filter (38) and the Doubly Filled COMP Filter (59). Moreover, an analysis like (132) violates a featural uniqueness principle posited by Cinque & Rizzi (2008) which was outlined informally in §2.8 as follows:

(135)    **One Feature One Head Principle**
Each functional head carries only one interpretable feature

The violation of (135) is incurred because (132) treats *that* as marking both factivity and interrogativity.

A further objection to the analysis in (132) is that it has been argued by numerous linguists that factive projections contain a null operator as their specifier, with the operator serving to mark factivity or definiteness.[50] If so, the specifier position in a projection with a factive head will be filled by the null operator, and cannot therefore be filled by *how come* – thus ruling out an analysis like (132). This in turn leads to the conclusion that *how come* is contained in a separate projection from *that*. Given that there are numerous languages which have a distinctive factive complementiser,[51] one implementation of this idea (which I shall adopt here) is to suppose that in *how come that* structures, *that* is a factive complementiser which serves as the head of a FACTP projection. On this view, a sentence like 'How come that he lied?' will have the peripheral structure shown below (perhaps with

---

[50]    See, among others Melvold (1991), Roussou (1992), Watanabe (1993a, 1993b), Bianchi (2000), Zubizarreta (2001), Starke (2004), de Cuba (2007), and Haegeman (2012).

[51]    These include *sto* in Serbo-Croatian (Bibović 1973), *wé* in Krio (Nylander 1985), *vos* in Yiddish (Diesing 1990), *pu* in Greek (Roussou 1992, 2010), *ma* in Akan (Osam 1994, 1996, 1998), *ḍĕ* in Gbe (Aboh 2005), *háybɔ* in Meiteilon (Kidwai 2010), *deto* in Bulgarian (Krapova 2010), *xe* in Nêlêmwa (Bril 2010), and *ko* in Pulaar (Ba 2015).

a null factive operator as the specifier of FACTP, although this is not shown here):

(136)   [FORCEP [FORCE ∅] [INTP how come [INT ∅] [FACTP [FACT that] [FINP [FIN ∅] he lied]]]]

Such a structure seems plausible from a diachronic perspective, if the historical antecedent of *how come* clauses is a *how did/does it come (about/to be) that . . .* structure in which the *that*-clause is factive.

One aspect of the FACTP analysis which might at first sight seem potentially problematic is positing that the overt factive complementiser *that* can appear not only in embedded clauses, but also in root clause structures like (132): this is at odds with the traditional view that the complementiser *that* serves to introduce embedded clauses. However, as we saw in §3.5, exclamative clauses (for some speakers) can also contain *that* not only in embedded clauses like those bracketed in (137) below but also in root clauses like (138):

(137)   a.  You will be amazed [*how quickly* **that** people you care about come round to the idea . . .] (community.babycentre.co.uk)
        b.  It's amazing [*how well* **that** they did with the likeness] (ladydickson.com)
        c.  You would be surprised [*how often* **that** people forget and later wonder why they aren't live] (searchenginewatch.com)
        d.  It just shows you [*how invincible* **that** they have been at the Etihad] (Dominic McGinnis, Talksport Radio)
        e.  No, I'm agreeing with you, John, saying [*what a hard job* **that** it's been to make that happen] (Ian McGarry, BBC Radio 5)

(138)   a.  *How quickly* **that** people turned this into a totally different place! (naira land.com)
        b.  *How pretty* **that** she looks in this photo! (web)
        c.  *What a legend* **that** Frank Lampard is! (John Cross, Talksport Radio)

Given that exclamative clauses are themselves factive (Grimshaw 1979; Zanuttini & Portner 2003; Abels 2010), it may be that the complementiser *that* in exclamatives like (137–8) marks factivity (as suggested by Wolfram Hinzen, pc). This in turn raises the possibility of extending the FACTP analysis to exclamatives, by treating *that* as the head of a FACTP projection which serves as the complement of an exclamative wh-projection, so that (138b) has the peripheral structure below:

(139)   [FORCEP [FORCE ∅] [EXCLP how pretty [EXCL ∅] [FACTP [FACT that] [FINP [FIN ∅] she looks in this photo]]]]

There would then be a potential structural parallelism between *wh+that* exclamatives like (139) and *how come that* interrogatives like (136). For speakers who use such structures, it would seem that the restriction on *that* is not that it can't occur in a root clause, but rather that it can't occur in a root projection (i.e. in the highest projection in a root clause): since *that* does not occur in the root (=FORCEP) projection in (136/139), the relevant constraint is not violated.

Potential cross-linguistic support for the factive analysis outlined above comes from the observation by Endo (2015a) that the Japanese counterparts of factive clauses, wh-exclamatives and *how come* questions all contain the factive complementiser *koto* (below glossed as FACT) – as illustrated by the following examples (from Endo 2015a, fn. x):

(140)   a. John-wa    [(zibun-ga)    sake-o     nonda   koto]-o     kookaisita
           John-TOP    [(self-NOM)    sake-ACC   drank   fact]-ACC   regretted
           'John regretted that he drank sake'
        b. Nante    hayaku    wasureru    koto!
           How      quickly   forget      fact
           'How quickly people forget'
        c. Ko-nai-to-wa          dooiu    koto?
           Come-not-that-TOP     how      fact
           'How come you won't come?'

These examples show that *koto* is used not only in typical factive clauses like that bracketed in (140a) above, but also in exclamatives like (140b) and in *how come* questions like (140c). The FACTP analyses in (136) and (139) capture this parallelism in English.

Returning now to *how come* sentences in English, it can be argued that the FACTP analysis in (136) accounts for a number of characteristics of *how come that* sentences. One such is why *that* cannot be stranded under Sluicing in a structure like that below:

(141)   I know he was arrested, but I don't understand how come (**that**) ~~he was arrested~~

If Sluicing deletes the complement of (the INTP projection housing) *how come* in (136), it will delete the FACTP containing *that*, so accounting for why *that* cannot be stranded in (141).

The FACTP analysis will also account for a further property of *how come* questions observed by Fitzpatrick (2005), namely that they do not license polarity items like those italicised below:

(142)   *How come that John *ever* said *anything*?

Fitzpatrick argues that this is because a polarity item must be locally c-commanded by an appropriate licenser, and 'a factive complementizer $C_{FACT}$ creates an island that blocks this local relation' (Fitzpatrick 2005: 141). So, for example, the negative auxiliary *didn't* is prevented by the intervening factive complementiser *that* from licensing the polarity item *anyone* in a sentence such as the following (Fitzpatrick 2005: 141, ex. 17):

(143)   *John *didn't* find out [**that** <u>anyone</u> left]

The same intervention effect is found in a *how come* structure like that below:

(144)   *[$_{FORCEP}$ [$_{FORCE}$ Ø] [$_{INTP}$ *how come* [$_{INT}$ Ø] [$_{FACTP}$ [$_{FACT}$ **that**] [$_{FINP}$ [$_{FIN}$ Ø] John <u>ever</u> said <u>anything</u>]]]]

In (144), the intervening factive complementiser prevents *how come* from licensing the polarity items *ever/anything*.[52]

If *how come that* sentences do indeed contain a FACTP projection, the question arises of whereabouts in the clause periphery the FACT head is positioned – i.e. what position it occupies in the template in (78) above. If *how come* is housed in a projection of an INT head which has a FACTP complement (as in 136 above), this would suggest that FACT is positioned immediately below INT, so that we have the following ordering of peripheral heads:

---

[52] The islandhood may well be created by a null operator in spec-FACTP (see fn. 50 for references). I note that the robustness of the claim that *how come that* questions do not license polarity items is seemingly called into question by the occurrence of (italicised) polarity items in sentences such as the following:

  (i)   But, Grandpa, how come **that** *anyone* is still interested in a poor Native American people? (M. Horvat, *Dreams of the Soul*, Author House, Bloomington, IN, 2013: 201)
  (ii)  How come **that** *anyone* actually believes that a handful of bureaucrats can possibly know better than the free market? (web)
  (iii) How come **that** *anyone* can access the phone system without additional authentication or VPN – from outside of their network? (community.spiceworks.com)

Chris Collins (pc) queries whether these may involve free choice *any*. Possible support for his suggestion comes from the observation that *any* is stressed in the relevant examples above (like free choice *any*), whereas in its use as a (partitive) polarity item it can be unstressed and even have its initial vowel truncated, as in:

  (iv)  He wouldn't say *'nything*

Moreover, *anyone* can be modified by *absolutely* in (i–iii), just like free choice *anyone* in:

  (v)   Absolutely ANYONE can access the network, if they know how to

(145)    FORCE > TOP* > INT > **FACT** > TOP* > FOC > TOP* > MOD > TOP* > FIN

This in turn would lead us to expect that the factive complementiser *that* can be followed by a topicalised or focused constituent – and this is indeed the case, as we see from the sentences below:

(146)    a. How come **that** <u>the things you did last night</u>, you say you can't remember (them)? (=129a)

b. How come **that** *nowhere in the paper* do you explain what exactly, in your opinion, a nanobot is? (=128b)

c. How come **that** <u>the dinosaurs that roamed the earth millions of years ago</u>, *nowhere in the Bible* do they get mentioned?

The examples in (146) show (bold-printed) factive *that* followed by an an (underlined) topic in (146a), by an (italicised) fronted focused negative phrase in (146b), and by both in (146c) – in conformity with the template in (145). Under the factive analysis, (146c) will have the peripheral structure shown below:

(147)    [FORCEP [FORCE ø] [INTP *how come* [INT ø] [FACTP [FACT **that**] [TOPP the dinosaurs that roamed the earth millions of years ago [TOP ø] [FOCP nowhere in the Bible [FOC ø] [FINP [FIN do] they get mentioned]]]]]]

And a structure like (147) is consistent with the template in (145).[53]

Furthermore, the FACTP analysis outlined above would account for why neither *wh+that* exclamatives nor *how come that* questions allow Auxiliary Inversion, e.g. in sentences like the following:

(148)    a. *How come that *were you* late?

b. *How quickly that *do people* forget!

The ungrammaticality of Inversion in such sentences could be attributable to either/both of two factors. One is that (as noted by Henry 1995), a projection headed by the complementiser *that* does not license Inversion, as is illustrated by contrasts such as the following in Belfast English:

(149)    I wonder *which dish* (***that**) did they pick (adapted from Henry 1995: 108)

---

[53] A potential objection to the factive analysis of *that* is that it has been widely assumed in the literature (in work dating from Hooper & Thompson 1973 to Haegeman 2012) that factive clauses do not allow internal Topicalisation. However, recall that I argued in relation to the examples in (74) in §2.6 that the empirical basis of this claim is questionable. Interestingly, Krapova (2002: 111) reports that a topic can likewise be positioned below (but not above) a FACT projection in Bulgarian.

Even though Belfast English allows *wh+that* structures and also allows Inversion in embedded wh-questions, it does not allow Inversion if the complementiser *that* is used. A second factor blocking Inversion in sentences like (148) is that factive clauses are resistant to Interrogative Inversion for many speakers – as we see from contrasts such as the following reported by McCloskey (2006) to be found in some varieties of Irish English:

(150)    a. I asked him [from what source could the reprisals come] (McCloskey 2006: 87, ex. 2a)
       b. *I found out [how did they get into the building] (McCloskey 2006: 88, ex. 3a)

These examples suggest that Auxiliary Inversion (in the relevant varieties) is permitted in non-factive interrogative complement clauses like that bracketed in (150a) but not in factive/resolutive interrogatives like that bracketed in (150b). They thus provide evidence that factive heads do not license Interrogative Inversion.[54] More generally, the considerations outlined above lend plausibility to the idea of taking the *that* following *how come* to be a factive complementiser which serves as the head of a FACTP projection which is selected as the complement of a null INT head whose specifier is *how come*.

The factive analysis of *how come that* structures outlined above suggests that the complementiser *that* in such cases spells out the head of a FACTP complement of *how come*. But what of other occurrences of the complementiser *that* in *how come* clauses? As a case in point, consider the bold-printed complementiser in (71c) above, repeated as (151) below (and see fn. 23 for authentic examples of such structures):

(151)   He protested [**that** *how come* <u>that</u> they had searched his flat without a warrant?]

Under the analysis of reportative complementisers in §3.2, the bold-printed occurrence of *that* here can be taken to be a REP(ort) head with an interrogative FORCEP complement. Given this assumption (and the factive analysis outlined above), the bracketed complement clause in (151) will have the peripheral structure in (152) below:

(152)   He protested [REPP [REP **that**] [FORCEP [FORCE ø] [INTP *how come* [INT ø]
    [FACTP [FACT <u>that</u>] [FINP [FIN ø] they had searched his flat without a warrant]]]]]

---

[54] Note that Auxiliary Inversion in sentences like (146b) is licensed by the fronted focused negative phrase, not by (the FACT head which serves as the complement of the INTP projection housing) *how come*.

On this view, the bold-printed occurrence of *that* lexicalises a reportative head, and the underlined occurrence lexicalises a factive head, so resulting in a double-*that* structure.

Now consider the rather different kind of double-*that* structure reported in (105a) above and repeated as (153) below (which is fine for speakers like me):

(153)    How come *that* <u>after a long drawn-out conflict</u>, **that** the Israelis and Palestinians still haven't made peace?

Given the factive analysis of *how come that* outlined in this section, the first (italicised) occurrence of *that* will be a FACT head. But what of the second (bold-printed) occurrence of *that*? Recall that in the discussion of secondary spellout in §3.3, I argued that some speakers allow a form of secondary spellout in which a non-verbal peripheral head with a criterial specifier can be spelled out as *that*. I argued in particular that a MOD head with a circumstantial adjunct as its specifier can be spelled out as *that*, e.g. in a structure such as that below (repeated from 59 in Chapter 3):

(154)    Major League Soccer has a program in place (and they have for some time) saying [FORCEP [FORCE ø] [TOPP any former Major League Soccer player [TOP ø] [MODP when he is finished with playing his career [MOD ø] [MODP *if they wanna be a referee* [MOD **that**] [FINP [FIN ø] there is money allocated so that they can be put on a fast-track system to become a referee in Major League Soccer]]]]]

Under the analysis in §3.3, the bold-printed complementiser in (154) lexicalises a MOD head with an italicised clausal adjunct as its specifier. This analysis can be extended to the secondary use of *that* in *how come* clauses, if (153) is analysed in the manner shown below:

(155)    [FORCEP [FORCE ø] [INTP how come [INT ø] [FACTP [FACT *that*] [MODP <u>after a long drawn-out conflict</u> [MOD **that**] [FOCP at no point [FOC ø] [FINP [FIN have] the Israelis and Palestinians managed to agree on terms for a lasting peace]]]]]]

For speakers who allow secondary spellout in such structures, the underlined adjunct in spec-MODP will license the use of *that* to spell out the MOD head in (155) as *that*. The fact that the bold-printed complementiser is followed by a fronted focused negative phrase provides us with evidence that the complementiser is not in FIN (since FIN does not allow a FOCP complement) but rather is in MOD. On the assumptions made in §3.6, this kind of secondary spellout is locally licensed and thus independent of the presence of the higher *that*. This means that the resulting sentence is equally grammatical (for speakers like me who allow the relevant kind of secondary spellout) without factive *that*, as in (156) below:

(156)    How come, *after a long drawn-out conflict*, **that** at no point have the Israelis and Palestinians managed to agree on terms for a lasting peace?

It also means that sentences like that below which contain more than one (underlined) circumstantial adjunct will allow more than one (bold-printed) secondary use of *that*:

(157)    How come *that*, if you are in a bilingual classroom, **that** once you have completed the homework in one language, **that** you have to do it all over again in the second one?

On the assumptions made here, (157) will have the peripheral structure below:

(158)    [FORCEP [FORCE ø] [INTP how come [INT ø] [FACTP [FACT *that*] [MODP if you are in a bilingual classroom [MOD **that**] [MODP once you have completed the homework in one language [MOD **that**] [FINP [FIN ø] you have to do it all over again in the second one]]]]]]

Given the account of secondary spellout in §3.3, each bold-printed occurrence of the complementiser *that* will be licensed by the underlined adjunct immediately preceding it. Speakers who do not allow secondary spellout will not accept the bold-printed uses of *that* in structures like (154), (155) and (158), and speakers who do not allow use of factive *that* with *how come* will not accept the italicised uses of *that* in structures like (155) and (158). It may be that a copy of the factivity feature on the FACT head percolates down onto the MOD heads beneath it, allowing these to be spelled out as *that*.

Although the FACTP analysis outlined above can be argued to account for a wide range of properties of *how come that* questions, there are a number of issues arising from it. One is why, since factive *that* can be substituted by *the fact that* in a sentence like (159a) below, this is not possible after *how come* in (159b):

(159)    a. I resent (*the fact*) **that** you take me for granted
         b. How come (\**the fact*) **that** you take me for granted?

A plausible answer is that *the fact that* is a DP, and hence can serve as the complement of a transitive factive predicate like *resent*, but not as the complement of the head INT constituent of the INTP projection housing *how come*, since INT is not a transitive head.

A related question is why (if *that* is a factive complementiser in *how come that*) it cannot be replaced by *how* (as we see from 160b below), since *how* can function as a factive complementiser in sentences like (160a), as noted by Willis (2007), van Gelderen (2009), Legate (2010) and Nye (2013):

(160)   a. They didn't tell me [**how** the tooth fairy doesn't really exist] (Legate 2010: 127, ex. 17a)
        b. *They didn't tell me [*how come* **how** he managed to escape]

It may be that the unacceptability of sentences like (160b) is attributable (in part, at least) to repetition of *how,* in violation of a constraint against multiple occurrences of like constituents which are too close to each other (Radford 1979). Another factor may be that constraints on the selection of factive *how-*clauses rule out the possibility of an INT head selecting a *how-*complement, just as they prevent a factive predicate like *sorry* from selecting a *how-*complement in a sentence such as:

(161)   I am *sorry* [**that/*how** I treated you badly]

See Nye (2013) for discussion of constraints on the use of factive *how.*

A further problem that the FACTP analysis runs into is that use of *that* in *how come that* structures would appear to violate the following constraint which operates in the grammars of speakers like me (see the relevant discussion in §3.8):

(162)   **Complementiser Licensing Condition/CLC**
        In standard varieties of English, the complementiser *that* cannot be licensed by a superordinate peripheral head

Recall from §3.8 that CLC bars the use of *that* in structures like those bracketed below:

(163)   a. I went home [$_{SUBP}$ [$_{SUB}$ *because*] [$_{FORCEP}$ [$_{FORCE}$ ø/*that] [$_{FINP}$ [$_{FIN}$ ø] I felt unwell]]]
        b. She told me [$_{FORCEP}$ [$_{FORCE}$ *how*] [$_{FINP}$ [$_{FIN}$ ø/*that] she hadn't been feeling well]]
        c. I wonder [$_{FORCEP}$ [$_{FORCE}$ ø] [$_{INTP}$ *Op* [$_{INT}$ *whether/if*] [$_{FINP}$ [$_{FIN}$ ø/*that] it will rain]]]
        d. I don't know [$_{FORCEP}$ [$_{FORCE}$ ø] [$_{WHP}$ [$_{WH}$ *what*] [$_{FINP}$ [$_{FIN}$ ø/*that] she has in mind]]]

It follows from CLC that peripheral heads like the subordinating conjunction *because* in (163a), the factive complementiser *how* in (163b), the interrogative complementisers *whether/if* in (163c), and the WH head *what* in (163d) cannot license the use of *that* in varieties of English like mine. However, the problem is that the FACTP analysis of *How come that he lied?* presented in (136) above (repeated as 164 below) also violates CLC:

(164)    [FORCEP [FORCE ø] [INTP how come [INT ø] [FACTP [FACT that] [FINP [FIN ø] he lied]]]]

This is because the complementiser *that* in (164) is licensed via a selectional relation with INT, in violation of the condition in CLC that a peripheral head (like INT) cannot license a *that*-complement.

In order for the FACTP analysis to be tenable, we need to find some way of accounting for why *that* is possible in structures like (164) for speakers like me (in spite of violating CLC), but not possible in structures like (163). One possibility would be to simply stipulate that (the head of the INTP projection housing) *how come* is an exception to CLC, perhaps because (unlike the INT head in 163c) it is null. However, this is an inelegant, stipulative and non-explanatory account; so let's try and find a more principled analysis.

One intriguing possibility would be to suppose that for *how come that* speakers like me, *how* and *come* are separate constituents, with *how* in spec-INTP and *come* in INT, as outlined in schematic form in (97b) above. This would mean that a sentence like 'How come that he lied?' has the structure in (165) below:

(165)    [FORCEP [FORCE ø] [INTP how [INT come] [FACTP [FACT that] [FINP [FIN ø] he lied]]]]

As noted in §4.5, such an analysis could be argued to be appropriate for speakers like me who position postmodifiers like those underlined below immediately after *how* in sentences such as the following:

(166)    a. And *how the hell come* **that** such ignorant and plain stupid people make laws? (aaa-mazing.livejournal.com)
         b. *How the heck come* **that** everything is nerfed compared to its real life equivalent? (foolz.fireden.net)
         c. *How the fuck* come **that** grand larceny [*sic*] ensued? (genius.com)
         d. *How on earth come* **that** the rating change values are different? (therugby forum.com)
         e. *How else come* that eighty percent of the juvenile delinquents in our prisons are Moroccans and Turkish? (=55c)
         f. And *how exactly come* **that** ADA focus helps to understand as well, rather than just help you memorize things? (dreamviews.com)

Moreover, for speakers like me, such sentences become ungrammatical if the postmodifier is positioned after *come* (as in \**How come the hell that ...*).

An analysis like (165) could suggest that *come* (in the course of its diachronic development) has evolved from being a lexical head to becoming a functional head located in the clause periphery: and we might then draw parallels with the way in which in some African, South Asian and Pidgin/Creole languages the counterpart of a lexical verb like *say* became reanalysed as a peripheral head (with a quotative or declarative function).[55] If we adopted the analysis in (165), we could replace the Complementiser Licensing Condition in (162) above by an alternative constraint along the following lines:

(167)   **Lexical Licensing Condition/LLC**
        The complementiser *that* can be licensed by a lexical head, but not by a non-lexical one

If *come* in (165) retains enough of its diachronic origin as a lexical verb to allow it to select a *that*-complement, we could then suppose that LLC is satisfied in (165) because (by hypothesis) *come* is a verb-like head, but not in (163) because the SUB head in (163a), the FORCE head in (163b), the INT head in (163c) and the WH head in (163d) are not lexical heads. Interestingly, Claridge (2012: 191) claims that '*How come* consists of one functional (*how*) and one lexical (*come*) element', and thus implicitly treats *come* as a lexical head.[56]

The idea that an INT head can be verbal is by no means far-fetched. After all, it could be argued that in yes-no questions such as (168a) below, INT is a verbal

---

[55] On this type of re-analysis, see Lord (1973, 1976, 1993), Alleyne (1980), Frajzyngier (1984), Heine & Reh (1984), Byrne (1987), Holm (1988), Saxena (1988), Kihm (1990), Ebert (1991), Heine et al. (1991), Hopper & Traugott (1993), Veenstra & den Besten (1995), Klamer (2000), Miller (2000), Güldemann (2001), Simpson & Wu (2002), Chappell (2008), Finney (2012).

[56] If (as suggested here) *how come* only selects a *that*-complement when *come* is in INT, we'd expect not to find structures like *how come the fuck that, how come the hell/heck that* etc. As noted in the text, these are ungrammatical for me, and indeed I was unable to find any such structures on the web. On the other hand, I did find:

    (i)   *How come <u>exactly</u>* **that** quotes don't count towards the character limit? (forums .3dtotal.com)

    (ii)  *How come <u>else</u>* **that** players time after time come up with the idea that you should be able to leave something behind you in Azeroth? (pinkpigtailinn.blogspot.com)

It is not clear how best to analyse these, but one possibility is the following. An interesting property of *exactly* (and also *else*, in some varieties) is that it can be stranded in a projection below the constituent it modifies – as in the sentences below:

    (iii)  *Who did they blame <u>exactly</u>?* (Zyman 2016: 1)

    (iv)  *What have you got <u>else</u> for us, Matt?* (Danny Kelly, Talksport Radio)

This opens up the possibility that *exactly/else* in (i) and (ii) occupy the specifier position of a projection below INT, with *that* being used to spell out the head of the relevant projection as an instance of secondary spellout.

head which attracts the (auxiliary) verb *is* to raise from T through into INT, as in (168b), perhaps in order to ensure that the INTP projection which houses the null yes-no question operator (*Op*) is visible at PF:

(168)   a. Is it raining?
        b. [$_{FORCEP}$ [$_{FORCE}$ ø] [$_{INTP}$ *Op* [$_{INT}$ is] [$_{FINP}$ [$_{FIN}$ ~~is~~] [$_{TP}$ it [$_T$ ~~is~~] raining]]]]

We might then suppose that a non-verbal INT head is filled by directly merging *whether/if* in INT, and that a verbal INT head is filled either by attracting an auxiliary to move into INT as in (168b) above, or by directly merging *come* in INT as in (165). If *come* is directly merged in INT, it follows that (because it is not within the local domain of a T-constituent) it will not inflect for tense and so will be spelled out in the default form *come*, unlike the inverted auxiliary *is* in (168b) which originates in T, or moves into T from some lower (e.g. Aspect) position in the course of the derivation. It may be that speakers who don't like using *how come* in embedded clauses have a constraint to the effect that they only allow non-verbal clauses (e.g. *whether*-clauses) to be used in embedded contexts, and restrict verbal clauses to use in root contexts: such speakers might also be expected to reject sentences such as 'I asked *was he going there*', where the italicised embedded clause is verbal and undergoes Auxiliary Inversion.

Intriguing though the analysis in (165) is, it faces a potential problem in accounting for the ungrammaticality which results from coordinating two structures like those bracketed below:

(169)   *How [*come* **that** you cheated on your wife with me] and [*come* **that** you cheated on me with her]?

Under the analysis in (165), both bracketed constituents in (169) would be intermediate projections of the INT head lexicalised as *come* (i.e. both would be INT-bar constituents), and so the analysis in (165) would seemingly lead us to expect that they can be coordinated, contrary to fact.

A plausible way of dealing with this problem would be to treat *how come* as a frozen lexical chunk with the property that *come* can only head an INTP whose specifier is *how* (or *why*, for speakers who allow *why come* sentences like those in 53 above). On this view, the lexical entry for *come* when used as an INT head specifies that it occurs in structures of the following form (where *Op* is the operator in factive projections posited in the research cited in fn. 50):

(170)   ... [$_{INTP}$ *how* (postmodifier) [$_{INT}$ *come*] [$_{FACTP}$ *Op* [$_{FACT}$ ø/%that] ...]] ...

An analysis along the lines of (170) provides a way of capturing the intuition that *how come* is an idiosyncratic lexical collocation in present-day English.

Such an analysis would also account for why *come* is obligatorily stranded under Sluicing in sentences such as that below:

(171)     You're always grinning about something. *How* \*(*come*)? (=35)

If (as generally supposed) Sluicing involves deletion of the complement of the head of the projection housing the interrogative expression, then under the analysis in (170), Sluicing in (171) will involve deleting the FACTP complement of the INT head housing *come*, thereby leaving *how come* intact.[57]

To summarise: in this section, I have argued that the complementiser *that* in *how come that* questions is a FACT head, and I have shown how such a factive analysis can account for a wide range of properties of such questions. I have also suggested (albeit tentatively) that it may well be that for speakers like me who allow *how come that*, the item *come* functions as an INT head whose specifier is *how* (plus any postmodifier that *how* may have). I further noted that this analysis seems appropriate for speakers like me who say *how the hell come that*, but not \**how come the hell that*.

Having looked at *how come that* questions, in the next section I turn to analyse two other types of *how come* questions – namely *how come*+subject and *how come*+auxiliary questions.

## 4.8     Other *how come* Questions

The discussion of *how come that* questions in the previous section begs the question of how to deal with *how come*+subject structures in which *how come* occurs without *that*. One possible answer is that such questions have a less complex structure which lacks the FACTP projection found in *how come that* structures. On this (simpler structure) view, a sentence like 'How come he lied?' would have the (FACT-free) structure below:

(172)     [FORCEP [FORCE ø] [INTP how come [INT ø] [FINP [FIN ø] he lied]]]

---

[57] A potential problem posed by Sluicing in (171) is that if *come* is an INT head, it potentially violates the Sluicing Constraint (42) which specifies that overt complementisers don't allow Sluicing of their complements. However, this constraint appears not to be inviolable, since Villa-García (2015: 49–56, 73–81) reports cases in Spanish where an overt complementiser allows ellipsis of its complement. It may be that the verbal origins of *come* make it behave more like a lexical than a functional head, and hence able to allow complement ellipsis, as (perhaps) with the verb *come* below:

    (i)   But how did it come? (C.B. Haynes, *The other side of death*, Southern Publishing Association, Nashville, TN, 1944: 8)

Speakers who have this kind of structure would be expected to reject *how come that* questions because there is no constituent that can house *that* in (172): for example, *that* could not occupy the INT position, for the reasons noted in our earlier discussion of (132) above; nor could *that* occupy the FIN position, if (as claimed in Chapter 3), secondary spellout of *that* is generally only permitted where the relevant head has a criterial specifier to license it (which is not the case in 172, since FIN has no specifier). Thus, an analysis along the lines of (172) might at first sight seem to be appropriate for speakers who don't allow *that* to be used after *how come*.

And yet, the structure in (172) is problematic in a number of respects. For one thing, it fails to account for *how come*+subject questions being factive in the same way as *how come that* questions. For another, the analysis in (172) would fail to account for why we don't find the use of (italicised) polarity items in sentences such as:

(173)    *How come John *ever* said *anything*?

This is because (under the analysis in 172) there is no FACTP projection in (173) to serve as a barrier to *how come* licensing polarity items like *ever/anything*. In addition, the analysis in (172) would fail to account for why many speakers who don't allow the use of *that* immediately after *how come* nonetheless accept its use in coordinate structures like:

(174)    *How come* [you cheated on your wife with me] and [**that** you cheated on me with her]?

Under the analysis in (172), the bracketed structure in the first conjunct would be a FINP, whereas under the analysis of *how come that* questions in (136), the bracketed structure in the second conjunct would be a FACTP projection. Given the traditional assumption that only like constituents can be conjoined, we would then wrongly expect sentences like (174) to be ungrammatical for all speakers.

An alternative approach which would overcome the problems identified in the previous paragraph would be to suppose that *how come* always has a FACTP complement in *how come (that)*+subject structures, with the FACT head either being spelled out overtly as *that* or receiving a null spellout – as shown below:

(175)    [$_{FORCEP}$ [$_{FORCE}$ ø] [$_{INTP}$ *how come* [$_{INT}$ ø] [$_{FACTP}$ [$_{FACT}$ **that/ø**] [$_{FINP}$ [$_{FIN}$ ø] he lied]]]]

Such an analysis would provide a straightforward account of speakers like me who freely alternate between 'How come that he lied?' and 'How come he lied?' It would also enable us to provide a relatively straightforward account of coordinate structures such as (174), since it would then be the case that both bracketed conjuncts are FACTP projections (the first headed by a null complementiser, and the second headed by *that*).

However, the assumption made in (175) that a FACT head can have a null spellout is at variance with the following generalisation proposed by Ormazabal (2005):

(176)    **Factive Complementiser Generalisation** (Ormazabal 2005: 95, ex. 9)
         Factive predicates do not allow complements headed by a null complementiser

Ormazabal argues that this generalisation gains empirical support from the (supposed) obligatoriness of *that* in factive clauses like that below:

(177)    Mary pointed out [*(**that**) Sue wasn't there]

However, it is clear from sentences like (178) below that there are speakers for whom *that* is not obligatory in factive clauses like those bracketed:

(178)    a. Why do Trump supporters get upset when it's pointed out [he hired a self-defined racist to be the CEO of his campaign]? (answers.yahoo.com)
         b. My boyfriend has stopped talking to me after I pointed out [he doesn't make time for me anymore] (answers.yahoo.com)
         c. I started writing instrumentals but Roma pointed out [they were very visual], so she started writing lyrics (Enya, interview in *The Times Magazine*, 2005)

Sentences like those in (178) are also fine in my variety of English, which shows the following broader spellout pattern for complementisers in factive complement clauses:

(179)    a. The FBI is very sorry [*that/ø* it sabotaged the CIA's operation]
         b. The FBI very much regrets [*that/*ø* it sabotaged the CIA's operation]
         c. The fact [*that/ø* the FBI had sabotaged their operation] annoyed the CIA
         d. The discovery [*that/*ø* the FBI had sabotaged their operation] annoyed the CIA
         e. [*That/*ø* the FBI had sabotaged their operation], the CIA only found out about it later

The contrast between (179a) and (179b) suggests that a factive clause which is the complement of the predicate *sorry* allows its (italicised) complementiser to have a null spellout, but one which is the complement of *regret* does not: this seems to be a lexical effect whereby use of a null complementiser is permitted after a high-frequency/informal-style predicate like *sorry*, but not after a low-frequency/formal-style predicate like *regret*. A similar lexical effect is found in non-factive predicates, as we see from use of a null complementiser being permitted after *say* but not (for some people) after *quip*. For speakers like me, a parallel lexical effect is found in sentences like (179c, d), where use of a null complementiser is permitted after the noun *fact*, but not after the noun *discovery*; however, some speakers reportedly dislike the use of a null complementiser after any kind of noun, and for them the constraint seems to be structural, in that only a verbal or adjectival predicate licenses use of a null complementiser. A clearer case of a structural constraint against giving a complementiser a null spellout is found in (179e), where use of a null complementiser violates the Empty Category Principle of earlier work (e.g. Rizzi 1990), because the antecedentless empty complementiser in (179e) has no licenser (by virtue of not being head-governed, theta-governed or antecedent-governed), whereas the empty C in (179a) is licensed by *sorry*.

The generalisation that emerges from sentences like (179) is that we would expect a FACT head to have a dual spellout (either an overt spellout as *that* or a silent spellout), provided that relevant lexical or structural constraints are satisfied. For speakers like me who alternate freely between (e.g.) 'How come that he lied?' and 'How come he lied?' the situation is exactly as expected. But a question that remains to be answered is why the FACT head cannot be spelled out as *that* for the majority of speakers. One possible answer is that for many speakers, using *that* with *how come* gives rise to an interpretive (clause-typing) clash at LF: if the relevant speakers treat *that* as a complementiser which types a clause as non-interrogative, it will be incompatible with use of an expression like *how come* which types a clause as interrogative. Such speakers would also be expected to reject use of *that* in interrogative clauses like that bracketed below:

(180)    He didn't know [*for what reason/why/whether/if* (**that**) she had lied to him]

Speakers who impose a wider constraint against using *that* in any kind of wh-clause and thus treat *that* as a non-wh complementiser would be expected to reject use of *that* not only in questions like (180) above but also in wh-exclamatives like that below:

(181)    You'd be amazed at *what a big fuss* (**that**) there was

And speakers who restrict *that* to use in non-root clauses (or to use as the first word in an embedded clause) would also be expected to reject use of *that* in root clause structures like (175). On this view, the ban on use of *that* after *how come* would be attributable to one or more independent factors.

Having looked at *how come (that)*+subject structures, let's now turn to look at the *how come*+auxiliary questions used by a minority of speakers. As argued in §4.4, *how come* in this structure seems to have the status of an interrogative operator (like *why*) and (under the analysis in §4.5) originates in a REASONP projection below FIN, and moves through the edge of FINP (triggering Auxiliary Inversion) into its criterial position on the edge of INTP. On this view, a sentence like (182a) below would have the structure in (182b), as suggested in §4.5:

(182)   a. *How come, if he's the Devil Incarnate,* **does** *he spend half the book down there in that poxy little room?* (=63c/87a, Kim & Kim 2011)

   b. [FORCEP [FORCE ∅] [INTP *how come* [INT ∅] [MODP if he's the Devil Incarnate [MOD ∅] [FINP ~~how come~~ [FIN does] [REASONP ~~how come~~ [REASON ∅] he spend half the book down there in that poxy little room]]]]]

The fact that *does* is positioned after the underlined adjunct in (182) provides evidence that the auxiliary does not raise into INT in such sentences, but rather remains in FIN.[58]

However, given the arguments presented above that *how come (that)*+subject structures contain a FACTP projection, the question arises as to whether the same is true of *how come* questions with Auxiliary Inversion. If indeed we were to extend the FACTP analysis to *how come+ auxiliary* sentences, (182a) above would have the rather more articulated structure in (183) below:

(183)   [FORCEP [FORCE ∅] [INTP *how come* [INT ∅] [FACTP [FACT ∅] [MODP if he's the Devil Incarnate [MOD ∅] [FINP ~~how come~~ [FIN does] [REASONP ~~how come~~ [REASON ∅] he spend half the book down there in that poxy little room]]]]]]

However, a FACTP derivation for *how come*+auxiliary structures is problematic for a number of reasons. For one thing, the assumption embodied in the analysis in (183) that *how come* moves from an initial spec-REASONP position below FACTP into a superficial spec-INTP position above FACTP is problematic because FACTP is a factive island (Oshima 2006) and hence a barrier to movement; moreover, if (as suggested in the literature cited in fn. 50) there is a null operator in spec-FACTP, movement of *how come* across the operator would violate the Intervention Constraint outlined in §1.4, specifying that 'Likes cannot cross likes' (Abels 2012: 247). Furthermore, we have already

---

[58] An incidental issue which I set aside here is whether the auxiliary *does* transits through the head of REASONP on its way to FIN.

seen from sentences like (148) and (150b) above that factive complements generally do not allow Auxiliary Inversion. And in addition, the structure is ungrammatical for me (even though I allow *how come that*) if the FACT head in (183) is lexicalised as *that*, as in (184) below

(184)    *How come **that** (if he's the Devil Incarnate) *does* he spend half the book down there in that poxy little room?

The ungrammaticality of (184) deals a potentially fatal blow to the FACTP analysis in (183).

Moreover, there is reason to think that *how come* questions are not inherently factive when they involve Interrogative Inversion. In this connection, note that Fitzpatrick (2005) (building on an earlier observation by Collins 1991) argues in relation to the contrast below that *how come* questions are factive, but *why* questions are not:

(185)    a.  Why would John leave?
         b.  *How come John would leave?

Fitzpatrick notes that a *why*-question like (185a) can be used rhetorically with a negative bias to imply that John wouldn't leave, and in this use the question does not carry any presupposition about John leaving, and so is not factive. By contrast, (185b) can't be used rhetorically with a negative bias, and this is because it is factive and so carries the presupposition of John leaving.

In this connection, it is interesting to note that sentences like those below provide evidence that *how come* questions with Interrogative Inversion can be used with a negative bias:

(186)    a.  I mean, *how come* **would** I be crying? ... You know I don't cry (Janice Daugharty, *It's Okay to Cry*, Google Books, 2010)
         b.  If Conor can't even fight NATE for 3 rounds without gassing *how come* **would** he be able to box 12 rounds against a legit pro boxer? (forums .sherdog.com)
         c.  And if we're paying every month and on time for several years, *how come* **would** we suddenly stop making payments! (consumeraffairs.com)
         d.  *How come* **would** anyone choose lame Larry over that amazon bombshell? Are you fucking kidding me?! (zetaboards.com)
         e.  It's insane, she is only three years old, *how come* **would** she be married? (canadavisa.com)
         f.  He is a pure vegetarian that doesn't eat meat or any life (*sic*) animal; so *how come* **would** such a man be associated with murder or ritual? (allafrica.com)
         g.  *How come* **would** anyone delete replies you have made on a member's forum status? That's insane (teammuppet.eu)

The *how come* questions in (186) all have a negative bias, as is clear in some cases from accompanying remarks to the effect that the relevant proposition is implausible. This provides us with evidence that *how come* questions with Interrogative Inversion are not inherently factive; and this in turn means that they do not contain a FACTP projection.

Further evidence that there is no FACTP projection in *how come*+auxiliary structures comes from the observation that *how come* can license polarity items like those italicised below in such questions:

(187)   a. How come would *anyone* do less than they had to? (J. Dalmas, *The Regiment: A Trilogy*, Google Books, 2004)
  b. How come would he *ever* imagine that situation would end up in a kiss? (fanfiction.com)
  c. How come could *anyone* live without health care? (flaglerlive.com)
  d. How come could *anything* be doomed with someone like God around? (community.beliefnet.com)
  e. How come can *anyone* say the Luggones praised Lugh? (wikipedia.org)
  f. How come can *anything* bad happen under the sky so blue? (ss2.glossa.pl)

And indeed we find the polarity item *anyone* in (186d, g) above as well. Given the claim made earlier in relation to (142) and (173) above that the presence of a FACTP projection in *how come (that)* questions prevents *how come* from licensing polarity items, the occurrence of polarity items in *how come*+auxiliary questions like (187) leads to the converse conclusion that such questions do not contain FACTP.

Instead, a more plausible analysis of *how come* questions with Interrogative Inversion is a non-factive analysis in which *how come* is an interrogative operator which originates in spec-REASONP and transits through spec-FINP (thereby triggering Auxiliary Inversion), before moving on to spec-INTP in (183). It may well be that (in its operator use) *how come* mirrors the behaviour of *why*, which is characterised by Shlonsky & Soare (2011: 663) in the following terms: 'Short-moved *why* raises from Spec, Reason to Spec, Int and *cannot* target Spec, Wh, whereas long-moved *why* has exactly the opposite property, namely, it targets the matrix Wh and *not* the matrix Int.'

To summarise: I began this section by arguing that in *how come*+subject questions, *how come* is generated in situ on the edge of INTP and has the same FACTP complement as in *how come that* questions, differing only in that the FACT head has a null spellout. However, I argued that *how come*+auxiliary questions are non-factive in nature, and that (in this use) *how come* is an interrogative operator constituent which undergoes Wh-Movement and (like other interrogative operators) triggers Auxiliary Inversion in root clauses.

## 4.9   Summary

I began this chapter in §4.1 by reporting on an informal survey conducted by Yoshio Endo and me (see §4.10 for details) which showed that all 20 of our informants gave a high acceptability rating to *how come*+subject structures, but only 1 informant gave a high rating to *how come*+auxiliary structures, and likewise only 1 gave a high rating to *how come*+complementiser structures. In §4.2 I outlined Zwicky & Zwicky's (1973) claim that a sentence like 'How come you were arrested?' is derived from 'How ~~did it~~ come about ~~that you~~ were arrested?' via deletion of the material marked by strikethrough. However, I argued against the deletion analysis, noting that it would require an unparalleled and unprincipled deletion operation, and that it fails to account for numerous differences between *how come* and *how did it come about* questions (e.g. a parenthetical PP like *in your view* can be positioned immediately after *how* in *how did it come about* questions but not in *how come* questions). In §4.3 I outlined an alternative analysis of *how come* as a complementiser proposed in Collins (1991). However, I argued against this analysis on several grounds: for one thing, the occurrence of *how come* in root clauses is inconsistent with it being a complementiser because English does not allow an overt complementiser to introduce a root clause; and for another, the analysis would be unable to account for Sluicing after *how come* (because overt complementisers do not allow Sluicing of their complement). In §4.4 I outlined an alternative analysis proposed by Ochi (2004, 2011) under which *how come* is taken to be the specifier of a CP headed by a null C which selects a TP complement; I showed how this spec-CP analysis can account for a range of properties of *how come*+subject structures, and went on to argue that it can be extended to deal with *how come*+auxiliary structures, if the relevant speakers treat *how come* as an interrogative operator (like *why*) which moves from a position below T to spec-CP, and thereby triggers concomitant Auxiliary Inversion. However, I argued that analysing the clause periphery in *how come* questions as comprising a single CP layer containing *how come* as its specifier cannot account for the possibility of having a range of other peripheral constituents preceding or following *how come*. I further argued that handling *how come* clauses containing multiple peripheral constituents in terms of CP recursion would fail to account for constraints on the ordering of the relevant peripheral constituents. In §4.5, I outlined an alternative cartographic analysis proposed by Shlonsky & Soare (2011), under which *how come* is directly generated in spec-INTP. I showed how the INTP analysis accounts for a range of properties of *how come* questions, including why most speakers don't allow Interrogative Inversion after *how come* (e.g. in *'How come did he apologise?') but do allow Negative Inversion after *how come* (e.g. in 'How come at no point did he apologise?'). In §4.6, I went on to outline the FINP recursion analysis of Endo (2017), under which *how come* selects a FINP complement with a nominal head, which in turn can have a MODP complement whose head can select a further FINP projection. I discussed Endo's claim that his analysis can account for subject drop in *how come* questions, and for inter-speaker variation in the use of *that*. However, I cast doubt on these claims, and further argued that Endo's FINP analysis can't handle the occurrence of topicalised or focused constituents after *how come that*. In §4.7 I went on to present an alternative factive analysis of *how come (that)*+subject structures under which (the head INT of the INTP projection housing) *how come* selects a FACTP complement whose head can optionally be spelled out as *that* for speakers like me, but obligatorily has a null spellout for other speakers. I suggested that for speakers like me, *how come* is a frozen lexical chunk in which *come* is in INT and *how* is its specifier, with *come* retaining enough of its diachronic origins as a verb to allow it to select a factive *that*-complement (and to trigger Sluicing). In §4.8, I argued for a parallel FACTP analysis for *how come*+subject questions, with the difference that the FACT head has a null spellout. I also argued that *how come* questions which involve Interrogative Auxiliary Inversion are non-factive (and hence lack a FACTP projection) and that *how come* in such cases is an interrogative operator phrase which undergoes Wh-Movement and triggers Auxiliary Inversion.

## 4.10    Appendix: Questionnaire on *how come*

Yoshio Endo and I devised an informal (unscientific) questionnaire in which 20 native speakers of English were asked to judge the acceptability of the following 7 sentences:

    (i)   How come I fell in love with someone like you?
    (ii)   How come that I fell in love with someone like you?
    (iii)   How come I fell in love with someone like you, and that you fell in love with someone like me?
    (iv)   How come did I fall in love with someone like you?
    (v)   How come I ever fell in love with someone like you?
    (vi)   How come that I ever fell in love with someone like you?
    (vii)   How come did I ever fall in love with someone like you?

Informants were asked to rate the sentences on a 5-point scale (5 = OK, 4 = ?, 3 = ??, 2 = ?*, 1 = *). The results are presented in tabular form below, where the letters (A–S) denote different informants, the Roman numerals (i–vii) denote the correspondingly numbered sentences above, and the Arabic numerals (1–5) denote scores.

| | A | B | C | D | E | F | G | H | I | J | K | L | M | N | O | P | Q | R | S | T | Mean |
|---|---|---|---|---|---|---|---|---|---|---|---|---|---|---|---|---|---|---|---|---|---|
| **(i)** | 5 | 5 | 5 | 5 | 5 | 5 | 5 | 5 | 5 | 5 | 5 | 5 | 5 | 5 | 5 | 4 | 5 | 5 | 5 | 4 | 4.9 |
| **(ii)** | 1 | 1 | 2 | 3 | 3 | 2 | 2 | 2 | 2 | 1 | 5 | 1 | 2 | 3 | 1 | 2 | 3 | 1 | 1 | 1 | 2.0 |
| **(iii)** | 1 | 2 | 5 | 4 | 3 | 2 | 4 | 3 | 5 | 3 | 5 | 1 | 5 | 5 | 5 | 3 | 5 | 2 | 1 | 3 | 3.4 |
| **(iv)** | 1 | 1 | 1 | 1 | 1 | 1 | 1 | 1 | 1 | 1 | 1 | 1 | 1 | 1 | 1 | 1 | 1 | 5 | 2 | 1 | 1 | 1.3 |
| **(v)** | 5 | 5 | 3 | 5 | 4 | 5 | 5 | 4 | 4 | 5 | 5 | 5 | 5 | 4 | 2 | 5 | 5 | 2 | 2 | 1 | 4.1 |
| **(vi)** | 1 | 1 | 2 | 3 | 1 | 2 | 2 | 1 | 2 | 1 | 5 | 1 | 2 | 1 | 1 | 2 | 4 | 1 | 1 | 1 | 1.8 |
| **(vii)** | 1 | 1 | 1 | 1 | 1 | 3 | 1 | 1 | 3 | 1 | 1 | 1 | 1 | 1 | 1 | 3 | 5 | 3 | 1 | 1 | 1.6 |

The informants were university teachers of English or Linguistics: A–K were from the UK, L–Q from the USA, R from Canada, S from Australia and T from New Zealand.

# *Epilogue*

---

This book marks the culmination of a decade-long adventure for me, in which I have been able to combine a passion for (armchair) sport with a passion for analysing language, through a detailed study of a range of non-canonical structures found in live, unscripted radio and TV broadcasts (supplemented by data from other sources). I hope that the book has achieved the following aims:

- dispelling the prescriptive myth that colloquial English utilises sub-standard structures characterised by a sloppy form of language which has no proper structure and is thus not worthy of the attention of serious scholars
- showing how supposedly 'sloppy' structures in which (e.g.) topics and relative pronouns are seemingly unlinked to their associated proposi-tions actually involve a form of pragmatic linking which is found in other languages (e.g. Chinese, Japanese and Thai)
- highlighting the richness of non-standard English, illustrating this in terms of a vast panoply of novel authentic data sourced mainly from live, unscripted radio and TV broadcasts or the web
- adding to awareness of the range and nature of non-standard, non-dialectal variation in colloquial English, and contributing novel data to debates about language typology and microvariation
- showing that the range of syntactic structures found in colloquial English can profitably be studied and understood from a formal syntactic perspective
- contributing to understanding the cartography of the clause periphery, employing (what in terms of cartographic work is) a novel source of data from authentic examples of spoken English
- showing that the clause periphery is the locus of much variation in syntax, with parametric variation reducible to the feature composition and spellout of functional heads

- showing how a usage-based approach to linguistic analysis can provide a fertile additional source of data which complements other (e.g. introspective and experimental) approaches

I hope that you have had as much fun in reading the book as I had in collecting and analysing the data!

What's next for me? Well, I have a lot of data on relative clauses in colloquial English, so my next goal is to prepare a monograph on these, if my biological clock carries on ticking long enough!

# References

Abeillé, A. & Borsley, R.D. 2008. Comparative correlatives and parameters. *Lingua* 118: 1139–57.

Abels, K. 2010. Factivity in exclamatives is a presupposition. *Studia Linguistica* 64: 141–57.

2012. The Italian left periphery: A view from locality. *Linguistic Inquiry* 43: 229–54.

Abney, S.P. 1987. The English noun phrase in its sentential aspect. PhD diss. MIT.

Aboh, E. 2004. *The Morphosyntax of Complement-Head Sequences*. Oxford: Oxford University Press.

2005. Deriving relative and factive constructions in Kwa. In Brugé et al. (eds) 265–85.

2006. Complementation in Saramaccan and Gungbe: The case of C-type modal particles. *Natural Language and Linguistic Theory* 24: 1–55.

2010. Information structuring begins with numeration. *Iberia* 2: 12–42.

Aboh, E. & Pfau, R. 2010. What's a *wh*-word got to do with it? In Benincà & Munaro (eds) 91–124.

Ackema, P. 2010. Restrictions on subject extraction: A PF interface account. In *Interfaces in Linguistics: New Research Perspectives*, R. Folli & C. Ulbrich (eds) 225–41. Oxford: Oxford University Press.

Ackema, P. & Neeleman, A. 2003. Context-sensitive spell-out. *Natural Language and Linguistic Theory* 21: 681–735.

Ackerman, L., Frazier, M. & Yoshida, M. 2014. Resumptive pronouns salvage island violations in forced-choice tasks. Poster presented to CUNY Sentence Processing Conference 2014.

Adger, D. & Smith, J. 2010. Variation in agreement: A lexical feature-based approach. *Lingua* 120: 1109–34.

Adger, D., de Cat, C. & Tsoulas, G. (eds) 2004. *Peripheries: Syntactic Edges and their Effects*. Dordrecht: Kluwer.

Alexopoulou, T. 2006. Resumption in relative clauses. *Natural Language and Linguistic Theory* 24: 57–111.

2010. Truly intrusive: Resumptive pronominals in questions and relative clauses. *Lingua* 120: 485–505.

Alexopoulou, T. & Keller, F. 2002. Resumption and locality: A crosslinguistic experimental study. *Chicago Linguistic Society Papers* 38: 1–14.

2007. Locality, cyclicity and resumption: At the interface between the grammar and the human sentence processor. *Language* 83: 110–60.

Alleyne, M. 1980. *Comparative Afro-American*. Ann Arbor, MI: Karoma Publishers.

Alrenga, P. 2005. A sentential subject asymmetry in English and its implications for complement selection. *Syntax* 8: 175–207.

Anagnastopoulou, E., van Riemsdijk, H. & Zwarts, F. 1997 (eds). *Materials on Left Dislocation*. Amsterdam: Benjamins.

Aoun, J. 2000. Resumption and last resort. *Documentação de Estudos em Lingüística Teórica e Aplicada* 16: 13–43.

Aoun, J., Choueiri, L. & Hornstein, N. 2001. Resumption, movement, and derivational economy. *Linguistic Inquiry* 32: 371–403.

Asudeh, A. 2004. Resumption as resource management. PhD diss. Stanford, CA.

2011a. Local grammaticality in syntactic production. In *Language from a Cognitive Perspective: Grammar, Usage, and Processing*, E.M. Bender & J.E. Arnold (eds) 51–79. Chicago: The University of Chicago Press.

2011b. Parallel processing and sentence comprehension difficulty. *Language and Cognitive Processes* 26: 301–49.

2011c. Towards a unified theory of resumption. In *Resumptive Pronouns at the Interfaces*, A. Rouveret (ed.) 121–87. Amsterdam: Benjamins.

2012. *The Logic of Pronominal Resumption*. Oxford: Oxford University Press.

Authier, J.-M. 1992. Iterated CPs and embedded Topicalization. *Linguistic Inquiry* 23: 329–36.

Authier, J.-M. & Haegeman, L. 2016. On the syntax and semantics of Mirative Focus Fronting in French. Ms. Pennsylvania State University and Ghent University.

Ba, I. 2015. Factive relative clauses in Pulaar. *Kansas Working Papers in Linguistics* 36: 84–99.

Badan, L. 2007. High and low periphery: A comparison between Italian and Chinese. PhD diss. University of Padua.

Badan, L. & Del Gobbo, F. 2010. On the syntax of topic and focus in Chinese. In Benincà & Munaro (eds) 63–90.

Baker, C.L. 1970. Notes on the description of English questions: The role of an abstract morpheme. *Foundations of Language* 6: 197–219

Baltin, M. 1982. A landing site theory of movement rules. *Linguistic Inquiry* 13: 1–38.

2010. The non-reality of doubly filled Comps. *Linguistic Inquiry* 41: 331–5.

Barbiers, S. 2009. Locus and limits of syntactic microvariation. *Lingua* 119: 1607–23.

2013. Geography and cartography of the left periphery: The case of Dutch and German imperatives. In *Current Approaches to Limits and Areas in Dialectology*, E. Carrilho, C. Magro & X. Álvarez (eds) 267–92. Newcastle upon Tyne: Cambridge Scholars.

Barbosa, P. 2000. Clitics: A window into the null subject property. In *Portuguese Syntax: New Comparative Studies*, J. Costa (ed.) 31–94. Oxford: Oxford University Press.

Barton, E. 1998. The grammar of telegraphic structures: Sentential and nonsentential derivation. *Journal of English Linguistics* 26: 37–67.

Battye, A. 1989. Free relatives, pseudo-free relatives and the syntax of CP in Italian. *Rivista di Linguistica* 1: 219–50.

Bayer, J. 1984a. Towards an explanation of certain *that-t* phenomena: The COMP node in Bavarian. In *Sentential Complementation*, W. de Geest & Y. Putseys (eds) 23–32. Dordrecht: Foris.

1984b. COMP in Bavarian syntax. *The Linguistic Review* 3: 209–74.

2014. Syntactic and phonological properties of wh-operators and wh-movement in Bavarian. In *Bavarian Syntax: Contributions to the Theory of Syntax*, G. Grewendorf & H. Weiss (eds) 23–50. Amsterdam: Benjamins.

2015. Doubly-filled Comp, wh-head movement, and derivational economy. In *Representing Structure in Phonology and Syntax*, M. van Oostendorp & H. van Riemsdijk (eds) 7–40. Berlin: Mouton de Gruyter.

2016. Doubly-filled comp, wh-head-movement, and the doubly-filled-comp-filter. Ms. Universität Konstanz.

Bayer, J. & Brandner, E. 2008. On wh-head-movement and the doubly-filled-comp-filter. *Proceedings of the West Coast Conference on Formal Linguistics* 26: 87–95.

Bayer, J. & Dasgupta, P. 2016. Emphatic topicalization and the structure of the left periphery: Evidence from German and Bangla. *Syntax* 19: 1–45.

Belletti, A. 2004a. Aspects of the low IP area. In Rizzi 2004a: 16–51.

2004b (ed). *Structures and Beyond: The Cartography of Syntactic Structures*, vol. 3. Oxford: Oxford University Press.

2009. *Structures and Strategies*. London: Routledge.

Beltrama, A. 2013. Intrusive but not intruders. The processing of resumptive pronouns in Italian and English. Ms. University of Chicago.

Benincà, P. 2001. The position of topic and focus in the left periphery. In *Current Studies in Italian Syntax: Essays Offered to Lorenzo Renzi*, G. Cinque & G. Salvi (eds) 39–64. Amsterdam: Elsevier-North Holland.

2003. La frase relativa in fiorentino antico. Paper presented to the *V Incontro di Dialettologia*, University of Bristol, 26–7 September.

2006. A detailed map of the left periphery of medieval Romance. In *Crosslinguistic Research in Syntax and Semantics*, R. Zanuttini. H. Campos, E. Herburger & P. Portner (eds) 53–86. Washington, DC: Georgetown University Press.

2010. La periferia sinistra. In Salvi & Renzi (eds.) 27–59.

2012a. Lexical complementizers and headless relatives. In *Functional Heads*, L. Brugé, A. Cardinaletti, G. Giusti, N. Munaro & C. Poletto (eds) 29–41. Oxford: Oxford University Press.

2012b. Frasi relative e strutture copulari. In *Per Roberto Gusmani: Studi in Ricordo*, V. Orioles & P. Borghello (eds) 251–67. Udine: Forum editrice.

Benincà, P. & Cinque, G. 2010. La frase relativa. In Salvi & Renzi (eds.) 469–507.

Benincà, P. & Munaro, N. 2010 (eds). *Mapping the Left Periphery: The Cartography of Syntactic Structures*, vol. 5. Oxford: Oxford University Press.

Benincà, P. & Poletto, C. 2004. Topic, focus and V2: Defining the CP sublayers. In Rizzi 2004a: 52–75.

Bennis, H. 2000. On the interpretation of functional categories. In *Interface Strategies*, H. Bennis, M. Everaert & E. Reuland (eds) 37–53. Amsterdam: KNAW publications.

Berizzi, M. 2010. Interrogatives and relatives in some varieties of English. PhD diss. University of Padova.

Berizzi, M. & Rossi, S. 2010. 'Something here what made me think': Some new views on relative *what* in the dialects of English. *LangUE Proceedings 2009*: 14–26, University of Essex.

den Besten, H. 1983. On the interaction of root transformations and lexical deletive rules. In *On the Formal Syntax of the Westgermania*, W. Abraham (ed.) 47–131. Amsterdam: Benjamins.

Bever, T.G., Carroll, J.M. & Hartig, R. 1976. Analogy or ungrammatical sequences that are utterable and comprehensible are the origins of new grammars in language acquisition and linguistic evolution. In *An Integrated Theory of Linguistic Disability*, T.G. Bever, J.J. Katz & D.T. Langendoen (eds) 149–82. New York: T.Y. Crowell Press.

Bhatt, R. & Yoon, J. 1992. On the composition of Comp and parameters of V-2. *Proceedings of the West Coast Conference on Formal Linguistics* 10: 41–53.

Bianchi, V. 1999 *Consequences of Antisymmetry: Headed Relative Clauses*. Berlin: Mouton de Gruyter.

2000. On time adverbials. *Italian Journal of Linguistics* 12: 77–106.

2008. Resumptives and LF chains. Ms. University of Siena.

Bianchi, V. & Frascarelli, M. 2010. Is topic a root phenomenon? *Iberia* 2: 43–88.

Biber, D., Johansson, S., Leech, G., Conrad C. & Finegan E. 1999. *Longman Grammar of Spoken and Written English*. Harlow: Pearson Education Limited.

Bibović, L. 1973. The structural possibilities of Serbo-Croatian related to the English structure adjective+prepositional sentential complement. Ms. University of Novi Sad.

Biloa, E. 2013. *The Syntax of Tuki: A Cartographic Approach*. Amsterdam: Benjamins.

Birner, B.J. & Ward, G. 1998a. *Information Status and Non-canonical Word Order in English*. Amsterdam: Benjamins.

1998b. Discourse and information structure. Ms. Northwestern University, IL.

Blythe, H. 2016. Resumption in English: An investigation of usage and acceptability. *Cambridge Occasional Papers in Linguistics* 9: 156–83.

Bocci, G. 2004. Contrastive focalisation on topics and preverbal subjects in Italian. *Rivista di Grammatica Generativa* 29: 3–60.

2007. Criterial positions and left periphery in Italian. *Nanzan Linguistics* 3: 35–70.

2009. On syntax and prosody in Italian. PhD diss. Siena.

2013. *The Syntax–Prosody Interface: A Cartographic Perspective with Evidence from Italian*. Amsterdam: Benjamins.

Boeckx, C. 2003. *Islands and Chains: Resumption as Derivational Residue*. Amsterdam: Benjamins.

2007. *Understanding Minimalist Syntax*. Oxford: Blackwell.

2012. *Syntactic Islands*. Cambridge: Cambridge University Press.

Boeckx, C. & Grohmann, K.K. 2005. Left dislocation in Germanic. In *Focus on Germanic Typology*, W. Abraham (ed.) 131–44. Berlin: Akadamie-Verlag.

Boeckx, C. & Jeong, Y. 2004. The fine structure of intervention in syntax. In *Issues in Current Linguistic Theory: A Festschrift for Hong Bae Lee*, C. Kwon & W. Lee (eds) 83–116. Seoul: Kyungjin.

Bolinger, D. 1961. Syntactic blends and other matters. *Language* 37: 366–81.

1970. The lexical value of *it*. *University of Hawaii Working Papers in Linguistics* 2.8: 57–76.

Bondaruk, A. 1995. Resumptive pronouns in English and Polish. In *Licensing in Syntax and Phonology*, E. Gussmann (ed.) 27–55. Lublin: Folium.

Borsley, R.D. 1984. Free relatives in Polish and English. In *Contrastive Linguistics: Prospects and Problems*, J. Fisiak (ed.) 1–18. Berlin: Mouton.

2011. Constructions, functional heads and comparative correlatives. In *Empirical Issues in Syntax and Semantics* 8: 7–26. http://www.cssp.cnrs.fr/eiss8

Bošković, Ž. 1997. *The Syntax of Non-finite Complementation: An Economy Approach.* Cambridge, MA: MIT Press.

2002. On multiple wh-fronting. *Linguistic Inquiry* 33: 351–83.

2005. On the locality of left branch extraction and the structure of NP. *Studia Linguistica* 59: 1–45.

2008a. What will you have, DP or NP? *Proceedings of the North East Linguistic Society* 37: 101–14.

2008b. On successive cyclic movement and the freezing effect of feature checking. In *Sounds of Silence: Empty Elements in Syntax and Phonology*, J. Hartmann, V. Hegedüs & H. van Riemsdijk (eds) 195–233. Amsterdam: Elsevier North-Holland.

2009a. More on the no-DP analysis of article-less languages. *Studia Linguistica* 63: 187–203.

2009b. Unifying first and last conjunct agreement. *Natural Language and Linguistic Theory* 27: 455–96.

Bošković, Ž. & Lasnik, H. 2003. On the distribution of null complementisers. *Linguistic Inquiry* 34: 527–46.

Branigan, P. 2005. The phase-theoretic basis for Subject-Aux Inversion. Ms. Memorial University.

Bresnan, J. 1970. On complementizers: Toward a syntactic theory of complement types. *Foundations of Language* 6: 297–321.

1972. Theory of complementation in English syntax. PhD diss. MIT (published as Bresnan 1979).

1976. Evidence for a theory of unbounded transformations. *Linguistic Analysis* 2: 353–93.

1979. *Theory of Complementation in English Syntax.* New York: Garland.

1994. Locative inversion and the architecture of Universal Grammar. *Language* 70: 72–131.

Bresnan, J. & Grimshaw, J. 1978. The syntax of free relatives in English. *Linguistic Inquiry* 9: 331–91.

Bril, I. 2010. Informational and referential hierarchy: Clause-linking strategies in Austronesian-Oceanic languages. In *Clause Linking and Clause Hierarchy: Syntax and Pragmatics*, I. Bril (ed.) 269–312. Amsterdam: Benjamins.

Broekhuis, H. 2008. *Derivations and Evaluations: Object Shift in the Germanic Languages.* Berlin: Mouton.

Brovetto, C. 2002. Spanish clauses without complementizers. In *Current Issues in Romance Languages: Selected Proceedings from the 29th Linguistic Symposium on Romance Languages (LSRL-29)*, T. Satterfield, C. Tortora & D. Cresti (eds) 33–46. Amsterdam: Benjamins.

Browning, M.A. 1996. CP recursion and *that*-t effects. *Linguistic Inquiry* 27: 237–55.

Brucart, J.M. 1993. Sobre la estructura de SComp en español. In *Sintaxi: Teoria y Perspectives*, A. Viana (ed.) 59–102. Lleida: Pagès Editors.

Brugé, L., Giusti, G., Munaro, N., Schweikert, W. & Turano, G. (eds) 2005. *Proceedings of the XXX Incontro di Grammatica Generativa*. Venice: Cafoscarina.

Buchstaller, I. 2004. The sociolinguistic constraints on the quotative system: US English and British English compared. PhD diss. University of Edinburgh.

Büring, D. 1997. *The Meaning of Topic and Focus: The 59th Street Bridge Accent*. London: Routledge.

1999. Topic. In *Focus: Linguistic, Cognitive and Computational Perspectives*, P. Bosch & R. van der Sandt (eds.) 142–65. Cambridge: Cambridge University Press.

2003. On D-trees, beans and B-Accents. *Linguistics and Philosophy* 26: 511–45.

Byrne, F. 1987. *Grammatical Relations in a Radical Creole*. Amsterdam: Benjamins.

Camacho-Taboada, V., Jiménez-Fernández, Á, Martín-González, J. & Reyes-Tejedor, M. (eds). 2013. *Agreement, Information Structure and the CP*. Amsterdam: Benjamins.

Campos, H. 1992. Los bearneses que quequean, ¿y nosotros qué? *Hispanic Linguistics* 4: 329–49.

Cann, R., Kaplan, T. & Kempson, R. 2005. Data at the grammar–pragmatics interface: The case of resumptive pronouns in English. *Lingua* 115: 1551–78.

Caponigro, I. 2002. Free relatives as DPs with a silent D and a CP complement. In *Proceedings of WECOL 2000*, V. Samiian (ed.) 140–50. Fresno, CA: California State University.

Caponigro, I. & Pearl, L. 2008. Silent prepositions: Evidence from free relatives. In *The Syntax and Semantics of Spatial P*, A. Asbury, J. Dotlačil, B. Gehrke & R. Nouwen (eds) 365–85. Amsterdam: Benjamins.

2009. The nominal nature of *where, when* and *how*: Evidence from free relatives. *Linguistic Inquiry* 40: 155–64.

Caponigro, I., Torrence, H. & Cisneros, C. 2013. Free relative clauses in two Mixtec languages. *International Journal of American Linguistics* 79: 61–96

Cardinaletti, A. 2004. Towards a cartography of syntactic positions. In Rizzi 2004a: 115–65.

2009 On a (wh-)moved topic in Italian, compared to Germanic. *Linguistics Today* 141: 3–40.

Cardinaletti, C., Cinque, G. & Endo, Y. (eds). 2014. *On Peripheries: Exploring Clause Initial and Clause Final Positions*. Tokyo: Hituzi Syobe Publishing.

Casielles-Suárez, E. 2004. *The Syntax–Information Structure Interface: Evidence from Spanish and English*. New York: Routledge.

Cattell, R. 1976. Constraints on movement rules. *Language* 52: 18–50.

Chapman, C. & Kučerová, I. 2016. Two base-generated positions of *why*: Evidence from English. Ms. McMaster University, Canada.

Chao, W. & Sells, P. 1983. On the interpretation of resumptive pronouns. *Proceedings of the North East Linguistic Society* 13: 47–61.

Chappell, H. 2008. Variation in the grammaticalization of complementizers from *verba dicendi* in Sinitic languages. *Linguistic Typology* 12: 45–98.

Chaves, R. 2012. On the grammar of extraction and coordination. *Natural Language and Linguistic Theory* 30: 465–512.

Cheng, L. & Corver, N. (eds) 2006. *Wh-Movement: Moving On*. Cambridge, MA: MIT Press.

Chevalier, J.-C., Blanche-Benveniste, C., Arrivé, M. & Peytard, J. 1991. *Grammaire du Français Contemporain*. Paris: Larousse.

Chomsky, N. 1955. *The Logical Structure of Linguistic Theory*, mimeo, MIT (published as Chomsky 1975).

1957. *Syntactic Structures*. The Hague: Mouton.

1964. *Current Issues in Linguistic Theory*. The Hague: Mouton.

1965. *Aspects of the Theory of Syntax*. Cambridge, MA: MIT Press.

1966. *Topics in the Theory of Generative Grammar*. The Hague: Mouton.

1968. The formal nature of language. In *Biological Foundations of Language*, E. H. Lenneberg (ed.) 397–442. New York: John Wiley & Sons.

1972. *Language and Mind*. New York: Harcourt Brace Jovanovich Inc.

1973. Conditions on transformations. In *A Festschrift for Morris Halle*, S.R. Anderson & P. Kiparsky (eds) 232–86. New York: Holt, Rinehart and Winston.

1975. *The Logical Structure of Linguistic Theory*. New York: Plenum Press.

1977a. *Essays on Form and Interpretation*. New York: North-Holland.

1977b. On Wh-movement. In *Formal Syntax*, P.W. Culicover, T. Wasow & A. Akmajian (eds) 71–132. New York: Academic Press.

1980. On binding. *Linguistic Inquiry* 11: 1–46.

1981. *Lectures on Government and Binding*. Dordrecht: Foris.

1986. *Barriers*. Cambridge, MA: MIT Press.

1995. *The Minimalist Program*. Cambridge, MA: MIT Press.

1998. Minimalist inquiries: The framework. *MIT Occasional Papers in Linguistics* 15; also published in *Step by Step: Essays on Minimalism in Honor of Howard Lasnik*, R. Martin, D. Michaels & J. Uriagereka (eds) (2000), 89–155. Cambridge, MA: MIT Press.

2001. Derivation by Phase. In *Ken Hale: A Life in Language*, M. Kenstowicz (ed.) 1–52. Cambridge, MA: MIT Press.

2007. Approaching UG from Below. In Sauerland & Gärtner (eds) 1–29.

2008. On Phases. In *Foundational Issues in Linguistic Theory: Essays in Honor of Jean-Roger Vergnaud*, R. Freidin, C. Otero & M.L. Zubizarreta (eds) 133–65. Cambridge, MA: MIT Press.

2013. Problems of projection. *Lingua* 130: 33–49.

Chomsky, N. & Lasnik, H. 1977. Filters and Control. *Linguistic Inquiry* 8: 425–504.

Cinque, G. 1977. The movement nature of left dislocation. *Linguistic Inquiry* 8: 397–412.

1978. Towards a unified treatment of island constraints. In *Proceedings of the Twelfth International Congress of Linguists*, W.U. Dressler & W. Meid (eds) 344–8. Innsbrücker Beiträge zur Sprachwissenschaft.

1983. Topic constructions in some European languages and connectedness. *Tilburg Studies in Language and Literature* 4: 7–41. Reprinted in Anagnastopoulou et al. (eds) 93–118.

2002 (ed.) *The Structure of DP and IP: The Cartography of Syntactic Structures*, vol. 1. Oxford: Oxford University Press.

2008. Two types of non-restrictive relatives. In *Empirical Issues in Syntax and Semantics*, vol. 7, O. Bonami & P. Cabredo Hofherr (eds) 99–137. Paris: CNRS.

2017. On the double-headed analysis of 'headless' relative clauses. Ms. University of Venice.

Cinque, G. & Benincà, P. 2014. Kind-defining relative clauses in the diachrony of Italian. In *Diachrony and Dialects*, P. Benincà, A. Ledgeway & N. Vincent (eds) 257–78. Oxford: Oxford University Press.

Cinque, G. & Rizzi, L. 2008. The cartography of syntactic structures. *Studies in Linguistics* 2: 42–58.

2010. The cartography of syntactic structures. In *The Oxford Handbook of Grammatical Analysis*, B. Heine & H. Narrog (eds) 51–65. Oxford: Oxford University Press.

Citko, B. 2000. Parallel merge and the syntax of free relatives. PhD diss. State University of New York at Stony Brook.

2002. (Anti)reconstruction effects in free relatives: A new argument against the Comp account. *Linguistic Inquiry* 33: 507–11.

2004. On headed, headless, and light-headed relatives. *Natural Language and Linguistic Theory* 22: 95–126.

2008. Missing labels. *Lingua* 118: 907–44.

2011. *Symmetry in Syntax: Merge, Move and Labels*. Cambridge: Cambridge University Press.

Claridge, C. 2012. The origins of *how come* and *what ... for*. In *English Historical Linguistics 2010: Selected Papers from the Sixteenth International Conference on English Historical Linguistics*, I. Hegedüs & A. Fodor (eds) 177–95. Amsterdam: Benjamins

Cocci, G. & Poletto, C. 2007. Complementizer deletion and double complementizers. In *Proceedings of the 32nd Incontro di Grammatica Generativa*, M.C. Picchi et al. (eds) 49–62. Florence: Edizioni dell'Orso.

Cohen, G.L. 1987. *Syntactic Blends in English Parole*. New York: Peter Lang.

Collins, C. 1991. Why and how come. *MIT Working Papers in Linguistics* 15: 1–45.

2005. A smuggling approach to the passive in English. *Syntax* 8: 81–120.

2007. Home sweet home. *NYU Working Papers in Linguistics* 1: 1–34.

Collins, C. & Radford, A. 2015. Gaps, ghosts and gapless relatives in spoken English. *Studia Linguistica* 69: 191–235.

Conroy, A. 2006. The semantics of *how come*: A look at how factivity does it all. *University of Maryland Working Papers in Linguistics* 14: 1–24.

Contreras, H. 1976. *A Theory of Word Order with Special Reference to Spanish*. Amsterdam: North-Holland.

1991. On resumptive pronouns. In *Current Studies in Spanish Linguistics*, H. Campos & F. Martinez-Gil (eds) 143–63. Washington, DC: Georgetown University Press.

Coppock, E. 2006. Alignment in syntactic blending. *MIT Working Papers in Linguistics* 53: 239–55.

2010. Parallel encoding of alternatives in sentence production: Evidence from syntactic blends. *Language and Cognitive Processes* 25: 38–49.

Cowart, W. 1997. *Experimental Syntax: Applying Objective Methods to Sentence Judgments*. Thousand Oaks, CA: Sage Publications.

van Craenenbroeck, J. 2004. Ellipsis in Dutch dialects. PhD diss. Leiden University.

2010. *The Syntax of Ellipsis: Evidence from Dutch Dialects*. Oxford: Oxford University Press.

Cresswell, C. 2002. Resumptive pronouns, wh-island violations, and sentence production. In *Proceedings of the 6th International Workshop on Tree-Adjoining Grammar and Related Frameworks (TAG+6)*, 101–9. Università di Venezia.

Cruschina, S. 2006. Informational focus in Sicilian and the left periphery. In Frascarelli (ed.) 363–85.

2008. Discourse-related features and the syntax of peripheral positions: A comparative study of Sicilian and other Romance languages. PhD diss. University of Cambridge.

2010a. Fronting as focalization in Sicilian. In D'Alessandro et al. (eds.) 247–60.

2010b. Aspetti morfologici e sintattici degli avverbi in siciliano. In *Quaderni di Lavoro ASIt n.11: Studi sui Dialetti della Sicilia*, J. Garzonio (ed.) 21–42. Padua: Unipress.

2011a. On the syntactic status of sentential adverbs and modal particles. *Sprachtypologie und Universalienforschung (STUF)* 63: 345–57.

2011b. Grammaticalization and the expression of evidentiality and epistemicity in Italian and in Sicilian. Unpublished handout, University of Manchester.

2012. *Discourse-Related Features and Functional Projections*. Oxford: Oxford University Press.

Cruschina, S. & Remberger, E.-M. 2008. Hearsay and reported speech: Evidentiality in Romance. *Rivista di Grammatica Generativa* 33: 99–120.

de Cuba, C. 2007. On (non)factivity, clausal complementation and the CP-field. PhD diss. Stony Brook University.

de Cuba, C. & MacDonald, J. 2013a. Referentiality in Spanish CPs. In Camacho-Taboada et al. (eds) 117–40.

2013b. On the referential status of embedded polarity answers in Spanish. In *Selected Proceedings of the 16th Hispanic Linguistics Symposium*, J.C. Amaro, G. Lord, A. de Prada Pérez & J. E. Aaron (eds) 312–23. Somerville, MA: Cascadilla Proceedings Project.

Cukor-Avila, P. 2002. She say, she go, she be like: Verbs of quotation over time in African American Vernacular English. *American Speech* 77: 3–31.

Culicover, P. 1982. *Though-attraction*. Indiana University Linguistics Club.

1996. On distinguishing A' movements. *Linguistic Inquiry* 27: 445–63.

2013. *Explaining Syntax: Representations, Structures and Computation*. Oxford: Oxford University Press.

Culicover, P. & Jackendoff, R. 1999. The view from the periphery: The English comparative correlative. *Linguistic Inquiry* 40: 543–71.

Culicover, P. & Levine, R.D. 2001. Stylistic inversion in English: A reconsideration. *Natural Language and Linguistic Theory* 19: 283–310.

Culy, C. 1996. Null objects in English recipes. *Language Variation and Change* 8: 91–124.

Cutting, J.C. & Bock, K. 1997. That's the way the cookie bounces: Syntactic and semantic components of experimentally elicited idiom blends. *Memory and Cognition* 25: 57–71.

Dąbrowska, E. 2010. Naive v. expert intuitions: An empirical study of acceptability judgments. *The Linguistic Review* 27: 1–23.

D'Alessandro, R., Ledgeway, A. & Roberts, I. 2010 (eds). *Syntactic Variation: The Dialects of Italy*. Cambridge: Cambridge University Press.

Danckaert, L. 2011. On the left periphery of Latin embedded clauses. PhD diss. University of Ghent.

2012. *Latin Embedded Clauses: The Left Periphery*. Amsterdam: Benjamins.

Danckaert, L., D'Hulster, T. & Haegeman, L. 2016. Deriving idiolectal variation: English *wh*-raising. *Linguistics Today* 234: 145–76.

Dekkers, J., van der Leeuw, F. & van der Weijer, J. (eds.). 2000. *Optimality Theory: Phonology, Syntax and Acquisition*. Oxford: Oxford University Press.

Delahunty, G. 1983. But sentential subjects do exist. *Linguistic Analysis* 12: 379–98.

Demirdache, H. 1991. Resumptive chains in restrictive relatives, appositives, and dislocation structures. PhD diss. MIT.

Demonte, V. & Fernández Soriano, O. 2009. Force and finiteness in the Spanish complementizer system. *Probus* 21: 23–49.

2013. El *que* citativo en español y otros elementos de la periferia oracional: Variación inter e Intralingüística. In *Autour de 'que'*, D. Jakob & K. Plooj (eds) 47–69. Frankfurt: Peter Lang.

2014. Evidentiality and illocutionary force: Spanish matrix *que* at the syntax–semantics interface. *Linguistics Today* 214: 217–251.

Diesing, M. 1990. Verb movement and the subject position in Yiddish. *Natural Language and Linguistic Theory* 8: 41–79.

den Dikken, M. 2005. Comparative correlatives comparatively. *Linguistic Inquiry* 36: 497–532.

2006. *Either* float and the syntax of co-*or*-dination. *Natural Language and Linguistic Theory* 24: 689–749.

Donati, C. 2006. On Wh-Movement. In Cheng & Corver (eds) 21–46.

Donati, C. & Cecchetto, C. 2011. Relabeling heads: A unified account for relativization structures. *Linguistic Inquiry* 42: 519–60.

Douglas, J. 2016. The syntactic structures of relativization. PhD diss. University of Cambridge.

Duffield, N. 2015. Where not to put *why*, and why not? *The Journal of Konan University Faculty of Letters* 165: 57–68.

Durrleman, S. 2008. *The Syntax of Jamaican Creole: A Cartographic Perspective.* Amsterdam: Benjamins.

Ebert, K.H. 1991. Vom Verbum dicendi zur Konjunktion: Ein Kapitel universaler Grammatikalisierung. *Arbeiten des Seminars für Allgemeine Sprachwissenschaft* 11: 77–95.

Elsness, J. 1984. That or zero? A look at the choice of object clause connective in a corpus of American English. *English Studies* 65: 519–33.

Emonds, J.E. 1970. Root and structure-preserving transformations. PhD diss. MIT.

1976. *A Transformational Approach to English Syntax.* New York: Academic Press.

1987. The Invisible Category Principle. *Linguistic Inquiry* 18: 613–32.

2004. Unspecified categories as the key to root constructions. In Adger et al. (eds) 75–120.

Endo, Y. 2007. *Locality and Information Structure: A Cartographic Approach to Japanese.* Amsterdam: Benjamins.

2014. Variations of *why, how come* and new topic in C. Handout for talk presented to *Variation in C Workshop*, 21 October 2014, Venice.

2015a Two ReasonPs: What are(*n't) you coming to the US for? In *Beyond Functional Sequence: The Cartography of Syntactic Structures*, vol. 10, U. Shlonsky (ed.) 220–31. Oxford: Oxford University Press.

2015b. *Why, what … for, how come* and *why the hell.* In *Papers from the International Spring Forum of the English Linguistic Society of Japan*, 7: 10–16.

2017. Inter-speaker variation and subject drop in *how come* questions in English. Ms. Kanda University of International Studies.

Engdahl, E. 1984. Why some empty subjects don't license parasitic gaps. *Proceedings of the West Coast Conference on Formal Linguistics* 3: 91–104.

Epstein, S.D., Pires A., & Seely, T.D. 2005. EPP in T: More controversial subjects. *Syntax* 8: 65–80.

Erteschik-Shir, N. 1992. Resumptive pronouns in islands. In *Island Constraints: Theory, Acquisition and Processing*, H. Goodluck & M. Rochemont (eds) 89–108. Dordrecht: Kluwer.

Escribano, J.L.R.G. 1991. *Una Teoría de la Oración*, Oviedo: University of Oviedo Publications Service.

Espinal, M.T. 1991. The representation of disjunct constituents. *Language* 67: 726–62.

Etxepare, R. 1997. The grammatical representation of speech events. PhD diss. University of Maryland.

2010. From hearsay evidentiality to same-saying relations. *Lingua* 120: 604–27.

Fábregas, A. & Jiménez-Fernández, Á. 2012. Extraction from fake adjuncts and first phase syntax. Poster presented at *Going Romance*, KU Leuven, 1–8 December.

Fay, D. 1981. Substitutions and splices: A study of sentence blends. *Linguistics* 19: 717–49.

Fernández-Rubiera, F.J. 2009. Clitics at the edge: Clitic placement in western Iberian Romance languages. PhD diss. Georgetown University.

Ferreira, F. & Swets, B. 2005. The production and comprehension of resumptive pronouns in relative clause 'island' contexts. In *Twenty-First Century Psycholinguistics: Four Cornerstones*, A. Cutler (ed.) 263–78. Mahwah, NJ: Lawrence Erlbaum Associates.

Ferreira, V.S. 2003. The persistence of optional complementiser production: Why saying 'that' is not saying 'that' at all. *Journal of Memory and Language* 48: 379–98.

Fiengo, R. 1977. On Trace Theory. *Linguistic Inquiry* 8: 35–61.

Finney, M.A. 2012. The interaction of declarative and procedural memory in the process of creolization: The case of Sierra Leone Krio. Special edition of the *Legon Journal of the Humanities* 83–118.

Fiorentino, G. 2007. European relative clauses and the uniqueness of the relative pronoun type. *Rivista di Linguistica* 19: 263–91.

Fitzpatrick, J. 2005. The whys and how comes of presupposition and NPI licensing in questions. *Proceedings of the West Coast Conference on Formal Linguistics* 24: 138–45.

Fontana, J.M. 1993. Phrase structure and the syntax of clitics in the history of Spanish. PhD diss. University of Pennsylvania.

Frajzyngier, Z. 1984. On the origin of *say* and *se* as complementizers in Black English and English-based creoles. *American Speech* 59: 207–10.

Franco, I. 2009. Verbs, subjects and stylistic fronting: A comparative analysis of the interaction of CP properties with verb movement and subject positions in Icelandic and Old Italian. PhD diss. University of Siena.

Franks, S. 2000. A PF-insertion analysis of *that*. *Syntaxis* 3: 1–27.

2005. What is *that*? *Indiana University Working Papers in Linguistics* 5: 33–62.

Frascarelli, M. (ed.) 2006. *Phases of Interpretation*. Berlin: Mouton de Gruyter.

Frascarelli, M. & Hinterhölzl, R. 2007. Types of topics in German and Italian. In *On Information Structure, Meaning and Form*, S. Winkler & K. Schwabe (eds) 86–116. Amsterdam: Benjamins.

Frascarelli, M. & Puglielli, A. 2007. Focus in the Force-Fin system: Information structure in Cushitic Languages. In *Focus Strategies: Evidence from African Languages*, E. Aboh, K. Hartmann & M. Zimmermann (eds) 161–84. Berlin: Mouton de Gruyter.

Frey, W. 2004. Notes on the syntax and pragmatics of German left dislocation. In *The Syntax and Semantics of the Left Periphery*, H. Lohnstein & S. Trissler (eds) 163–209. Berlin: Mouton de Gruyter.

2005. Pragmatic properties of certain German and English left peripheral constructions. *Linguistics* 43: 89–129.

Friedmann, N., Belletti, A. & Rizzi, L. 2009. Relativized minimality: Types of intervention in the acquisition of A-bar dependencies. *Lingua* 119: 67–88.

Friedmann, N., Novogrodsky, R., Szterman, R. & Preminger, O. 2008. Resumptive pronouns as a last resort when movement is impaired: Relative clauses in hearing impairment. In *Current Issues in Generative Hebrew Linguistics* 7: 267–90.

Garrett, J. 2013. Which *que* is which? A squib on reduplicative *que* complementizers in Iberian Spanish embedded clauses. *Indiana University Working Papers in Linguistics* 13: 1–9.

Garzonio, J. 2005. Struttura informazionale e soggetti nulli in russo: Un approccio cartografico. PhD diss. University of Padua.

van Gelderen, E. 2009. Renewal in the left periphery: Economy and the complementiser layer. *Transactions of the Philological Society* 107: 131–95.

Geluykens, R. (1992) *From Discourse Process to Grammatical Construction: On Left Dislocation in English*. Amsterdam: Benjamins.

Giorgi, A. 2014. Prosodic signals as syntactic formatives in the left periphery. In Cardinaletti et al. (eds) 161–88.

Giusti, G. 1996. Is there a FocusP and a TopicP in the Noun Phrase? *University of Venice Working Papers in Linguistics* 6: 105–28.

2006. Parallels in clausal and nominal periphery. In Frascarelli (ed.) 151–72.

2012. On Force and Case, Fin and Num. In *Enjoy Linguistics: Papers Presented to Luigi Rizzi on the Occasion of his 60th Birthday*, V. Bianchi & C. Chesi (eds) 205–17. Siena: CISCL Press.

González i Planas, F. 2010. Cartografia de la recomplementació en les llengües romàniques. MA diss. University of Girona.

2014. On quotative recomplementation: Between pragmatics and morphosyntax. *Lingua* 146: 39–74.

Greenberg, G. 1984. Left dislocation, topicalization, and interjections. *Natural Language and Linguistic Theory* 2: 283–7.

Gregory, M. & Michaelis, L. 2001. Topicalization and left dislocation: A functional opposition revisited. *Journal of Pragmatics* 33: 1665–706.

Grewendorf, G. 2002. Left dislocation as movement. *Georgetown University Working Papers in Theoretical Linguistics* 2: 31–81.

Grewendorf, G. & Poletto, C. 2009. The hybrid complementizer system of Cimbrian. *Studies in Linguistics* 3: 181–94.

Grewendorf, G. & Zimmermann, T.E. (eds) 2012 *Discourse and Grammar: From Sentence Types to Lexical Categories*. Berlin: De Gruyter.

Griffiths, J. & de Vries, M. 2013. The syntactic integration of appositives: Evidence from fragments and ellipsis. *Linguistic Inquiry* 44: 332–44.

Grimshaw, J. 1979. Complement selection and the lexicon. *Linguistic Inquiry* 10: 279–326.

1993. Minimal projection, heads, and optimality. Ms. Rutgers University.

1997. Projection, heads and optimality. *Linguistic Inquiry* 28: 373–422.

Grohmann, K.K. 1997. On left dislocation. *Groninger Arbeiten zur Germanistischen Linguistik* 40: 1–33.

2000. Prolific peripheries: A radical view from the left. PhD diss. University of Maryland.

2003. *Prolific Domains: On the Anti-Locality of Movement Dependencies*. Amsterdam: Benjamins

2006. Top issues in questions: Topics-topicalization-topicalizability. In Cheng & Corver (eds) 249–88.

Grolla, E. 2005. Resumptive pronouns as last resort: Implications for language acquisition. *Penn Working Papers in Linguistics* 11: 71–84.

Groos, A. & van Riemsdijk, H. 1981. Matching effects in free relatives: A parameter of core grammar. In *Theory of Markedness in Generative Grammar*, A. Belletti, L. Brandi & L. Rizzi (eds) 171–216. Pisa: Scuola Normale Superiore.

Grosu, A. 1989. Pied-piping and the matching parameter. *Linguistic Review* 6: 41–58.
    1996. The proper analysis of missing-P free relative constructions. *Linguistic Inquiry*
        27: 257–93.
    2003. A unified theory of standard and transparent free relatives. *Natural Language
        and Linguistic Theory* 21: 247–331.
Gruber, J.S. 1967. Topicalization in child language. *Foundations of Language* 3: 37–65.
Guasti, M.T., Thornton, R. & Wexler, K. 1995. Negation in children's questions:
    The case of English. *Proceedings of the Boston University Conference on
    Language Development* 19: 228–39.
Güldemann, T. 2001. Quotative constructions in African languages: A synchronic and
    diachronic survey. Habilitation thesis. Leipzig: Universität Leipzig, Institut für
    Afrikanistik.
Gundel, J.K. 1975. Left dislocation and the role of topic-comment structure in linguistic
    theory. *Ohio State Working Papers in Linguistics* 18: 72–131.
    1985. Shared knowledge and topicality. *Journal of Pragmatics* 9: 83–107.
    1988. Universals of topic-comment structure. In *Studies in Syntactic Typology*,
        M. Hammond, E.A. Moravcsik & J. Werth (eds) 209–42. Amsterdam:
        Benjamins.
Gupton, T. 2010 The syntax–information structure interface: Subjects and clausal word
    order in Galician. PhD diss. University of Iowa.
van Haaften, T., Smits, R. & Vat, J. 1983. Left dislocation, connectedness and
    reconstruction. *Linguistics Today* 3: 133–54.
Haddican, W. & Zweig, E. 2012. The syntax of manner quotative constructions in
    English and Dutch. *Linguistic Variation* 12: 1–26.
Haegeman, L. 1983. *Die* and *dat* in West-Flemish relative clauses. In *Linguistics in the
    Netherlands 1983*, H. Bennis & W.U.S. van Lessen Kloeke (eds) 83–91.
    Dordrecht: Foris.
    1987. Complement ellipsis in English: Or, how to cook without objects. In *Studies in
        Honour of René Derolez*, A.M. Simon-Vandenbergen (ed.) 248–61. Ghent:
        University of Ghent.
    1990a. Non-overt subjects in diary contexts. In *Grammar in Progress*, J. Mascaró &
        M. Nespor (eds) 167–74. Dordrecht: Foris.
    1990b. Understood subjects in English diaries. *Multilingua* 9: 157–99.
    1992 *Theory and Description in Generative Grammar: A case study of West Flemish*.
        Cambridge: Cambridge University Press.
    1994. *Introduction to Government and Binding Theory* (2nd edn). Oxford: Blackwell.
    1996. Verb second, the split CP and null subjects in early Dutch finite clauses.
        *GenGenP* 4: 133–75. <lingBuzz/001059>
    1997. Register variation, truncation and subject omission in English and in French.
        *English Language and Linguistics* 1: 233–70.
    2000a. Inversion, non-adjacent inversion and adjuncts in CP. *Transactions of the
        Philological Society* 98: 121–60.
    2000b. Adult null subjects in non pro-drop languages. In *The Acquisition of Syntax*,
        M.-A. Friedemann & L. Rizzi (eds), 129–69. London: Addison, Wesley and
        Longman.

2003. Notes on long adverbial fronting in English and the left periphery. *Linguistic Inquiry* 34: 640–9.

2004. Topicalization, CLLD and the left periphery. In *Proceedings of the Dislocated Elements Workshop*, B. Shaer, W. Frey & C. Maienborn (eds) 157–92. Berlin: ZAS.

2006a. Argument fronting in English, Romance CLLD and the left periphery. In Zanuttini et al. (eds) 27–52.

2006b. Conditionals, factives and the left periphery. *Lingua* 116: 1651–69.

2007. Operator movement and topicalization in adverbial clauses. *Folia Linguistica* 18: 485–502.

2009. The movement analysis of temporal adverbial clauses. *English Language and Linguistics* 13: 385–408.

2010. The internal syntax of adverbial clauses. *Lingua* 120: 628–48.

2012. *Adverbial Clauses, Main Clause Phenomena, and Composition of the Left Periphery*. Oxford: Oxford University Press.

2013. The syntax of registers: Diary subject omission and the privilege of the root. *Lingua* 130: 88–110.

2015. Unspeakable sentences. Ms. Ghent University.

Haegeman, L. & Greco, C. 2016. 'V > 2'. Handout for paper presented to the conference on 'Rethinking Verb Second', University of Cambridge, 22–4 March.

Haegeman, L. & Guéron, J. 1999. *English Grammar: A Generative Perspective*. Oxford: Blackwell.

Haegeman, L. & Hill, V. 2014. Vocatives and speech-act projections: A case study in West Flemish. In Cardinaletti et al. (eds) 209–36.

Haegeman, L. & Ihsane, T. 1999. Subject ellipsis in embedded clauses in English. *Journal of English Language and Linguistics* 3: 117–45.

2001. Adult null subjects in the non-pro drop languages: Two diary dialects. *Language Acquisition* 9: 329–46.

Haegeman, L., Jiménez-Fernández, Á. & Radford, A. 2014. Deconstructing the Subject Condition in terms of cumulative constraint violation. *The Linguistic Review* 31: 73–150.

Hallman, P. 1997. Reiterative syntax. In *Clitics, Pronouns and Movement*, J.R. Black & V. Motapayane (eds) 87–131. Amsterdam: Benjamins.

Han, C.-H. 1998. The structure and interpretation of imperatives: Mood and Force in Universal Grammar. PhD diss. University of Pennsylvania.

2001. Force, negation and imperatives. *The Linguistic Review* 18: 289–325.

Harbert, Q. 1983. On the nature of the matching parameter. *Linguistic Review* 2: 237–84.

Harris, J. 1993. The grammar of Irish English. In Milroy & Milroy (eds) 139–86.

Hartman, J. & Ai, R.R. 2009. A focus account of Swiping. In *Selected Papers from the 2006 Cyprus Syntaxfest*, K.K. Grohmann & P. Panagiotidis (eds) 92–122. Newcastle upon Tyne: Cambridge Scholars.

Hawkins, J. 2001. Why are categories adjacent? *Journal of Linguistics* 37: 1–34.

Heestand, D., Xiang, M. & Polinsky, M. 2011 Resumption still does not rescue islands. *Linguistic Inquiry* 42: 138–52.

Heine, B., Claudi, U. & Hünnemeyer, F. 1991. *Grammaticalization: A Conceptual Framework*. Chicago: The University of Chicago Press.

Heine, B. & Reh, M. 1984. *Grammaticalization and Reanalysis in African Languages.* Hamburg: Helmut Buske.

Henry, A. 1995. *Belfast English and Standard English: Dialect Variation and Parameter Setting.* Oxford: Oxford University Press.

Hernanz, M.L. 2007. From polarity to modality: Some (a)symmetries between *bien* and *sí* in Spanish. In *Coreference, Modality, and Focus*, L. Eguren & O. Fernández Soriano (eds) 133–69. Amsterdam: Benjamins.

Hernanz, M.L. & Rigau, G. 2006. Variación dialectal y periferia izquierda. In *Andolin Gogoan: Essays in Honour of Professor Eguzkitza*, B. Fernández & I. Laka (eds) 435–45. Gipuzkua: Euskal Herriko Unibersitatea.

Herrmann, T. 2003. Relative clauses in dialects of English: A typological approach. PhD diss. Albert-Ludwigs-Universität, Freiburg.

    2005. Relative clauses in English dialects of the British Isles. In *A Comparative Grammar of British English Dialects*, B. Kortmann, T. Herrmann, L. Pietsch & S. Wagner (eds) 21–124. Berlin: Mouton.

Higgins, F.R. 1973. On J. Emonds' analysis of Extraposition. In J. Kimball (ed.) *Syntax and Semantics* 2: 149–95. New York: Academic Press.

    1988. Where the Old English sentence begins. Unpublished ms. University of Massachusetts, Amherst.

Hill, V. 2007. Romanian adverbs and the pragmatic field. *The Linguistic Review* 24: 61–86.

Hiramatsu, K. 2003. Children's judgments on negative questions. *Language Acquisition* 11: 99–126.

Hirschbühler, P. 1973. La dislocation à gauche en français. *Le Langage et l'Homme* 23: 19–125.

    1974. La dislocation à gauche comme construction basique en français. In *Actes du Colloque Franco-Allemande de Grammaire Transformationelle*, C. Rohrer & N. Ruwet (eds) vol. 1, 9–17, Tübingen: Max Niemeyer Verlag.

    1975. On the source of lefthand NPs in French. *Linguistic Inquiry* 6: 155–65.

    1976. Two analyses of free relatives in French. *Proceedings of the North East Linguistic Society* 6: 137–52.

    1978 The syntax and semantics of *wh*-constructions. PhD diss. University of Massachusetts, Amherst.

Hirschbühler, P. & Rivero, M.L. 1983. Remarks on free relatives and matching phenomena. *Linguistic Inquiry* 14: 505–19.

Hoffmann, T. 2011. *Preposition Placement in English.* Cambridge: Cambridge University Press.

Hofmeister, P. & Norcliffe, E. 2013. Does resumption facilitate sentence comprehension? In *The Core and the Periphery: Data-driven Perspectives on Syntax Inspired by Ivan A. Sag*, P. Hofmeister & E. Norcliffe (eds) 225–46. Stanford: CSLI Publications.

Holm, J. 1988. *Pidgins and Creoles*, vol. 1: *Theory and Structure.* Cambridge: Cambridge University Press.

Holmberg, A. 2010. Answers to yes-no questions: A comparative study. Paper presented at conference on *Generative Grammar in the 21st Century*, University of Essex, 7 July.

Honegger, M. 2004. Review of Ginsburg & Sag *Interrogative Investigations. Journal of English Linguistics* 32: 151–8.

Hoomchamlong, Y. 1991. Some issues in Thai anaphora: A Government and Binding approach. PhD diss. University of Wisconsin, Madison.

Hooper, J.B. & Thompson, S.A. 1973. On the applicability of root transformations. *Linguistic Inquiry* 4: 465–97.

Hopper, P.J. & Traugott, E.C. 1993. *Grammaticalization.* Cambridge: Cambridge University Press.

Hopper, R. 1992. *Telephone Conversation.* Bloomington: Indiana University Press.

Hornstein, N. 2007. Pronouns in a minimalist setting. In *The Copy Theory of Movement,* N. Corver & J. Nunes (eds) 351–85. Amsterdam: Benjamins.

Horsey, R. 1998. Null arguments in English registers: A Minimalist account. BA thesis, La Trobe University.

Huang, C.-T.J. 1982. Logical relations in Chinese and the theory of grammar. PhD diss. MIT.

Huddleston, R. 1994. The contrast between interrogatives and questions. *Journal of Linguistics* 30: 411–39.

Hudson, R. 2003. Trouble on the left periphery. *Lingua* 113: 607–42.

Iatridou, S. 1991. Topics in conditionals. PhD diss. MIT.

Iatridou, S. & Kroch, A. 1992. The licensing of CP-recursion and its relevance to the Germanic verb-second phenomenon. *Working Papers in Scandinavian Syntax* 50: 1–24.

Ihalainen, O. 1980. Relative clauses in the dialect of Somerset. *Neuphilologische Mitteilungen* 81: 187–96.

Ioannou, G. 2011. On the nature of T-to-C movement in English wh-interrogatives. PhD diss. University of Essex.

Iwasaki, E. & Radford, A. 2009. Comparative correlatives in English: A minimalist-cartographic analysis. *Essex Research Reports in Linguistics* 57.6: 1–14.

Izvorski, R. 2000. Free adjunct free relatives. In *Proceedings of the West Coast Conference on Formal Linguistics* 19: 232–45.

Jacobs, R.A & Rosenbaum, P.S. 1968. *English Transformational Grammar.* Waltham, MA: Blaisdell Publishing Co.

Jacobson, P. 1995. On the quantificational force of English free relatives. In *Quantification in Natural Languages,* E. Bach, E. Jelinek, A. Kratzer & B.H. Partee (eds) 451–86. Dordrecht: Kluwer.

Jaeger, T.F. 2010. Redundancy and reduction: Speakers manage syntactic information density. *Cognitive Psychology* 61: 23–62.

2012. Phonological optimization and syntactic variation: The case of optional 'that'. *Berkeley Linguistics Society Proceedings* 32: 175–87.

Janda, R.J. 1985. Note-taking English as a simplified register. *Discourse Processes* 8: 437–54.

Jayaseelan, K.A. 2008. Topic, focus and adverb positions in clause structure. *Nanzan Linguistics* 4: 43–68.

Jiménez-Fernández, Á. 2011. On the order of multiple topics and discourse-feature inheritance. *Dilbilim Araştırmaları* 2011: 5–32. < lingBuzz/001216>

2015. Towards a typology of focus: Subject position and microvariation at the discourse–syntax interface. *Ampersand* 2: 49–60.

Kameshima, N. 1989. The syntax of restrictive and nonrestrictive relative clauses in Japanese. PhD diss. University of Wisconsin-Madison.

Kathol, A. 2001. Positional effects in a monostratal grammar of German. *Journal of Linguistics* 37: 35–66.

Katz, J.J. & Postal, P.M. 1964. *An Integrated Theory of Linguistic Descriptions*. Cambridge, MA: MIT Press.

Kayne, R.S. 1984. *Connectedness and Binary Branching*. Dordrecht: Foris.

1994. *The Antisymmetry of Syntax*. Cambridge, MA: MIT Press.

1998. Overt vs covert movement. *Syntax* 1: 128–91.

2008. Why isn't *this* a complementiser? <lingBuzz/000726>

2016. What is suppletive allomorphy? On *went* and on *\*goed* in English. Ms. New York University.

Keenan, E. & Schieffelin, B. 1976a. Foregrounding referents: A reconsideration of left dislocation in discourse. *Berkeley Linguistics Society Proceedings* 2: 240–57.

1976b. Topic as a discourse notion: A study of topic in the conversations of children and adults. In Li (ed.) 335–84.

Kenesei, I., Vágo, R.M. & Fenyvesi, A. 1998. *Hungarian*. London: Routledge.

Kidwai, A. 2010. The cartography of phases: Fact and inference in Meiteilon. In *Edges, Heads and Projections: Interface Properties*, A.M. Di Sciullo & V. Hill (eds) 233–62. Amsterdam: Benjamins.

Kihm, A. 1990. Complementizer, verb or both? Kriyol Kuma. *Journal of Pidgin and Creole Languages* 5: 53–70.

Kim, J.-B. & Kim, O. 2011. English *how come* construction: A double life. Paper presented to Arizona Linguistics Circle 5, 28–30 October.

Kitagawa, C. 1982. Topic construction in Japanese. *Lingua* 57: 175–214.

Kjellmer, G. 1988. Conjunctional/adverbial *which* in substandard English. *Studia Anglica Posnaniensia* 21: 125–37.

Klamer, M. 2000. How report verbs become quote markers and complementisers. *Lingua* 110: 69–98.

Koeneman, O. 2000. The flexible nature of verb movement. PhD diss. University of Utrecht.

Koizumi, M. 1995. Phrase structure in minimalist syntax. PhD diss. MIT.

Koopman, H. 2000. *The Syntax of Specifiers and Heads*. London: Routledge.

Koster, J. 1978. Why subject sentences don't exist. In *Recent Transformational Studies in European Languages*, S.J. Keyser (ed.) 53–64. Cambridge, MA: MIT Press.

Kramer, R. & Rawlins, K. 2011. Polarity particles: An ellipsis account. *Proceedings of the Annual Meeting of the North East Linguistic Society* 39: 479–92.

Krapova, I. 2002. On the left periphery of the Bulgarian sentence. *University of Venice Working Papers in Linguistics* 12: 107–28.

2010. Bulgarian relative and factive clauses with an invariant complementiser. *Lingua* 120: 1240–72.

Krapova, I. & Cinque, G. 2008. On the order of *wh*-phrases in Bulgarian multiple *wh*-fronting. In *Formal Description of Slavic Languages*, G. Zybatow, L. Szucsich, U. Junghanns & R. Meyer (eds) 318–36. Frankfurt am Main: Peter Lang.

Kroch, A. 1981. On the role of resumptive pronouns in amnestying island constraint violations. *Chicago Linguistic Society Papers* 17: 125–35.

Kuha, M. 1994. Attitudes towards users of coordinate *which*. Unpublished paper: Indiana University, Bloomington.

Kuno, S. 1976. Subject, theme and speaker's empathy: A reexamination of relativization phenomena. In Li (ed.) 417–44.

Laenzlinger, C. 1999. *Comparative Studies in Word Order Variation: Adverbs, Pronouns, and Clause Structure in Romance and Germanic*. Amsterdam: Benjamins.

Lahiri, U. 1991. Embedded interrogatives and predicates that embed them. PhD diss. MIT.

Lakoff, G. 1969. On derivational constraints. *Chicago Linguistic Society Papers* 5: 117–39.

Lambrecht, K. 1994 *Information Structure and Sentence Form*. Cambridge: Cambridge University Press.

Larson, R.K. 1985. On the syntax of disjunction scope. *Natural Language and Linguistic Theory* 3: 217–64.

1987. Missing prepositions and the analysis of English free relative clauses. *Linguistic Inquiry* 18: 239–66.

Lasnik, H. & Saito, M. 1992. *Move α: Conditions on its Application and Output*. Cambridge, MA: MIT Press.

Law, P. 1991a. Effects of head-movement on subjacency and proper government. PhD diss. MIT.

1991b. Verb movement, expletive replacement and head government. *The Linguistic Review* 8: 255–85.

Ledgeway, A. 2000. *A Comparative Syntax of the Dialects of Southern Italy: A Minimalist Approach*. Publications of the Philological Society 33. Oxford: Blackwell.

2004. Il sistema completivo dei dialetti meridionali: La doppia serie di complementatori. *Rivista Italiana di Dialettologia* 27: 89–147.

2005. Moving through the left periphery: The dual complementizer system in the dialects of Southern Italy. *Transactions of the Philological Society* 103: 339–96.

2006. The dual complementiser system in southern Italy: Spirito greco, materia romanza? In *Rethinking Languages in Contact: The Case of Italian*, A.L. Lepschy & A. Tosi (eds) 112–26. Oxford: Legenda.

2009. Aspetti della sintassi della periferia sinistra del cosentino. In *Studi sui Dialetti della Calabria (Quaderni di Lavoro ASIt n. 9)*, D. Pescarini (ed.), 3–24. Padua: Unipress.

2010. The clausal domain: CP structure and the left periphery. In D'Alessandro et al. (eds) 38–51.

2012a. La sopravvivenza del sistema dei doppi complementatori nei dialetti meridionali. In *Atti del II Convegno Internazionale di Dialettologia – Progetto A.L.Ba*, ed. P. Del Puente, 151–76. Rionero in Vulture: Calice Editore.

2012b. *From Latin to Romance: Morphosyntactic Typology and Change*. Oxford: Oxford University Press.

2013. Greek disguised as Romance? The case of Southern Italy. In *Proceedings of the 5th International Conference on Greek Dialects and Linguistic Theory*, M. Janse, B.D. Joseph, A. Ralli & M. Bagriacik (eds) 184–228. University of Patras: Laboratory of Modern Greek Dialects.

2015. Reconstructing complementiser-drop in the dialects of the Salento: A syntactic or phonological phenomenon? In *Syntax Over Time: Lexical, Morphological, and Information-Structural Interactions*, T. Biberauer & G. Walkden (eds) 146–62. Oxford: Oxford University Press.

2016. Complementation. In *The Oxford Guide to the Romance Languages*, A. Ledgeway & M. Maiden (eds) 1013–28. Oxford: Oxford University Press.

Ledgeway, A. & Lombardi, A. 2014. The Development of the southern subjunctive: Morphological loss and syntactic gain. In *Diachrony and Dialects: Grammatical Change in the Dialects of Italy*, P. Benincà, A. Ledgeway & N. Vincent (eds) 25–47. Oxford: Oxford University Press.

Lee, M.-W. & Gibbons, J. 2007. Rhythmic alternation and the optional complementiser in English: New evidence of phonological influence on grammatical encoding. *Cognition* 105: 446–56.

Lees, R.B. 1960. *The Grammar of English Nominalizations*. Bloomington: Indiana University Press.

Legate, J.A. 2002. Warlpiri: Theoretical implications. PhD diss. MIT.

2010. On how *how* is used instead of *that*. *Natural Language and Linguistic Theory* 28: 121–34.

Legendre, G., Grimshaw, J. & Vikner, S. (eds) 2001. *Optimality-Theoretic Syntax*. Cambridge, MA: MIT Press.

Li, C.N. 1976 (ed). *Subject and Topic*. New York: Academic Press.

Llinàs-Grau, M. & Fernández-Sánchez, J.F. 2013. Reflexiones en torno a la supresión del complementante en inglés, español y catalán. *Revista Española de Lingüística* 43: 55–88.

Lobeck, A. 1990. Functional heads as proper governors. *Proceedings of the North East Linguistic Society* 20: 348–62.

Loock, R. 2005 Appositive relative clauses in contemporary written and spoken English: Discourse functions and competitive structures. PhD diss. University of Lille III.

2007. Are you a good *which* or a bad *which*? The relative pronoun as a plain connective. In *Connectives as Discourse Landmarks*, A. Celle & R. Huart (eds) 71–87. Amsterdam: Benjamins.

2010. *Appositive Relative Clauses in English: Discourse Functions and Competing Structures*. Amsterdam: Benjamins.

López, L. 2009. *A Derivational Syntax for Information Structure*. Oxford: Oxford University Press.

Lord, C. 1973. Serial verbs in transition. *Studies in African Linguistics*: 4: 269–96.

1976. Evidence for syntactic reanalysis: From verb to complementizer in Kwa. In *Papers from the Parassession on Diachronic Syntax*, S. Steever, C. Walker & S. Mufwene (eds) 179–91. Chicago: Chicago Linguistic Society.

1993. *Historical Change in Serial Verb Constructions*. Amsterdam: Benjamins.

McCawley, J.D. 1988. Adverbial NPs: Bare or clad in see-through garb? *Language* 64: 583–90.

McCloskey, J. 1979. *Transformational Syntax and Model-Theoretic Semantics: A Case Study in Modern Irish*. Dordrecht: Reidel.

1990. Resumptive pronouns, A'-binding, and levels of representation in Irish. In *Syntax and Semantics,* vol. 23: *The Syntax of Modern Celtic Languages*, R. Hendrik (ed.) 199–248. New York: Academic Press.

1992. Adjunction, selection and embedded verb second. *Working Paper LRC-92–07*, Linguistics Research Center, University of California, Santa Cruz.

2002. Resumption, successive-cyclicity, and the locality of operations. In *Derivation and Explanation*, S.D. Epstein & D. Seely (eds) 184–226. Oxford: Blackwell.

2006. Questions and questioning in a local English. In Zanuttini et al. (eds) 87–126.

2017a. Observations and speculations on resumption (in Irish). Ms. University of California, Santa Cruz.

2017b. Resumption. In *The Wiley Blackwell Companion to Syntax* (2nd edn), M. Everaert & H. van Riemsdijk (eds) 3809–38. Hoboken, NJ: John Wiley & Sons.

McKee, C. & McDaniel, D. 2001. Resumptive pronouns in English relative clauses. *Language Acquisition* 9: 113–56.

Macaulay, R. 2001. You're like 'why not?' The quotative expression of Glasgow adolescents. *Journal of Sociolinguistics* 5: 3–21.

Maekawa, T. 2007. *The English Left Periphery in Linearisation-based HPSG*. PhD diss. University of Essex.

Maki, H. & Kaiser, L. 1998. Implications of embedded topicalization. *English Linguistics* 15: 290–300.

Manetta, E. 2007. Unexpected left dislocation: An English corpus study. *Journal of Pragmatics* 39: 1029–35.

Martín-González, J. 2002. The Syntax of Sentential Negation in Spanish. PhD diss. Harvard University.

Mascarenhas, S. 2007. Complementizer doubling in European Portuguese. Unpublished ms. New York University. <http://homepages.nyu.edu/_sdm330/docs/mascaren has_cdoubling.pdf>

Massam, D. 1989. Null objects and non-thematic subjects, *Journal of Linguistics* 20: 134–9.

2017. Extra *be*: The syntax of shared shell-noun constructions in English. *Language* 93: 121–52.

Massam, D. & Roberge, Y. 1989. Recipe context null objects in English. *Linguistic Inquiry*, 20: 134–9.

Matsumoto, Y. 1997. *Noun-Modifying Constructions in Japanese: A Frame Semantic Approach*. Amsterdam: Benjamins.

316    *References*

Matushansky, O. 1995. Le sujet nul dans les propositions à temps fini en anglais. Maîtrise paper. University of Paris VIII.

Meier, G. 1989. The postpositive conjunctions *though, as* and *that*. *International Review of Applied Linguistics* 27: 307–24.

Melvold, J. 1991. Factivity and definiteness. *MIT Working Papers in Linguistics* 15: 97–117.

Merchant, J. 2002. Swiping in Germanic. In *Studies in Comparative Germanic Syntax*, W. Abraham & J.-W. Zwart (eds) 295–321. Amsterdam: Benjamins.

  2004. Resumptivity and non-movement. *Studies in Greek Linguistics* 24: 471–81.

  2006. Why No(t)? *Style* 40: 20–23.

  2013. Voice and ellipsis. *Linguistic Inquiry* 44: 77–108.

Miller, C. 2000. The grammaticalisation of the verb 'to say' in Juba Arabic. In *Proceedings of the Third International Conference of Aïda*, M. Mifsud (ed.) 213–18. Malta: University of Malta.

Miller, J. 1988. *That*: A relative pronoun? In *Edinburgh Studies in the English Language*, J.M. Anderson & M. Macleod (eds) 113–19. Edinburgh: John Donald.

  1993. The grammar of Scottish English. In Milroy & Milroy (eds) 99–138.

Miller, J. & Fernandez-Vest, J. 2006. Spoken and written language. In *Pragmatic Organization of Discourse in the Languages of Europe*, G. Bernini, & M.L. Schwartz (eds) 9–66. Berlin: De Gruyter.

Miller, J. & Weinert, R. 1998. *Spontaneous Spoken Language: Syntax and Discourse*. Oxford: Clarendon Press.

Milroy, J. & Milroy, L. 1993. *Real English*. London: Longman.

Miyagawa, S. 2017. Topicalization. Ms. MIT/University of Tokyo.

Morgan, A.M. & Wagers, M. in press. English resumptive pronouns are more common where gaps are less acceptable. In press with *Linguistic Inquiry*.

Morgan, J. 1972. Some aspects of relative clauses in English and Albanian. In Peranteau et al. (eds) 63–72.

Müller, G. 1995. *A-bar Syntax: A Study in Movement Types*. Berlin: De Gruyter.

  2000. Shape conservation and remnant movement. *Proceedings of the North East Linguistic Society* 30: 525–39.

  2001. Order preservation, parallel movement, and the emergence of the unmarked. In *Optimality-Theoretic Syntax*, G. Legendre, J. Grimshaw & S. Vikner (eds) 113–42. Cambridge, MA: MIT Press.

Munaro, N. 2003. On some differences between exclamative and interrogative wh-phrases in Bellunese: Further evidence for a split-CP hypothesis. In *The Syntax of Italian Dialects*, C. Tortora (ed.) 137–51. Oxford: Oxford University Press.

Nakamura, T. 2009. Headed relatives, free relatives, and determiner-headed free relatives. *English Linguistics* 26: 329–55.

Nakao, C., Yoshida, M. & Ortega-Santos, I. 2012. On the syntax of *Why*-Stripping. *Proceedings of the West Coast Conference on Formal Linguistics* 30: 270–80.

Nariyama, S. 2006. Pragmatic information extraction from subject ellipsis in informal English. *Proceedings of the 3rd Workshop on Scalable Natural Language Understanding*, 1–8. New York: Association for Computational Linguistics.

Neubauer, P. 1970. On the notion chopping rule. *Chicago Linguistic Society Papers* 6: 400–7.

Newmeyer, F.J. 2003. Grammar is grammar and usage is usage. *Language* 79: 682–707.

2005. A reply to the critiques of 'Grammar is grammar and usage is usage.' *Language* 81: 229–36.

2006a. On Gahl and Garnsey on grammar and usage. *Language* 82: 399–404.

2006b. Grammar and usage: A response to Gregory R. Guy. *Language* 82: 705–6.

Nunes, J. (1995) The copy theory of movement and linearization of chains in the minimalist program. PhD diss. University of Maryland at College Park.

2001. Sideward movement. *Linguistic Inquiry* 32: 303–44.

2004. *Linearization of Chains and Sideward Movement*. Cambridge, MA: MIT Press.

Nye, R. 2013. How complement clauses distribute: Complementiser-*how* and the case against clause type. PhD diss. University of Ghent.

Nylander, D.K. 1985. Factivity, presupposition and the relativized predicate in Krio. *Studies in African Linguistics* 16: 323–36.

Ochi, M. 2004. *How come* and other adjunct *wh*-phrases: A cross-linguistic perspective. *Language and Linguistics* 5: 29–57.

2011. Multiple wh-questions and left periphery. *Nanzan Linguistics* 7: 23–42.

Omaki, A. & Nakao, C. 2010. Does English resumption really help to repair island violations? *Snippets* 21: 11–12.

Ormazabal, J. 1995. The syntax of complementation. PhD diss. University of Connecticut.

2005. The syntactic distribution of factive complements. *Recherches Linguistiques de Vincennes* 33: 91–110.

Ortega-Santos, I. 2013. Corrective focus at the right edge in Spanish. *Lingua* 131: 112–35.

Ortega-Santos, I., Yoshida, M. & Nakao, C. 2014. On ellipsis structures involving a wh-remnant and a non-wh-remnant simultaneously. *Lingua* 138: 55–85.

Osam, E.K. 1994. Aspects of Akan grammar: A functional perspective. PhD diss. University of Oregon.

1996. The history of Akan complementizers. *Journal of Asian and African Studies* 51: 93–103.

1998. Complementation in Akan. *Journal of African Languages and Linguistics* 19: 21–43

Oshima, D.Y. 2006. On factive islands: Pragmatic anomaly vs. pragmatic infelicity. In *New Frontiers in Artificial Intelligence. Lecture Notes in Computer Science*, vol. 4384: 147–61. Dordrecht: Springer.

Ott, D. 2011. A note on free relative clauses in the theory of phases. *Linguistic Inquiry* 42: 183–92.

2012. Movement and ellipsis in contrastive left-dislocation. *Proceedings of the West Coast Conference on Formal Linguistics* 30: 281–91.

2014. An ellipsis approach to contrastive left-dislocation. *Linguistic Inquiry* 45: 269–303.

2015. Connectivity in left-dislocation and the composition of the left periphery. *Linguistic Variation* 15: 225–90.

Paoli, S. 2003. COMP and the left periphery: Comparative evidence from Romance. PhD diss. University of Manchester.

2007. The fine structure of the left periphery: COMPs and subjects: Evidence from Romance. *Lingua* 117: 1057–79.

Paul, W. 2005. Low IP area and left periphery in Mandarin Chinese. *Recherches Linguistiques de Vincennes* 33: 111–34.

2014. *New Perspectives on Chinese Syntax*. Berlin: De Gruyter.

Pearce, E. 1999. Topic and focus in a head-initial language: Maori. *Toronto Working Papers in Linguistics* 16: 249–63.

Peranteau, P.M., Levi, J.N & Phares, G.C. (eds). 1972. *The Chicago Which Hunt: Papers from the Relative Clause Festival*. Chicago: Chicago Linguistic Society.

Pérez-Leroux, A.T. 1995. Resumptives in the acquisition of relative clauses. *Language Acquisition* 4: 105–38.

Perlmutter, D.M. 1972. Evidence for shadow pronouns in French relativization. In Peranteau et al. (eds) 73–105.

Pesetsky, D. 1982a. Paths and categories. PhD diss. MIT.

1982b. Complementizer-trace phenomena and the Nominative Island Condition. *The Linguistic Review* 1: 297–345.

1989. Language-particular processes and the Earliness Principle. Ms. MIT.

1998. Some optimality principles of sentence pronunciation. In *Is the Best Good Enough?*, P. Barbosa, D. Fox, P. Hagstrom, M. McGinnis & D. Pesetsky (eds) 337–83. Cambridge, MA: MIT Press.

Plann, S. 1982. Indirect questions in Spanish. *Linguistic Inquiry* 13: 297–312.

Platzack, C. 2001. Multiple interfaces. In *Cognitive Interfaces: Constraints on Linking Cognitive Information*, U. Nikanne & E. van der Zee (eds) 21–53. Oxford: Oxford University Press.

2004. Cross-linguistic word order variation at the left periphery: The case of object-first main clauses. In Adger et al. (eds) 191–210.

Platzack, C. & Holmberg, A. 1989. The role of AGR and finiteness. *Working Papers in Scandinavian Syntax* 44: 101–17.

Poletto, C. 2000. *The Higher Functional Field: Evidence from Northern Italian Dialects*. Oxford: Oxford University Press.

Polinsky, M., Clemens, L.E., Morgan, A.M., Xiang, M. & Heestand, D. 2013. Resumption in English. In *Experimental Syntax and Island Effects*, J. Sprouse & N. Hornstein (eds) 341–59. Cambridge: Cambridge University Press.

Portner, P. & Yabushita, K. 1998. The semantics and pragmatics of topic phrases. *Linguistics and Philosophy* 21: 117–57.

Postal, P.M. 1971. *Cross-over Phenomena*. New York: Holt, Rinehart and Winston.

1972. On some rules that are not successive cyclic. *Linguistic Inquiry* 3: 211–22.

1998. *Three Investigations of Extraction*. Cambridge, MA: MIT Press.

Prince, E. 1981a. Topicalization, Focus-Movement, and Yiddish-Movement: A pragmatic differentiation. *Berkeley Linguistics Society Proceedings* 7: 249–64.

1981b. Toward a taxonomy of given-new information. In *Radical Pragmatics*, P. Cole (ed.) 222–55. New York: Academic Press.

1984. Topicalization and left dislocation: A functional analysis. *Annals of the New York Academy of Sciences* 433: 213–25.

1985. Fancy syntax and shared knowledge. *Journal of Pragmatics* 9: 65–81.

1990. Syntax and discourse: A look at resumptive pronouns. *Berkeley Linguistics Society Proceedings* 16: 482–97.

1995. On *kind*-sentences, resumptive pronouns, and relative clauses. In *Towards a Social Science of Language: A Festschrift for William Labov*, G. Guy, J. Baugh & D. Schiffrin (eds) 223–35. Cambridge: Cambridge University Press.

1997 On the functions of left-dislocation in English discourse. In *Directions in Functional Linguistics*, A. Kamio (ed.) 117–43. Benjamins: Amsterdam.

Puskás, G. 2000. *Word Order in Hungarian: The Syntax of Ā-positions*. Amsterdam: Benjamins.

Radford, A. 1979. The functional basis of transformations. *Transactions of the Philological Society* 77: 1–42.

1980. On English exclamatives. Ms. Bangor, University College of North Wales.

1981. *Transformational Syntax*. Cambridge: Cambridge University Press.

1988. *Transformational Grammar: A First Course*. Cambridge: Cambridge University Press.

1989. The status of exclamative particles in French. In *Essays on Grammatical Theory and Universal Grammar*, D. Arnold, M. Atkinson, J. Durand, C. Grover & L. Sadler (eds) 223–84. Oxford: Oxford University Press.

1997a. *Syntactic Theory and the Structure of English*. Cambridge: Cambridge University Press.

1997b. *Syntax: A Minimalist Introduction*. Cambridge: Cambridge University Press.

1997c. Verso un'analisi delle frasi esclamative in italiano. In *La Linguistica Italiana Fuori d'Italia*, L. Renzi & M. Cortelazzo (eds) 93–123. Rome: Bulzoni, Società Linguistica Italiana.

2004a. *Minimalist Syntax: Exploring the Structure of English*. Cambridge: Cambridge University Press.

2004b. *English Syntax: An Introduction*. Cambridge: Cambridge University Press.

2009a. *Analysing English Sentences*. Cambridge: Cambridge University Press.

2009b. *An Introduction to English Sentence Structure*. Cambridge: Cambridge University Press.

2010a. Real relatives: The syntax of relative clauses in live radio and TV broadcasts. Talk given at 'Essex Which Hunt' conference, University of Essex, 4 June.

2010b. The syntax of wh-clauses in live radio and TV broadcasts. Paper presented at conference on 'Generative Grammar in the 21st Century', University of Essex, 7 July.

2010c. On the Doubly Filled COMP Filter and complementiser spellout in English. Ms. University of Essex.

2011a. Take *that*. Paper presented to meeting of the Irish Network in Formal Linguistics, City University, Dublin, 16 September.

2011b. Complementizer use in spoken English. Ms. University of Essex.

2013. The complementiser system in spoken English: Evidence from broadcast media. In Camacho-Taboada et al. (eds) 11–54.

2014. How come questions with *how come* are different? Ms. University of Essex.

2016. *Analysing English Sentences* (2nd edn). Cambridge: Cambridge University Press.

2017. Relative clauses in colloquial English. Ms. University of Essex.

Radford, A., Boxell, O. & Felser, C. 2014. Complementiser spellout in indicative clauses in present-day English. Ms. Universities of Essex & Potsdam.

Radford, A. & Felser, C. 2011. On preposition copying and preposition pruning in wh-clauses in English. *Essex Research Reports in Linguistics* 60.4: 1–35.

Radford, A., Felser, C. & Boxell, O. 2012. Preposition copying and pruning in present-day English. *English Language and Linguistics* 16: 403–26.

Radford, A. & Iwasaki, E. 2015. On Swiping in English. *Natural Language and Linguistic Theory* 33: 703–44.

Reiman, P.W. 1994. Subjectless sentences in English. *UTA Working Papers in Linguistics* 1: 141–52.

Reinhart, T. 1981. Pragmatics and linguistics: An analysis of sentence topics. *Philosophica* 27: 53–94.

Ribeiro, I. 2010. Sobre os usos de ênclise nas estruturas subordinadas no português arcaico. *Estudos da Lingua(gem)* 8: 15–40.

Richards, N. 2010. *Uttering Trees*. Cambridge, MA: MIT Press.

van Riemsdijk, H. 2017. Free relatives. In *The Wiley Blackwell Companion to Syntax* (2nd edn), M. Everaert & H. van Riemsdijk (eds) 1665–1710. Hoboken, NJ: John Wiley & Sons.

van Riemsdijk, H. & Zwarts, F. 1974. Left dislocation in Dutch and the status of copying rules. Ms. MIT and University of Amsterdam. Reprinted as van Riemsdijk (1997).

1997. Left dislocation in Dutch and the status of copying rules. In Anagnastopoulou et al. 13–30.

Rigau, G. & Suïls, J. 2010. Microvariation in Catalan and Occitan complementisers: The so-called expletive *se*. *Catalan Journal of Linguistics* 9: 151–65.

Rivero, M.-L. 1978. Topicalization and wh-movement in Spanish. *Linguistic Inquiry* 9: 513–17.

1980. On left-dislocation and topicalization in Spanish. *Linguistic Inquiry* 11: 363–93.

1994. On indirect questions, commands, and Spanish quotative que. *Linguistic Inquiry* 25: 547–54.

Rizzi, L. 1990. *Relativised Minimality*. Cambridge, MA: MIT Press.

1996. Residual verb-second and the *wh*-criterion. In *Parameters and Functional Heads*, A. Belletti & L. Rizzi (eds) 63–90. Oxford: Oxford University Press.

1997. The fine structure of the left periphery. In *Elements of Grammar*, L. Haegeman (ed.) 281–337. Dordrecht: Kluwer.

2000a. Remarks on early null subjects. In *The Acquisition of Syntax*, M.-A. Friedemann & L. Rizzi (eds) 269–92. London: Longman.

2000b. *Comparative Syntax and Language Acquisition*. London: Routledge.

2001. On the position 'Int(errogative)' in the left periphery of the clause. In *Current Issues in Italian Syntax*, G. Cinque & G. Salvi (eds) 287–96. Amsterdam: Elsevier.

2004a (ed). *The Structure of IP and CP: The Cartography of Syntactic Structures*, vol. 2. Oxford: Oxford University Press.

2004b. Locality and left periphery. In Belletti 2004b: 223–51.

2005. On some properties of subjects and topics. In Brugé et al. (eds) 203–24.

2006a. On the form of chains: Criterial positions and ECP effects. In Cheng & Corver (eds) 97–133.

2006b. On intermediate positions: Intervention and impenetrability. Handout for talk presented to Ealing 2006. Paris: ENS.

2006c. Grammatically-based target-inconsistencies in child language. *University of Connecticut Occasional Papers in Linguistics* 4: 19–49.

2010. On some properties of criterial freezing. In *The Complementizer Phase: Subjects and Operators*, E.P. Panagiotidis (ed.) 17–32. Oxford: Oxford University Press.

2011. Syntactic cartography and the syntacticisation of scope-discourse semantics. Ms. universities of Siena and Geneva.

2012. Delimitation effects and the cartography of the left periphery. In Grewendorf & Zimmermann (eds) 115–45.

2013a. Notes on cartography and further explanation. *Probus* 25: 197–226.

2013b. A Note on locality and selection. In *Deep Insights, Broad Perspectives: Essays in Honor of Mamoru Saito*, Y. Miyamoto, D. Takahashi & H. Maki (eds) 325–41. Tokyo: Kaitakusha.

2013c. Focus, topic and the cartography of the left periphery. In *The Bloomsbury Companion to Syntax*, S. Luraghi & C. Parodi (eds) 436–51. London: Bloomsbury Publishing.

2014a. Some consequences of criterial freezing. In *Functional Structure from Top to Toe: The Cartography of Syntactic Structures*, vol. 9, P. Svenonius (ed.) 19–45. Oxford: Oxford University Press.

2014b. The cartography of syntactic structures: Locality and freezing effects on movement. In Cardinaletti et al. (eds) 29–59.

2015a. Cartography, criteria and labelling. In *Beyond Functional Sequence: The Cartography of Syntactic Structures*, vol. 10, U. Shlonsky (ed.) 314–38. Oxford: Oxford University Press.

2015b. Notes on labelling and subject positions. In *Structures, Strategies and Beyond: Studies in Honour of Adriana Belletti*, E. Di Domenico, C. Hamann & S. Matterini (eds) 17–46. Amsterdam: Benjamins.

Rizzi, L. & Bocci, G. 2017. Left periphery of the clause: Primarily illustrated for Italian. In *The Wiley Blackwell Companion to Syntax* (2nd edn), M. Everaert & H. van Riemsdijk (eds) 2171–200. Hoboken, NJ: John Wiley & Sons.

Rizzi, L. & Cinque, G. 2016. Functional categories and syntactic theory. *Annual Review of Linguistics* 2: 139–63.

Rizzi, L. & Shlonsky, U. 2006. Satisfying the Subject Criterion by a non-subject; Locative Inversion and Heavy NP Shift. In Frascarelli (ed.) 341–61.

2007. Strategies of subject extraction. In Sauerland & Gärtner (eds) 115–60.

Roberts, I. 1993. *Verbs and Diachronic Syntax*. Dordrecht: Kluwer.

2004. The C-system in Brythionic Celtic languages and the EPP. In Rizzi 2004a: 297–328.

2010. *Agreement and Head Movement: Clitics, Incorporation and Defective Goals*. Cambridge, MA: MIT Press.

Roberts, I. & Roussou, A. 2002. The extended projection principle as a condition on the tense dependency. In *Subjects, Expletives and the EPP*, P. Svenonius (ed.) 125–55. Oxford: Oxford University Press.

Rochemont, M. 1989. Topic islands and the Subjacency Parameter. *Canadian Journal of Linguistics* 34: 145–70.

Rodman, R. 1974. On left dislocation. *Papers in Linguistics* 7: 437–66. Reprinted as Rodman (1997).

1997. On left dislocation. In Anagnastopoulou et al. (eds) 31–55.

Rodríguez Ramalle, T. 2003. *La Gramática de los Adverbios en -mente o cómo Expresar Mañeras, Opiniones y Actitudes a través de la Lengua*. Madrid: UAM Publications.

Rohdenburg G. 1998. Clausal complementation and cognitive complexity in English. In *Anglistentag, Erfurt*, F.-W. Neumann & S. Schülting (eds) 101–12. Trier: Wissenschaftlicher Verlag.

Rohrbacher, B. 1999. *Morphology-Driven Syntax: A Theory of V-to-I Raising and Pro-Drop*. Amsterdam: Benjamins.

Romaine, S. & Lange, D. 1991. The use of *like* as a marker of reported speech and thought: A case of grammaticalization in progress. *American Speech* 66: 227–79.

Rooryck, J. 1994. Generalized transformations and the *wh*-cycle: Free relatives as bare *wh*-CPs. In *Minimalism and Kayne's Asymmetry Hypothesis*, C. J.-W. Zwart (ed.) 195–208. Groningen: Groningen University.

Rosenbaum, P.S. 1965. The grammar of English predicate complement constructions. PhD diss. MIT (published as Rosenbaum 1967).

1967. *The Grammar of English Predicate Complement Constructions*. Cambridge, MA: MIT Press.

Ross, J.R. 1967. Constraints on variables in syntax. PhD diss. MIT (published as Ross 1986).

1969. Guess who. *Chicago Linguistic Society Papers* 5: 252–86.

1970. On declarative sentences. In *Readings in English Transformational Grammar*, R. Jacobs & P. Rosenbaum (eds) 222–72. Waltham, MA: Ginn.

1973. The same side filter. *Chicago Linguistic Society Papers* 9: 549–67.

1986. *Infinite Syntax!* Norwood, NJ: Ablex.

Roussou, A. 1992. Factive complements and Wh-Movement in modern Greek. *UCL Working Papers in Linguistics* 4: 123–47.

2000. On the left periphery: Modal particles and complementizers. *Journal of Greek Linguistics* 1: 65–94.

2010. Selecting complementizers. *Lingua* 120: 582–603.

Rouveret, A. 2002. How are resumptive pronouns linked to the periphery? *Linguistic Variation Yearbook* 2: 123–84.

2011 (ed.) *Resumptive Pronouns at the Interfaces*. Amsterdam: Benjamins.

Safir, K. 1986. *Syntactic Chains*. Cambridge: Cambridge University Press.

Sag, I. A. 2010. English filler-gap constructions. *Language* 86: 486–545.

Saito, M. 2012. Sentence types and the Japanese right periphery. In Grewendorf & Zimmermann (eds) 147–76.

Saito, M. & Murasugi, K. 1990. N'-deletion in Japanese: A preliminary study. *University of Connecticut Working Papers in Linguistics* 3: 87–107.

Salvi, G. 2005. Some firm points on Latin word order: The left periphery. In *Universal Grammar and the Reconstruction of Ancient Languages*, K.E. Kiss (ed.) 429–56. Berlin: Mouton de Gruyter.

Salvi, G. & Renzi, L. (eds). 2010. *Grammatica dell'Italiano Antico*. Bologna: Il Mulino.

Samek-Lodovici, V. 2006.When right dislocation meets the left-periphery: A unified analysis of Italian non-final focus. *Lingua* 116: 836–73.

2009. Topic, focus and background in Italian clauses. In *Focus and Background in Romance Languages*, A. Dufter & D. Jacob (eds) 333–57. Amsterdam: Benjamins.

Sauerland, U. & Gärtner, H.-M. 2007 (eds). *Interfaces + Recursion = Language?* Berlin: Mouton de Gruyter.

Saxena, A. 1988. On syntactic convergence: The case of the verb 'say' in Tibeto-Burman. *Berkeley Linguistics Society Proceedings* 14: 375–88.

Schönenberger, M. 2010. Optional doubly-filled COMPs (DFCs) in wh-complements in child and adult Swiss German. In *Variation in the Input*, M. Anderssen, K. Bentzen & M. Westergaard (eds) 33–64. Dordrecht: Springer.

Schütze, C. 1996. *The Empirical Basis of Linguistics: Grammaticality Judgments and Linguistic Methodology*. Chicago: The University of Chicago Press.

2001. On the nature of default case. *Syntax* 4: 205–38.

2009. Web searches should supplement judgements, not supplant them. *Zeitschrift für Sprachwissenschaft* 28: 151–6.

Schütze, C. & Sprouse, J. 2014. Judgment data. In *Research Methods in Linguistics*, R.J. Podesva & D. Sharma (eds) 27–50. Cambridge: Cambridge University Press

Sells, P. 1984. Syntax and semantics of resumptive pronouns. PhD diss. University of Massachusetts, Amherst.

1987. Binding resumptive pronouns. *Linguistics and Philosophy* 10: 261–98.

2001. *Structure, Alignment and Optimality in Swedish*. Stanford, CA: CSLI Publications.

Seppänen, A. 1994. Subject gap phenomena in English and Swedish. In *Proceedings of the XIVth Scandinavian Conference of Linguistics and the VIIIth Conference of Nordic and General Linguistics*, C. Hedlund & A. Holmberg (eds) 127–44. Department of Linguistics, University of Göteborg.

Seppänen, A. & Trotta, J. 2000. The *wh+ that* pattern in present-day English. In *Corpora Galore: Analyses and Techniques in Describing English*, J.M. Kirk (ed.) 161–75. Amsterdam: Rodopi.

Shaer, B. & Frey, W. 2004. Integrated and non-integrated left-peripheral elements in German and English. *ZAS Papers in Linguistics* 35: 465–502.

Sharvit, Y. 1999. Resumptive pronouns in relative clauses. *Natural Language and Linguistic Theory* 17: 587–612.

Shlonsky, U. 1992. Resumptive pronouns as a last resort. *Linguistic Inquiry* 23: 443–68.

1997. *Clause Structure and Word Order in Hebrew and Arabic: An Essay in Comparative Semitic Syntax*. Oxford: Oxford University Press.

2010. The cartographic enterprise in syntax. *Language and Linguistics Compass* 4: 417–39.

2014. Subject positions, subject extraction, EPP, and the Subject Criterion. In *Locality*, E. Aboh, M.T. Guasti & I. Roberts (eds) 58–85. Oxford: Oxford University Press.

Shlonsky, U. & Soare, G. 2011. Where's *why*? *Linguistic Inquiry* 42: 651–69.

Sichel, I. 2014. Resumptive pronouns and competition. *Linguistic Inquiry* 45: 655–93.

Sigurdsson, H.A. & Maling, J. 2007. Argument drop and the empty left edge condition. Ms. Lund University and Brandeis University.

Simon-Vandenbergen, A.M. 1981. *The Grammar of Headlines in The Times 1870–1970*. Brussels: AWLSK.

Simpson, A. & Wu, Z. 2002. IP-raising, tone sandhi and the creation of S-final particles: Evidence for cyclic spell-out. *Journal of East Asian Linguistics* 11: 67–99.

Sobin, N. 1987. The variable status of Comp-trace phenomena. *Natural Language and Linguistic Theory* 5: 33–60.

2002. The Comp-trace effect, the adverb effect and minimal CP. *Journal of Linguistics* 38: 527–60.

2003. Negative Inversion as non-movement. *Syntax* 6: 183–222.

Speas, M. 1994. Null arguments in a theory of economy of projection. *University of Massachusetts Occasional Papers in Linguistics* 17: 179–208.

Speas, P. & Tenny, C. 2003. Configurational properties of point of view roles. In *Asymmetry in Grammar*, A.M. di Sciullo (ed.) 315–45. Amsterdam: Benjamins.

Sprouse, J. 2011. A test of the cognitive assumptions of magnitude estimation: Commutativity does not hold for acceptability judgments. *Language* 87: 274–88.

Sprouse, J. & Almeida, D. 2011a. Power in acceptability judgment experiments and the reliability of data in syntax. Ms. University of California, Irvine and Michigan State University.

2011b. A formal experimental investigation of the empirical foundation of generative syntactic theory. <lingBuzz/001195>

2012a. Assessing the reliability of textbook data in syntax: Adger's *Core Syntax*. *Journal of Linguistics* 48: 609–52.

2012b. The empirical status of data in syntax: A reply to Gibson and Fedorenko. *Language and Cognitive Processes*. iFirst: 1–7.

Sprouse, J., Schütze, C. & Almeida, D. 2013. A comparison of informal and formal acceptability judgments using a random sample from *Linguistic Inquiry* 2001–2010. *Lingua* 134: 219–48.

Starke, M. 2001. Move dissolves into Merge: A theory of locality. PhD diss. Geneva.

2004. On the inexistence of specifiers and the nature of heads. In Belletti (ed.) 225–67.

Staum Casasanto, L., Futrell, R. & Sag, I.A. 2008. Non-repeated extra complementizers increase syntactic predictability. Poster, Stanford University and Max Planck Institute for Psycholinguistics.

Staum Casasanto, L. & Sag, I.A. 2008. The advantage of the ungrammatical. *Proceedings of the 30th Annual Conference of the Cognitive Science Society*, 601–6. Austin, TX: Cognitive Science Society.

Stemberger, J.P. 1982. Syntactic errors in speech. *Journal of Psycholinguistic Research* 11: 313–45.

Stowell, T. 1981. Origins of phrase structure. PhD diss. MIT.

1991. Abbreviated English. *Glow Newsletter*, March 1991.

1996. Empty heads in abbreviated English. Ms. UCLA.

Stuurman, F. 1990. *Two Grammatical Models of Modern English: The Old and the New from A to Z*. London: Routledge.

Suñer, M. 1991. Indirect questions and the structure of CP: Some consequences. In *Current Studies in Spanish Linguistics*, H. Campos & F. Martinez-Gil (eds) 283–312. Georgetown: Georgetown University Press.

1993. About indirect questions and semi-questions. *Linguistics and Philosophy* 16: 45–77.

1998. Resumptive restrictive relatives: A crosslinguistic perspective. *Language* 74: 335–64.

Tagliamonte, S. & Hudson, R. 1999. *Be like* et al. beyond America: The quotative system in British and Canadian youth. *Journal of Sociolinguistics* 3: 147–72.

Tamburelli, M. 2007. The role of lexical acquisition in simultaneous bilingualism. PhD diss. University College London.

Taraldsen, K.T. 1978. The scope of *wh*-movement in Norwegian. *Linguistic Inquiry* 9: 623–40.

Teddiman, L. & Newman, J. 2010. Subject ellipsis in English: Construction of and findings from a diary corpus. In *Handbook of Research on Discourse Behaviour and Digital Communications: Language Structures and Social Interaction*, R. Taiwo (ed.) 281–95. Hershey, PA: IGI Global.

Thornton, R. 1995. Referentiality and Wh-Movement in Child English: Juvenile D-Linkuency. *Language Acquisition* 4: 139–75.

Torrence, H. 2013. *The Clause Structure of Wolof: Insights into the Left Periphery*. Amsterdam: Benjamins.

Traugott, E.C. 1972. *A History of English Syntax: A Transformational Approach to the History of English Sentence Structure*. New York: Holt, Rinehart and Winston.

Travis, L. 1984. Parameters and effects of word order variation. PhD diss. MIT.

Truswell, R. 2007. Extraction from adjuncts and the structure of events. *Lingua* 117: 1355–77.

2009. Preposition stranding, passivisation, and extraction from adjuncts in Germanic. *Linguistic Variation Yearbook* 8: 131–77.

2011. *Events, Phrases, and Questions*. Oxford: Oxford University Press.

Tsai, W.-T. D. 1997. On the absence of island effects. *Tsing Hua Journal of Chinese Studies* 27: 125–49.

2008. Left periphery and *why-how* alternations. *Journal of East Asian Linguistics* 17: 83–115.

Uriagereka, J. 1995. An F position in Western Romance. In *Discourse Configurational Languages*, K.É. Kiss (ed.) 153–75. Oxford: Oxford University Press.

Vangsnes, Ø. 2005. Microparameters for Norwegian wh-grammars. *Linguistic Variation Yearbook* 5: 187–226.

Varlokosta, S. & Armon-Lotem, S. 1998. Resumptives and wh-movement in the acquisition of relative clauses in modern Greek and Hebrew. *Proceedings of the Boston University Conference on Language Development* 22: 737–46.

Vat, J. 1981. Left dislocation, connectedness and reconstruction. *Groninger Arbeiten zur Germanistischen Linguistik* 20: 80–103.

Veenstra, T. & den Besten, H. 1995. Fronting. In *Pidgins and Creoles: An Introduction*, J. Arends, P. Muysken & N. Smith (eds) 303–15. Amsterdam: Benjamins.

Vikner, S. 1995. *Verb Movement and Expletive Subjects in Germanic Languages*. Oxford: Oxford University Press

Villa-García, J. 2010. Recomplementation and locality of movement in Spanish. Second general examination paper, University of Connecticut, Storrs (published as Villa-García 2012c).

2011a. On COMP-*t* effects in Spanish: A new argument for rescue by PF deletion. Paper presented to GLOW 34, University of Vienna.

2011b. On the Spanish clausal leftedge: In defence of a TopicP account of recomplementation. Paper presented to 41st Linguistic Symposium on Romance Languages, University of Ottowa.

2012a. Characterizing medial and low complementizers in Spanish: Recomplementation *que* and jussive/optative *que*. In *Current Formal Aspects of Spanish Syntax and Semantics*, M. González-Rivera & S. Sessarego (eds) 198–228. Newcastle upon Tyne: Cambridge Scholars.

2012b. The Spanish complementizer system: Consequences for the syntax of dislocations and subjects, locality of movement, and clausal structure. PhD diss. University of Connecticut, Storrs.

2012c. Recomplementation and locality of movement in Spanish. *Probus* 24: 257–314.

2015. *The Syntax of Multiple-que Sentences in Spanish: Along the Left Periphery*. Amsterdam: Benjamins.

Villalba, X. 2000. *The Syntax of Sentence Periphery*. Universitat Autònoma de Barcelona. Barcelona: Servei de Publicacions.

Vogel, R. 2001. Case conflict in German free relative constructions: An optimality theoretic treatment. In *Competition in Syntax*, G. Müller & W. Sternefeld (eds) 341–75. Berlin: Mouton de Gruyter.

2006. The simple generator. *Linguistics in Potsdam* 25: 99–136. <http://www.ling.uni-potsdam.de/lip.>

de Vries, M. 2002. The syntax of relativization. PhD diss. University of Amsterdam.

Ward, G. & Prince, E. 1991. On the topicalization of indefinite NPs. *Journal of Pragmatics* 15: 167–77.

Watanabe, A. 1993a. Agr-based case theory and its interaction with the A-bar system. PhD diss. MIT.

1993b. Larsonian CP recursion, factive complements and selection. *Proceedings of the North East Linguistic Society* 23: 523–37.

Weir, A. 2008. Subject pronoun drop in informal English. MA thesis, University of Edinburgh.

2009. Subject pronoun drop in informal English. Ms. University College London.

2012. Left-edge deletion in English and subject omission in diaries. *English Language and Linguistics* 16: 105–29.

2014a. *Why*-Stripping targets Voice Phrase. *Proceedings of the North East Linguistic Society* 43: 235–48.

2014b. Fragments and clausal ellipsis. PhD diss. University of Massachusetts, Amherst.

2018. Object drop and article drop in reduced written register. To appear in *Linguistic Variation*, special issue on register variation

Weskott, T. & Fanselow, G. 2011. On the informativity of different measures of linguistic acceptability. *Language* 87: 249–73.

Westergaard, M.R. 2003. Word order in wh-questions in a north Norwegian dialect: Some evidence from an acquisition study. *Nordic Journal of Linguistics* 26: 81–109.

2005. Optional word order in wh-questions in two Norwegian dialects: A diachronic analysis of synchronic variation. *Nordic Journal of Linguistics* 28: 81–109.

Westergaard, M.R. & Vangsnes, Ø. 2005. Wh-questions, V2 and the left periphery of three Norwegian dialect types. *Journal of Comparative Germanic Linguistics* 8: 117–58.

Wexler, K. & Culicover, P.W. 1980. *Formal Principles of Language Acquisition*. Cambridge, MA: MIT Press.

White, L. 1986. Island effects in second language acquisition. *Montreal Working Papers in Linguistics* 3: 1–27.

Williams, E. 1974. Rule ordering in syntax. PhD diss. MIT.

1980. Predication. *Linguistic Inquiry* 11: 203–38.

Willis, D. 2007. Specifier-to-head reanalyses in the complementiser domain: Evidence from Welsh. *Transactions of the Philological Society* 105: 432–80.

Wurmbrand, S. 2017. Stripping and topless complements. *Linguistic Inquiry* 48: 341–66.

Yoshida, M., Nakao, C. & Ortega-Santos, I. 2015. The syntax of *Why*-Stripping. *Natural Language and Linguistic Theory* 33: 323–70.

Zaenen, A. 1997. Contrastive dislocation in Dutch and Icelandic. In Anagnastopoulou et al. (eds) 119–48.

Zanuttini, R., Campos, H., Herburger, E. & Portner, P.H. (eds) 2006. *Crosslinguistic Research in Syntax and Semantics: Negation, Tense, and Clausal Architecture*. Georgetown: Georgetown University Press.

Zanuttini, R. & Portner, P. 2003. Exclamative clauses: At the syntax–semantics interface. *Language* 79: 39–81.

Zhang, N. 2008. Gapless relative clauses as clausal licensors of relational nouns. *Language and Linguistics* 9: 1005–28.

Ziv, Y. 1994. Left and right dislocations: Discourse functions and anaphora. *Journal of Pragmatics* 22: 629–45.

Zwicky, A.M. 2002. I wonder what kind of construction that this example illustrates. In *The Construction of Meaning*, D. Beaver, L.D. Casillas Martínez, B.Z. Clark & S. Kaufmann (eds) 219–48. Stanford: CSLI Publications.

Zwicky, A.M. & Zwicky, A.D. 1973. How come and what for? In *Issues in Linguistics: Papers in Honor of Henry and Renée Kahane*, Braj B. Kachru et al. (eds) 923–33. Urbana, IL: University of Illinois Press.

Zubizaretta, M.-L. 1998. *Prosody, Focus and Word Order*. Cambridge, MA: MIT Press.

2001. The constraint on preverbal subjects in Romance interrogatives. In *Subject Inversion in Romance and the Theory of Universal Grammar*, A. Hulk & J.-Y. Pollock (eds) 183–204. Oxford: Oxford University Press.

Zyman, E. 2016. Adjunct stranding, late merger, and the timing of syntactic operations. Ms. University of California, Santa Cruz.

# Index